A Hebraic Inkling

A Hebraic Inkling

C.S. Lewis on Judaism and the Jews

P.H. Brazier

The Lutterworth Press

THE LUTTERWORTH PRESS
P.O. Box 60
Cambridge
CB1 2NT
United Kingdom

www.lutterworth.com
publishing@lutterworth.com

Paperback ISBN: 978 0 7188 9656 0
PDF ISBN: 978 0 7188 9655 3

British Library Cataloguing in Publication Data
A record is available from the British Library

First published by Pickwick Publications, 2021

This edition published by The Lutterworth Press, 2023,
by arrangement with Wipf and Stock Publishers

Copyright © Paul Brazier, 2021

All rights reserved. No part of this edition may be reproduced, stored electronically or in any retrieval system, or transmitted in any form or by any means, electronic, mechanical, photocopying, recording, or otherwise, without prior written permission from the Publisher (permissions@jamesclarke.co).

For Hilary

Contents

Acknowledgements / IX

Foreword / XIII

A Hebraic Inkling / XVII

Introduction / 1

PART I REVELATION / 23

1. The Young C. S. Lewis / 25

2. The Hebrews, the Jews, . . . and God: I / 47

3. The Hebrews, the Jews, . . . and God: II / 61

4. God's Chosen: Holiness,
Theology and Spirituality, . . . Pride / 77

PART II SCRIPTURE / 87

5. The Hebrew Scriptures:
Historicity and Humanity / 89

6. The Psalms I:
Hebrew Theological Poetry / 105

7. The Psalms II:
Judgements and Cursings—Imprecatory Poems / 117

8. The Psalms III:
A Hebraic Doctrine of Creation / 133

9. The Psalms IV:
Hebraic Prefigurement and Meaning / 145

10. The Psalms V:
Yeshua, *Mashiach*: Second Meanings in the Psalms / 165

PART III FAMILY / 185

11. Sarai-Sarah: Identity . . . in the LORD / 187

12. The Incarnation Nation: the People and the Savior / 199

13. Joy Davidman and the Mature C. S. Lewis:
Race, Semitism . . . and Family / 217

Conclusion / 249

Bibliography / 255

Index of Names / 269

Index of Subjects / 272

Acknowledgements

Extracts quoted from works in German, such as those by Karl Barth, are my own translation.

Acknowledgment and thanks is given to the C. S. Lewis Co. Pte., for permission to quote from the following works used.

C. S. Lewis. *A Grief Observed*. (N. W. Clerk, pseudonym for C. S. Lewis). London: Faber & Faber, 1961. Extracts by C. S. Lewis, © copyright C. S. Lewis Co. Pte. Ltd., 1961. Extracts reprinted by permission.

C. S. Lewis. *Christian Reflections*. Edited by Walter Hooper. London: Fount, 1967. Extracts by C. S. Lewis, © copyright C. S. Lewis Co. Pte. Ltd., 1967, 1980. Extracts reprinted by permission.

C. S. Lewis. *Collected Letters, Vol. I: Family Letters 1905–1931*. Edited by Walter Hooper. San Francisco: Harper San Francisco, 2004. Extracts by C. S. Lewis, © copyright C. S. Lewis Co. Pte. Ltd., 2000. Extracts reprinted by permission.

C. S. Lewis. *Collected Letters, Vol. III: Narnia, Cambridge and Joy 1950–1963*. Edited by Walter Hooper. San Francisco: Harper San Francisco, 2007. Extracts by C. S. Lewis, © copyright C. S. Lewis Co. Pte. Ltd., 2006. Extracts reprinted by permission.

C. S. Lewis. *Letters of C. S. Lewis.* Edited, with a memoir, by W. H. Lewis. London: Geoffrey Bles, 1966, 1988. Extracts by C. S. Lewis, © copyright C. S. Lewis Co. Pte. Ltd., 1966, 1988. Extracts reprinted by permission.

C. S. Lewis. *Letters to an American Lady.* Edited by Clyde S. Kilby. Grand Rapids: Eerdmans, 1967. Extracts by C. S. Lewis, © copyright C. S. Lewis Co. Pte. Ltd., 1967. Extracts reprinted by permission.

C. S. Lewis. *Letters to Malcolm: Chiefly on Prayer.* London: Geoffrey Bles, 1964. Extracts by C. S. Lewis, © copyright C. S. Lewis Co. Pte. Ltd., 1963, 1964. Extracts reprinted by permission.

C. S. Lewis. *Mere Christianity.* London: Bles, 1952. Extracts by C. S. Lewis, © copyright C. S. Lewis Co. Pte. Ltd., 1942, 1943, 1944, 1952. Extracts reprinted by permission.

C. S. Lewis. *Miracles* (1st ed., 1947). London: Bless, 1947. Extracts by C. S. Lewis, © copyright C. S. Lewis Co. Pte. Ltd., 1947, 1960. Extracts reprinted by permission.

C. S. Lewis. *Miracles* (2nd ed. 1960). London: Bless, 1960. Extracts by C. S. Lewis, © copyright C. S. Lewis Co. Pte. Ltd., 1960. Extracts reprinted by permission.

C. S. Lewis. *Reflections on the Psalms.* London: Bles, 1958. Extracts by C. S. Lewis, © copyright C. S. Lewis Co. Pte. Ltd., 1958. Extracts reprinted by permission.

C. S. Lewis. *Screwtape Letters and Screwtape Proposes a Toast.* London: Bles/Centenary, 1961. Extracts by C. S. Lewis, copyright © C. S. Lewis Co. Pte. Ltd., 1961. Extracts reprinted by permission.

C. S. Lewis. *Surprised by Joy.* London: Bles, 1955. Extracts by C. S. Lewis, © copyright C. S. Lewis Co. Pte. Ltd., 1955. Extracts reprinted by permission.

Acknowledgements

C. S. Lewis. *The Chronicles of Narnia—The Magician's Nephew*. London: Bles, 1955. Extracts by C. S. Lewis, © copyright C. S. Lewis Co. Pte. Ltd., 1955. Extracts reprinted by permission.

C. S. Lewis. *The Four Loves*. London: Geoffrey Bles, 1960. Extracts by C. S. Lewis, © copyright C. S. Lewis Co. Pte. Ltd., 1960. Extracts reprinted by permission.

C. S. Lewis. *The Great Divorce: A Dream*. London: Macmillan. 1945. Extracts by C. S. Lewis, © copyright C. S. Lewis Co. Pte. Ltd., 1946. Extracts reprinted by permission.

C. S. Lewis. *The Pilgrim's Regress: An Allegorical Apology for Christianity, Reason and Romanticism*. London: J. M. Dent and Sons, 1933. Extracts by C. S. Lewis, © copyright C. S. Lewis Co. Pte. Ltd., 1949. Extracts reprinted by permission.

C. S. Lewis. *The Problem of Pain*. London: Centenary Press, 1940. Extracts by C. S. Lewis, © copyright C. S. Lewis Co. Pte. Ltd., 1940. Extracts reprinted by permission.

C. S. Lewis. *They Asked for a Paper: Papers and Addresses*. London: Bles, 1962. Extracts by C. S. Lewis, © copyright C. S. Lewis Co. Pte. Ltd., 1962. Extracts reprinted by permission.

C. S. Lewis. *They Stand Together. They Stand Together: The Letters of C. S. Lewis to Arthur Greeves 1914–1963*. Edited by Walter Hooper. London: Collins, 1979. Extracts by C. S. Lewis, © copyright C. S. Lewis Co. Pte. Ltd., 1979. Extracts reprinted by permission.

C. S. Lewis. *Transposition and Other Addresses*. London: Bless, 1949. Extracts by C. S. Lewis, © copyright C. S. Lewis Co. Pte. Ltd., 1970. Extracts reprinted by permission.

C. S. Lewis. *Undeceptions: Essays on Theology and Ethics*. London: Bles, 1971. Extracts by C. S. Lewis, © copyright C. S. Lewis Co. Pte. Ltd., 1949. Extracts reprinted by permission.

Extracts from the Bible are in most instances my own translations from the original Greek text:

Extracts from the Bible used with permission:

Revised Standard Version of the Bible, copyright 1952 [2nd edition, 1971] by the Division of Christian Education of the National Council of the Churches of Christ in the United States of America. Used by permission. All rights reserved.

New Revised Standard Version Bible, copyright 1989, Division of Christian Education of the National Council of the Churches of Christ in the United States of America. Used by permission. All rights reserved.

New Revised Standard Version Bible: Anglicized Edition, copyright 1989, 1995, Division of Christian Education of the National Council of the Churches of Christ in the United States of America. Used by permission. All rights reserved.

THE HOLY BIBLE, NEW INTERNATIONAL VERSION®, NIV® Copyright © 1973, 1978, 1984, 2011 by Biblica, Inc.™ Used by permission. All rights reserved worldwide.

Nestle-Aland, *Novum Testamentum Graece*, 27th Revised Edition, edited by Barbara Aland, Kurt Aland, Johannes Karavidopoulos, Carlo M. Martini, and Bruce M. Metzger in cooperation with the Institute for New Testament Textual Research, Münster/Westphalia, © 1993 by Deutsche Bibelgesellschaft, Stuttgart. Used by permission.

Foreword

A modern-day Kohelet might word the warning in the megillah a little differently—"Of making many books about C.S. Lewis there is no end." In 2005, writing for *The New Yorker*, critic Adam Gopnik[1] takes the C. S. Lewis industry to task, deploring the extent to which the lovers of his work, conservative American Evangelicals in particular, have made of Lewis something akin to the deceased leader of a cult. Gopnik's article, which points to Lewis' less exalted reputation in Britain and takes quite a few pot shots at Lewis himself along the way, is written in a snide tone that displays an often-tone-deaf religious sensibility. Nonetheless, he has a point. Lewis' life story has had numerous iterations in the form of books, plays, and film. I have read and seen a number of them myself. In the end, the interpreters of his life often unconsciously tell us more about themselves than about their subject.

So, why is this book different from all other books? I will admit that what drew me to the opportunity to contribute the foreword was the intriguing angle of approach: *A Hebraic Inkling—C. S. Lewis on Judaism and the Jews*. I had to admit I had not come across that one before.

I was attracted for two main reasons. The first is that I am and have been a Jewish believer in the gospel for close to fifty years. The second reason is that Lewis played a formative role in that faith decision. The privilege of supplying this forward is a welcome pretext to bring to mind my first encounter with Lewis as a young seeker and the effect he had on

---

1. Adam Gopnik, "Prisoner of Narnia," *The New Yorker*, Nov 21, 2005: https://www.newyorker.com/magazine/2005/11/21/prisoner-of-narnia

me then, as well as from that point on as I read most of his books and have revisited many of them over the years.

I never encountered Narnia in my childhood years and had never heard of Lewis when someone loaned me a copy of *Mere Christianity* while my struggle to understand the Christian message was already under way. Pausing at the threshold, I came to realize later that I was seeking intellectual permission from myself to exercise a manner of faith that I have come to view as an epistemological category all its own. Lewis helped me get there, and it was not easy.

Although a religiously uncommitted Jew, like many of my peers I had nonetheless a well-formed commitment to the history and heritage of my people, as well as a cultural identity passed down as second nature by my parents and other relatives. Christianity was the bells of the Catholic Church and the crucifixes that seemed to greet my eyes virtually everywhere I looked. It was foreign and threatening. A child of the 1950s, I may have known the number six million before I could count to six and I think I must actually have believed at one point that the Nazis were a species of Christian who simply worked more efficiently to eliminate us than the others had.

This hedge of misunderstanding, suspicion, and distrust I had almost unconsciously erected around the gospel prevented me from encountering its message until a series of dance steps in what I like to call God's choreography upset my complacency. As I found myself increasingly attracted to the gospel's message of forgiveness and new birth, I was simultaneously terrified, wondering what would happen to my "*pintele yid*," the Jewish spark that animated my personhood. If I came too near Christians or their churches, would I have to learn to hunt and play golf or do whatever else gentiles did with themselves on weekends? At that point, a Jewish Jesus or any knowledge whatsoever of the Jewish context of what eventually emerged as Christianity was still unknown to me.

Like many others before me, I was much taken by the patient and friendly tone of Lewis' apologetic writing as he adduced the arguments to make his case. Almost despite myself, I was disarmed, then charmed, and finally convinced. That is, Lewis brought me to the place where I was able

Foreword

to say I no longer had a justifiable reason to withhold my faith. And for that, I am eternally grateful. Over the years, Lewis' work has continued to delight, edify, and challenge me.

I also read enough about him to be at least somewhat aware of the path of his pilgrim's way and the milestones that marked its progress: the first gentle context of his childhood, the rude thrust from the nest brought about by his mother's death, the Orwellian horrors of the public school, rescue in the form of "Old Knock" Kirkpatrick, the war, the budding career of the young academic, his atheism, his romance with "Northerness" and myth, his encounter with McDonald's "goodness," his famous walk and talk with Tolkien and Dyson and his self-identification as "the most dejected and reluctant convert in all England."

Paul Brazier covers this familiar territory, as many other have done, but he has done so in a way that has provided insight into an element of Lewis' faith that has been, up to now, as far as I'm aware, quite overlooked. It is that not only did Lewis arrive by incremental steps to acceptance of the gospel, once he has accepted it, he seems to have come fairly quickly to the realization that the gospel he had surrendered to and the God he had encountered through it were integrally bound to the wider context of salvation history borne witness to by the children of Israel and their prophets. In short, because C. S. Lewis' God was integrally connected with the both the history and the destiny of the Jewish people, so was he.

And, of course, who would have dreamed that this seemingly insulated don would encounter the embodiment of this realization literally in the flesh in the person of Joy Davidman. Dr. Brazier truly brings Davidman to life. I frankly had no idea we had so much in common. She attended Hunter College; I attended Hunter College. She lived on the Grand Concourse in the Bronx; so did I, albeit when it was in a seedier condition. She had some of her formative spiritual experiences in Central Park as I did. Although she was a generation behind me, I clearly recognize the type of Jew she perceived herself to be prior to her faith decision. My own field of study has certainly taught me that the subculture of artistic, politically active, urban, secular Jews that flourished in New York in the early to mid-twentieth century is a world well worth exploring. And like her, my own understanding of Jewish identity was truly revolutionized after my surrender to Yeshua.

Dr. Brazier also brings to the fore the extent to which Lewis' reverence for the Hebrew Bible informs his understanding on the new covenant. One of his most penetrating analyses that draws upon this sensibility is that of the portrait of Frank and Sarah Smith in *The Great Divorce*. Here, as Brazier leads us to realize, Lewis has consciously echoed the style and cadence of the prophet Isaiah and the Book of Psalms.

Dr. Brazier's work is replete with well-researched, surprising nuggets. My favorite is Lewis' observation in his foreword to Davidman's *Smoke on the Mountain* that the Jewish follower of Yeshua (my preferred designation) is the only normal human being.

Who knew?

Alan Shore, PhD
Missionary, serving in Washington State
"Modern Jewish History and Culture"

A Hebraic Inkling

Hebraic
*. . . of, relating to, or characteristic of the Hebrews
or their language, religion, or culture.*

First used in the fourteenth century, from the Middle English *Ebrayke*, from Late Latin *Hebraicus*, from Greek *Hebraikos, Hebraios*. Thus, relating to the Jewish people, especially the Hebrews of ancient Israel, and to Judaism, the religion of the chosen people of God, the stories recounting God's dealings with the Jewish peoples: a student of Hebraic religion, the Hebrew people, and their religious literature.

Inkling
*. . . a feeling that something is true or likely to happen,
although not certain.*

The Inklings were a literary discussion group based in the University of Oxford from the early 1930s to c.1950. The Inklings were literary enthusiasts who praised the value of narrative in fiction and encouraged the writing of fantasy, and centered much of their discussion and belief on traditional Christian belief: C. S. Lewis, J. R. R. Tolkien, Owen Barfield, Charles Williams—and others—often meeting in pubs in the centre of Oxford, or in the college rooms of university lecturers. Participants read from works in progress, and much of their discussion fed back into countless published works, often religious and theological, especially by
J. R. R. Tolkien and C. S. Lewis.

"... to remind all us Gentile Christians—who forget it easily enough and even flirt with anti-Semitism—that the Hebrews are spiritually senior to us, that God did entrust the descendants of Abraham with the first revelation of Himself, to put us in our place...."

C. S. Lewis writing to Mrs Johnson, May 14, 1955.

A Hebraic Inkling:
C. S. Lewis on Judaism and the Jews

Introduction

"If we are not Christians we shall dismiss this with the old gibe, 'How odd of God to choose the Jews.' This is impossible for us who believe that God chose that race for the vehicle of His own Incarnation, and who are indebted to Israel beyond all possible repayment."

C. S. LEWIS[1]

1. C. S. LEWIS . . . AND THE JEWISH QUESTION

This work originated in a comment by an old and dear friend, an Anglican religious in her eighties, who commented that a guest staying within their monastic community dismissed C. S. Lewis as anti-Semitic. The guest, a seeker, had come to stay in visitors' quarters, joining in with the chapel services and meals, but she slept separate from the enclosed contemplative community. There were many discussions, intense, as is the way with seekers, and the woman—who by the sister's description was something of "a 1970s liberal Anglican"[2]—had categorized his whole

---

1   Lewis, *Reflections on the Psalms*, 24.
2   The term appears to have been coined by the Revd Andrew Wakefield (1956–2016), letter to *The Church Times*, July 21, 2006. In essence, a form of identity politics where Revd Wakefield identified himself as such and lamented how the progress represented by his education and training as "a 1970s liberal Anglican" was being eroded. The priest was looking back nostalgically at his theological education and formation in the 1970s, where the gospel was re-written to accommodate the socio-sexual, cultural-political revolution of the late 1960s. This also encompassed a liberal theological agenda that questioned the supernatural, the divinity of Christ, and the authority of the Bible,

oeuvre and belief system as anti-Semitic on the basis of one line in Lewis's *The Great Divorce*. This belief about Lewis, it appeared, was a relatively ill-informed but common one amongst those who self-identify as liberal Anglicans. The seeker's comment was about a character in Lewis's story *The Great Divorce*, a hard-bitten character, a left-wing progressive who is dead, in hell, and rails against the Jews (and the Vatican and all political parties except the one he still ideologically believes in).[3] The man is indeed a left-wing anti-Semite, but he does not reflect Lewis's views. In fact, the portrait is accurately presented as a *criticism* of such a man (with echoes of the anti-Semitism of the National Socialists in the early years of the political party, always blaming the Jews for whatever goes wrong). Indeed, the portrait, though written in the early 1940s, could equally apply to certain politicians in the British Labour party today, which is currently having to face accusations of endemic anti-Semitism in its policies and approach to Israel, Zionism, and Hebrew revelation.[4] This anti-Semitism, wrote Lewis, in the character, is one reason, among others, why the man is condemned to an eternity in hell, and can no longer change his beliefs. There is another character later in the book who is Jewish, a young woman who is presented as saintly, altruistic, and Christ-like! That is, after Yeshua the Nazarene: Jesus Christ the Jewish Messiah. The two characters could not be more opposite: and one, the anti-Semite, is hell-bound by his own prejudiced political identity politics; the other, a Jewish woman, is beautifully, paradisiacally, heaven-bound; she will descend to the fringes of hell to attempt to draw some souls out of damnation into their own salvation. She is Jewish but hides not in identity politics.

These portraits are not painted by an anti-Semite. But what did Lewis have to say about Judaism and the Jews, the ancient Hebrews and the Jewish Bible (the church's "Old Testament"), supersessionism, replacement theology, identity politics, and Israel, and therefore the status before humanity of God's chosen people?

---

and refuted most of the propositions within the Creed. See also, on the perceived decline and threat to 1970s liberal Anglicanism, Revd Maggie Guillebaud, letter to *The Church Times*, Aug. 13, 2008. See also, https://en.wikipedia.org/wiki/Liberal_Christianity.

3   Lewis, *The Great Divorce*, ch. 7.

4   See: https://en.wikipedia.org/wiki/Antisemitism_in_the_UK_Labour_Party.

Introduction

2. AIMS AND OBJECTIVES

The aim of this book is to examine precisely what C. S. Lewis believed and wrote about the ancient Hebrews, their scriptures, their status as God's chosen people, and about today's Jews. It also asks, what can we conclude about Lewis's political beliefs, particularly in regard to contemporary humanity's obsession with tribalistic identity politics?

Lewis commented about how many of his contemporaries, especially at Oxford (essentially British academics, a cultural elite, especially high-ranking Anglican clerics), considered it questionable that God chose the Jews for his people, especially in the context of the cursings and violence, vitriolic vindictiveness, even lasciviousness in the Psalms; often the criticism was that they were not "Christian"—or pertinently, the Jews did not hide behind polite pietism! Lewis's proleptic response was to assert how orthodox/traditional Christians, essentially Catholic-Evangelical, found no quarrel with this choice, ". . . God chose that race for the vehicle of His own Incarnation" therefore we are "indebted to Israel beyond all possible repayment."[5] The key to humanity and the world comes through the Jews (not through the European Enlightenment), likewise a right understanding of fallen humanity before God comes from the ancient Hebrew tradition, salvation comes through the Jews, through a Jewish Messiah: "Jesus wasn't actually a Christian. He was a temple worshipping, kosher-keeping, circumcised, first-century Jew, who loved the Book of Isaiah and called God 'Abba.' . . . [He was a respecter of] God's promises as laid out in the Hebrew scriptures."[6]

Neither Lewis nor the detractors of Judaism fully understood the objection that questioned God's choice of the Jewish peoples: God did not "choose" the Jews as individuals; God selected, nominated, adopted, ordinary people—indeed an ordinary man: Abram—to be his chosen (Abraham) and Abra(ha)m's descendants to become the Jewish people, God's chosen. God did not choose a people that already existed; instead, through his election of Abraham, he created a people, whose very existence and identity was constituted by divine election. What the detractors should

---

5 Lewis, *Reflections on the Psalms*, 24.

6 Revd Giles Fraser, speaking on the "Thought for the Day" three-minute broadcast, as part of the Today news and current affairs radio program on BBC R4 (Mon–Fri, 06:00–09:00am; Sat, 0700–9:00). Broadcast, Jan. 1, 2018, 07:47–07:50. See, https://www.bbc.co.uk/programmes/p00szxv6. Archive of recordings: https://www.bbc.co.uk/programmes/p00szxv6/clips

have said, in their pagan politicized prejudices, was that they, in their expertise, were not satisfied with God's creation of a chosen people. The Jews were not already in existence and subsequently chosen: did not God create them, mold and forge them from the stuff of ordinary humanity? As we shall see, Lewis's understanding of Israel in God's purposes may not be flawless—indeed, he failed to understand what "chosen" and a "created people" meant. Nevertheless, his stand against anti-Semitism was grounded in a deeper biblical appreciation of the Jewish people than many of his contemporaries. Therefore, there is a need to assess his understanding of the Jews and Judaism, the Hebrews and their scriptures.

It is important to remember against the backdrop of somber religion that there is an important thread of humor in the Hebrew Bible, a thread that continues through Jewish culture and tradition to this day. Perhaps most Christians fail to see the humor in the Bible, indeed, fail to see how humor can have a parabolic/analogic role to play in illumining God's truth; indeed, C. S. Lewis noted in correspondence to a Mr. Lucas that he had learned from his wife, Joy Davidman, who had been born and raised an American Jew, how God's chosen people see humor in the Hebrew Bible where we Christians do not. Or do we sometimes fail to perceive the paradoxical humor in a religious context?[7] How important is this thread of humor to Lewis in his works? Does it give him a distance from the establishment at Oxford? Lewis understood this long before he met and married Joy Davidman because throughout *The Screwtape Letters* (1942) there is in every chapter a self-effacing mild humor in heaven amongst the redeemed whereas by contrast hell is defined by a cold, steel-hard, absolute deadly seriousness—thus, hell's inhabitants have made themselves unalterable, irredeemable. Generally speaking, Lewis believed that we must picture hell as a state where everyone is perpetually concerned about his or her own dignity, and particularly about advancement, where all have a grievance, a complaint, and where everyone subsists with deadly serious passions: envy and self-importance, superiority and resentment. Laughter in heaven can be self-effacing; it brings us down to size, keeps us in our place, defeats pride, where pride has been traditionally seen as the root and heart of irredeemable sin. As the senior tempter and demon Screwtape notes regarding the humor found in heaven, "Humor and laughter of this kind does us no good and should always be discouraged. Besides, the phenomenon is of itself disgusting and

---

7   "Lewis writing to Mr Lucas, Dec 6, 1956." In Lewis, *Collected Letters, Vol. III*, 814–15.

Introduction

a direct insult to the realism, dignity, and austerity of Hell."[8] Lewis may have been writing in the early 1940s—and could see something of this in the development of nationalistic socialist movements (Marxism in Russia; Nazism in Germany), but there is something of an epidemic of this deadly seriousness in the West since Lewis's death in 1963 given the development of (individualistic) identity politics, often through tribalistic sexual identities.

Many Jews see humor and hyperbole in the sayings of Jesus. Hyperbole is also found in poetry (often known as known as auxesis), hence it can be found in the Book of Psalms, and also the Proverbs, to evoke strong feelings and impressions. Such is not meant to be taken straightforwardly but analogically. For example, Jesus's use of the mustard seed,[9] which is not actually, scientifically speaking, the smallest of all seeds and does not become the largest of trees, but the intention of Jesus is to draw attention to the contrast between the size of the tiny seed and that of the mature plant, and then to draw an analogy between this and how salvation and the kingdom of heaven develops from seemingly insignificant beginnings yet appears, in some ways, limitless.

Why speak of *A Hebraic Lewis*? Why we might talk of Lewis as Hebraic? Because this is something of a hidden side of Lewis that is quite distinct from your average Church of England theologian and philosopher (remembering that Lewis was an Anglican) and this element contradicts the implicit anti-Semitism that has marked the British political and religious establishment, to an extent. It is fair to say that today, in the early decades of the twenty-first century, we are, perhaps, more conscious of the need to see something of a balance between the Christian West (or what is left of it) and the Jews, the eternal Israel, and the ancient Hebrew witness and scriptures. Therefore, the aim and objective of this book is to uncover and analyze this Hebraic seam to C. S. Lewis: the man and his work.

---

8   Lewis, *The Screwtape Letters*, 54; Chapter 11 features Screwtape's complaint with the subject of humor as compared to the seriousness of hell, though the dialectic as such is spread throughout the work.

9   Matt 13:31–32; Mark 4:30–32; and Luke 13:18–19.

3. EXPLANATIONS, QUALIFICATIONS

A few terms need to explained, and qualified in their use, before we proceed. Some readers familiar with Lewis's books may not appreciate the full meaning and use of the terms used here. Professionals familiar with these terms may still gain some understanding of the Hebraic context in which they are used in this book. Many Catholics and Evangelicals are familiar with these terms derived from New Testament Greek, and from *ecclesial* (i.e., church) Latin—ironically it is often Lewis's Anglicans who are ignorant of them.

Election

In a sense, this is a book about election: rhetorically we may ask, Who is elected, and for what? Elected to serve? Elected to represent? Elected to salvation? But first we must ask, who elects? God elects. Election is about God's search for humanity—fallen humanity; it is about those elected to demonstrate and guide humanity, those elected to salvation: but saved from what and to what? The ancient Hebrews were elected by God through Abraham to be a chosen people. What does Lewis say about this? Jews are elected to this status, and how does this affect us? Are we gentiles elected too, through the death and resurrection of Jesus, the Jewish Messiah? The apostle Paul says much on this and how gentiles are enfolded into the election of the Jews. Lewis confirms this. The need for election originates with the fall—original sin: humanity separated themselves from God. The process of election starts in essence with one person: Abraham, and culminates with Jesus. Election is about atonement: how we are forgiven and thereby reconciled to God, and therefore no longer lost, but saved. There are many words and concepts here, but in essence Lewis sees the ancient Hebrew patriarchs as the root of atonement and election. Now, the conflicting and often contradictory propitiatory elements in doctrines of atonement have been, and still are, the cause of profound disagreements amongst the churches, and have caused much disagreement and deep puzzlement, as we will see in the young Lewis. Why should atonement focus down onto a dead Jewish religious man two thousand years ago? Yet, the gospel claims that through his death and resurrection we gentiles are enfolded into God's chosen and saved from ourselves to the glorious life of heaven, though only if we so wish! Many reject their election,

Introduction

preferring the nihilistic chaos of hell. Or as Lewis said in relation to this, "All get what they want, they don't always like it."[10]

A Rose by Any Other Name?[11]

At the center of this work is Jesus Christ. Jesus and Christ are modern English names, but are the same reality as their counterparts in Greek *iēsuos christos* (Greek) and *Yeshua Ha Mashiach* (Hebrew). Yeshua is Jesus' proper name: Yeshua ("the one who delivers," "rescues/rescuer"; "God is savior") is what he was named shortly after he was born, the name above all names given to Mary by the messenger Gabriel. Yeshua is an ancient Hebrew name, all Jews are given Hebrew names, for it has been the language of Jews for nigh on 4,000 years! The name "Jesus" is simply Yeshua in an Anglicized form. *Ha Mashiach* means the Anointed One (derived from the ancient Hebrew tradition of anointing the king with oil). The word "Christ" (from *Christos*, the Greek translation of *Mashiach*) has taken on a global meaning in the West, and is often divorced from its Hebraic roots.

Like many ancient names that had cultural or religious meanings, the name Jesus, Yeshua—given to Mary by Gabriel, the angel/messenger at the annunciation—was known to those who heard it as signifying "God is savior," or "Jehovah is savior," "the one who delivers"; Christ means "Anointed One," Messiah. The word Messiah was commonly used in the intertestamental era (i.e., the time between the end of the Old Testament and the start of the New), the concept of messiahship having developed in later Judaism from its earlier roots in the anointing of kings and priests. Messiah was not necessarily a name, but a label, an office, a role, essentially a title. By the time of Jesus of Nazareth, the title "Messiah" was often attributed to those set apart by God for certain roles, such as priests and kings (though there were no more Jewish kings after the exile). It's not about those whom the people "like"—popular votes were nothing to do with it. However, to be the Messiah was to be the one anointed at the end of days, chosen to deliver and rule Israel. Jesus is taken by many of those around him to be the Messiah; hence the early attribution that he is the Christ. Therefore, Jesus Christ, in name and title, was God's salvation, the Anointed One. This is not to be confused with the idea that Jesus was

10   Lewis, *The Magician's Nephew*, 162.
11   William Shakespeare, *Romeo and Juliet*, Act II, Scene I

the second person of the Trinity. The trinitarian perception, however, is part of the dawning realization in the early church, with ample pointers and examples of Jesus's divine nature in the books that became the New Testament (texts produced by the earliest church in the years after the resurrection and ascension): starting immediately after the resurrection with the concept, Son of God; the title "son of God" in the NT often simply means Messiah—as the Davidic king was the "son" of God (for example, Ps 2:7); later, based on Jesus of Nazareth's assertion that he was *Huios tou Patéra* (Son of the Father: to quote the Greek of the Gospel narrative, written later in the first century).

Around the time of Jesus's birth, messiahship carried expectations. Some saw the coming messiah as a political leader who would expel the Romans; others expected a messiah who would be a partisan revolutionary whose aims were unclear; to yet more, the messiah would return the temple religion back to a happier time, he would oversee the restoration of Israel. To an extent, these can be seen as purely human offices. During the intertestamental period there were many false messiahs, men raised up to realize a revolutionary, political, or religious role supported by a group or sect to save Israel in some way or other. However, false messiahs lapsed, disappeared, or were killed by the Romans or the Jewish religious authorities. The Jews were left still hoping.

The idea of redemption, of salvation, was part of these multitudinous expectations of a messiah figure during the intertestamental period—but saved *from what*, redeemed *to what*? The answers to those questions were as varied as the messianic expectations of these would-be messiahs. As a redeemer figure, expected and foretold, Jesus does not necessarily live up to the expectations of his fellow Jews. However, on reflection, the clues were there all along in Jesus's life and ministry, and crucially in the Old Testament. The ancient Hebrew priests and kings were anointed, they were messiahs (Exod 30:22–25); later, this messiahship became focused on one anointed by God as a leader, a king from the line of David. Therefore, Jesus of Nazareth was perceived by many who saw and heard him to be the long-awaited Messiah, with different and often subjective expectations as to his role. What is important is that *a posteriori*, after the event, the earliest church interpreted this messiahship in the context of Jesus's role as God descended to earth to judge and forgive humanity, hence the use of the Greek word *Christos* by the writers of the New Testament. Jesus is then the final Messiah of messiahs.

Introduction

In Christian thinking, the Messiah/Christ is ultimately revealed to be a trinitarian truth: God anoints God, *his* Son, to descend to save his chosen people, in potential, along with all humanity, reascending with them into the divine life. Only in the fullness of the incarnation-cross-resurrection and the ascension is messiahship finally defined by Jesus. Then his life and ministry, his sayings and actions, take on new meaning, a significance and understanding veiled to many during his lifetime. Whatever the expectations of messiahship, Jesus of Nazareth is *the* Messiah (therefore, *the* Christ), not *a* messiah, political or otherwise. It is fair to say that some of the Hebrew expectations were blown away by God's final revelation; whatever people expected, it fell short of what was given by God in this Jesus. People could not see or fully understand what Messiah was to be, even though with hindsight the evidence was there in the Old Testament.

The witness of the apostles, disciples, and the early church is then a form of revelation equal to Jewish scripture. The early church tradition replaces the old Hebrew categories of messiahship; the expectations of the contemporaries of Yeshua, those who knew him, saw him, and spoke with him, were fulfilled by God's revelation (even if they did not fully realize his ontic status), but not necessarily in accordance with what they desired or expected. This divergence also extended to the interpretation of messiahship that the Jewish religious authorities held to in Jerusalem. For many years the Western church concentrated only on the early church tradition and the conclusions of the church councils in the fourth and fifth centuries, often, in effect, ignoring the Hebrew tradition that Jesus of Nazareth was born into. In recent years, many theologians and Bible scholars, for example the N. T. Wright, derive most of their conclusions about Jesus of Nazareth from an understanding of the New Testament's Jewish background, a setting in the life of the times in some ways. Perhaps the answer is to hold in balance the Hebrew tradition and categories, the perceptions of the earliest church, and also the conclusions of the later church councils, about the person and nature of Jesus. This is how to see and understand the term Messiah, the Christ. In his middle years, Lewis's work is, we may assert, dominated by Greek philosophical categories and concepts; this gives way more-and-more in his mature years to Hebraic categories and concepts.

It is the intention with this work to switch between the Hebrew and English names for Jesus Christ simply to emphasize that he is not simply an historic, English-speaking, religious professional! In addition, we err if we forget or marginalize the fact that Jesus is a Jew, and represents nigh on two thousand years of Hebrew culture and tradition, embodying a unique religious development as representative of God's chosen people: the flock of Israel.

"What's in a name? That which we call a rose, by any other name would smell as sweet," Shakespeare had Juliet say.[12] What underpins the name Yeshua, and its modern equivalents, is the same: Jesus Christ, the Jewish Messiah, God's only Son, born in and through the chosen people.

"Hegelianism"

Another piece of contextual information we need to set in place is the philosophical background in Lewis' time. Hegelianism was the dominant philosophy and "religion" of C. S. Lewis as a young man, as an atheistic apostate. It is from Hegelianism that Lewis struggles to escape as, over years, the realization that "God is" dawns on him. Hegelianism was a philosophical system issuing from Georg Hegel and can be defined by the statement, "the rational alone is real."[13] Therefore, to the young Lewis, only the rational categories existed. This absolute idealism dictated any religious beliefs he began to have an inkling of, so he began to invent his own pagan religion! But the Holy Spirit pressed on him—which is the story of the first chapter here.

"Revelation"

In the context of Lewis's philosophical roots, we need to be clear on his understanding of revelation. Revelation is personal, as in the realization of perception and understanding many people will have—a *eureka* moment when one finds something, or when something is revealed to an individual. But it is also more than that, more than the personal and subjective. Revelation is about God's self-disclosure to humanity. Lewis understood and accepted how God had revealed of God's own self to humanity in multifarious and diverse ways down the millennia and across vast geographical and cultural eons, but as an orthodox Christian

---

12   Juliet to Romeo: William Shakespeare, *Romeo and Juliet*, Act II, Scene I

13   "*Vorrede: Was vernünftig ist, das ist Wirklich; und was wirklich ist, das ist vernünftig.*" G. W. F. Hegel, *Elements of the Philosophy of Right* (1821):" "What is rational is real; what is real is rational."

Introduction

he knew both as fact and from personal encounter that Christ was unique, the highest form of self-revelation of the one true living God. So to talk about Christ is to talk about God; to speak of Christ is to speak of revelation (John 14:7–14). Over recent centuries revelation has often been pitted against reason, against philosophical rationalism. Because of the confidence emanating from the Age of Reason and the Enlightenment, a confidence issuing from the belief that the human capacity to reason things out was all that was needed, revelation became in certain quarters, obsolete. Lewis seeks to try to hold both revelation and reason in balance; as a trained philosopher he knew and understood the background against which he was writing.

"Doctrine of God"/"Names for God"

Lewis the philosopher reasoned; but the distinction between reason and revelation was, for him, a supplementary dialectic between philosophical reasoning and Hebrew revelation, therefore we are "given" what we need to know and, pertinently, do: beliefs and actions. Hence, the evolving understanding and behavior of the ancient Hebrews into the Jews of the intertestamental period, even when it clashes with or contradicts rationalism: therefore, the academy and the temple stand, often offset or seeming to contradict, but this is a supplementary dialectic between the academy (Greek) and the temple (Hebrew): and the temple will replace the academy in the eschaton.

What were the Hebrews given to know about God? The names given to the Hebrews for knowing God develop, evolve, over time. Within a name is a relationship and an understanding about the nature of God in God's infinity: we can understand something of this in how Lewis came to know God and was converted.

Messianic–Hebraic

Messianic (of the Messiah, the Anointed One) Jews are ethnic Jews who believe that Jesus is the Christ, the Son of God, with all that is implied and asserted from the Hebrew Bible and the Christian New Testament. Messianic Jews usually seek to live in obedience to *Halakha*, religious law, including Talmudic and Rabbinic declarations and traditions in addition to the Mosaic Law.[14]

14   The Talmud is the central text of Rabbinic Judaism and the primary source of Jewish religious law (*halakha*) and Jewish theology.

A HEBRAIC INKLING

By comparison Hebraic Christians (essentially Christians who embrace the Jewish roots of their faith) are people of any cultural background who acknowledge that Jesus Christ is the Son of God and worship and proclaim Yeshua of Nazareth, *bar Yoseph*, Lord and God; they seek to worship in the way the ultra-early church did (for example, as recorded in the Acts of the Apostles). Hebraic Christians are children of Abraham by faith, even if gentiles by birth, and will emphasize and cite Paul's comments to the church in Galatia: "Understand, then, that those who have faith are children of Abraham" (Gal 3:7). Therefore, all who genuinely believe are the descendants of Abraham.[15] This was something Lewis affirmed, as we shall see.

Jewish Christian

C. S. Lewis, in all probability unaware of the term Messianic Jew (the term was not really in use in his time), referred to his wife Joy Davidman as a Jewish Christian. Born to East European Jewish parents in New York, she did not seek to live in obedience to Halakha, following her conversion, but was critically aware of the need to see how the two covenants interrelated and showed no mercy to Oxford academics and establishment Anglicans who had not even thought about these issues. In retrospect, the main difference between Jewish Christians and Messianic Jews is the crucial emphasis on the Law.

The question this work addresses then is in what manner, and how evidently Hebraic, was C. S. Lewis, and how does this awareness/consciousness change over the course of his life.

Identity Politics

The West today—indeed much of the rest of the developed world—is obsessed with asserting and projecting identity politics, that is, self-beliefs and values, an identity, based on culture and anthropological detail, that claims uniqueness and therefore special treatment by governments and other people. This identity is essentially a projection of vanity and pride, self-importance (such identities are often the result of psychological delusions). However, we err if we believe that being a Jew is just another form of identity politics. That said, the Jews should not, perhaps, be considered a separate race: there is but one race—the human race. This

---

15   See: https://www.myshalom.org/hebraic_christianity

applies to all forms of identity politics (especially where questions of ethnicity are considered): all we can claim in terms of identity before God the Lord is that we are *human*, if more elucidation is needed, then we are *merely human*. The people that were the ancient Hebrews were selected, chosen by God; this gave them a special rank or position, but they were not a different humanoid race. (The last one available that stood alongside humanity—*homo sapiens*—were the Neanderthals!)[16] However, Jews have had what can be seen as a crucial witness for thousands of years as God's chosen, to which they have by-and-large held faithful.

4. A HEBRAIC INKLING: C. S. LEWIS ON JUDAISM AND THE JEWS: SYNOPSIS

This work is divided into three parts, thirteen chapters in all. Each chapter opens with quotes from C. S. Lewis, from the Hebrew Bible and the New Testament, or from some other sources. These quotes form the basis of the analysis in each chapter.

PART I: REVELATION

In the first chapter, **1. The Young C. S. Lewis**, we need to examine Lewis's life, the development of his religious beliefs, and his implicit political beliefs, all of which betray a mixed, developing attitude towards the Jewish people. Lewis's youth, as a boy and a young man, reflected much of the implicit anti-Semitism inherent to the public-school-educated Edwardian establishment. As a young man, he not only saw Judaism as replaced (i.e., irrelevant) but also Christianity as relegated: a form of Enlightenment-led atheistic supersessionism grounded in Hegelianism, logical positivism, individualism, and private morality. From the time of his conversion, the more Lewis studied the Bible and the Christian theological tradition the more he moved away from the Edwardian Anglican civic religion he had been raised in and imbued with in the English public school system, though he remained a stalwart of the Church of England, albeit not uncritically.

---

16   Neanderthals (*homo neanderthalensis*) are an extinct species of ancient humans who lived in Europe and Asia until c. 40,000 years ago. They became extinct due to what is now seen as assimilation into the modern human genome, climatic change, disease, and other factors.

Chapter 2, The Hebrews, the Jews, ... and God. I: Lewis's conversion happened in several stages (though, indeed, the final stage of his conversion happened with the death of his wife, Joy). Of concern to us is how in the early 1930s he re-evaluates everything in his life, particularly the demands of God in the gospel and in particular the question of sacrifice: from the ancient Hebrew practices to the temple in the intertestamental period, through to the nature of and necessity for Jesus's sacrifice. This puzzled him. The solution, the reconciliation, is in acceptance of the uniqueness of Jesus's sacrifice, in relation to pagan sacrifice as a precursor: he must see Jesus as the one true sacrifice: from a Jewish perspective. How does Lewis's conversion compare with other leading theologians, for example, the Swiss Reformed Minister and theologian Karl Barth? Different though they are, they share a common ground in relation to the Jews, and the ancient Hebrew scriptures. Their relationship to God as Christians could not exist apart from this approach, which requires acceptance of all that is Hebrew along with the continued validity of the Jewish testament. Lewis, like Karl Barth, needs to approach God from a whole new perspective: God as "God is . . . ." This leads to understanding Exodus 3:14 in a whole new light: The Lord as "I Am": leading to what we may consider to be the personal relationship of, and with, *YHWH*.

C. S. Lewis and Karl Barth are examined together in the third chapter—**3. The Hebrews, the Jews, ... and God: II**. Lewis and Barth can be considered dissimilar. Indeed, to many from a more extreme position they could be seen as incompatible. Yet, as secularism, dominated by consumerism, has taken hold in the West since their respective deaths in the 1960s, both seem closer than their denominational categories might suggest. What we can discover is how, like Lewis, the Edwardian young gentleman with an empire mentality, the young Karl Barth reflected the *Weltanschauung* of German society and its attitude towards the Jews. At least, he did prior to his conversion, his *retraktation*, his return to a traditional and orthodox Christianity and church. How does Lewis compare with his fellow inklings? Lewis's comments in relation to the Jews were more progressive than the Inklings, with the exception of J. R. R. Tolkien. There was as pervasive a veiled anti-Semitism in the innate beliefs and cultural background to some of the Inklings as there was amongst the Oxbridge common-room staff. Therefore, we will consider Barth on the Davidian Israelite, and the importance of *Israelitisch*; likewise, at this formative time, Lewis's comments in *The Pilgrim's Progress* (1933), and

Introduction

the approach of both to what may be considered to be at the heart of Judaism and the Hebrew covenant: the Law?

What can we establish about Lewis's understanding of supersessionism, replacement theology, and the relation of the Christian West with Israel and the Jews? This is the subject of the fourth chapter: **4. God's Chosen: Holiness, Theology and Spirituality, . . . Pride.** Lewis swam against the tide during the 1930s: he spoke out strongly against the rise of National Socialism in Germany. All ideas of a replacement theology go, along with supersessionism: Christianity and Judaism stand in complement.

For Lewis, "chosenness" is the belief that the Jews, having descended from the ancient Israelites and Hebrews, are *ha'am hanivhar* ("the chosen people"): chosen to be in a direct covenant with God as *'am qadosh* ("holy people," Deut 7:6; 14:2); cf. *goy qadosh*[17] ("holy nation," Exod 19:6). Why do so many find such a difficulty with the concept of a chosen people? Lewis asserts that the ancient Hebrews through to the Jews today were chosen *for the sake of the unchosen*: Abraham is weighted down with a heavy burden through which "all nations will be blest" (Gen 22:18. Cf. Acts 3:25; Gal 3:8, 16). Why does C. S. Lewis reject so firmly any belief in "supersessionism" or "replacement theology"? He does not see the church as a *replacement* of Israel, considering both in some ways complementary, but how does he arrive at such a position? Lewis points always to Paul's Letter to the church in Rome (Rom 11:17–21) about how the gentiles are grafted into the holy root of Israel. Lewis looks at the question of supersessionism and replacement theology in terms of the sins of "pride" and "superiority." Essentially, we can see how Lewis's approach to supersessionism and replacement theology is to cut through the pretense of categorizing such theories as academic, impartial propositions, and to expose them as instances of the sin of pride, which they are.

PART II: SCRIPTURE

In the fifth chapter—**5. The Hebrew Scriptures: Historicity and Humanity**—we can examine Lewis on the Bible—essentially the Hebrew scriptures? What did he write and how do these missives compare? What

---

17   This is in biblical Hebrew, as distinct from modern Hebrew or Yiddish. The word goy is, in some circles in Yiddish and Modern Hebrew, regarded as a derogative for gentiles, but not so in biblical Hebrew.

does Lewis consider in terms of a doctrine of creation? Lewis insists that we regard the Hebrew Bible as holy and inspired,[18] and therefore he deals with the question of the miraculous as part of creation.

For Lewis, genre is to be seen as closely related to the aims and objectives of the writer: Is a particular text intended to be factual, historic, or scientific? Is it meant to teach something spiritual or moral through story, allegory, or parable? Is it to be seen as simply entertaining or an amusing insight into the superstitions and magic of primitive people, as some skeptics or atheists would assert? Specifically, regarding the Hebrew Bible as literature, as Lewis does, as it is elevated into something more than itself, then the vehicle is greater than the merely human; and the range and wealth of meanings will be limitless, provided we hold to the reality of what we read. Therefore, we must consider that the pertinent question, in relation to Lewis on scripture is, what exactly is the function of the Hebrew Bible, and what is it that scripture teaches us generally? All of this adds up to what Lewis refers to in broad terms as the humanity of scripture specifically, and the historicity of the Hebrew Bible, generally. Lewis stresses how infinite wisdom comes down and is beyond complete human comprehension. Therefore, we can see how for Lewis the Bible is ruled over by a divine presence that inspires but does not dictate.

Chapter 6. The Psalms I: Hebrew Theological Poetry: Why did Lewis devote an entire book to a study of the Psalms: *Reflections on the Psalms* (1958)? Is this book biblical studies? Or, more pertinently, is it a personal theological survey in relation to salvation history amongst God's chosen for all humanity? We will discover how this is one of Lewis's last books and reflects considerable maturity. Professionally, from the mid-1920s, Lewis earned his daily bread as a teacher of English Literature at Oxford, then as a professor at Cambridge. He was an academic of some distinction, albeit within his primary expertise in literature. Lewis knew poetry and literature (he was an acknowledged and published poet himself). When reading, he noted how the Hebrew Bible as literature was taken up to be the medium of something that is more than merely human. For Lewis, the Psalms are primarily poems—poems that are to be sung! Lewis demonstrated how the Psalms do have a unique poetic structure, grammar, and syntax that survives translation, having been translated into hundreds of world languages.

---

18   Lewis, *Reflections on the Psalms*, 93f.

Introduction

What did Lewis write about judgement in the Psalms? Cursings, death, . . . and the fair beauty of the Lord. In **Chapter 7. The Psalms II: Judgements and Cursings—Imprecatory Poems**, Lewis sees the judgement and cursings in the Psalms as almost dialectical. While Christians of a traditional persuasion fear judgement, the Hebrew mindset in the Psalms welcomes judgement—like a plaintiff does who has been wronged and trusts the integrity of the judge. Why does Lewis digress to examine justice in the sayings of Jesus (e.g., Luke 18:1–5)? It is to emphasize an illustration of the psalmist's Hebraic cry for the plaintiff in a civil case—the poor woman deprived of justice, faced with a corrupt judiciary calls for a judgment. Therefore, Lewis asks, why are we surprised to find in the Book of the Psalms a deep longing for judgement, without the fear of a traditional Christian? So how does Lewis define our "rightness" with God? The desire for justice must not be equated with the demand for vengeance, and vengeance must not be allowed to turn over into cursings.

So how does Lewis tackle the thorny question of cursing in the imprecatory psalms? He handles it with difficulty. For he is blind to the vast multitude of sins in the West that involve such criticisms, often cursings out of self-righteousness, backed by assumed superiority. Lewis relates all of this to the Hebraic concept of death: with the promise of eternal life withheld. Therefore, Lewis begins to identify a temporal paradox in the Psalms: have we already been saved or is salvation still to come?

Chapter 8. The Psalms III: A Hebraic Doctrine of Creation: Lewis understood that the Psalms can give us a sound doctrine of creation in terms of a model that complements the account in the Book of Genesis. What exactly is this understanding? At the center of any doctrine of creation is the biblical account: the Book of Genesis, the prologue to John's Gospel, and, for example, Psalms 104 and 148: the "speech-act" model—God conceives and speaks, and creation is created. Therefore, it is important that Lewis can present this as fundamental to an ancient Hebrew agrarian economy with small urban developments—towns—merging seamlessly with the land and its crops. The majority of people were rural, living off the land: livestock and crops. This was celebrated through festivals when the harvest was gathered in. Lewis notes how when the poets write of seeing *YHWH*, indeed, longing to see God, we would be in error to see this as only a desire to be "religious" in a social setting: they were meeting with the source and sustainer of their lives. This Hebrew praise for the functional beauty of a landscape was commonplace. Unlike the creation myths of many of the world's religions, Lewis considers the Hebraic revelation unique: nature and God are considered *distinct*.[19] All is created by God, ex nihilo. This is clearly read from the Psalms, writes Lewis, and the condition of creation (including humanity) is to honor the Lord in love and obedience. Creation can turn away and rebel, but if it does it must live with the consequences.

Lewis takes further this detail in his Hebraic doctrine of creation. A doctrine that empties nature of any sense of pagan divinity, allows creation to be a symbol of God-like action, an expression, even as an appearance from God. What place does Lewis afford the ancient Hebrews? The Jews are the chosen people of God, and have a unique role before humanity, but they are not necessarily (along with the rest of humanity) the center of creation, and the rest of creation is not necessarily organized around humanity. All wait upon God for their sustenance, their livelihood, their very existence to be.

An important question is addressed in **Chapter 9. The Psalms IV: Hebraic Prefigurement and Meaning**. This relates pertinently to the Book of the Psalms: what is the relationship of the Hebrew Bible to other religions, but specifically, to other forms of God's revelation to humanity? This question arises explicitly from the ancient pagan religions Lewis studied (North-West European, ancient Indian, Egyptian, *et al.*). This we examine next.

If there are links of intimation between religions (for example, pagan models of the Christ), in the same way that there are intimations of God's purposes through salvation history, centered on the revelation in and through the ancient Hebrew people and their scriptures, then this raises questions, for Lewis, about subsequent interpretations, or, as he termed it, "second meanings." At the heart of agrarian societies the world over were myths of death and resurrection. A "god" who dies and is often raised up again, a "god" who through death brings life to people bears an uncanny relationship—an intimation—of what happened to Jesus on the cross and in the tomb. We will see how Lewis notes that although the story of Yeshua has remarkable parallels with the principle of descending and re-ascending within nature myths, there is no suggestion in the Gospels of a

---

19   Lewis, *Reflections on the Psalms*, 66.

Introduction

self-awareness of this parallel in Jesus or his disciples. In the incarnation story, God descends to reascend.

Lewis does consider a digression with reference to a degree of prefigurement that is comparable to the evolution of the understanding of monotheism—an analogical model—and the names for God in the ancient Hebrews. To this extent Lewis considers an ancient Egyptian poem, The Hymn to the Sun, by Akhenaten (circa fourteenth century BC).[20] What is Lewis dealing with? Some may consider there to be a problem with such prefigurement because it appears to do an injustice to the original aims and intentions of the author of the myth in asserting a second, a subsequent, level of meaning? We will see what Lewis proposed.

A consideration of second meanings leads us to **Chapter 10. The Psalms V: Yeshua, Mashiach: Second Meanings in the Psalms**. The greatest evidence of prefigurement in the Hebrew Bible is of course the promise of the Messiah: the deliverer, the rescuer, the one to save—Yeshua Ha Mashiach. So what can we read of Jesus Christ from the Book of the Psalms: prophetic previsions at the heart of the Hebrew Bible? And what did Lewis note? He analyzes typical messianic psalms; second, directly predictive (prophetic) psalms; third, mystically messianic psalms; fourth, psalms of trust in Christ; fifth, creation–new creation messianic psalms. In many ways, the second meaning issuing from prefigured interpretations represent the Christological movement of the entire Hebrew scriptures.

In an interim conclusion, we may ask, how did the Hebrews relate to the God, to their identity and status as God's chosen, in Lewis's estimation? How through the Davidian poems, that are the Psalms, is humanity blessed? And, we ask, what are other scholars' assessments, judgements, criticisms of Lewis in his work on the Psalms?

PART III: FAMILY

Chapter 11. Sarai-Sarah: Identity . . . in the Lord, opens with the one scholar who had begun to examine Lewis on the Jews generally, and the question of anti-Semitism specifically: Kathryn Lindskoog (1934–2003). In a brief five-page essay,[21] she presents a study of Lewis's position on the Jews, in particular the historical events of the 1930s and 1940s, the National Socialist dictates in relation to the Jews, the role of legislation

---

20   Lewis, *Reflections on the Psalms*, 73–76
21   Lindskoog, "C. S. Lewis's Anti-Anti-Semitism."

in the oppression and denial of the Jews (essentially grounded in the 1935 Nuremberg Race Laws), but also his whole understanding of the Jews, contemporary and historic: that is the Hebrew-Jewish witness of thousands of years . . . as God's chosen people. She refers to Lewis's position as "anti- anti-Semitism." This attack on anti-Semitism focuses on Lewis's *The Great Divorce* (1945). How accurate is Lingskoog's assessment? Lewis's story sketch focuses on a character named Sarah Smith (a typically Jewish name, with an English family name): Sarah exudes Christ-like love—*agápē*—to her own loss.

Lindskoog demonstrates how at the fall of Western Europe in 1940, Lewis and Tolkien both realized that there were statements in their works that would have marked them as sympathetic to the Jews and also as anti-Nazi!—however, they were prepared to face the onslaught of "the tyrant Hitler and his legions" if England fell to invasion. To what extent, we may ask, do people fail to know of this stand, but also to perceive and understand Lewis's dismissal of the stereotypical picture of Jews common to the British people? To what extent is Lewis's portrait of a Messianic Jew or Jewish Christian complimentary? We will see how a key biblical text, for Lewis, that may resolve these questions is Ephesians 2:11-15.

Moving into **Chapter 12. The Incarnation Nation: The People and the Savior** we are beginning to focus more and more on the heart of Judaea-Christian revelation: Jesus of Nazareth—properly *Yeshua ben Yoseph, Ha Mashiach*. But this is more than merely one person; this is a man who has a cataclysmic role for the nation of Israel, and for humanity: beyond Abraham—people, nations, humanity. Ancient Israel consistently failed: it struggles through mistake after mistake as to what it should do and be; it kept reverting to pagan religious practices, and when it did appear to get the temple worship right, it becomes a fixed civic religion that sacrifices the prophets and refutes their warnings: thus says the Hebrew Bible. Yet it endured and bore witness, testimony, against the surrounding pagan gentiles in all their worldly success.

In general terms, Lewis warns of the dangers of nationalism and the religious confusion and nihilism that gentile nations produce. In this context, we need to consider skepticism and the scandal of particularity. likewise, we must consider, with Lewis, why God spent thousands of years forging and creating, honing and refining, at times even seeming to brutalize, a people into the right character, the right religion, the right belief and obedience—why was this so? Lewis often wrote of the desire amongst modern, usually Western, Christians to reduce Jesus to a universal mystic, or to a non-denominational religious teacher. This marginalized the nation and Yeshua's nationality and status as a Jew. Lewis was clear on this question. God, for Jesus, raised in an orthodox Jewish culture, is the God of the Jews, the creator, *YHWH* the righteous Lord, the one true God outside of the world and beyond all other "gods." If nation is important so is blood for Lewis. We then need to consider the Passover, and specifically why blood? (This question was a stumbling block to the young Lewis, when he was ripe for conversion.) With maturity he saw the answer: simple—because the ancient Hebrews conceptualized the very life-force of an individual as being in, with, contained by, but essentially part of, the blood; people bled to death: The answer is, we will see, in the issue of blood and death; to grasp this we need to understand and comprehend Hebrew religious culture: the death and resurrection of Yeshua is at the heart of this life and death, though it can be seen as a Hebrew paradox.

Why the nation? Lewis has no intellectual qualms about naming the Hebrews as the chosen people, with Yeshua representing and carrying all with him. The people are the nation: Lewis notes how a special illumination was given to the Jews, and subsequently to Christians, but, in the context of prefigurement, there is also some divine light—fragments of the true light—that were given, and are still being offered, to other peoples, irrespective of how flawed their own religious scheme-of-things was or is. Therefore, we emphasize Lewis's often repeated aphorism that all that was best in Judaism survives in Christianity.

The final chapter, **Chapter 13. Joy Davidman . . . and the Mature C. S. Lewis**, considers further Lewis's anti-anti-Semitism, and his prophetic anti-racism! In his maturity he not only raises the Jews up as the model and template for humanity but warns of the cost of the racism he had witnessed as a privileged member of a public-school-educated elite: Lewis is unswerving in naming and shaming racism.

Lewis's view of the Jews—and associated anti-Semitism—was, as we have seen so far, turned on its head initially by his conversion in the early 1930s, but also by his marriage to Helen Joy Davidman, an American Jewish convert to Christianity, in 1956. Further, she comes to him with two sons from her first marriage and this too left its mark on him in relation to his view of Judaism. We need to consider Joy's life story and her religious pilgrimage so as to understand the profound influence she had on Lewis: this was a woman who as a teenager glimpsed that beauty was a sacrament at the heart of all things. She was conditioned by her parents' cultural atheism, which led her to scorn all things Jewish, likewise as a young Marxist she espoused dialectic cultural atheism. But when she embraced Christ, she also re-embraced some of her Jewish heritage, which impacted Lewis. For Lewis, religion and theology gets deeply personal and Hebraic; when one of Davidman's children—Lewis's stepson, David—sought, as a teenager, to return to Joy's birth-faith, after her untimely death, Lewis moved all to accommodate his wishes and raise him as a Jew (seeking out kosher foods, special pots and pans, etc.).

We need also to consider the final—Job-like—stage of conversion following Joy's death. Lewis's theology grew out of his personal experience of God in Christ: the death of his mother and his wife Joy Davidman, both from cancer, and his conversion experiences. These events point not to a single Damascus Road epiphany but to a process with identifiable moments.

Lewis's invocation of the shadows of eternity, intimations through the veil of this world of the life to come, revealed through Christ, which characterize and define his theology, grew out of his personal experience of God in Christ-Yeshua: the death from cancer of his mother (in 1908), which contributed to his loss of faith (the clearing out, perhaps, of a false "god"?), his conversion back to faith (to theism in 1929), and then to the Christ (in 1931), and then the death of his wife Joy Davidman, again from cancer (1960), are all staging posts in the process of conversion and reorientation, redemption and salvation, driven by serious changes in his thinking and the ideas that formed his life and character: finally, he meets with the Hebraic Jobian God who hung on a cross for Lewis, for Joy, and their family.

PART I

REVELATION

"You will show me the path of life;
In Your presence is fullness of joy;
At Your right hand are pleasures forevermore."
PSALM 16:11

1

The Young C. S. Lewis

"I wonder will you ever get to the end of the Bible; the undesirable 'primitives' around you will enable you to appreciate the Hebrews who were class A primitives after all."

C. S. LEWIS[1]

"Do not think that I have come to abolish the law or the prophets; I have come not to abolish but to fulfil. For truly I tell you, until heaven and earth pass away, not one iota, not one stroke of a letter, will pass from the law until all is accomplished. Therefore, whoever annuls one of the least of these commandments, and teaches others to do the same, will be called least in the kingdom of heaven; but whoever does them and teaches them will be called great in the kingdom of heaven. For I tell you, unless your righteousness exceeds that of the scribes and Pharisees, you will never enter the kingdom of heaven."

MATTHEW 5:17-20

"My conversion involved as yet no belief in a future life. I now number it among my greatest mercies that I was permitted for several months, perhaps for a year, to know God and to attempt obedience without even raising that question. My training was like that of the Jews to whom He revealed Himself centuries before there was a whisper of anything better (or worse) beyond the grave than shadowy and featureless Sheol. And I did not dream even of that."

C. S. LEWIS[2]

1. INTRODUCTION

Born in Northern Ireland to educated professional parents in 1898, C. S. Lewis (Clive Staples—known to his family and friends, from childhood, at his instigation as "Jack"), professor of English literature, Oxbridge scholar,

  1 Lewis to his brother Warren ("Warnie") Lewis, c. 20 April 1921. In, Lewis, *Collected Letters Volume One: Family Letters 1905–1931*, 536–38.
  2 Lewis, *Surprised by Joy*, 179–80.

theologian, poet, and apologist—was a product of the English middle classes: educated by an Edwardian elite, he exhibited all the strength and weaknesses of empire. In this context, he classifies Jews as "class A primitives" similar to the "primitives" around his brother Warren, to whom he is writing, skeptical that "Warnie" is attempting to read through the whole of the Bible: New Testament and the Hebrew Bible referred to by his education, often dismissively, as the *Old* Testament (in Hebrew, *Tanakh*).

Lewis is a product of his age, his upbringing, his education at the University of Oxford, his formation in several boarding schools—strengths, benefits, . . . and brutality—all underpinned by arrogance and prejudice, racism and anti-Semitism, a patronizing superiority that served a global empire, which had only a few decades earlier finally relinquished imposing the yoke of slavery. It was reputedly said that the British Empire had been forged with the gun in one hand and the (Church of England) Bible in the other. Little did the colonialists realize how they were transmitting and distributing to the world (translated to almost every language they came across) not only the New Testament, but the ancient Hebrew scriptures—the Old Testament—to the nations!

And Jesus Christ? Yeshua Ha Mashiach was and still is eternally Jewish: God's chosen one from God's chosen people. His resurrected flesh is Jewish: Jesus was resolutely, determinedly, unwaveringly in the tradition and otology of the ancient Hebrews, of the house of David;[3] his friends were Jews, his first followers—women, and male disciples—were Jews, he studied the Hebrew scriptures, he heard them as a boy, he read and discussed them at the age of twelve with the elders in the temple courts (Luke 2:41–52), he worshiped in the synagogue, and he traveled to Jerusalem to observe the festivals. Jesus did not reject Judaism, he was no revolutionary—military, militant, or otherwise—he was no radical in relation to his Jewish religion and culture . . . and flesh. If we are correct to criticize the innate anti-Semitism in the British establishment, the English public-school system that formed Lewis in the past, then we may also argue that the British—like most European and American people—are *insufficiently Semitic*, as is the case with the establishment in Britain and America today.[4]

3   "Jesus the Messiah, the son of David, the son of Abraham." Matt 1:1
4   In recent years there has been much justified criticism in the media of the inherent anti-Semitism in the British Labour Party, but the political establishment now

1. The Young C. S. Lewis

As a child and as a young man C. S. Lewis unquestioningly and unconsciously absorbed something of the inherent racism and anti-Semitism of the British establishment, its mind-set and worldview. As a little child he created an imaginary world, wrote about it, but the names and creatures reflected—unconsciously—the racial stereotypes of the Edwardian Empire. As a young man he stereotypes the ancient Hebrews as "primitives";[5] he is writing after the brutal nihilism of the First Word War, which he had been injured out of (by so-called friendly fire) and had recuperated while reading philosophy in a medical station surrounded by the mud and blood of war and the daily bombardment of shells. This began his philosophical education in earnest. Wounded near Arras on April 15, 1918, Lewis read and studied the seventeenth-century philosopher John Locke, his essay on human understanding, while recovering in Étaples hospital.[6] Back at Oxford he was a proud atheist, but the establishment, so to speak, required that he should be quiet and attend public services in the Church of England into which he had been baptized and confirmed, as befits his education. His atheism was also influenced by the turn-of-the-century logical positivism that had swept through mid-European intellectuals, from its Viennese origins, arriving in post-war Oxford.[7] Relished by the nihilistic and cynical survivors of war, logical positivism had the advantage, we may say, of distancing Lewis from his cultivated education and formation: war had broken the mold of the Victorian/Edwardian worldview—empire-led and anti-Semitic. But it was becoming a Christian in his early thirties that finally changed Lewis's understanding of the Jews.

2. CHILDHOOD

Lewis journeyed. Lewis was a pilgrim. Lewis's pilgrimage is from a child with a sincere faith, to a self-confessed atheist, to a Hegelian idealist, to a

---

in Britain can be justifiably criticized as insufficiently Semitic, if God's chosen people are to be a model to us, along with their laws and their relationship with God (yes, culminating in the Messiah: Jesus of Nazareth, the Christ).

5   Lewis to his brother Warren ("Warnie") Lewis, c. 20 April 1921. In, Lewis, *Collected Letters Volume One*, 536–38.

6   Locke, *Essay Concerning Human Understanding*.

7   Central European in origin, logical positivism had taken a generation to travel from the salons of Vienna to take root in the fertile post-WWI nihilism of what was left of the intelligentsia at the University of Oxford.

theist, and then to a Christian. Lewis's teenage atheism is confirmed by his experiences in the trenches of the First World War. Nothing he came across as a student at Oxford after the war threatened this atheism. However, it is when he is teaching at Oxford that he begins to find difficulties with his atheistic belief system. At the center of Lewis's pilgrimage is what he termed "Joy," a mystical experience central to his conversion, his faith, and his work as a Christian theologian, philosopher, and apologist.

C. S. Lewis was born in Belfast, Ireland, to comfortable and well-off, educated and professional parents, and raised in a large, substantial, detached house. However, the settled secure and secluded life at home with his brother for companion was shattered and irretrievably lost when his mother died of cancer in 1908. Thereafter, from the age of ten years, Lewis is educated at several public schools. It is through these rigid Edwardian institutions that Lewis's religious, social, and personal development takes place.

Childhood Religion: Moments of Grace

Written over forty years after the childhood events it recalls, Lewis the intellectual, in his spiritual autobiography, *Surprised by Joy* (subtitled, *The Shape of My Early Life*), accounts for what was important in his childhood. Lewis values beauty and magnificence, feeling and emotion, he holds imagination in great esteem. Lewis writes of a moment of intense beauty that must been seen as a moment of grace: the Holy Spirit touching Lewis's mind and soul in a way that does not normally happen in everyday discourse and actions (in *The Talmud*[8] this is in effect named as *Shekhinah*—the divine presence). What we have here is the first hint of something that is of profound importance to Lewis, particularly the apostate atheistic young Lewis: *Sehnsucht*, a longing, a yearning. Several years afterwards, Lewis noted what he termed the memory of a memory, how these moments from his childhood returned to possess him momentarily:

> It is difficult to find words strong enough for the sensation which came over me; Milton's "enormous bliss" of Eden (giving the full, ancient meaning to "enormous") comes somewhere near it. It was a sensation, of course, of desire; but desire for what? not, certainly,

---

8   The Talmud is the central text of Rabbinic Judaism and the primary source of Jewish religious law (*halakha*) and Jewish theology.

for a biscuit tin filled with moss; . . . before I knew what I desired, the desire itself was gone, the whole glimpse withdrawn, the world turned commonplace again, or only stirred by a longing for the longing that had just ceased. It had taken only a moment of time; and in a certain sense everything else that had ever happened to me was insignificant in comparison.[9]

Lewis actually writes in *Surprised by Joy* that religious experiences were non-existent in his childhood;[10] he simply did not regard these moments of meeting as religious, in the way the ancient Hebrews did. He defines these moments as aesthetic experiences, simply an encounter with beauty. But is this an encounter with God, *YHWH*, of the Lord, Christ? Religion for the young Lewis was something external, cultural, imposed by his parents, by school, and by society, and as such was part of an incomprehensible adult world. He also asserts that his parents did not fit in with the stereotypical idea of puritanical Presbyterian Ulster religion, they were far more Anglican than most around him. Within the context of implicit religious experience, it is important to note how when the Lewis family moved to the new, large, detached house, Little Lea, Jack now saw himself as the product of "long corridors, empty sunlit rooms, upstairs indoor silences."[11] Lewis developed a degree of isolated quietude, which set him apart and contributed to him developing as a writer.

Lewis's glimpses of this spiritual world, the longing and yearning, seem at times more important than people to him. However, this sense of isolation also helped develop him as a poet. He noted how when reading he could be caught by something unexpected that triggered this sense of longing and yearning:

> There came a moment when I idly turned the pages of the book and found the unrhymed translation of Tegner's "Drapa" and read
>
> > I heard a voice that cried,
> > Balder the beautiful
> > Is dead, is dead—
>
> I knew nothing about Balder; but instantly I was uplifted into huge regions of northern sky, I desired with almost sickening intensity something never to be . . . and then, as in the other examples,

---

9   Lewis, *Surprised by Joy*, 14.
10 Lewis, *Surprised by Joy*, 5.
11 Lewis, *Surprised by Joy*, 8.

found myself at the very same moment already falling out of that desire and wishing I were back in it.[12]

Lewis regards these early spiritual experiences—though he does not necessarily see them in a religious context—as important, even key to anyone who seeks to understand his life and work.

Death

In 1908 the ten-year-old Lewis faced the death of his mother from cancer. Lewis writes poignantly of his mother's illness and loss, very much from a child's perspective: the innocence and yet apparent self-centered view of a child. Lost in puzzlement the Lewis boys were not told of the cancer till after she had died. Lewis wrote how his father, in his inconsolable grief, ignored the boys, resulting in Jack and Warnie seeking solace in their own company.[13]

It is at this point that Lewis owns up to what he considered some sort of religious experience: his mother's death. "When her case was pronounced hopeless I remembered what I had been taught; that prayers offered in faith would be granted. I accordingly set myself to produce by will power a firm belief that my prayers for her recovery would be successful; and, as I thought, I achieved it."[14] Lewis was not gripped by a crisis of faith when his prayers were apparently unanswered, he comments that he thought no more about it. Lewis prayed for healing; then with his mother's death presumably he prayed for resuscitation-resurrection, which if it had happened would have been reminiscent of Lazarus in John's Gospel. However, Lewis does see something of this:

> I think the truth is that the belief into which I had hypnotized myself was itself too irreligious for its failure to cause any religious revolution. I had approached God, or my idea of God, without love, without awe, even without fear. He was, in my mental picture of this miracle, to appear neither as Saviour nor as Judge, but

---

12   Lewis, *Surprised by Joy*, 15. Lewis is referring to Esaias Tegnér's poem, "Drapa," in Longfellow, *The Seaside and the Fireside*. Esaias Tegnér (1782–1846), Professor of Greek, Swedish writer, and folklorist composed poems derived from the Norse myths, for instance, Frithjof's Saga.

13   Lewis, *Surprised by Joy*, 16–17.

14   Lewis, *Surprised by Joy*, 18.

merely as a magician; and when He had done what was required of him I supposed he would simply—well, go away.[15]

This is Lewis's first experience of the cross—but it is so rarely recognized. For the child this was a profound encounter from which he reacted. The death of his mother, the intensity of his prayer, the result which may have appeared as no answer but was still an answer, all of this we may consider to be intensely religious: "With my mother's death all settled happiness, all that was tranquil and reliable, disappeared from my life."[16]

3. YOUTH

Within weeks of his mother's death C. S. Lewis was sent away by his father, with Warnie, to boarding school. Lewis records with poignancy the journey, the reliance on his brother (for whom this was not the first time away at school), and the lack of reconciliation in him regarding his mother's death. He was still grieving; indeed, the repression of grief and feeling amongst the Victorian-Edwardian middle class was considered essential, mandatory. He was not allowed to grieve or to miss his mother. In some ways this was the social norm.

Schooling

Boarded at the Wynyard School in Watford, Hertfordshire, an education characterized by mathematics lessons, Latin grammar (but never any Roman literature), and—to Lewis—an unusual and excessive brutality (the school closed when the Headmaster was certified insane). Lewis was then sent to Campbell College in Belfast, then to Cherbourg House public school, Malvern, England. Considered a good English public school without the sadism and paucity of curriculum that had characterized Wynyard, Lewis hated the traditional Edwardian public-school ethos at Malvern, dominated by class and social status, pecking order, fagging, and sports; nothing but sports, gymnastics, rugby, and ambition. Lewis's father acquiesced and withdrew Lewis, sending him to be privately tutored by William T. Kirkpatrick, a retired headmaster living in Surrey. Kirkpatrick—who had tutored Lewis's father, Albert—was a formidable intellect, very much a logician who could expose the weaknesses in an

---

15   Lewis, *Surprised by Joy*, 18–19.
16   *Lewis, Surprised by Joy*, 19.

opponent's argument without mercy. Kirkpatrick was also a passionately committed philosophical atheist. It is to Kirkpatrick—"The Great Knock" as Lewis called him—that we must attribute a sound base to Jack's education, but also the incisive skill in logic that so often characterizes Lewis's mature Christian writings. Lewis's use of logic was grounded in the unforgiving teaching technique that Kirkpatrick used: he would accept absolutely no sloppy thinking or undefended argument or position.

Anglo-Catholicism

Where was religion and spirituality in Lewis's youth and schooling? What was it that was of value to him? Whilst at Wynyard School Lewis began to attend an Anglo-Catholic church, the parish church of St. John the Apostle and Evangelist in Watford.[17] Lewis regards it as the most important thing that befell him at Wynyard: "There first I became an effective believer."[18] Lewis notes how as an Ulster Protestant he reacted against much that was high Anglo-Catholic in the church, in later life he claimed to be filled with disgust at the excessively Anglo-Catholic practices of St. John's. However, this was an important grounding and he was perceptive enough at the time to realize that it was in hearing Christian doctrine as distinct to what he terms religious uplift that was crucially important: "I began seriously to pray and to read my Bible and to attempt to obey my conscience."[19] Despite the nihilistic brutality of Wynyard School, St. John's gave Lewis a grounding, the value of which, coming soon after his mother's death, is to be seen as immeasurable. However much he would walk away from this start during the coming years, the grounding was there and his prayers were answered: he was hooked to invoke a fishing analogy common in the early church. St. John's Church fished for men and women and children and through the vicar, the Revd. Canon R. H. L. James (incumbent from 1904–54, who must be seen as one of the most important people in Lewis's life, yet he rarely if ever gets a mention), God had hooked Lewis. However much Lewis wandered, the Lord God played him like a fish, giving him

---

17   The parish church of St. John the Apostle and Evangelist, Sutton Road, Watford, WD17 2QQ, was consecrated in 1873, a temporary building was replaced with the present church in 1893 with a rood screen by architect and designer Sir John Ninian Comper; for Lewis's reaction to St. John's, see Green and Hooper, *C. S. Lewis: A Biography*.

18   Lewis, *Surprised by Joy*, 31.

19   Lewis, *Surprised by Joy*, 32.

line, to wear himself out with all manner of philosophical, cultural, and pseudo-religious thought systems, before reeling him in nearly twenty years later.

But whichever Edwardian public school he attended, appearance at Church of England chapel services was obligatory. This often included confirmation, though many saw this as a social right-of-passage and perhaps did not take their vows and commitment seriously. Whether a Sunday morning Holy Communion service, or daily prayer, they would have been reciting hymns and prayers and Bible readings invoking such phrases as "Oh people of Zion, behold the LORD (*YHWH*?) is at hand to redeem the nations," "The LORD (*YHWH*) shall cause his glorious voice to be heard," "The LORD's anointed," "Judah's champion mounts on high," "Son of David," "Once in Royal David's City," "Almighty God (*El Shaddai*)," "*YHWH*," endless readings from the Psalms and the Book of Isaiah . . . the list is endless: at every turn they were evoking the Hebrew Bible, salvation history, and perhaps the Ten Commandments, but somehow separated from their source: Moses and the Israelites. How little was the thought and consideration as to what they were saying and why, and how they related to the chosen people of God, while drinking in anti-Semitism at every turn, and also anti-Roman Catholicism, such was the prejudiced nature and confusion still echoing from the Henrician/English Reformation. The Evangelical churches displayed, generally, a deep respect for the Hebrew scriptures, the Torah,[20] the Pentateuch,[21] the unfolding of salvation history through God's chosen people, but this did not inoculate them against the anti-Semitic mindset of the day.

Northernness

The first flush of belief from Wynyard/St John's waned as Lewis reacted against the public-school civic religion and ethos. During his teen years Lewis developed a strong passionate interest in pagan Norse myth,

---

20   Torah has a range of meanings. It can most specifically mean the first five books of the Hebrew Bible. This is commonly known as the Written Torah. It can also mean the continued narrative from all the twenty-four books, from the Book of Genesis to the end of the *Tanakh*. (Wikipedia)

21   Pentateuch means the first five books of the Bible. These books are Genesis, Exodus, Leviticus, Numbers, and Deuteronomy. The word Pentateuch comes from two Greek words that mean "five books" or "five scroll." According to tradition, the books were written by the Israelite leader, Moses. (Wikipedia)

Wagner, Icelandic sagas, Irish mythology, and Celtic mysticism. This was epitomized in a word: "Northernness." A Northernness that became like a religion to him, characterized by sheer wide open spaces, skies hung over vast forests and mountains, infinite seascapes with the fall of a winter sun behind the horizon. There was a coldness in this Northernness, coupled with a love for nature, for landscape, for sunrises and sunsets, and autumn evenings. What characterized all of these phenomena for Lewis was "otherness"; an otherness where eternity, what was really real, could be glimpsed through the veil, the curtain, of our reality. Lewis was a Romantic in the artistic and cultural sense of the word. Although it is fair to say that Lewis was something of a loner, he did develop a deep friendship at this time with another teenager by the name of Arthur Greeves—both realized their deep love for Wagner, illustrated by Arthur Rackham, and this sense of Northernness, mythology, and saga. Both Lewis and Greeves shared a life-long correspondence.

Atheism

Lewis's childhood faith, from the days attending St. John's Church when he was ten to eleven years of age, was genuine; however, he lapsed into apostasy as he grew up and embraced atheism in his teens. While Lewis was boarding at Cherbourg House (the preparatory feeder school for Malvern College), the Matron[22]—cited as Miss C, by Lewis—was the person who perhaps unwittingly triggered Lewis's crisis of faith and descent into atheism. Lewis notes how caring she was in her professional role but that also she was lost in a sea of belief systems with no ability to discern: Theosophy, Rosicrucianism, Spiritualism, and what Lewis terms "the whole Anglo-American Occultist tradition."[23] Lewis writes about

---

22   The Matron of a boarding/residential public school was the person responsible for the care, welfare and well-being, and health of the residential pupils. This was not a teaching/academic role and in Edwardian England it was always a woman.

23   Lewis, *Surprised by Joy*, 56. Theosophy is a study of religion, philosophy, and metaphysics developed from the late nineteenth century (though is rooted in many ancient religions) as a spiritual philosophy by Helena Blavatsky (1831–91), who also co-founded of the Theosophical Society. As a belief system it holds that all religions are equal, or that there are elements in all religions that point to truth (truth being the highest form of religion): there is therefore in this context nothing unique, superior, or revelatory in Judaism and Christianity. Religions are an effort by the so-called spiritual hierarchy to show people how to develop excellence. Theosophy is, as with all religions, characterized by diversity of belief. Some hold to reincarnation; often the human spiritual self is

how discussions with this Matron triggered his interest in and desire for the preternatural, the supernatural, which he describes as a spiritual disease, a lust.[24] Lewis notes how one reason why the devil, the enemy, could so easily destroy his true understanding of God with false religion was because he was ripe for atheistic spirituality. He notes how his practice of the Christian religion had become burdensome, particularly as he had become more and more anxious and even neurotic in his prayer. When he first came to "a serious belief" through St. John's Church he was eager to pray, but as the years passed he was concerned about the genuineness of his prayer, the efficacy of it.[25]

Lewis the intellectual was also confused by the apparent truthfulness of the Christianity as the one religion that he was asked to subscribe to, when he was exposed to the existence of other religions, philosophies, and thought systems. The only solution to Lewis as a fifteen-year-old was to dismiss all religion as nonsense, but to dip into some of them, as seemed to satisfy his desires and pleasures. Although Lewis now moved away from Christianity and claimed to be an atheist (it is always important to remember that from the age of ten to around thirteen years Lewis was a seriously believing Christian), it is fair in reality to assert that he was a religious atheist. He dismissed the existence of the Christian God, called himself an atheist, but was actually very religious. However, his religion was a religion of feeling, of myth and story, of nature, of experience, all of which was orientated around self, around Lewis's ego. Despite this personal, experiential, mythological religion (which to Lewis was not religion); despite his avowed disbelief—or more pertinently lack of acknowledgement of God and the truth of the Christian gospel—Lewis still went forward for confirmation into the Church of England, again at public school, very much to please his father, and because it was a rite of passage for good middle-class Edwardian young gentlemen. What does Lewis have to say, in an attempt at self-analysis almost half-a-century later? "Asgard and the Valkyries seemed to me incomparably more important

---

known as "the monad": this is the higher self. Originating in the seventeenth century, Rosicrucianism was a secretive order where inner realms or worlds aided people in their spiritual development. Both Theosophy and Rosicrucianism contain what appears to many to be an unhealthy element of Gnosticism.

24   Lewis, *Surprised by Joy*, 57.
25   Lewis, *Surprised by Joy*, 57–61.

than anything else in my experience."[26] What is more, these pagan myths were more important than his Christian beliefs, plagued as the latter were by doubts. Lewis asserts that the phenomenon of Northernness was, or at least appeared to be to him, greater and more important than religion, yet he can see that part of this Northernness was religious, that it contained elements that his religion, or church practice, ought to have contained. Yet he asserts that it was not itself a new religion,[27] because, he argues, it contained no trace of belief in a "god" or "gods/idols" and was not externally imposed. Here Lewis's understanding of religion is somewhat off the mark: religion does not necessarily require belief in a god, and is not always externally imposed. Lewis is prepared to admit something of this, "There was in it something very like adoration, some kind of quite disinterested self-abandonment to an object which securely claimed this by simply being the object it was. . . . Sometimes I can almost think that I was sent back to the false gods there to acquire some capacity for worship against the day when the true God should recall me to Himself."[28]

Sehnsucht

A literal translation of the German concept *Sehnsucht*—for it is more than simply a word—is "a yearning," "a longing." The problem is that there is no direct translation: it is a German concept that is only really covered by several related words in English. A yearning for, a longing for, implies an object, an object of desire, but there is so often with *Sehnsucht* no object, it is the sensation itself. Therefore, *Sehnsucht* is often seen to have mystical overtones relating to something unattainable. It is then characterized by a fervent and passionate desire or longing, a yearning or craving, a hunger or even an addiction. In many ways this feeling, the concept of this desire, is destructive, negative, even seen by some as self-defeating because of the regret and, simultaneously, the deeply corrosive sense of unattainability and loss.

As a teenager and as a young man C. S. Lewis experienced *Sehnsucht*. He saw it as an inconsolable longing for an ill-defined or unknown object, a longing that struck with a sickening intensity: "That unnameable something, desire for which pierces us like a rapier at the smell of bonfire,

---

26   Lewis, *Surprised by Joy*, 72.
27   Lewis, *Surprised by Joy*, 72–73.
28   Lewis, *Surprised by Joy*, 73.

1. The Young C. S. Lewis

the sound of wild ducks flying overhead, the title of *The Well at the World's End*, the opening lines of *Kubla Khan*, the morning cobwebs in late summer, or the noise of falling waves."[29] There is, then, sometimes a sense of nostalgia about the longing/yearning because if the object of desire is not known, or is ill-defined, there is then the association of "it" being from or in the past—often it is associated with childhood, or childhood memories, or simply past times, better times. For many like Lewis the ache, the yearning or longing—Lewis often uses the term "pang," because it was so like a stabbing—was transient and short-lived but was so intense that the sense of *Sehnsucht* was in itself the object desired. Lewis considered the longing better than fulfillment. There is then an element of the secretive, the esoteric, about the longing because it is always different for each individual. Despite these individualistic characteristics, Lewis considered that *Sehnsucht* was widespread, a common occurrence in humanity. Lewis occasionally uses the German word/concept, but defines this experience, this pang of *Sehnsucht* in himself, as "Joy" (which hereafter will be set with a capital J). In essence, this is the religion of the pagan North, but also of the powerful nations that surrounded and preyed upon ancient Israel.

Sehnsucht—Lewis's "Joy"—is a human concept, it is real, but the name, the concept, is to a degree a human imposition. As the person experiences this yearning, this longing, which pierces the soul, cuts to the core of the very being, strikes and disables with a sickening intensity, there is an external cause, a trigger. However, this is no psychological illusion or projection. So what triggers, what creates, these experiences? We may assert that it is caused by the sway of the Holy Spirit. There have been secular—self-proclaimed—atheistic writers who have written on this yearning, this un-nameable longing, but the intellectual construction they employ to name and explain falls short of what is happening. Lewis, like so many others who had focused on the experience of *Sehnsucht*, found after his conversion, after he had surrendered to God, that the pain and the disabling nature of this longing was satiated. However, if this sense of the Holy Spirit (which is essentially convicting the person of sin in not living a life orientated to God in Christ) is ignored, and if this sense of *Sehnsucht* is then cultivated for the experience in itself, then it becomes idolatrous and often amongst an educated and cultured elite it leads

---

29   Lewis, "Preface to Third Edition." Lewis, *The Pilgrim's Regress*, xiv.

to suicide. This intimation of the Holy Spirit which is *Sehnsucht*/"Joy" therefore must be seen as an element of conscience—in these instances, an element of a *guilty* conscience.

Lewis's sense of *Sehnsucht*/"Joy" can be seen as idolatrous. Such idolatry is a form of religion. Religion itself then can become an idol that works against the purposes of God in seeking the salvation of humanity. Lewis writing of the experience commented: "It is that of an unsatisfied desire which is itself more desirable than any other satisfaction. I call it 'Joy,' which is here a technical term and must be sharply distinguished both from Happiness and from Pleasure. 'Joy' (in my sense) has indeed one characteristic, and one only, in common with them; the fact that anyone who has experienced it will want it again."[30] *Sehnsucht* is eschatological: if *Sehnsucht* is a glimpse of the judgment of God—not directed to any specific behavior but at the orientation of the individual person towards God, or not as the case may be—then for those who do turn it is a glimpse of heaven; for those who do not turn to God this is a glimpse of hell. Some may see the unfulfilled longing of *Sehnsucht* as disabling agony that has the potential of driving the sinner mad.

4. THE YOUNG DON

Returning from the First World War, Lewis picked up his studies at Oxford. It is fair to assert that there was an element of nihilistic sadness in many of the returning soldiers/scholars. Lewis, like others, found comfort, we may assert, in logical positivism—a reasoned rigid structure to atheism. It is at this time he comments to his brother, cynically dismissive of Warnie's reading through the whole Bible, that "I wonder will you ever get to the end of the Bible; the undesirable 'primitives' around you will enable you to appreciate the Hebrews who were class A primitives after all."[31] We see the culmination of his Edwardian public school education, the arrogance of the Empire mentality, the dismissal of virtually all other people as "primitive," in particular ethnic groups outside of the European Caucasian; this is an anti-Semitism that permeates the individual and the collective: the British establishment.

---

30 Lewis, *Surprised by Joy*, 15–16.

31 "Lewis to his brother Warren ("Warnie") Lewis, c. 20 April 1921." In Lewis, *Collected Letters Volume One*, 536–38.

Later in life, speaking of the world he grew up in and the attitude of his family and peers to the Jews, Lewis wrote how the very name "Jew" was associated with finance, trade, and so forth. But such associations were not the heart of what being Jewish was about; in many ways they were attempts to avoid facing up to the God-given status of the Jewish people as "chosen. In many ways it avoided accepting their God-given status as the chosen people, to bear witness to humanity for humanity's sake. Of the Jews and the early twentieth century stereotype—

> They belong to a nation chiefly of peasants. For us the very name Jew is associated with finance, shop-keeping, moneylending and the like. This however, dates from the Middle Ages when the Jews were not allowed to own land and were driven into occupations remote from the soil. Whatever characteristics the modern Jew has acquired from millennia of such occupations, they cannot have been those of his ancient ancestors. . . . Everyone was close to the land; everyone vividly aware of our dependence on soils and weather.[32]

5. PILGRIMAGE: CONVERSION

Lewis wrote of his conversion in two books. The first, *The Pilgrim's Regress* (1933), is disguised; it is somewhat allegorical; that is, the degree to which the story's hero is based on Lewis is open to speculation and conjecture. *Surprised by Joy* (1955) is much more transparent and open: it is a spiritual autobiography. The chapters on Lewis's adult conversion, his return to faith, are a detailed and intensely existential attempt at charting his development from not just the childhood faith we have explored but also his atheism and then the struggle to break free of various belief systems (mostly philosophical) in his twenties to return to the gospel. *Surprised by Joy* is a seminal conversion story and rightly ranks with Augustine's *Confessions*. Essentially Lewis's struggle with God is charted in two chapters—XI *Check* and XIV *Checkmate*. The first of these two chapters is set in 1915 when Lewis is seventeen years of age and receiving private tuition from William T. Kirkpatrick; the second charts the development of his beliefs as a young don from 1922 through to 1929.

---

32 *Lewis, Reflections on the Psalms*, 65.

A HEBRAIC INKLING

"gods" & "temples"

Lewis writes much about *Sehnsucht*/"Joy," a sense of desire with no object, characterized, for Lewis, by regret, unattainability, and loss. Transient, it filled him with a sense of pure beauty, pure joy, a beauty independent of the world of flesh and desire, ambition and lust. Lewis wrote that this mystical experience was often generated by "huge waves of Wagnerian music and Norse and Celtic mythology."[33] Lewis admits candidly that as a teenager he sought to cultivate this sense of "Joy," he longed for it, searched for it, but found that he could not replicate it. "Joy" was elusive; it was not in his command. Lewis writes that he came to see how he made the mistake of believing that this mystical experience was the *object* of his desire in itself. However, he was to realize it was merely a pointer—the *source* of this mystical pang was the true *object* of his desire. If what was happening for Lewis was the Holy Spirit attempting to point him, re-orientate him, towards God, Lewis did not realize this, that the source was outside of this world, outside of this reality, and therefore the true enjoyment that lasts was not to be attained in this world: you cannot grasp and keep the beauty of a sunrise enveloped in white mist, you cannot own or freeze in time the music that so captivates. To seek leads to inconsolable loss, the sickening intensity of longing for what cannot be grasped, when "it" does not really exist: only the source of the beauty exists: God—the triune Godhead. Lewis wrestled with trying to understand this sense of "Joy" for several years, from his late teens through into his twenties. Eventually he realizes that he is trying to capture the unattainable. But he has to overcome intellectual hurdles: therefore, he initially thinks his way to faith and then justifies this conversion.

What he did not realize until much later was that this pseudo-religious busyness was in itself something of a pilgrimage, but "the very moment when I longed to be so stabbed again, was itself again such a stabbing. The Desirable which had once alighted on Valhalla was now alighting on a particular moment of my own past; and I would not recognize him there because, being an idolater and a formalist, I insisted that he ought to appear in the temple I had built him; not knowing that he cares only for temples' building and not at all for temples built."[34] Reflecting further on

---

33 Lewis, *Surprised by Joy*, 159.
34 Lewis, *Surprised by Joy*, 161. See also 174–75 for Lewis's own analysis of what he believed was happening in these experiences and his reaction to them.

this some forty years after the event, Lewis compared this with "that error which the angel at the Sepulchre rebuked when he said to the women, 'Why seek ye the living among the dead? He is not here, He is risen.'"[35] Ever the poet, Lewis continued, "The comparison is of course between something of infinite moment and something very small; like comparison between the Sun and the Sun's reflection in a dewdrop."[36]

Lewis wrestled. The horror of the Christian universe was that it had no door marked exit.[37] At the center of Christianity, so Lewis concluded at this time, was a transcendental interferer, which jarred with his desire for independence and insularity. Lewis realized even at the age of eighteen years that there was no possibility of a treaty with this Christian reality: "there was no region even in the innermost depth of one's soul which one could surround with a barbed wire fence and guard with a notice, 'No Admittance!'"[38] However, a matter of months before call-up to war service Lewis was visited by a profound mystical experience that effectively scattered and annihilated all these various pseudo-religious belief systems—the discovery of a book by a Christian writer, George MacDonald, entitled *Phantastes, a Faerie Romance* (something of a precursor to the work on Christian fantasy that both the mature Lewis and Tolkien were to produce—i.e., Narnia and Middle Earth). In addition, he discovered the work on a station bookstall on a profoundly beautiful autumn evening, shrouded in mist in the heart of the Surrey countryside. Travelling by train through the Surrey countryside and arriving at Leatherhead station Lewis wrote lyrically about the moment of dusk, the violet hills, the sky tinged green, of the air frost, when the dusk light is on the cusp of turning to the night, when the steam train's fire box glowed in the mist, his senses were enlivened by the cold: "Turning to the bookstall, I picked out an Everyman in a dirty jacket, *Phantastes: A Faerie Romance*, George MacDonald. Then the train came in . . . ." That evening I began to read my new book."[39] So what sort of religious/spiritual experience was this for Lewis? Lewis actually begins to struggle for words to describe what was happening as he read *Phantastes*: "It is

35	Lewis, *Surprised by Joy*, 161.
36	Lewis, *Surprised by Joy*, 161.
37	Lewis, *Surprised by Joy*, 165.
38	Lewis, *Surprised by Joy*, 166.
39	Lewis, *Surprised by Joy*, 172–73.

as if I were carried sleeping across the frontier, or as if I had died in the old country and could never remember how I came alive in the new. . . . It was Holiness. It was as though the voice which had called to me from the world's end were now speaking at my side."[40] Lewis, though he did not know it at the time, was encountering the Holy Spirit: God the Holy Spirit was using all that was in Lewis's life experience to try to change, to re-orientate him: "It was with me in the room, or in my own body, or behind me. If it had once eluded me by its distance, it now eluded me by proximity—something too near to see, too plain to be understood, on this side of knowledge."[41] The pang, the longing, of *Sehnsucht*/"Joy" returned just when he was most unprepared, unaware, with his defenses down, just when he believed he had intellectualized it, and thereby dismissed it. The pang then left him to try to understand, with all his theories in tatters. After the war, when he returned to Oxford as an undergraduate, he dismissed all this as romantic longing, as nonsense. This new-look, post-war Oxford excluded *Sehnsucht*/"Joy" in the sense that it was to be categorized as internal; all such experience was part of, contained within, a closed, single-level universe. Therefore *Sehnsucht*/"Joy" was now to be dismissed only as a psychological projection from his deepest unfulfilled desires. Realism had taken over.

Philosophy & Belief

Lewis graduated in Greats; his father agreed to finance him to read English in the hope of a fellowship. From his reading of philosophy Lewis had developed a belief system more akin to Gnostic Hegelianism. Among his new friends in the English school were several whom Lewis believed had all the right ideas, but—like Nevill Coghill—they were Christian. As he read English, he also found that all the books he rated highly turned against him: Milton, MacDonald, Chesterton, and medieval literature. Lewis wrote that:

> Absurdly . . . I thought that "the Christian myth" conveyed to unphilosophic minds as much of the truth, that is of Absolute Idealism, as they were capable of grasping, and that even that much put them above the irreligious. Those who could not rise to the notion of the Absolute would come nearer to the truth by belief

---

40   Lewis, *Surprised by Joy*, 173.
41   Lewis, *Surprised by Joy*, 173.

1. The Young C. S. Lewis

in a god than by disbelief. . . . The implication—that something which I and most other undergraduates could master without extraordinary pains would have been too hard for Plato, Dante, Hooker, and Pascal—did not yet strike me as absurd.[42]

Realism had to be abandoned, the new look was damaged; also his belief in chronological snobbery (the idea that humanity today is innately more advanced and superior to people in previous ages) was shaken, particularly after he had read G. K. Chesterton's *The Everlasting Man*. Further, he wrote that "the great Angler played his fish but he never dreamed that the hook was in his tongue."[43] Furthermore, he was now in regular long discussions with people like Hugo Dyson and J. R. R. Tolkien. Lewis wrote that a crucial step came in reading Samuel Alexander's *Space, Time and Deity*,[44] where he came across the distinction between "enjoyment" and "contemplation"—it was this, in part, that enabled him to see how he had mistaken the mystical pang of *Sehnsucht*/"Joy" for an end in itself.[45] Alexander distinguishes between *enjoyment* and *contemplation*, between *enjoying* the act of seeing a table whilst *contemplating* the table: the two acts cannot be simultaneous. Therefore, Lewis could understand that attention to the object was essential. If you love someone, they are the object of your love. To cease attending, to cease focusing on the other, is therefore—for Alexander and for Lewis—to cease to love. To attend to your own feeling of love and not to the object of your love is, therefore, to cease loving. Lewis could then see how all his waiting and watching for *Sehnsucht*/"Joy" was vain and hopeless: the sensation of *Sehnsucht*/"Joy" had been not the wave, but, as Lewis asserts, the wave's imprint on the seashore. To mistake the wave's imprint on the sand for the wave itself led to the idolatry of worshipping the effect the Holy Spirit had on his mind rather than redirecting his attention to God at the invitation of the Holy Spirit. Conversion was near.

Lewis wrote that as God closed in he was given a choice. He recounts how whilst on a bus travelling up Headington Hill he was being presented with a choice—without words or images. Lewis was aware how he was holding something at bay, that he was not moved by desire: this was an

---

42   Lewis, *Surprised by Joy*, 208.
43   Lewis, *Surprised by Joy*, 208.
44   Alexander, *Space, Time and Deity—The Gifford Lectures 1910–1918* (1920).
45   Lewis, *Surprised by Joy*, 210.

existential moment, a decisive moment, when he appeared the nearest it is possible to be to a free agent: "The fox," wrote Lewis "had been dislodged from the Hegelian wood."[46]

Submission & Conversion

Lewis realizes of the separateness, aseity, and utter difference between God and humanity; yet this is a God who wills that we should know, contemplate, and become aware of God. This is not the result of philosophical speculation. Lewis realized that this God was what the experiences of *Sehnsucht*/"Joy" were pointing towards—the desiring that became close to what is in some ways religious experience at the height of his atheistic period. Lewis:

> [This] was no state of my own mind or body at all. In a way, I had proved this by elimination. I had tried everything in my own mind and body; as it were, asking myself, "Is it this you want? Is it this?" Last of all I had asked if "Joy" itself was what I wanted; and, labelling it "aesthetic experience," had pretended I could answer "Yes." But that answer too had broken down. Inexorably "Joy" proclaimed, "You want—I myself am your want of—something other, outside, not you nor any state of you." I did not yet ask, "Who is the desired?" only "What is it?"[47]

This realization brought Lewis into a region of awe, the intimation of a realization that there was a God who was beyond all that he could conjure, think, or construct that was utterly "other," purely perpendicular to our world (tangential even). Lewis wrote:

> For I thus understood that in deepest solitude there is a road right out of the self, a commerce with something which, by refusing to identify itself with any object of the senses, or anything whereof we have biological or social need, or anything imagined, or any state of our own minds, proclaims itself sheerly objective. Far more objective than bodies, for it is not, like them, clothed in our senses; the naked Other, imageless (though our imagination salutes it with a hundred images), unknown, undefined, desired.[48]

---

46   Lewis, *Surprised by Joy*, 217.
47   Lewis, *Surprised by Joy*, 213.
48   Lewis, *Surprised by Joy*, 214.

But this was only a realization of the existence beyond self of the absolute otherness of God. In effect this was a step between the Hegelian absolute spirit and the Platonic otherness of God—but this was not God as Lord of all, the origin and creator of all, the God revealed through the incarnation. In some ways Lewis, in the space of a few years, goes from the absolute utter distance and difference of the self-existing absolute (*Elohim*?) to the authority and purity of Almighty God (*El Shaddai*) to a knowable God, and submitting to a relational God and Lord (*YHWH*): this mirrors in some way the journey of the ancient Hebrews over several millennia, as recorded in the Bible.

This realization had fatally damaged Lewis's atheism: "Really," Lewis wrote, "a young atheist cannot guard his faith too carefully."[49] And so he was forced to consider this absolute spirit, in effect the Hegelian "absolute" separated from humanity and human desire, yet he convinced himself that this contemplation was not prayer. But there was a problem—if this was so, that this absolute spirit was independent of humanity, then how could the initiative lie on Lewis's side? "It might, as I say, still be true that my 'spirit' differed in some way from 'the God of popular religion.' My adversary waved the point. It sank into utter unimportance. He would not argue about it. He only said 'I am the Lord'; 'I am that I am.'"[50] And so Lewis wrote of his moment of surrender:

> You must picture me alone in that room in Magdalen, night after night, feeling, whenever my mind lifted even for a second from my work, the steady unrelenting approach of him whom I so earnestly desired not to meet. That which I greatly feared had at last come upon me. In the Trinity Term of 1929 I gave in, and admitted that God was God, and knelt and prayed: perhaps that night, the most dejected and reluctant convert in all of England.[51]

This is crossing the Rubicon. Lewis wrote that at least the prodigal son walked home on his own feet, but he had surrendered to a Love that opened the gates to a kicking, struggling, resentful prodigal. Lewis staggered, we may say, across the Rubicon and acknowledged that "*God was God.*" But what was this a conversion to? This was not necessarily, in Lewis's mind, the *Christian* God; it was not the God revealed in and through

---

49   Lewis, *Surprised by Joy*, 219.
50   Lewis, *Surprised by Joy*, 220.
51   Lewis, *Surprised by Joy*, 221.

the incarnation. Or was it? It was, in the sense that Lewis had said yes to God, the God above all gods, and now the Holy Spirit would re-orientate him to the full revelation displayed in the incarnation. Therefore, initially this was only a conversion to theism; the second conversion to the gospel followed after a lengthy debate with J. R. R. Tolkien and Hugo Dyson that lasted all of one night, and a motorbike journey with his brother, after which Lewis simply knew that Jesus was the Christ, the incarnate, crucified, and resurrected Son of God, *Elohim, El Shaddai, YHWH, Adonai*—the Lord. Upon this foundation stands Lewis's faith, and his work as theologian of orthodoxy.

2

The Hebrews, the Jews, . . . and God: I

"For the life of the flesh is in the blood, and I have given it to you on the altar to make atonement for your souls; for it is the blood by reason of the life that makes atonement."
LEVITICUS 17:11

"The sorrows of those who have bartered for another god will be multiplied;
   I shall not pour out their drink offerings of blood,
   Nor will I take their names upon my lips."
PSALM 16:4

"And according to the Law, one may almost say, all things are cleansed with blood, and without shedding of blood there is no forgiveness."
HEBREWS 9:22

"I might agree that the Allies are partly to blame, but nothing can fully excuse the iniquity of Hitler's persecution of the Jews, or the absurdity of his theoretical position. Did you see that he said 'The Jews have made no contribution to human culture and in crushing them I am doing the will of the Lord.' Now as the whole idea of the 'Will of the Lord' is precisely what the world owes to the Jews, the blaspheming tyrant has just fixed his absurdity for all to see in a single sentence, and shown that he is as contemptible for his stupidity as he is detestable for his cruelty. For the German people as a whole we ought to have charity: but for dictators, 'Nordic' tyrants and so on—well, read the chapter about Mr. Savage in *The Regress* and you have my views."
C. S. LEWIS[1]

1. INTRODUCTION

Those familiar with the life and works of C. S. Lewis can be forgiven for being mildly confused as to where and when Jack finally gave in and was converted. However, his journey may be longer and more protracted

---

1   "Lewis to Arthur Greeves, 5 Nov 1933." In *They Stand Together*, 466–687.

than many others, but it does bear witness to the situation many find themselves in: life is often full of steps where we can become closer to God. But there may be specific Damascus Road moments, which Lewis often wrote of.

2. DEBATE: AWARENESS AND COMPREHENSION

Lewis's final conversion to the God witnessed by the Gospel writers and affirmed by the creeds was in many ways foisted onto Lewis by the young Oxford don, the Roman Catholic Professor of Anglo Saxon, John Ronald Reuel Tolkien. This was the God who had been revealed, unfolding by meeting and encounter, to the ancient Hebrews, to the Jews in the temple and synagogues, distinct and apart from the multitudinous gods and goddesses of pagan Rome and Greece (and the seemingly multitudinous nations and tribes, with their "gods" and "goddesses" that came and went with alarmingly rapidity in the Eastern Mediterranean, preying on the ancient Hebrews): *Elohim, El Shaddai, YHWH*. Two years after Lewis's conversion to theism, a conversation took place on the evening of Saturday September 19, 1931, between J. R. R. Tolkien and Hugo Dyson, on the one hand, and Lewis, on the other. This debate was about myth and Christianity (part of the debate took place in Magdalen water meadows, along the tree-lined Addison Walk). It was, by all accounts, a heated conversation that lasted through the night till the early hours of the morning of Sunday September 20, and it finally convinced Lewis of the veracity of the claims of the Gospel writers and the creeds: that *Yeshua bar Yosef* was the Messiah, the Christ, the incarnate Son of God, eternally begotten of the Father, God from God. Writing to Arthur Greeves two days later on Tuesday September 22, 1931,[2] Lewis outlines the meeting, how Dyson came to talk in his rooms at Magdalen, how Tolkien joined them, discussing late into the night, then leaving at 3.00am, Lewis and Dyson seeing him out by the postern on Magdalen Bridge. Lewis and Dyson then retraced the walk through the water meadows and Addison walk talking further and recapitulating on their conversation, till 4.00am. Writing again to Greeves on the October 18, he explains how Tolkien and Dyson showed him how redemption was achieved, for it was this in many ways that proved the obstacle to Lewis. What had been holding him

---

2   "Lewis writing to Arthur Greeves, Sept. 22, 1931." In, Lewis, *Collected Letters Vol. I*, 969–72.

2. The Hebrews, the Jews, ... and God. I

back from full belief was puzzlement over how the event of the cross and resurrection should achieve salvation for mankind:

> My puzzle was the whole doctrine of Redemption: in what sense the life and death of Christ "saved" or "opened salvation to" the world. . . . What I couldn't see was how the life and death of Someone Else (whoever he was) two thousand years ago could help us here and now—except in so far as his example helped us. And the example business, tho' true and important, is not Christianity: right in the centre of Christianity, in the Gospels and St Paul, you keep on getting something quite different, . . . "propitiation"—"sacrifice"—"the blood of the Lamb."[3]

It was this which Lewis found shocking, it led to an immediacy: the implications of the sacrifice of Christ were in the *here and now*, not isolated in the event two thousand years ago. Also, Lewis could not see how, when the world was full of stories of dying and resuscitated gods in pagan myths and world religions, this one story could be unique and true. Lewis, from his atheistic apostate days, was suffering from a form of puzzling multi-religion syncretism: this was, in part, because Lewis had immersed himself so much during his youth in Northernness and the pagan myths (eschewing anything to do with the ancient Hebrews, the Jews, and their scriptures and traditions). However, now he could see that the doctrines we get out of the "true myth," to use Lewis's own words, are separate, a dilution in some ways, they are "translations into our concepts and ideas of what God has already expressed in a language more adequate, namely the actual Incarnation, Crucifixion, and Resurrection."[4]

This conversation with Tolkien and Dyson was still not the final giving-in by Lewis to full Christian belief. Intellectually he could not see how God had acted unilaterally, uniquely, and there was still the problem of what Lewis saw as the language of atonement: propitiation, the sacrament of communion, the emphasis on the blood of Christ. It is fair to assert that much of this was cultural prejudice on Lewis's part, but there was also a deep ingrained resistance to finally giving in to this God. It was required that Lewis lay down his intellectual ego, his intellectual crown (cf. Rev

---

[3] "Lewis writing to Arthur Greeves, Oct. 18, 1931." In Lewis, *Collected Letters Vol. I*, 975–77. Quote, 974.

[4] "Lewis writing to Arthur Greeves, Oct. 18, 1931." In Lewis, *Collected Letters Vol. I.*, 977.

4:10),[5] but somehow this required more than belief, it was not simply a suspension of the intellect, it was something different. This moment came eight days later on Monday September 28, 1931; the realization of who and what Christ was suddenly became real to Lewis, while he was riding in the sidecar of his brother's motorcycle to Whipsnade Zoo!

> I was driven to Whipsnade one sunny morning. When we set out I did not believe that Jesus Christ is the Son of God, and when we reached the zoo I did. Yet I had not exactly spent the journey in thought. Nor in great emotion. "Emotional" is perhaps the last word we can apply to some of the most important events. It was more like when a man, after long sleep, still lying motionless in bed, becomes aware that he is now awake. And it was, like that moment on top of the bus, ambiguous.[6]

This realization was, in many ways, the gift of the Holy Spirit; an example of grace: the spiritual action of God affecting the human mind. But Lewis had to prepare himself by slowly, painfully slowly, exorcizing his false gods and the philosophical barriers that prevented him seeing God, and understanding the why of the crucifixion. Warnie, incidentally, had returned to belief in Christianity eight months earlier on the May 9, 1931.

Lewis up to this point is too ignorant of the Hebrew Bible to understand the significance and the necessity of a blood sacrifice to end all sacrifices.[7] What he heard through attendance at Holy Communion, either as a boy at public school or obligatory attendance at college chapel services in the University of Oxford, clearly puzzled him. Yet what happens in the Mass/Eucharist/Communion, so the apostle Peter asserts, is how the precious blood of the Anointed One offered as an unblemished lamb was part of God's plan from before "the foundations of the world" (1 Pet 1:19–20). This resonates with depictions of Melchizedek, Abraham, and the Passover in the Hebrew Bible. But he does acknowledge the personal God he has submitted to; the idea of "the Will of the Lord" comes not from all the wide and contradictory history of religions across the world,

---

5   "[T]he twenty-four elders fall before the one who is seated on the throne and worship the one who lives forever and ever; they cast their crowns before the throne." Rev 4:10.

6   Lewis, *Surprised by Joy*, 229.

7   For example, a small number of pertinent references: Exodus 23:18; 24:6; 44:7; 44:15. Hebrews 9:7, 22, 25; 10:4; 13:11; Isaiah 1:11; 66:3. Leviticus 4:5, 16; 6:27, 30; 17:11; Luke 13:1; Psalms 16:4; 50:13; Romans 3:25.

but from the Jews, from the ancient Hebrews: and it comes as revelation to humanity.[8]

3. WISDOM: THE CHRISTIAN LEWIS

We cannot underestimate the immediate change of heart towards European Jews, the ancient Hebrews, and their scriptures, engendered in Lewis by his conversion to Christianity. The anti-Semitism—from his upbringing and his schooling—has disappeared. Writing to his brother in 1933 on the rise of National Socialism in Germany and Hitler's politicized prejudices towards the Jews, Lewis—who had shown little interest in politics before his conversion—comments that Warnie might be correct that the Western forces share much of the responsibility for the present growth of National Socialism in Germany, "but nothing can fully excuse the iniquity of Hitler's persecution of the Jews, or the absurdity of his theoretical position."[9] Lewis quotes some of the more ridiculous of Hitler's comments about the Jews, the absurd argument that the Jews have made no contribution to human culture, further that Hitler has argued that by destroying the Jews he will be undertaking the will of the Lord. This is regarded by Lewis as contradictory: "Now as the whole idea of the 'Will of the Lord' is precisely what the world owes to the Jews, the blaspheming tyrant has just fixed his absurdity for all to see in a single sentence, and shown that he is as contemptible for his stupidity as he is detestable for his cruelty."[10] Lewis expresses charity towards the German peoples, but gives no quarter to Nordic dictators and tyrants, as he terms them. It is fair to assert that this new approach is down to his conversion(s), which culminated with the motorcycle ride two years prior to his writing this letter. It was like a switch was thrown in his brain, he merely accepted and knew God's truth in the incarnation-crucifixion-resurrection, with all that flowed from this event, and how it was grounded in and issued from millennia of witness from the Jews. His conversion changes utterly his approach to, and value given to the Jews of Europe, and the ancient Hebrews and their testimony. Lewis's position is quite different also to the mainstream attitude amongst the British people at that time towards the Jewish question—particularly amongst the intelligentsia elite at Oxford.

8 Lewis, *Surprised by Joy*, 220.
9 "Lewis to Arthur Greeves, 5 Nov 1933." In *They Stand Together*, 466–687.
10 "Lewis to Arthur Greeves, 5 Nov 1933." In *They Stand Together*, 466–687.

4. "I AM THAT I AM" (EXOD 3:14)

The Lord as "I Am."

For Lewis, that "God was God"[11] was more of an acknowledgement than a realization and he qualifies this by invoking the present tense: the realization that God stood over and against him simply, sheerly, and purely as Lord: "'I am the Lord'; 'I am that I am.'"[12] For Lewis, this is a paradoxical statement as it tells little about God except for utter transcendence, and diametric being over and against the world. He is still coming from a position redolent with nineteenth-century German philosophy—the obvious influence of Hegelian metaphysics prior to his conversion/re-conversion is clear. (His starting point is not with the Hebrew *El, Elohim*[13]—the eternal self-existing One—but with nineteenth-century Enlightenment-led philosophy.) Perhaps this is why he stresses the absolute transcendence and separation, aseity and independence of God from human reality so much. But this realization is more than the acknowledgement of an abstract absolute spirit over and against the world: this is a personal Lord that knows us intimately and seeks a response. As we have seen, Lewis makes the link explicitly with Exodus 3:14: "God said to Moses, 'I Am that I Am.' He said further, 'Thus you shall say to the Israelites, I Am has sent me to you.'"

Eberhard Busch has noted (in the context of a similar conversion experience by the Swiss Reformed theologian Karl Barth, early in his career) how this new starting point (for Barth more of a *Retraktation*) was in many ways an explication of God's revelation to Moses in the Book of Exodus (Exod 3:14).[14] Busch describes how Barth began to use this phrase, how he sought to deny the "god" that parts of the church revered as a no-god; further, how the position "God is God" does not exclude a Christocentric position. Neither does "God is God" mean "God is everything;" for if God is everything then God is not God. What is

---

11   Lewis, *Surprised by Joy*, 220.

12   Lewis, *Surprised by Joy*, 220.

13   *Elohim*, singular *Eloah*, (Hebrew: God), the God of Israel in the Old Testament. . . . When referring to *YHWH*, *Elohim* very often is accompanied by the article *ha-*, to mean, in combination, "the God," and sometimes with a further identification *Elohim ḥayyim*, meaning "the living God."

14   Busch, "God Is God: The Meaning of a Controversial Formula and the Fundamental Problem of Speaking about God."

more, explains Busch, this is not a mathematical equation: "The equation, therefore, is not self-evident because it implies the critical thesis that our speaking about God does not automatically speak about God." To say that "God is God" invokes the realization that what we take for God is not God: therefore, God is not acknowledged as God. Even in saying thus, all we can proclaim is that we fall short in our perceiving. Our speech is inevitably inadequate. As Busch notes, by placing our "god" "on the throne of the world we enthrone in him only ourselves."[15] Furthermore, to say, "God is God, is so unprotected that it seems to cry out for further explanatory definition."[16] Lewis finds himself in the same position, which is why he struggles in the period in his life from the conversion to theism in his rooms in Magdalen in 1929 through to the conversation with Dyson and Tolkien, this is followed by the motorcycle ride in 1931, which sees the end of his wrestling with God in his mind, by which time he is as exhausted as Jacob (Gen 32:22–32) and God can finally, preveniently gift Lewis true faith. (And unlike Jacob, at least Lewis escaped with his skeleton and musculature intact.)

The Paradoxical Difficulties of Defining the Complement in "God is God"

The proposition, "God is God" is subject-complement. This is to invoke, deliberately, the language of grammar. In calling God *subject*, this is as the *nominative* in a sentence; not the *object* (*accusative*), the object that we may study, investigate. In his mature work, Barth asserted that God allows us to turn God into an object of study so as to gain some understanding, but this self-objectification does not deny the primacy of God as the *eternal* subject, the eternal origin from which all that is created flows. Grammatically the complement is not less than the subject.[17] Therefore, such a construct is in essence Trinitarian, or, more particularly, points to the Trinitarian—the relationship between the Father and the Son can be seen as subject-complement: the Son is not less than the Father; the Father does not exist before the Son; the Spirit is co-eternal, it proceeds

---

15   Busch, "God Is God," 105.
16   Busch, "God Is God," 105
17   For example, in NT Greek *Theos ēn ho Logos*: The Word is God (John 1:1). The position of the article indicates the subject; the complement drops the article and is placed before the verb.

from both the Son and the Father. They are, however, different persons. This question of personhood is important. However, what is predicated requires further elucidation. The complement in "God is God" implies unknowing; the complement opens up distance and hiddenness, aseity and sovereignty. This becomes a safeguard that prevents God being merged utterly into human affairs. Therefore, for Karl Barth and for Lewis, without this safeguard we have only a noetic idol: the no-"god" of human-centered churches/religion for Barth,[18] or C. S. Lewis's "absolute spirit" from his Hegelian phase. In his commentary on Romans, Barth faces the paradox that we *must* speak about God—it is a divine imperative—but we are human and therefore *cannot* speak about God. We must replace the complement "God" in both Barth and Lewis's declaration with a qualifier, but herein lies danger, for whenever we declare God is *love*, God is *glorious*, is *truth*, is *goodness*, God is *immeasurable, infinite, immutable*, there is compromise—we reduce God to a concept. And we so often draw these concepts from ancient Greek philosophy not from the ancient Hebrews, from the Hebrew Bible, where God again and again stops the Hebrew patriarchs, the prophets, the kings, and tribes from creating idols and little "gods" out of an idea or thought about God: they had to suffice again and again with this blank canvas—the, "I am that I am:" that God is.

For hundreds and hundreds of years the "Lordship" of the Holy Spirit restrained and prepared the ancient Hebrews until qualification of the great "I am" happened as an event in human history. Therefore, we must always keep before us the paradoxical revelation of this hidden God, the *Deus abscondus*,[19] rooted in the name given in Exodus: "I am that I am." Therefore, the qualifier can only be "Lord." This then opens up space for the self-revealing of God in Christ Jesus: "God is God" is qualified by Lordship; personhood is thereby revealed as the nature of this Lordship—this person acts in love toward humanity. But this love, forgiveness, and mercy do not deny God's Lordship. This is rooted in the first commandment: "*I am* the LORD your God, and you shall have no other gods before me" (Exod 20:2). Therefore, to return to Busch, "The

---

18   This is best expounded by Barth in a scathing attack on religion, an address delivered in the Town Church of Aarau on Jan. 16, 1916. See, Karl Barth, "*Die Gerechtigkeit Gottes.*"

19   Busch, "God Is God," 104. The phrase (or "name"?) God is God is in one sense apophatic, yet it does not point to nothingness. Is it not a form of unknowing-knowing, kataphatic-apophatic?

equation 'God is God' seeks initially to avoid the equating of God and our concepts of God."[20] Only if this is no definition at all can we avoid the pitfalls of qualifying and reducing God to a human idol. Busch rightly notes how the acknowledgement/declaration is a reflection of the revelation of God's name given to Moses. In Barthian terms, this is simultaneously a revealing and a concealing, a veiling and unveiling, visible yet shrouded: "I am that I am": as both Abraham and Moses found in their own particular ways. This name is both informative and given, yet obtuse and cryptic. Therefore, any conversion must be initiated by God and on God's terms: otherness and Lordship are essential to this, as both Barth and Lewis realized. It is this realization that separates Barth and Lewis's conversions from the Hegelian metaphysics they were both moving away from. There is perhaps a way in which the Holy Spirit rehearses and prepares individuals, such as Lewis (and his wife to be—the American Jew, Joy Davidman—over the other side of the Atlantic); is this how the Holy Spirit converted many ancient Hebrews to a closer relationship with God? If so, this is fundamental to the Hebrew understanding of God as revealed and is given to the rest of humanity by the chosen people: a blank canvas is how to start a great painting.[21] Lewis and Barth in particular had to clear out all false conceptions of God and start with this basic axiom—that God was indeed God.

fides quaerens intellectum

There is another factor in this understanding—namely the realization that faith precedes doctrine, or more pertinently, *faith is a necessary prerequisite for understanding*. The acceptance of God as God, of the Lord as "I am," is the correct prerequisite for any degree of understanding; it is also the basis of a sound Christology. This is the basis of faith in the Hebrew Bible and the New Testament; intellectualization (something of the approach of the Greek academy) comes after. What then follows is as Anselm of Canterbury (1033–1109), churchman, theologian, and philosopher, wrote, "I do not seek to understand so that I can believe, but I believe so that I may understand; and what is more, I believe that unless

---

20   Busch, "God Is God," 107.

21   And if the painting goes wrong, does not work, fails, then scrub-off the painting and re-prime to a bare canvas!

I do believe I shall not understand."[22] Anselm accepted that any degree of understanding of God initially involved accepting the Lordship of God. Hence, *fides quaerens intellectum* (faith seeking understanding): faith may seek understanding but faith can only understand if such understanding is built upon faith. Lordship, however, is a constant: thus, Anselm could write that he was not trying to make his way to the height, to penetrate the light inaccessible, he knew in humility that his understanding was not equal or capable. But out of love he desires to understand a little of the truth about God. For Lewis he had to take the step of faith; then he could seek to understand, but an important factor was humility—a trait that was lacking in the pseudo-Hegelian beliefs prior to his conversion. If he had remained with his own innate theological speculation, he would have got no further than the idea he called "absolute spirit," which merely complemented all that he had become as a person. By comparison, Barth attempts to solve the crisis of faith manifested in his preaching and beliefs through left-wing politics. However, the year of the new starting point, 1915, for Barth is characterized by a realization of the distance and hiddenness, aseity, and sovereignty of God. This is a position that in Barth is redolent with humility. Both conversion/re-conversion for Barth and Lewis bear the hallmark of what Anselm asserted. It is of no mere coincidence that both Barth and Lewis developed a profound appreciation of Anselm of Canterbury in their mature work.

5. . . . TO CALL UPON THE NAME OF THE LORD

C. S. Lewis's protracted conversion was about perceiving a supernatural influence, listening and assessing, measuring and responding to the LORD. But the name does not come out of nowhere, it is given by God— revealed. If the complement in the paradoxical title of Lewis and Barth's "God is God" ("I am that I am") is Lord then the will of the Lord is known through relationship: listening and perceiving, hearing, knowing and understanding, . . . and receiving. This happens preveniently if we are open to the grace: so that the will is known through the name, a name that encapsulates what is known and understood. The revealed reality of knowing of God focused down from the point of the incarnation onto a triune understanding—Father, Son, and Holy Spirit, co-eternal,

---

22   Anselm of Canterbury, *The Proslogion*. Anselm is quoting from Isa 7:9. See, Davies and Evans, *Anselm of Canterbury—The Major Works*, 82–104.

2. The Hebrews, the Jews, ... and God. I

three persons in one God—but we need briefly to remind ourselves, as Lewis did, of the development, some might say evolution, in the human understanding of God that was given to the ancient Hebrews and formed the foundation of the triune revelation. This was a right understanding that was mirrored, to a degree, in Lewis's protracted stages of conversion. What happened for Lewis over a few years happened for the Hebrews over a period of nearly four thousand years.

Rabbinic Judaism regards seven names of God to be so holy that written down, they must never be expunged or removed: *YHWH*, *El* ("God"), *Eloah* ("God"), *Elohim* ("God"), *Shaddai* ("Almighty"), *Ehyeh* ("I Am"), and *Tzevaot* ("of Hosts").[23] The name *Yah*, which forms the first part of the name *YHWH*, is regarded by some of worthy of similar protection. There are other names but they are seen as titles or epithets reflecting different aspects of God, however, often out of respect—even exclusivity—special care is taken when writing of God in English: hence, "G-d."[24]

We need to look a little deeper at the name "I am." In the Septuagint this is "I am the one being"—*egō eimi ho ōn* (in the Hebrew: *ehyeh 'asher 'ehyeh*—"I-am who I-am" or "I-will-be who I-will-be."). However, the name *YHWH*—referred to as the Tetragrammaton,[25] and often translated as "LORD"—is, according to Jewish culture, forbidden to be pronounced, being substituted or replaced by the word *Adonai* (the Lord); but what is evoked by *YHWH* is often seen as more, yes, lordship, to a degree, but also, and essentially, the personal God and relation (which Lewis began to submit to in the final stages of his protracted conversions: was Lewis in effect visited by the *Shekhinah*[26]—the divine presence?).[27] *YHWH* has often

---

23 Maimonides. Mishneh Torah, Yesodei ha-Torah §6:2. See, http://www.mechon-mamre.org/i/1106.htm. Compiled by Maimonides, the Mishneh Torah is a code of ethics, advice/answers to moral questions, regarding Jewish law authored by Maimonides, as compiled between 1170–80 AD, in Egypt.

24 See, "Names of God," in Karesh and Hurvitz, *Encyclopedia of Judaism*, 179.

25 The Tetragrammaton or Tetragram (from Greek; meaning four letters, the four-letter Hebrew word *YHWH*, and is the name of the biblical God of Israel: from right to left, *yodh*, *he*, *waw*, *he*.

26 A title used freely in the Talmud.

27 There is nothing in the Torah that prohibits the speaking of the name and it is liberally cited in the Hebrew Bible (the people calling on the name of the LORD); however, the name had ceased to be spoken aloud by the third century BC (Second Temple Judaism). The writers of the New Testament consistently follows this practice.

been interpreted as meaning, "He who makes that which has been made, he brings into existence whatever exists." It is important to remember that the ancient Hebrews were surrounded by pagan tribes and nations that had invented "gods" and "goddesses," distant and unknowable—except, that is, knowable by a religious elite of mystical priestesses, shamans, shrine prostitutes, and patriarchal priest-kings. Many ordinary Jews living in an agrarian economy would suffice with *HaShem* (meaning, The Name). The evolving understanding of God as the one, the one true living deity, is potentially perceivable by all. Yes, there is a priestly tribe (the Levites) who handle sacrifice and intercede, to a degree, but God is perceivable and knowable and all can partake in this understanding, depending on how they have personally developed, and how life has shaped them. But many turn away and invent their own gods and idols (the Book of Judges, 2 Kings, et al.).

The name for God used by the Hebrews evolves over centuries, it develops over millennia, and it is fine-tuned, to a degree, through encounter and therefore revelation; it is often asserted that there are around 270 names, or combinations of names, for God in the Hebrew Bible.[28] The names are presented so as to reveal some facet of God: life,

See R. Kendall Soulen, *The Divine Name(s) and the Holy Trinity*, vol. 1

28   The Hebrew names for God fall into two categories: conceptual or proper. The original significance of divine names is often lost and indeterminate. Proper nouns are often found in ancient literature, conceptual or abstract names are more of a recent development (i.e., from the time of Second Temple Judaism). Each name is not exclusive but has significance and represents a specific tradition. *YHWH* and Elohim represent two biblical traditions. The Tetragrammaton appears the most frequently used and is an essential name of God invoking eternal monotheistic existence (Exod 3:14). *Shem ha-Meforash* ("the Ineffable Name") referring to "the holiest one" was never pronounced, except by the high priest in the Holy of Holies on Yom Kippur. Many other names occur in the Bible, but are regarded as secondary: *El, Eloha, Elohim* (plural; taken as a singular when applied to the God of Israel) with various suffixes—*El Shaddai*, and *El Zebaoth* (though there is some doubt about the validity of this last one according to the Talmud). The word *elohim* was also used in secular terms for heathen gods (Exod 20:3) and human judges (Exod 22:7). The names of God became ontological representations of God's relationship to creation and his creatures: often representative of compassion and mercy. Because of the perceived sanctity of God's name and the authority of the Third Commandment—taking the name of the LORD in vain—this caused a reluctance to overuse a particular name especially in the Talmudic period. See, as a good example of the cumulative Hebraic names and uses thereof, Auret, "The Theological Intent of the Use of the Names of God in the Eighth-Century Memoir of Isaiah"; furthermore, Broadie, "Maimonides and Aquinas on the Names of God." Regarding the difficulties of discerning intent and meaning see, de Blois, "Translating the Names of God: Tryggve

personhood, particularity, God's unfathomable enormity, his glory and beauty. A root for many of the names is *El, Elohim*—as in *El Shaddai*, God Almighty, *Beth El*, the house of God, *Immanu-el*, God with us. At the centre of this revelation is *Y-hw-h*: properly, *YHWH* (the vowels omitted out of respect for the holiness and purity which is inherent to the name). As we have noted, this is much more personal, indeed it is the very name of God, not a mere title. and is the name reserved for the covenant God of Israel.

The key biblical passage in attempting to understand the name is Exodus chapter 3: Moses and the burning bush. The revelation is fine-tuned in its ontological purity as "I am who I am," "I will be what I will be." (Exod 3:14). This is divine speech about the name:

> Moses said to God, Suppose I go to the Israelites and say to them, The God of your fathers has sent me to you, and they ask me, What is his name? Then what shall I tell them? God said to Moses, I am who I am. This is what you are to say to the Israelites: I am has sent me to you. God also said to Moses, Say to the Israelites, The LORD, the God of your fathers—the God of Abraham, the God of Isaac and the God of Jacob—has sent me to you.
> This is my name forever,
>   the name you shall call me
>   from generation to generation.
>
>   Exod 3:13–15

As we saw with Karl Barth and C. S. Lewis' conversions. God is therefore the eternal self-existing One. This is associated with the covenant with Israel, a covenant that builds on the encounters with Abraham, Isaac, and Jacob, and the twelve tribes. God was revealed to the patriarchs as *El Shaddai*, but to Moses as something other. To Moses this is a binding relational covenant: *YHWH*. There are multiple uses and forms to reflect this throughout the Hebrew Bible which mirror the developing understanding in Lewis during the 1930s as he explores his way forward in faith: "*YHWH Shammah*," "I am the One who is there" (Ezek 48:35); "*YHWH Sabbaoth*," "I am the Almighty" (1 Sam 1:3); "*YHWH Shalom*," "The LORD our Peace," (Judg 6:24); "*YHWH Yireh*," "the LORD your provider" (1 Sam 1:3); "*YHWH m'qaddesh*," "The LORD

Mettinger's Analyses Applied to Bible Translation"; also, Marmorstein, *The Old Rabbinic Doctrine of God*, 17–145.

who sanctifies you,"/"The LORD our Holiness," (Exod 31:13; Lev 20:8b); "*YHWH Tsidkenu*," "The LORD Our Righteousness" (Jer 23:5–6); "*YHWH Ro'i*," "The LORD is my Shepherd" (Ps 23:1). Hence when we come to the pivot point of revelation we find the apostles struggling to realize what has happened and what is before them: the Son of God? the Son of *YHWH*? Yeshua Ha Mashiach: before Abraham was, I am that I am—"'Yes, in very truth I tell you,' Jesus answered, 'before Abraham was, *I am!*'" (John 8:58).

Lewis is not alone amongst theologians and intellectual Christians who reflect an evolving conversion measured in some ways by the named revelation of God in the Hebrew Bible.

3

The Hebrews, the Jews, . . . and God: II

"Then Moses said to God, 'If I come to the people of Israel and say to them, The God of your fathers has sent me to you, and they ask me, What is his name? What shall I say to them?' God said to Moses, 'I am that I am.' And he said, 'Say this to the people of Israel, I am has sent me to you.' God also said to Moses, 'Say this to the people of Israel, The LORD, the God of your fathers, the God of Abraham, the God of Isaac, and the God of Jacob, has sent me to you:' this is my name for ever, and thus I am to be remembered throughout all generations."
EXODUS 3:13–15

"He was by necessity a Jew. We cannot be blind to this fact; it belongs to the concrete reality of God's work and God's revelation. For Jesus Christ is the fulfilment of the covenant concluded by God with Abraham, Isaac and Jacob. . . . The man who is ashamed of Israel is ashamed of Jesus Christ and therefore of his own existence."
KARL BARTH ON JESUS'S JEWISHNESS[1]

"The valley is a regular warren of caves inhabited by dwarfs. There are several species of them, I gather, though I only distinguished two—a black kind with black shirts and a red kind who call themselves Marxomanni. They are all very fierce and apparently quarrel a good deal but they all acknowledge some kind of vassalage to this man Savage. At least they made no difficulty in letting me through when they heard that I wanted to see him—beyond insisting on giving me a guard."
LEWIS, ON HITLER AND NATIONAL SOCIALISM[2]

---

1   Karl Barth, *Dogmatik im Grundriß*, 67. My translation.
2   Lewis *The Pilgrim's Regress*, 96–97.

1. C. S. LEWIS, KARL BARTH: THE JEWISH QUESTION

C. S. Lewis and Karl Barth can be considered dissimilar; indeed, to many from a more extreme position they could be seen as incompatible. Yet, as secularism, dominated by consumerism, has taken hold in the West since their respective deaths in the 1960s, Lewis and Barth have seemed closer in their thinking because of their respect for an orthodox traditional creedal basis for Christian doctrine, a basis grounded in the revelation of the triune God: the Word of God as person (Christ), and as scripture, with the church as the forgiving community. Though not poles apart, Barth and Lewis were operating from characteristically individual and personal positions when at the height of their powers in the 1940s and 1950s: Lewis the Anglican Oxford scholar, children's storywriter, religious broadcaster, and Christian apologist, philosopher, and theologian; Barth the Swiss Reformed Church minister, professor of dogmatics, whose career spanned Germany and Switzerland, who had created a revival of orthodox, creedal, Trinitarian theology. There is also a degree of similarity and convergence in their conversions: Lewis's protracted conversion, c.1929–31, which we have looked at, and Barth's dramatic change of heart in 1915—both cases characterized by a profound realization of God's aseity. The freedom by which God exists of and from God's-self, grounded in the utter reality of God, in Hebraic terms, the eternal self-existing One (*El, Elohim*), this is for Lewis a realization that changed them. Lewis and Barth both arrive at a point where they must own that "God is God," which leads them to acknowledge the unique self-revelation of God in Jesus—"God is God, in Christ."[3] In their mature work both are "muscular," intellectual Christians; notwithstanding the individual denominational characteristics of each as a theologian, Lewis and Barth are orthodox-traditional, biblical-creedal Christians who argue against the *zeitgeist*, the spirit of an Enlightenment-spawned modernism. However there remain, as we have noted, significant differences.

Like Lewis, the empire-minded Edwardian young gentleman, the young Karl Barth reflected the *Weltanschauung* of German society and its attitude towards the Jews; at least he did prior to his conversion, his *retraktation*, his return to a traditional and orthodox Christianity and church. He was not explicitly anti-Semitic; but neither did he repudiate

---

3   See Brazier, "C. S. Lewis and Karl Barth's Conversions," 31, essentially 34–36.

the self-generated identity of the Enlightened European with its assumed superiority over the Jews, and its dismissal of them. In 1913 Barth was critical of the nationalist basis in German politics, society, and theology—an agenda that was inherently anti-Semitic as it demanded that all Jews become perfect Aryan Germans—for he was prepared to comment publicly, "The ancient Hebrews should not become Germans, rather the Germans should become ancient Hebrews."[4] This expresses the Pauline tenet that gentiles are grafted onto the wild olive tree of the true Israel by faith in Christ (Rom 11:17). In the 1930s, Barth would come to articulate this position with much greater dogmatic sophistication. It is clear that at this time the German establishment—and in all probability the majority of its people—believed the Jews should become Germans, fully fledged, without a trace of Semitism, with Synagogues politely out of sight of the public. Barth was prepared to go against this, and stand out against his lecturers, his education, the establishment that paid his salary. Within a year, his lecturers, theological professors, had publicly backed the German war effort and all it stood for in terms of nationalism. Barth stood against them. Barth had been horrified to discover many of his respected teachers amongst the signatories when in August 1914 ninety-three intellectuals attempted to impress German public opinion by proclaiming support for the war policy of Kaiser Wilhelm II. Barth believed he could no longer subscribe to their ethics, or to their understanding of the Bible and of history, in particular ancient Hebrew history.[5] And at the heart of this was Germanic nationalistic anti-Semitism: hence his inversion of the demand by the establishment that Jews should become more like Germans. Barth questioned the validity of their teaching and doctrine, he concluded that it was grounded in the work of Schleiermacher: "He [Schleiermacher] was unmasked. In a decisive way all the theology expressed in the manifesto and everything that followed it (even in *Die Christliche Welt*) proved to be founded and governed by him."[6]

---

4   "*Die alten Hebr[äer] sollen keine Deutschen warden, aber Sie alten Hebräer.*" Barth, *Konfirmandenunterricht 1909–1921*, 2

5   See, Barth "Evangelische Theologie im 19. Jahrhundert," 14; an address delivered at the meeting of the Goethegsellschaft in Hanover, 8th January 1957.

6   Barth, "Nachwort" 293.

2. KARL BARTH AND *ISRAELITISCH*

Born in the second half of the nineteenth century, into a Europe dominated by agnostic freedom and global empire building, Karl Barth achieved the near impossible, by turning the mainland European (and to a degree American) theological status quo away from Friedrich Schleiermacher and G. W. F. Hegel and back to Christ. When asked by the eminent logician and mathematician Heinrich Scholz (originally trained in theology) what was the basis on which theology operated as an intellectual discipline in the university, Barth is reported to have answered, assertively, "the resurrection of Jesus Christ from the dead."[7] With Barth there was no beating about the bush, no obfuscatory, embarrassed apologetic squirming, no hedging around religious emotionalism, no putting any notion of a "god" into a box to be analyzed from the safe, secure position of the Enlightenment-endorsed human intellect. Nor did he seek refuge from the question by invoking an ill-defined semi-divine substance, invisible, but as comforting as a goddess of human desires, nor yet in paradox and mysticism. No, to Barth the resurrection was the only basis on which you could do theology as a distinctive Wissenschaft: all was related to this single event that had cosmic implications. Herein lies the intellectual responsibility that underpinned Barth's massive *Church Dogmatics* (*Kirchliche Dogmatik*, circa 6 million words),[8] issuing from the *analogia fidei*.

As with Lewis's conversion, Barth's led to an acknowledgment of the indisputable election of the ancient Hebrews and the Jews as the chosen people of God, yet also the undeniable failure of the majority Jewish people now to accept and acknowledge the Christ, their Messiah. Barth develops a kind of dynamic theology whereby the history of the ancient Hebrews, the progress of salvation history, the Christ-event, are all time-bound, particular, and yet also universal, where the first axiom—of crucial and fundamental importance—is God speaking to Israel: Deus dixit. For Barth, as Colin Gunton has identified, "the first commandment makes it a different sort of science to all others. You might say history is

---

7   Gunton, *The Barth Lectures*, 44.

8   Barth, *The Church Dogmatics* (14 vols.). References hereafter are given as CD, followed by the volume, section number (§) and page reference from The Church Dogmatics (UK, 1st edition, hardback, not the new translation, paperback 31-volume, edition).

similar but the point Barth is making is the distinctiveness of theology."[9] Barth himself on this question commented, "The fact that God does not permit Israel, the righteous, or the Church to perish means that he cannot allow them to go their way un-accused, un-condemned, un-punished; so grace includes a kind of holy judgement."[10] Israel's calling is eternal: "This is the point about Israel; Israel is called to be God's people."[11] Barth relies heavily on Paul's (i.e., Saul the Pharisee) Epistle to the Romans, in particular the fact that Israel has been chosen and can't be rejected, unchosen, or de-selected, but also that the gentiles have been "chosen" in order to invite Israel to come, to reconsider, and turn to the Messiah, Yeshua, one of them:[12] this is the primary mission of the church: to the Jew first, then the gentile! (Rom 1:16.)

This is a position that we will see C. S. Lewis comes to in the 1940s and explicates more and more in his maturity in the 1950s. Israel has set the terms, not so much by rejecting the Christ but rather by *not accepting him, just yet*. If we look at the present situation, there is rejection; but eschatologically it is "not yet," with the potential ever open. For Lewis—a position clear from his life and mature work in the 1950s—Israel and the church stand side-by-side.[13] This is indeed *resistance*—for a time. But it is no rejection of Israel, wrote Barth, but a temporary set-back. Israel's election is particular but of universal intent: Abraham is called that all nations might be blessed, thus Israel is called on behalf of *all nations*.[14] All have committed disobedience, and all may know God's mercy (Rom 11:30–32). This theological position is, for Barth (and becomes so for Lewis), universal in intent and is grounded in Israel's election as God's chosen and beloved. Barth commented: "Israel is the people of the Jews who resists its election—it doesn't reject—it resists it, the Church is the gathering of Jews and Gentiles called on the ground of its election."[15]

9   Gunton, *Barth Lectures*, 50.

10   Barth, *CD* II/1, §30, 357.

11   Gunton, *Barth Lectures*, 111, on Barth, *CD* II/2.

12   Barth, *CD* II/1, §30, 148 ff.

13   We will see this in the coming chapters through an analysis of Lewis's *Reflections on the Psalms*.

14   Barth, *CD* II/1, on Romans 11:30–32

15   Barth, CD II/2, §34, 236. It is important to remember that the church consists, in this context, of Western Christians—broadly speaking, Roman Catholics and Protestants—but also Hebraic Christians/Messianic Jews. (The Western churches err to

Some of the gentiles, for Barth, accept this election, but Israel still resists (*widerstehen, sich widersetzen*): the two sides of this are brought out by him. But where does this leave Israel? The popular Christian idea that Israel rejected and continues to reject the Messiah tends to forget that the very earliest church was entirely Jewish—until God's monumental extension of salvation to the gentiles, through Peter (Acts 10:9–16). This popular misconception also ignores the existence of Jewish Christ-believers down the centuries: Israel's rejection is, therefore, *partial*. Israel for Barth and for Lewis is still Israel. Even in its refusal it remains the people of Yeshua, the Anointed One, the resurrected universal Christ (*Christos*): "the electing God and the elected community embrace even this Israel that steps into the void."[16] Israel's partial resistance is, therefore, not the final word . . . and Israel is still listening, *simul iustus et peccator*?

Therefore, for Barth, even Israel is included in this election; everybody is amongst the elect —*in Christ*; where Christianity so willfully has forgotten how he *is* the Hebraic Messiah, of the House of David, Judah's champion![17] He commented "Both Jews and Gentiles are shut up by God in the same prison—then the prison opens and again they are all together. Because God has determined the Gentiles for the mercy in which they now participate and the Jews for future participation and the same mercies."[18] So for Barth there are two communities: Israel and the gentiles—but they are one community in the sense that they are both in different ways called and elected.[19] And the married Lewis's family represented these two communities: his Jewish wife who converted to being a Christian, and the elder of his two step-sons who re-embraced Judaism, while the younger embraced his parents Christian faith![20]

Barth never ceased to emphasize the fact—lost in much European theology from the time of the so-called Enlightenment—of Jesus's

---

dismiss the Orthodox churches and indigenous forms of the *ecclesia* in other parts of the world.)

16   Barth, *CD* II/2, §34, 303.

17   There is a long discussion of the biblical evidence for this (and the importance of emphasizing this Jewish identity). See: Barth, *CD* II/2, §34, 305 ff. However, it may be argued that Barth falls short in acknowledging the willfulness of humanity in resisting this election and therefore its salvation.

18   Barth, *CD* II/2, §34, 305; Romans 11.

19   Gunton, *Barth Lectures*, 118–19.

20   We will examine this in ch. 13.

Jewishness. Yeshua is *Jewish* flesh; we are saved by *Jewish* blood; atonement is grounded in the shedding of blood: holy Jewish blood, of Yeshua, one of the chosen people in the land of Israel: can we emphasize this enough?[21] And this assertion was before the Second World War and the Holocaust, and the guilt-trip many Europeans experienced following the discovery of Hitler's death camps. If we ignore or marginalize Christ's Jewishness, then

> The Church's whole doctrine of the Incarnation and the Atonement becomes abstract and valueless and meaningless to the extent that this comes to be regarded as something accidental and incidental. . . . Jewishness prevents this rounding of the picture of Jesus into a kind of ideal picture of human existence.[22]

The very word "Christ"—rooted in Greek linguistics—can becomes for some a vague universal term for homogenous humanity: is not *Ha Mashiach*, the Anointed One, the Hebrew who was touched, adopted, chosen, ontologically by God? For many in a late twentieth- and early twenty-first-century post-modern generation, this very Jewishness thwarts the attempts by Enlightenment-led theologians and philosophers—for example, Schleiermacher and Hegel, or today's self-confessed liberals, also multi-faith religionists[23]—to remove Jesus, the historic Yeshua, from his Jewish roots.[24] Jesus's Jewishness is a stumbling-block to those who would seek to reinvent him into an archetype of ideal human—for example, the idealized super-religious shaman that Schleiermacher tried to make Jesus into: European pseudo-divinity without Jewish flesh. Lewis was only too aware looking back on his childhood and youth from the perspective of his conversion how the socio-cultural education system he was schooled in was infected with such a modernist anti-Semitism. In central Europe, this heresy was epitomized by Germanic art in the late nineteenth and early twentieth centuries. For example, such idiomatic imagery reached its height in German civic religious art where Jesus was often reduced to a mere human presented with neo-Classical pagan imagery derived from

---

21   Indeed, Jesus's flesh, because of the nature of the incarnation, is Mary's Jewish flesh.

22   Barth, *CD* IV/1, §59.1, 166 and 167.

23   However it needs to be noted how many like the idea of a Jewish Jesus—because it sounds multi-faith to them, but this is often in a synchronistic context, therefore attempting to conflate all religions.

24   Gunton, *Barth Lectures*, 165.

Greek and Roman culture. An example of this was Max Klinger's *Christ on Mount Olympus* (1897): Jesus as a wise Germanic religious leader, a blond-haired, pale-skinned "Nordic/Aryan," a fair-haired, blue-eyed young man conversing with young Greek men and women. In effect, this was an early version of Hitler's vision of the Darwinian triumph of the ideal human, a German, representative of an obedient German Christian and a German Christianity: do we see here god-like Germanic flesh in the place of incarnated Jewish flesh? Barth's agenda is to work explicitly against this heterodox humanism that had come to represent European theology. Colin Gunton, writing on Barth's emphasis on the central importance of the Jewishness of Yeshua and the danger of reducing Jesus to an idealized human, asserted—

> You must not produce some ideal of humanity which is independent of the *israelitisch* equivalent of the New Testament. Therefore, of course, you rule out all forms of Docetism—the doctrine that Jesus only appeared to be human—and you do that by keeping the Old Testament in the picture.[25]

Barth commented that by retaining the Old Testament, the adherents of the new covenant are protected against all of the multiple forms of Docetism that had bedeviled the church throughout its history.[26] It is of fundamental importance, and this is clear from Barth's early works (the two commentaries, for example, on the *Epistle to the Romans*, 1919 and 1921), that we are talking about an unflushed Jewish Messiah, sent for the lost sheep of Israel. Yes, *he* is representative of universal humanity, but this is a Jewish Messiah, a real human reality, who represents God's purposes for the world, purposes that teleologically will be realized through what *he* did: first through Israel, then through the resurrected Christ, and finally through his present people, the church (composed of both Jew and gentile).

In 1934 Barth was largely responsible for the writing of the *Barmer Erklärung* (*The Barmen Declaration*), which explicitly rejected the National Socialist Party and its ideology, repudiated Hitler's messianic pretensions, and rejected the idea of the Third Reich. It also lamented the influence of Nazism on Germanic Christianity. The declaration argued for the allegiance of the church to Jesus Christ—God incarnate—and therefore

---

25   Gunton, *Barth Lectures*, 165 (referring to *CD* IV/1, §59.1, 160 f.)
26   Barth, *CD* IV/1, §59.1, 168.

all who claimed to be Christian should resist and repel false "gods" and false lords, such as the Führer (Barth is reputed to have personally mailed a copy of the Barmen Declaration to Hitler). Within months, Barth was dismissed from his post as professor at the University of Bonn and was exiled from Germany (returning to his native Switzerland), for refusing to take an oath of loyalty to Adolf Hitler. Most academics, whether they agreed with National Socialism or not, had capitulated; Barth could easily have done so, so as to maintain his exalted position, his chair at the University of Bonn, but he did not: history judges the others; Barth stands clear of the compromise. A few years earlier Hermann Otto Hoyer had painted a picture of Hitler in full rhetorical preaching mode entitled, "*Am Anfang war das Wort*" ("In the Beginning was the Word"): according to Hoyer's twisted version of John's Gospel, the Word did not descend into Yeshua the Jew, but into the Aryan-European pagan *supremo-"god"-and-"führer,"* Adolf Hitler. In Britain generally, Oxford specifically, such anti-Semitism was much more veiled, and polite, and challenging it carried little risk to career, status, and position.

3. LEWIS AND BARTH: WHY *YESHUA HA MASHIACH*, THE DAVIDIAN ISRAELITE?

Lewis: A Hebraic Inkling

In the 1950s Lewis moved more and more into a Hebraic mindset and study. This is reflected, for example, in his study *Reflections on the Psalms*, and was enhanced, in part, by his marriage to Joy Davidman—born and raised an American Jew in New York. The college staff at Oxford were skeptical for a variety of veiled reasons: Lewis's defense is spread across many of his works. The specific attitude from the esoteric elitist Oxbridge common-room skepticism was in part because Lewis, following on from his conversion, had broken etiquette by speaking out openly about his conversion and faith;[27] there was "religion" practiced amongst some tutors and professors in the colleges, but these people were supposed to keep their religion to themselves. Scientific and philosophical atheists

---

27   His witness in the common rooms of Oxford colleges led him, to a degree, to write his first Christian work—*Out of the Silent Planet* (1938)—which was scathing about the Enlightenment-led nihilism that characterized much of the academy.

were allowed to project their anti-religion in criticism of others, but believers were supposed to keep their faith veiled. Furthermore because of his professional status, teaching at Oxford, Lewis clearly saw himself in opposition to the "enlightened" and "modern" apostate elements within the common rooms as well as in the Church of England of his day. It is for this reason amongst several others that the professional group named the Inklings came together: primarily simply to discuss literature and theology, the arts, the state of the academy, the universities, and the churches. But etiquette dictated that such discussions were not in the common rooms (unless the debate was initiated by scientific and philosophical atheists, or by one whose faith was outside of the Judaic-Christian tradition). Discussion took place in their college rooms (hence, the Lewis-Dyson-Tolkien conversion debate) or in local pubs: The Eagle and Child and The Lamb and Flag, both in St Giles in the city center. Conversation, when initiated by the anti-religion contingent, in the common rooms of Oxford colleges was of a more defensive nature. Lewis had to justify first his conversion, then his faith, then his Christian works. By comparison, he could share his work with like-minded writers and critics in the Inklings (Tolkien and Lewis would share passages, chapters, from their works as they were writing them). However, although they shared his faith, his aims, and motives—to a degree—the other members of the Inklings did not allow Lewis to get away without a rigorous critical analysis. By the mid-1940s this had developed, alongside the Inklings meetings, into a Socratic society—based on explicit Greek philosophical principles.[28]

Lewis's comments in relation to the Jews were perhaps more progressive than his fellow Inklings. There was as pervasive a veiled anti-Semitism in the innate beliefs and cultural background to some of the Inklings as there was amongst the Oxbridge common-room staff. For example, Tolkien's assertion that the dwarves in *The Hobbit* (1937) were similar in many ways with the Jews, an assertion that cannot be seen as particularly complimentary; however, there is evidence that Tolkien sought to temper and alter this view later in *The Lord of the Rings* (1954–55) and in subsequent works.[29] Tolkien's approach can be seen as being

[28] The Oxford Socratic Club, 1942 to 1954, provided an open forum for the discussion of the intellectual questions connected with religion and with Christianity in particular. Papers were presented both for and against.

[29] See, Brackmann, "'Dwarves Are Not Heroes': Antisemitism and the Dwarves in J. R. R. Tolkien's Writing."

somewhat patronizing and condescending: a form of sublimated empire mentality? Lewis simply stood apart from the others.

Fellow Inkling Charles Williams portrayed Jews in his novels, including some strange ideas about Jewish mysticism. Concerns have been expressed over the stereotyping and anti-Semitism in these portrayals (and the works of other mid-twentieth-century authors), which for many are typical of the time in British middle- and upper-middle class intellectuals.[30]

Humphrey Carpenter notes how the Inklings were, by the 1950s,[31] politically conservative, seen by many of their students as reactionary, High Anglican or Roman Catholic, and hostile to the spirit of modernism and liberalism: Lewis started to find himself out of touch with the post-war generation of undergraduates, many of whom were beginning to be politically aware and to take the state of society rather more seriously than their predecessors had done. Lewis lamented this. "The modem world is so desperately serious," he remarked to Arthur Greeves.[32] Lewis found he was distanced, out of sympathy, with Oxbridge dons:

> It might or might not be true to say that Christians were in the minority in the senior common rooms of Oxford; but certainly those dons who did profess Christianity generally kept their religion to themselves, attending their college chapel or parish church but, not making any display of the fact, and certainly not writing popular books in the hope of converting others to their beliefs. Lewis, in fact, had offended against Oxford etiquette not by becoming a Christian, but by making a public matter of his conversion. He had refused to adopt the detached irony which Oxford has always regarded as an acceptable manner of cloaking one's true beliefs. He had indeed guyed this ironical detachment in the character of "Mr. Sensible" in The Pilgrim's Regress.[33]

But then Lewis was also out-of-step, to a degree, with the rest of the Inklings on the question of the ancient Hebrews, the Hebrew Bible, and his attitude to the Jews around them at Oxford (especially, to a degree,

---

30   See also, Patterson, "The Jewels of Messias: Images of Judaism and Antisemitism in the Novels of Charles Williams"; Loewenstein, *Loathsome Jews and Engulfing Women: Metaphors of Protection in the Works of Wyndham Lewis, Charles Williams and Graham Greene*.

31   Carpenter, *The Inklings*, 206–7.

32   Carpenter, *The Inklings*, 207.

33   Carpenter, *The Inklings*, 207–8.

in relation to the Church of England, specifically particularly modern Anglicans, who believed in a national civic, pseudo-Socialist religion and were, it seems, innately suspicious of any one group of people, one religion, claiming preference over others: how could one people, be "God's" chosen?).[34]

Barth: On the Davidian Israelite

Those who criticize Barth for not reflecting the current politically correct apologetic position devoid of value and meaning towards the Jews and towards the state of Israel, would do well to remember that this is the man who in front of thousands in 1946, in Germany (the land that gave us the Holocaust), in the ruins of the once magnificent *Kurfürsten schloss* in Bonn, stood and in a lecture asserted to people who were just recovering from the destruction of Nazi Germany, the absolute ground for Christian faith in the ancient Hebrews, the Hebrew Bible, and the Jews bearing witness as God's chosen people. Let us consider Barth in full flow, deeply relevant (and reflecting to a degree Lewis's position against something of the *Weltanschauung* and *Zeitgeist* among some of the academics at Oxford), pressing home the importance and significance of Israel in relation to Yeshua the Anointed One. Speaking of the evil that had engulfed Europe over the previous two decades Barth insisted that—

> . . . from its roots National Socialism was anti-Semitic, this movement was realized with a simple demonic clarity, that the enemy, to them, was the Jew: the enemy in this matter had to be Israel. Because in this Jewish nation there really lives to this day the extraordinariness of the revelation of God.
>
> Jesus, the Christ, the Savior, and God's Servant, is the one who sets forth and reveals the mission of the nation of Israel. He it is that fulfils the Covenant concluded between God and Abraham. When the Christian Church confesses Jesus Christ as Savior and the Servant of God for us, for all, also for the mighty majority of those who have no direct connection with the people of Israel, then it does not confess Him fully. This is because He was a Jew, this "Jewishness" in Jesus was often regarded as a *pudenda*.* No!

---

34   Read Rabbi Lionel Blue's account of his time at Oxford, as a post-WW2 undergraduate: Lionel Blue, *Hitchhiking to Heaven*; also, *A Backdoor to Heaven*, where Jewish students were regarded as a special case, inferior, and were regarded with suspicion due to their religious practices.

> Nor can the view be that we believe in Jesus Christ, who was just an Israelite, a Jew, by accident, but who might quite as well have sprung from another nation. No! We must strictly consider that Jesus Christ, in whom we believe, whom we Christians drawn out of the heathen call our savior, whom we praise as the consummator of God's work on our behalf: *He was by necessity a Jew*. We cannot be blind to this fact; it belongs to the concrete reality of God's work and God's revelation. For Jesus Christ is the fulfilment of the covenant concluded by God with Abraham, Isaac and Jacob; and it is the reality of this covenant—not the idea of any or every religious covenant—which is the basis, the meaning and goal of creation, that is, it is of everything that is real in distinction from God. The problem—if there is one—of Israel is, since the problem of Christ is inseparable from it, the problem of existence as such. The man who is ashamed of Israel is ashamed of Jesus Christ and therefore of his own existence.[35]

So, the self-revelation of God is in the person of Jesus Christ who was formed from and within God's chosen people: Mary's flesh. Therefore, if there is—from the perspective of neo-pagan European religion—a problem with Israel, then this problem is with existence itself: it represents the *krisis* of humanity. For Barth, if you deny Israel, you deny yourself as made in the image of God. Do most of the critics of Barth's regard for Israel hold a religiously syncretistic view, which expects Barth to write in an isolated pluralistically self-contained mode oblivious to contradiction and objective truth? By comparison does an academic Western elite marginalize or even remove Jesus's Jewishness so as to align him with the rest of universal humanity's invented religious fantasies? This is what is expected also of Lewis by his critics in the early twenty-first century, but Lewis contradicts them: Lewis is, in his maturity, more and more Israelitisch.

4. *THE PILGRIM'S REGRESS*—JEWISH CITATIONS

Therefore, writing to Arthur Greeves in 1933, shortly after his conversion, Lewis was well aware of what was happening in central Europe, despite being ensconced in the leafy English placidity of Oxford. He agrees

---

[35] Barth, *Dogmatik im Grundriß*, 67. My translation, but with Barth's emphasis. * *pudenda*: Latin, "shameful," "that whereof one ought to feel shame," "that which we must ignore!"

with Arthur Greeves that the conclusion of the First World War—the dictatorial terms of peace required by the allies—was responsible, in part, for the rise of Hitler, but this does not account for the evil injustice of the persecution, the scapegoating, of the Jews, a position Lewis describes as "absurd." He notes how Hitler asserts that the Jews made no input to European culture, no influence on what is taken to be Germanic culture and life, what is more, Hitler asserts that he is doing "The Will of the Lord." Lewis identifies how the concept of the will of the Lord issues precisely from the developing relationship of the ancient Hebrews with God. This intimate relationship between God and humanity was forged in God's relationship to the Jews (revealed to them by *El, Eloah, Elohim, El Shaddai: YHWH, HaShem*—the Name). The world owes this relationship and the salvation that issues from it precisely to the Jews. This, to Lewis, exposes the inaccuracy, absurdity, and irrelevance of Hitler—"the blaspheming tyrant"—and his protestations. Yes, writes Lewis, show charity to the German people, but not for absurd dictators.[36]

In the context of his spiritual autobiographies (*The Pilgrim's Regress*, 1933, and *Surprised by Joy*, 1955) what interests us is Lewis's allusions to the Jews. In the letter to this brother, he alludes to Mr. Savage in *The Pilgrim's Regress*.[37] Who is this? Why is he relevant? Allegory was important to Lewis. Written not long after his conversion, Lewis wrote explicitly following the structure and intent of John Bunyan's *The Pilgrim's Progress*. Writing on the rise of National Socialism in Germany Lewis is likening Hitler and his adherents to the character he created of Mr. Savage in *The Pilgrims Regress*. Why? because this character represents the political delusions of a dictator, who spins beliefs that the people flock to believe: all in contradiction to the revelation of God in the Jews. Therefore, Hitler's lies about the Jews were amongst the worst form of anti-Semitism precisely because this was a falsehood built out of lies.[38]

---

36   "Lewis to Arthur Greeves, 5 Nov 1933." In *They Stand Together*, 466–688.

37   Lewis *The Pilgrim's Regress: An Allegorical Apology for Christianity, Reason and Romanticism*. (1933).

38   Lewis's *The Pilgrim's Regress* is allegorical and was written early on after Lewis's conversion and lacks the considered approached to "chosen-ness" and the Jews we find in his mature work; see, generally, the following references.
Lewis on Mr. Savage: Bk. 5 "The Grand Canyon," Ch 6 Drudge; Bk. 7 "Southward Along the Canyon," Ch. 5, Tea on the Lawn.
On the Jews: Bk. 7 "Southward Along the Canyon," Ch. 10, Wisdom–Esoteric; Bk. 8 "At Bay," Ch. 8, History's Words.

3. The Hebrews, the Jews, . . . and God. II

5. THE LAW

But what about the heart of Judaism and the Hebrew covenant: the Law? Leviticus is not alone in laying out the incentive for obedience, and the results for disobedience.[39] Lewis's approach to the Law—the Mosaic Law, the Torah, the Pentateuch—is still, in the first few years after his protracted conversion, somewhat naive: critical, yet assertive. Mary Hennekes comments how Lewis projects this understanding into the character of John—in *The Pilgrims Regress*

> The rules themselves that John has been told he must keep are an allusion to the Bible, specifically the Old Testament. In the Old Testament, the Jews were given a strict list of rules by God that they were supposed to keep. The list of rules can be found in the chapters of Deuteronomy and Leviticus. . . . John, too, is told that he must keep the overwhelming list of rules given to him. Lewis' use of imagery entails how burdensome this list of rules was to John.[40]

But neither the character John nor Lewis could at this time understand what was going on in the role of law and rules in a relationship: in relation to *YHWH*. Nor could he see the freedom given by God's will, as compared with the constraints in a communal context: autonomous over heteronomous ethics. Or the importance of heteronomous Mosaic ethics

---

On Law: Bk. 1 "Data," Ch. 1 The Rules; Bk. 1 "Data," Ch. 2 The Island; Bk. 1 "Data," Ch. 6 *Quem Quaeritis in Sepulchro? Non est Hic*; Bk. 3 "Through Darkest Zeitgeistheim," Ch. 4 The Man Behind the Gun; Bk. 5 "The Grand Canyon," Ch. 7 The Gaucherie of Vertue; Bk. 6 "Northward Along the Canyon," Ch. 6 Furthest North; Bk. 7 "Southward Along the Canyon," Ch. 12 More Wisdom; Bk. 8 "At Bay," Ch. 8, History's Words; Bk. 10 "The Regress," Ch 2 The Synthetic Man.

39   "You must not make idols for yourselves or set up a carved image or sacred pillar; you must not place a sculpted stone in your land to bow down to it. For I am the LORD your God. . . . If you follow My statutes and carefully keep My commandments, I will give you rains in their season, and the land will yield its produce, and the trees of the field will bear their fruit . . . and will dwell securely in your land. And I will give peace to the land, and you will lie down with nothing to fear. . . . You will pursue your enemies, and they will fall by the sword before you. . . . I will turn toward you and make you fruitful and multiply you, and I will establish My covenant with you. You will still be eating the old supply of grain when you need to clear it out to make room for the new. And I will make My dwelling place among you, and My soul will not despise you. I will walk among you and be your God, and you will be My people." Lev 26:3 ff. See also, John 14:10, 15:10—"If you will keep my commandments . . ." See also, "72 Bible verses on keeping the commandments:" https://Bible.knowing-jesus.com/topics/Keep-The-Commandments

40   Hennekes, *C. S. Lewis: An In-Depth Study. The Pilgrim's Regress Analysis.*

over individualism, and the gradual evolving of the chosen people and the birth of the Messiah in the incarnation nation. Lewis is unaware of an evolving dialectic that features more and more in his thought between law and freedom—ethical givenness and liberty in Christ's grace and forgiveness. This is a supplementary dialectic. The resolution will be in the eschaton when a life will be weighed in the balance and be shown for what it is: hell-bound or heaven sent.

A simple truism is that Christianity emerged as part of the Jewish religion; Colin E. Gunton used to assert this regularly. The separation—in socio-political terms—may have come with the fall of Jerusalem in 70AD, but Christianity is to be seen as an extension of Judaism, of Hebrew revelation and the Jews as the chosen people of God. (Such an understanding was part of the revival of Trinitarian theology in the late twentieth century, which Gunton spearheaded, amongst others from King's College London.) A true Christian is by default enfolded into the chosen people of God. Christianity is a Jewish sect of sorts. Colin Gunton often used to quote in lectures and seminars how a Jewish rabbi he knew commented that the New Testament was really an appendix to the Hebrew Bible . . . ![41]

---

41   Colin Gunton, comments from a lecture course on the Swiss Reformed theologian Karl Barth at King's College London: B406, A Selected Modern Theologian—Karl Barth, 2000–2001, transcription of a lecture course delivered at King's College, London, Wednesday 4th October 2000, "Lecture 2. Barth's Development up to Romans." The lecture course, which was something of an internationally acclaimed annual event, was posthumously published as, Gunton, *The Barth Lectures* (2007); see 75, 88, 93, 111, 165, 170, 207–8.

4

God's Chosen:
Holiness, Theology and Spirituality, . . . Pride

"The 'chosen' people are chosen not for their own sake (certainly not for their own honour or pleasure) but for the sake of the unchosen. Abraham is told that 'in his seed' (the chosen nation) 'all nations shall be blest'. That nation has been chosen to bear a heavy burden. Their sufferings are great: but, as Isaiah recognised, their sufferings heal others."

C. S. LEWIS[1]

"I call heaven and earth as witnesses today against you, that I have set before you, life and death, blessing and cursing; therefore choose life, that both you and your descendants may live; that you may love the LORD your God, that you may obey His voice, and that you may cling to Him, for He is your life and the length of your days; and that you may dwell in the land which the LORD swore to your fathers, to Abraham, Isaac, and Jacob, to give them."

DEUTERONOMY 30:19

"I think myself that the shocking reply to the Syrophenician woman (it came alright in the end) is to remind all us Gentile Christians—who forget it easily enough and even flirt with anti-Semitism—that the Hebrews are spiritually senior to us, that God did entrust the descendants of Abraham with the first revelation of Himself. To put us in our place . . . ."

C. S. LEWIS[2]

---

1   Lewis *Miracles*. 2nd ed., 123–24.
2   Lewis to Mrs Johnson, May 14, 1955. In Lewis, *Collected Letters, Vol. III*, 607–8. Lewis is referring to Mark 7:24–30

A HEBRAIC INKLING

1. FOR THE UNCHOSEN

For up to four thousand years the Jews with their Hebrew forebears and religious traditions—much being held to from ancient times—have endured: bearing witness to the Eternal-Self-Existing-One, the God above and beyond all "gods," "idols" . . . also beyond transitory human-generated fantasy religions. For Jews, "chosenness" is the belief that they, having descended from the ancient Israelites and Hebrews, are "the chosen people" (*am hanivhar*): chosen to be in a direct covenant with God. This is most unswervingly stated in the Book of Deuteronomy,[3] and throughout the Hebrew Bible, often using the term "holy people"[4] (*'am qadosh*).[5] Judaism today broadly maintains the belief that the Jews have been chosen/elected for a unique purpose, commissioning the Jewish people with a mission: to be a light to the nations, and to bear witness to their covenant with God. Closest to C. S. Lewis's understanding and beliefs about "chosenness" (and bearing in mind the fragmentation of contemporary Judaism into different religious groupings from ultra-Orthodox to modern liberal) is a statement from The Jewish Theological Seminary in New York: being chosen does not imply any innate Jewish superiority, for they are to be a kingdom of priests and a holy nation with obligations and duties, this is not a license for special privileges, far from it, for they have additional responsibilities, not only to God, but to and before all people; the Jews should transcend their own self-interests as a people that take being covenanted with God seriously—thus they can thrive in the face of oppression and be a source of blessing to themselves and to others.[6]

  3   See, Clements, *God's Chosen People*.

  4   For example, Deut 7:6; 14:2. Often stated as "holy nation" (*goy qadosh*) Exod 19:6.

  5   See, Gurkan, *The Jews as a Chosen People*, 9ff; specifically § "Election & Covenant, 9, 16ff.

  6   "Few beliefs have been subject to as much misunderstanding as the 'Chosen People' doctrine. The Torah and the Prophets clearly stated that this does not imply any innate Jewish superiority. In the words of Amos (3:2) 'You alone have I singled out of all the families of the earth—that is why I will call you to account for your iniquities.' The Torah tells us that we are to be 'a kingdom of priests and a holy nation' with obligations and duties which flowed from our willingness to accept this status. Far from being a license for special privilege, it entailed additional responsibilities not only toward God but to our fellow human beings. As expressed in the blessing at the reading of the Torah, our people have always felt it to be a privilege to be selected for such a purpose. For the modern traditional Jew, the doctrine of the election and the covenant of Israel offers a purpose for Jewish existence which transcends its own self interests. It suggests that

4. God's Chosen: Holiness, Theology and Spirituality, ... Pride

That Israel are a chosen people should be indisputably acknowledged by Christians, yet it is often denied. Why do, amongst others, many in the West (often self-identifying as liberal) find such a difficulty with the concept of a chosen people. Is it because they were not chosen?[7] Perhaps they feel left out by assuming they have not been subject to equal opportunities? For millennia pagan religionists in the West have sought to solve the problem of existence and answer the question of life through their own efforts. The concept of "chosenness" appears to offend them, just as it does the modern sensibilities of equality. Does it generate fear that their own salvation is lost when they have worked so assiduously to invent salvation in their own image?[8] Lewis notes, that the Jews were chosen not for themselves, not for a reward, not for their own sake, not for honor or pleasure, nor because they were good and better than others. No, considers Lewis, the Jewish people were chosen "for the sake of the unchosen."[9] This is because Abraham is weighted down with a heavy burden through which "all nations will be blest":[10] Israel's sufferings will be great, but their sufferings will be the healing of others.[11] Lewis notes how the mention of the name Israel usually invokes disquiet about the concept of a "chosen people" because British history—post-Reformation and Enlightenment—specifically, Western history generally, makes us suspicious of such an undemocratic idea: we should prefer to think that all nations and individuals start level in the search for God, or even that all religions are equally true (an idea

---

because of our special history and unique heritage we are in a position to demonstrate that a people that takes seriously the idea of being covenanted with God can not only thrive in the face of oppression, but can be a source of blessing to its children and its neighbors. It obligates us to build a just and compassionate society throughout the world and especially in the land of Israel where we may teach by example what it means to be a 'covenant people, a light unto the nations.'" Emet Ve-Emunah: Statement of Principles of Conservative Judaism, 33–34

7 Are we correct to ask, if the West, particularly through its Reformations and Enlightenments, had remained faithful to the Jewish Messiah they would realize that they have been enfolded into the chosen people by faith, but have they remained faithful to Yeshua? And does modern Judaism and today's Israel still bear witness to the unchosen in the way it should? We will all be judged come the eschaton.

8 For example, the Viking Valhalla—heaven for the violent, the rapist, the mutilator, the dominant male, when entry is dependent upon such deeds with their weapon in hand (sword or axe).

9 Lewis, *Miracles*. 2nd ed., 123–24.

10 Gen 22:18; cf. Gen 12:1–4; 14:3 and Gal 3:7–9.

11 Isaiah 52 and 53.

A HEBRAIC INKLING

that has become something of general assumption throughout the West since Lewis's death).[12] Or do the objectors fear they are not the favorite, especially when they consider themselves superior and more worthy than the Jews? When the objectors accuse God of undue favor by and towards a "chosen," this often involves a charge of undue favor and disfavor to Western civilization in all its self-inflated glory.[13] The ancient Hebrews through to the Jews acquired a burden more than a blessing in being "chosen."[14] For the cynical atheist that sees all religion as about post-mortem reward, Lewis reminds them that for centuries the ancient Hebrews labored at trying to find the will of the Lord, and even more to be obedient to *YHWH* as the chosen people, yet that the secret of actual and real immortal life was withheld: "Believing as I do, that Jehovah is a real being, indeed the *ens realissimum*, I cannot sufficiently admire the divine tact of thus training the chosen race for centuries in a religion before even hinting the shining secret of eternal life."[15] Any religion that starts from the position of eternal life, notes Lewis, is "damned" from its inception. No, speculates Lewis, the creation of God's chosen people is like a wealthy man who courts the love of his life dressed and appearing as a beggar, then once she has accepted him he reveals his true identity and marries the maiden bestowing on her riches and a throne and a palace. Nonetheless, the average person is "bewildered to find the ancient Hebrews 'chosen' as they were."[16]

2. THE LOST SHEEP

If the Hebrews were and are chosen not for themselves, not for any benefit, but for the unchosen—the rest of humanity—how does this work out? Writing to a Mrs. Johnson in 1955,[17] Lewis explains in terms of the passage

12 Lewis, *Miracles*. 2nd ed., 122f.

13 Lewis, *Miracles*. 2nd ed., 123–24. See also, Lewis, *Undeceptions*. Published as, *God in the Dock* in US., Pt. 1, ch 9, 60–61; also, Lewis, *Christian Reflections*, ch. 10. It is worth noting that Mahatma Gandhi is reputed to have replied to a Western journalist, who asked him what he thought of Western civilization, that, yes, it would be a good idea.

14 Lewis, *Miracles*. 2nd ed., 121.

15 Lewis, "A Christian Reply to Professor Price." Published with related material in *Undeceptions* (1971) Pt. 1, Ch. 16, 99–114, quotation, 100–101. Lewis invokes the Latin *ens realissimum*: a philosophical term for God, reflecting the belief that reality, like goodness, comes in degrees, and that there must be a limiting, ultimately real, entity.

16 Lewis, "The Psalms." Written c. 1957–58. Published in Lewis, *Christian Reflections*, 114–28, quotation, 117.

17 "Lewis to Mrs Johnson, May 14, 1955." In, Lewis, *Collected Letters, Vol. III*,

in Matthew's Gospel about an encounter between a Canaanite woman and Jesus (referred to by Lewis as the Syrophoenician woman).

> Leaving that place, Jesus withdrew to the region of Tyre and Sidon. A Canaanite woman from that vicinity came to him, crying out, "Lord, Son of David, have mercy on me! My daughter is demon-possessed and suffering terribly." Jesus did not answer a word. So his disciples came to him and urged him, "Send her away, for she keeps crying out after us." He answered, "I was sent only to the lost sheep of Israel." The woman came and knelt before him. "Lord, help me!" she said. He replied, "It is not right to take the children's bread and toss it to the dogs." "Yes it is, Lord," she said. "Even the dogs eat the crumbs that fall from their master's table." Then Jesus said to her, "Woman, you have great faith! Your request is granted." And her daughter was healed at that moment.
>
> Matt 15:21–28

Lewis comments with twentieth-century modern, Western, sensitivities that Jesus's answer to the woman is shocking but at least it raises questions about the relationship between the unchosen and the Hebraic chosen, that there is a God-given order to salvation history. Yes, the Hebrews are first, they are elected. They are "spiritually senior" to all of us, which places us as—prior to the *eschaton*—"junior" before the Jews (however hard their selection may be to them, looking at the thousands of years of rigorous preparation throughout Hebraic history).[18] As Lewis rightly notes, this sequence goes back to Abraham's calling, God's revelation that through Abraham all nations will be blessed. But we must know our "place" in the pecking order: the Jew first, then to the gentile (Rom 1:16). Today's gentiles and heathens, pagans and postmodern liberals, can be enfolded into the community of Israel—in Christ. Many, however, reject this calling and become, in effect, spiritually illegitimate.

By turning away, initially, from the Canaanite woman, Jesus was not rejecting her: he needed to deal first with the appalling state of the religious authorities in Israel. By doing so salvation could then flow to the unchosen! By allowing himself to be sacrificed redemption opens up, *in potentia*, for all. However, he is prepared to answer the woman's plea because she is prepared to push the issue and not sit back complaining that her dependency culture was not being served (or her identity politics venerated). Like the

---

607–8. Lewis is referring to Mark 7:24–30.

18   "Lewis to Mrs Johnson, May 14, 1955," 607–8.

epileptic's father in Mark's Gospel she is prepared to demonstrate her faith to and in Jesus (Mark 9:22b–24).[19] Unlike many post-1960s liberal-socialist religious atheists who complain about Jesus's treatment of the woman from a feminist perspective,[20] Lewis understood the eschatological consequences of the encounter—beyond the transitory delusions of twentieth- and early twenty-first-century identity politics.

3. REPLACEMENT THEOLOGY AND SUPERSESSIONISM

C. S. Lewis does not ever display any firm belief in "supersessionism" or "replacement theology"; he does not see the church as a *replacement* of Israel. His apologetic works, numerous as they are, assert God's truth in the event of the incarnation-cross-resurrection-ascension. He will comment generally about how many of the Jews reject the coming of their Messiah yet thousands in the first century accepted (i.e., the very earliest church before it was extended to the gentile believers), but it is clear that he sees the old covenant—the Mosaic covenant—standing in relation to the *new covenant* in Yeshua.[21] The apostle Paul is often presented as believing that Jewish Law is no longer valid, but his comments about the Law are made in the context of drawing the gentiles into the chosen people and the *gentiles* are not required to observe Torah in the same way that Jewish believers are. There are numerous examples in the Acts of the Apostles of the heated arguments among the apostles in the development of this position (i.e., the Council of Jerusalem: Acts 15:1–41). While Messianic Jews today hold to and respect much of the Law, interpreted in the light of Jesus, gentile

---

19   The father cries out (the Greek verb used is *krazō*), he weeps (*dakruon*), and pleads for understanding, healing, and the faith to meet the Christ's expectations: "Immediately the boy's father exclaimed, 'I believe; help my unbelief'!" (Mark 9:24). Likewise, when Lazarus is brought out of the tomb Jesus weeps, the same verb is used. Jesus did not simply politely shed a few tears, but wept with convulsions of grief, the verb implied that he was torn apart with grief, that he shuddered with grief (John 11:43f.).

20   As a doctoral student at King's College London, I sat through the presentation of an hour-long paper on such issues by a fellow student who relied on Marxist dialectic and rhetoric to constantly repeat her demands for female divinization: God replaced by the oppressed human; God reduced to an in-the-pocket idol.

21   The whole idea of a new covenant comes from Jer 31; in Jeremiah the new covenant is the covenant with Israel but what is "new" is the eschatological transformation of Israel to enable them to obey the Law. So much Christian theology pulls the covenants apart, ignoring Jeremiah as the foundation, in many ways, of the "new covenant".

Christians appeared to have often abandoned traditional ethics that are grounded in the Pentateuch. Many Western Christians—something that applies to Lewis—have a basic respect for the Hebrew Law, unlike ancient Marcionites.[22] (That said, a local Anglican vicar said to me that the "Old Testament" was a terrible way to talk about God! My response, to question if he was a Marcionite, was met with puzzlement and ignorance.) In 1965, in the Second Vatican Council, despite centuries of asserting the church as the replacement to the temple in Jerusalem, and Christians as the new inheritors of Abraham, the Roman Catholic Church promoted the proposition that the church is the new people of God, without intending to make Israel irrelevant before God (i.e., they will be judged according to the traditions of Moses, at the eschaton).[23]

During Lewis's lifetime the term Hebraic Christian was not really known in the common rooms of Oxford. While most Christians do not really think about these issues, Lewis did because of the growing influence and place in his life of Jewish people (the obvious example being his wife and stepsons) and the manner in which his theology leaned towards the Hebraic in his middle and later years. While the apostle Paul's epistles are superficially seen in certain contexts as being supersessionist, he acknowledges the growing rift between the *ekklēsia* and the Jerusalem Temple. The comparison between the two covenants is seen in the analogy of an olive tree. In Romans chapter 11 Paul argues that if the root is holy, so are the branches

---

22   Marcion of Sinope (excommunicated in 144 AD) acknowledged Jesus as the savior, God's anointed, with the apostle Paul as missionary; however, he rejected the Hebrew Bible and the God of Israel, as if what the church believed could somehow be separated from Abraham's chosen people. (He also questioned the existence and validity of the material world.)

23   No official Roman Catholic doctrine either names or promotes supersessionism, however, Catholic teaching has reflected, to varying degrees, the idea that the church has replaced God's covenant with the Jews throughout its history, especially in the Middle Ages. Protestantism generally has, however, held to a fiercer supersessionist mentality. Protestant views vary, however there are three prominent Protestant approaches: covenant theology, new covenant theology, and dispensationalism. All Christian churches may exhibit a sense of judgmental superiority towards the Jews without realizing how such a view imperils their own salvation (the sin of pride). See, also, Mark Kinzer, *Searching Her Own Mystery Nostra Aetate, the Jewish People, and the Identity of the Church* (2015). The book arose from years of Messianic Jewish-Roman Catholic dialogue and is a model of such dialogue. (Mark Kinzer is a Messianic Jewish theologian.)

> If some of the branches have been broken off, and you, though a wild olive shoot, have been grafted in among the others and now share in the nourishing sap from the olive root, do not consider yourself to be superior to those other branches. If you do, consider this: You do not support the root, but the root supports you. You will say then, "Branches were broken off[24] so that I could be grafted in." Granted. But they were broken off because of unbelief, and you stand by faith. Do not be arrogant, but tremble. For if God did not spare the natural branches, he will not spare you either.
>
> Rom 11:17–21

And Paul continues that if "they" do not persist in unbelief they will be re-grafted in. Therefore, Christian are grafted[25] onto the origins of Judaism and cannot be Christians while cutting themselves off from Israel: do we not exist and subsist in "Jewish roots."[26]

Lewis looks at the question of supersessionism and replacement theology in terms of the sins of "pride," and "superiority." Lewis has Screwtape voice that people resent every kind of superiority in others (and not just the Jews as God's first chosen), seeking to belittle and disparage, seeking its eradication—driven by jealousy, even hatred.[27] If these people are church-goers then, writes Lewis, they should examine the New Testament where they will find clear unequivocal warnings against every kind of superiority, whether religious or cultural.[28] If and when these people claim pride in the apparent superiority of Christian ethics over, in particular, the Jews this may lead to "priggery," and anti-Semitic ignorance (do not Christian

---

24   See, Nanos, *Reading Romans within Judaism*, where the author argues that the branches are not "broken off" but merely damaged/bent, but still connected

25   This is often looked upon by today's Bible scholars as an odd and anachronistic word in this context, but it reflects the reality of a rural economy (vine growing, and the tortuous difficulties in grafting to create a new plant variety: one of the most difficult of agricultural practises) and also John 15:1–17

26   See Brian Tucker, *Reading Romans after Supersessionism*. See also, Nanos, Mark D. *Reading Paul within Judaism*, specifically, "The Myth of the 'Law-Free' Paul Standing between Christians and Jews," 77–85.

27   Lewis, *The Screwtape Letters*, ch. 3, 14 & ch. 22, 119. See also, related, Lewis, The World's Last Night, ch. 4, 60f., and *Mere Christianity*, Pt. 3, ch. 8 "The Great Sin." Generally in *Mere Christianity*, in terms of jealousy in relation to the sin of pride, see, 2, 74, 100, 188, & 215.

28   Especially in relation to the Jewish Law see, Lewis, *Christian Reflections*, ch. 2 Christianity & Culture, 14f.

ethics issue from Jewish ethics?).[29] Such is pride, which results in animosity, hostility, enmity, yes toward our neighbor, but ultimately towards God, claiming our beliefs and ethics are superior. "In God," Lewis notes, "you come up against something that is in every respect immeasurably superior to yourself. Unless you know God as that—and, therefore, know yourself as nothing in comparison—you do not know God at all."[30] Supersessionism and replacement theology are bedeviled by and issue from pride, and pride is the root of all sin: Lucifer's sin "is enmity. And not only enmity between man and man, but enmity to God."[31] This supersessionist pride and superiority replicates like a virus in the corporate, the communal: from a circle of friends, to Christian groups to secret societies and political parties: churches, Freemasons, the National Socialists, and the British Labor party (and the traditional shire county Tory). Or as Lewis terms it, "the inner ring."[32] People, notes Lewis, cannot tolerate being merely equal, thus they build themselves into groups set-off against the other, in which they generate pride and apparent superiority before the herd and its other inner rings.[33] Anti-Semitism is built, to a degree, on the desire to refute anything "better or stronger or higher than ourselves."[34] The antidote here is genuine humility.

> Whenever we find that our religious life is making us feel that we are good—above all, that we are better than someone else—I think we may be sure that we are being acted on, not by God, but by the devil. The real test of being in the presence of God is, that you either forget about yourself altogether or see yourself as a small, dirty object. It is better to forget about yourself altogether.[35]

Essentially Lewis's approach to supersessionism and replacement theology is to cut through the pretense of categorizing such theories as academic,

---

29   Lewis, *Reflections on the Psalms*, 64–66; also Screwtape Letters, ch. 24, 110f..
30   Lewis, *Mere Christianity*. see Book 3 Christian Behavior, ch. 8 "The Great Sin," specifically, 111.
31   Lewis, *Mere Christianity*, 111f.
32   Lewis, *The Four Loves*, ch. 4 "Friendship," specifically, 84–86.
33   Lewis, *The World's Last Night*, ch. 3, 41.
34   Lewis, *Mere Christianity*. See ch. 5 "Obstinate Toy Soldiers," specifically, 154; see also, ch. 8 "The Great Sin," specifically, 110–11.
35   Lewis, *Mere Christianity*. Book 3 Christian Behavior, ch. 8 "The Great Sin," 124–25. See also, Lewis, Letters to an American Lady. See, June 30, 1955 and Jun 6, 1958, where we can trap ourselves when we feel pride at being charitable.

impartial propositions, and exposing them for the sin of pride which they are.

Supersessionism and replacement theology relate directly to a doctrine of superiority and it is clearly to be avoided through the Christian virtue of humility. Superiority issues from pride. Lewis notes how a love of religion and religious knowledge underpins many of these prejudices[36] along with status and fame (today, celebrity-ism), which corrupts and generates pride, and the religious are not immune from this.[37] Lewis notes in criticism of himself how easy it is to be proud of being humble,[38] and how religious legalism—whether Jewish or Christian—can lead to self-righteousness and superiority.[39] Lewis notes how pride can hinder charity;[40] if you can identify religious pride in self, he notes, then you are looking in the right direction, but curbing it is another matter: writing to a Mrs Sonia Graham, Lewis notes, "Pride is a perpetual nagging temptation. Keep on knocking it on the head . . . as long as one knows one is proud one is safe from the worst form of pride."[41] Superiority and self-righteousness issued from the original or first sin;[42] indeed, notes Lewis, it was the cause of the first sin, and pride is the utmost sin and causes most of the other sins. It is impossible, voices Lewis's Screwtape, for the humble to be proud, so encourage pride as the entry to all the worst sins.[43] Pride and religious conceit are an obstacle to right living and a right judgement of our neighbor (especially if he or she is of another religious disposition).[44] The problem, insists Lewis, is that pride does not only come before a fall but causes the fall from grace in the first place because we turn from God to ourselves. God was not proud when he stooped to be incarnated a mere human baby.[45]

---

36   Lewis, "The Weight of Glory," 27–28.

37   Lewis, *The Screwtape Letters*, 65.

38   Lewis, *Christian Reflections*, 14.

39   Lewis, *Reflections on the Psalms*, 57–58.

40   Lewis, *Mere Christianity*, 82.

41   "Lewis writing to Mrs Sonia Graham, 15 May 1952." See, Lewis, *Letters of C. S. Lewis*, 2nd ed., 421–22.

42   Lewis, *Mere Christianity*, 111.

43   Lewis, *The Screwtape Letters*, 92–93.

44   Lewis, *Letters to Malcolm*, 90.

45   Lewis, *The Screwtape Letters*, 21. See also, Lewis, *The Problem of Pain*, ch. VI "Human Pain," 97; also, Lewis, *Letters to an American Lady*, 49.

PART II

SCRIPTURE

Hallelujah!
Praise God in His sanctuary.
Praise Him in His mighty heavens.
Praise Him for His mighty acts;
Praise Him for His excellent greatness.
PSALM 150:1–2

5

The Hebrew Scriptures: Historicity and Humanity

"So Philip ran to him and heard him reading Isaiah the prophet and asked, 'Do you understand what you are reading?' And he said, 'How can I, unless someone guides me?' And he invited Philip to come up and sit with him. Now the passage of the [Hebrew] scripture that he was reading was this:

> 'Like a sheep he was led to the slaughter
> and like a lamb before its shearer is silent,
> so he opens not his mouth.
>
> In his humiliation justice was denied him.
>
> Who can describe his generation?
> For his life is taken away from the earth.'

And the eunuch said to Philip, 'About whom, I ask you, does the prophet say this, about himself or about someone else?' Then Philip opened his mouth, and beginning with this [Hebrew] scripture he told him the good news."

ACTS OF THE APOSTLES 8:30–35

"The Hebrews, like other people, had mythology: but as they were the chosen people so their mythology was the chosen mythology—the mythology chosen by God to be the vehicle of the earliest sacred truths, the first step in that process which ends in the New Testament where truth has become completely historical."

C. S. LEWIS[1]

"That very day two of them were going to a village named Emmaus. . . . While they were talking and discussing together, Jesus himself drew near and went with them. But their eyes were kept from recognizing him. And he said to them, 'What is this conversation that you are holding with each other as you walk?' . . . And he said to them, 'O foolish ones, and slow of heart to believe all that the prophets have spoken! Was it not necessary that the Christ should suffer these things and enter into his glory?' And beginning with Moses and all the Prophets, he interpreted to them in all the [Hebrew] scriptures the things concerning himself."

LUKE 24:13–27

---

1   "Lewis to Corbin Scott Carnel, April 5, 1953," FN 114. See, Lewis, *Collected Letters Vol. III*, 318–19.

A HEBRAIC INKLING

1. INTRODUCTION

A full analysis of C. S. Lewis's doctrine of scripture—oral roots and a written tradition; revelation and illumination, inspiration and myth; legend and fact; homiletic, genre and language; historicity and the humanity of scripture; divine and human origins; inspiration and purpose; suspicion and skepticism: *Sitz im Leben*—is not warranted here. I have presented such an analysis elsewhere.[2] Here we can examine Lewis's approach to the Hebrew Bible as an Ulsterman, an Anglican, an Oxford academic, and its relationship to the people of God.

2. LEWIS ON THE HEBREW SCRIPTURES

What picture, or mental model, do we find from Lewis's beliefs, expressed in his writings, with regard to the Hebrew scriptures? What did he write and how do these missives compare?

In terms of creation, it is clear from scriptures—Jewish, Islamic, and Christian, notes Lewis—that the understanding that can be read from the universe is that there is something beyond nature that refutes the materialist scientists' picture of futility.[3] Unlike many of the nations and tribes that surrounded the ancient Hebrews, central to their Israelite belief was a coherent and explicit doctrine of creation, for the world, the universe, and for humanity and its standing before *El, Elohim*, so much so that this had significance for their religion, their daily lives, indeed, for Lewis, their entire way of thinking.[4] This is seen in the Book of Genesis, which promotes the idea of a true creation (a very real creation and not an illusion, as argued for in many ancient Middle Eastern and Oriental religions) and of a transcendent Creator.[5] Underpinning the Genesis account of creation is a folk tale that relays the concept of the eternal self-existing One who loves creation into being, yet does not suffer from

---

2   See Brazier, *C. S. Lewis—The Work of Christ Revealed*, Part One Scripture—Revelation Transposed, ch. 1 Scripture, Revelation, and Reason I: Skepticism and Suspicion; ch. 2 Scripture, Revelation, and Reason II: Mediation and the Bible; ch. 3 Scripture, Revelation, and Reason III: Idealism and Transposition. See Brazier, *In the Highest Degree Vol I.*, ch. 4 Scripture and the Christ, the Word of God: C. S. Lewis and Karl Barth—Convergence and Divergence; Brazier, "C. S. Lewis: A Doctrine of Transposition"; Brazier, "C. S. Lewis on Scripture and the Christ, the Word of God."

3   Lewis, "De Futilitate," in, *Christian Reflections*, 57–71, specifically, 59.

4   Lewis, *Reflections on the Psalms*, ch. 8, specifically, 77–85.

5   Lewis, *Reflections on the Psalms*, ch. 11, specifically, 110–11.

5. *The Hebrew Scriptures: Historicity and Humanity*

a need love,[6] a folk tale that gives us a rigorous doctrine of creation in the form of God's Word: God spoke, and it came into being.[7] Therefore, Lewis has no problem in acknowledging how the Genesis account of creation is rooted—derivative in many ways—from earlier stories and myths that were Semitic, pagan, and mythical.[8] If we acknowledge the pneumatological overlordship that scripture is subject to, and if we believe that all scripture is for our learning then, notes Lewis, we must struggle over difficult passages, especially from the ancient Israelites, and see relevance, and find use for them.[9] Furthermore, if you read and appreciate the Bible as a whole and do not marginalize the Hebrew scriptures, you can begin to see a process, a revelation of God's true nature, and Name.[10]

In terms of historicity, for Lewis, Deborah's song of triumph over Sisera may go back in oral tradition to the eleventh century BC.[11] By comparison, chapter 16 of Ezekiel (Jerusalem as an Adulterous Wife), Lewis considers to be deeply moving—and amongst the most graphic of accounts—in the Bible.[12] The point is, for Lewis, that we cannot approach all biblical texts with a single, simple, concept of historicity/unhistoricity. As Lewis comments, we must accept some Hebrew narratives to be unhistorical, including, he suggests, Jonah and Job.[13] In particular, the Book of Jonah has few historical attachments, though it does exhibit "a distinctly Jewish humour."[14] However, it is important to note that

---

6   God loves in freedom; God does not "need" to love (a very Barthian point) Humans "suffer" from need love. Altruistic love goes beyond the need: *agápē*—a Greco-Christian term referring to unconditional love, the highest form of love, charity (*caritas*), and the love of God for the human, and of humanity for God.

7   Lewis, *Miracles*, ch. 4 "Nature and Supernature," 33; cf. Lewis, "Myth Became Fact," in *Undeceptions*, pt. I ch. 5, 42; also Lewis, *Reflections on the Psalms*, 109–11.

8   Lewis, *Reflections on the Psalms*, 110.

9   Lewis, *Reflections on the Psalms*, 22.

10   Lewis, "Lewis writing to Mrs Ashton, May 14, 1955," in Lewis, *Letters of C. S. Lewis*, 448–49.

11   Lewis, "The Psalms," in, *Christian Reflections*, 115, referring to to Judg 5. (The actual timeline is heavily debated amongst Jewish scholars.)

12   Lewis, *Reflections on the Psalms*, 130.

13   "Lewis writing to Lewis writing to Arthur Greeves, September 22, 1931," in Lewis, *Letters of C. S. Lewis*, 2nd ed., 286–87. See also, Lewis, *The Problem of Pain*, 71–72 and; Lewis, "Myth Became Fact," in, *Undeceptions* pt. 1, ch. 5, 42, and "The Grand Miracle," pt. 1, ch. 9, 57–58; See also, Lewis, *Miracles*, 33, 133–34.

14   Lewis, "Modern Theology and Biblical Criticism," 154–55. See also, Lewis writing to Arthur Greeves, September 22, 1931, in Lewis, *Letters of C. S. Lewis*, 2nd ed., 286.

the Pentateuch presents many truths that are—for Lewis, in terms of genre—legends and myths, and even exhibit rich and, for some, fabulous elements, as demonstrated, asserted Lewis, by Milton in *Paradise Lost*.[15] Therefore, not every sentence of the Hebrew scriptures exhibits historical or scientific truth, for Lewis, but this is not to its detriment.[16] For example, Lewis notes, whether the eating of the fruit in the Garden of Eden was literal or not is of no consequence, for its symbolism projects a profound truth about humanity, particularly as the fruit is clearly metaphorical and relates to our epistemological downfall and moral corruption.[17] In terms of chosenness, we tend to forget, considers Lewis, how much "time" God spent—millennia—"selecting" the Jews and forging, "hammering" into them, "exactly what sort of God he was."[18] This is what is important when we consider the question of historicity/un-historicity in the Hebrew Bible.[19] Ironically, although Lewis extols the profound symbolism of the Hebrew stories he does state that they are much "less rich and imaginative and beautiful" than the stories we find in pagan mythologies: this is Lewis's personal view and harks back to his pre-Christian period in his teens and twenties.[20] The stories and myths, the literature, we encounter in the Hebrew Bible "Thus something originally merely natural—the kind of myth that is found among most nations—will have been raised by God above itself, qualified by Him and compelled by Him to serve purposes which of itself it would not have served."[21] In addition, the stories and accounts we read there are the basis of so much that we find in the New Testament.[22] So much so that we can read a sound Christian theology, in

---

15 "Lewis writing to Wayne Schumaker, 21 March 1962," in Lewis, *Letters of C. S. Lewis*, 2nd ed., 303. See also, Lewis, "Myth Became Fact," pt. I ch. 5, 42; "The Grand Miracle," and, "The Grand Miracle," pt. 1, ch. 9, 57–58, in, *Undeceptions*; see also, "Modern Theology and Biblical Criticism," in *Christian Reflections*, 152–66, specifically, 154f. For related, concepts, see: "Lewis writing to Lewis writing to Arthur Greeves, September 22, 1931," in Lewis, *Letters of C. S. Lewis*, 2nd ed., 286; Lewis, *Miracles*, 33, 133–34; Lewis, *The Problem of Pain*, 71.

16 C.f. "Lewis writing to Wayne Schumaker, 21 March 1962," in Lewis, *Letters of C. S. Lewis*, 2nd ed. Lewis, *Reflections on the Psalms*, 109.

17 Lewis, *The Problem of Pain*, 80.

18 Lewis, *Mere Christianity*, 54.

19 Lewis, *The Problem of Pain*, 109.

20 Lewis, *Miracles*, 133–34.

21 Lewis, *Reflections on the Psalms*, 111.

22 Lewis, *Reflections on the Psalms*, 26–27.

5. The Hebrew Scriptures: Historicity and Humanity

many ways, from the older testament.[23] Yet it is important to remember that many of the authors saw their material, and their aims and objective as essentially "secular," for example, the poets who composed the Song of Songs.[24] Lewis regards it as entirely fitting that the speech of God should often be in the form and genre of Hebraic poetry,[25] despite the times in the Psalms, for example, when we come across distortions and sentiments that appears to affront today's religious sensitivities.[26] The poetry we find in these scriptures is comparable to secular poetry, but it has been taken up into the service of God's Word.[27] But Proverbs and Psalms, and many poetic examples throughout the Bible, can still be read and respected as literature. Lewis is, of course, writing as a *literatus*, who taught literature at the University of Oxford, which is why he distrusted the modem Bible scholar and theologians as critics, because their understanding of literature and knowledge of literary form was poor and lacking.[28] In addition their misuse of literary form, and misappropriation of genre, was often in the service of what we may term religious atheism, while making sure their status and livelihood as religious professionals was protected.

3. THE HEBREW BIBLE AND THE NEW TESTAMENT

Biblical Reflections

By the time of his sixtieth birthday Lewis's understanding and respect for Judaism in relation to the New Testament and the Christian churches exhibits some of the enlightened approach that has come to be expected in the early twenty-first century among Bible scholars and theologians in the Western churches and academies. He commented in one of his last books to be published—*Reflections on the Psalms*—on the paucity of knowledge and understanding with regards to the Hebrew Bible amongst the average churchgoer and in academic circles. In particular, Lewis noted what he termed the rewards of reading the Hebrew Bible frequently, habitually,

---

23 Lewis, *Reflections on the Psalms*, Ch. 4, specifically, 34f.
24 Lewis, *Reflections on the Psalms*, 111.
25 Lewis, *Reflections on the Psalms*, 5.
26 Lewis, *Reflections on the Psalms*, 114.
27 Lewis, *Reflections on the Psalms*, 111.
28 Lewis, "Modern Theology and Biblical Criticism," 154–55 & 161

because it was possible to discover how so much of the New Testament consisted of quotations from the Hebrew scriptures: "how constantly Our Lord repeated, reinforced, continued, refined, and sublimated, the Judaic ethics," and thereby seldom brought in something new, or a "novelty" as he terms it.[29] What is more, this was common knowledge for generations of "unlearned Christians as long as Bible-reading was habitual."[30] By the mid-twentieth century, notes Lewis, ignorance of all but the most superficial of understanding amongst churchgoers leads to a suspicion of any respect for the Hebrew Bible as if this was leading to a denial of Christ himself; anticipations (Hebraic) and prefigurements (pagan) were deemed, so Lewis found amongst many of his contemporaries, to be a contradiction of the Christ-event:

> Every good teacher, within Judaism as without, has anticipated Him. The whole religious history of the pre-Christian world, on its better side, anticipates Him. It could not be otherwise. The Light which has lightened every man from the beginning may shine more clearly but cannot change. The Origin cannot suddenly start being, in the popular sense of the word, "original."[31]

The Authorship, Nature, and Genre of Scripture

Lewis insists that we regard the Hebrew Bible as holy and inspired,[32] and therefore deals with the question of the miraculous. He refuses to dismiss a story in the Bible as unhistorical just because it contains the miraculous: he notes how he has never found any philosophical grounds for the universal negative proposition, as he terms it, that miracles do not happen.[33] Lewis has no qualms about the authorship of books of the Hebrew Bible. He can readily accept that the creation account in Genesis may have been derived in some ways from earlier ancient Semitic stories, which were pagan and mythical in nature, because these proto-creation stories lead to a true creation story authored by and reflecting a transcendent creator: the mind of the original authors and that of the Genesis account were guided by God—no good work, notes Lewis, is

29   Lewis, *Reflections on the Psalms*, 22–23.
30   Lewis, *Reflections on the Psalms*, 23.
31   Lewis. *Reflections on the Psalms*, 23.
32   Lewis, *Reflections on the Psalms*, 93f.
33   See Lewis, *Miracles*, ch. 1.

5. *The Hebrew Scriptures: Historicity and Humanity*

done anywhere without aid from the Father of Lights.[34] Therefore, the entirety of the Hebrew Bible consists of multiple genres where different sources and authors come together over time leading to the text as it is endorsed by God, having been inspired by God in the first place.

As the style or category of art and literature, that is, the style or type of writing that is represented by a biblical book, genre is to be seen as closely related to the aims and objectives of the writer. Genre raises questions: Is a particular text intended to be factual, historic, or scientific? Is it meant to teach something spiritual or moral through story, allegory, or parable? Is it to be seen as simply entertaining or an amusing insight into the superstitions and magic of primitive people, as some atheists would assert? For Lewis, genre is of vital importance; he clearly distinguishes genres: that is, between parables, sacred fiction, and history where such books as the accounts of David's reign are concerned—they are "everywhere dovetailed into a known history and genealogies." By comparison, books like Ester and Jonah, even Job, "proclaim themselves to be sacred fiction."[35] Lewis here is responding to a Mrs. Janet Wise who wrote from the Middle East concerned by some letters in *The Times*, which claimed that there was now a widespread disbelief in the authority of the Bible, especially the Pentateuch. She wrote that, "it appeared that the unforgivable sin to these clerics was to be a fundamentalist. I regard myself, and still do, as an intelligent fundamentalist."[36] Fundamentalism is, in effect, pressing the Bible too much, pushing it too far. Lewis commented (writing in 1960) that the Hebrew Bible avoids descriptions of other worlds, excepting parable or allegory.[37] A similar misuse of the Bible for Lewis, which is related to genre, is in proof texting, that is, taking sayings or verses or a few words out of context, quoting them as a proof for some personal belief or ethic: Lewis notes how the habit of picking-out isolated texts and interpreting them as direct messages from God is wrought with problems.[38] This leads to presumptions. However, treating the Bible as an intellectual curiosity is likewise questionable; he was not

---

34   Lewis, *Reflections on the Psalms*, 95.
35   Lewis, *Reflections on the Psalms*, 652.
36   Lewis, *Reflections on the Psalms*, 652 n.284.
37   "Lewis writing to Vera Gebbert, Oct. 16, 1960." Lewis, *Collected Letters, Vol. III*, 1198.
38   "Lewis writing to Mrs Green, Jun. 18, 1962." Lewis, *Collected Letters, Vol. III*, 1353.

against the academic dissecting of the Bible, but saw little value in such antiquarianism when the Bible was clearly addressed to our conscience, to our fallen will, when it was concerned with our salvation.[39] Nor, we may say, building on what Lewis wrote, is scripture primarily for our intellectual curiosity or for career development in academia.

Lewis therefore classifies the material in the Hebrew Bible as (1) chronicle (essentially historical, though perhaps different to concepts of historicity today), (2) poetry (Song of Solomon, Job, and the Book of Psalms—but the Psalms also represent other genres), (3) moral and political diatribe (pietistic and spiritual teaching), (4) romances and myths (the creation stories—for example, Genesis and Psalm 104), however, there is also (5) material that is essentially unclassifiable according to twentieth-century conceptions of genre, model, and type of literature.[40] He explains that the poet who wrote the Song of Songs did not, in all probability, conceive the work for anything other than what he terms a secular and natural purpose.

From a Christian perspective, such a classification should not lead us to consider scripture as a merely human product: God inspires, God directs the various people involved in the composition and production of the books of the Bible. With regard to both testaments Lewis regards scripture as less than perfect: "To a human mind this working up (in a sense imperfectly), this sublimation (incomplete) of human material, seems, no doubt, an untidy and leaky vehicle."[41] The meaning scripture takes on, the relevance and context changes as salvation history unfolds. But underpinning scripture are certain facts, certain truths, certain revelation. The question is how do these multiple genres (chronicle; historical; poetry; moral; romances and myths; unclassifiable material by contemporary assessment) of the Hebrew Bible inform us objectively?

Specifically regarding the Hebrew Bible as literature, as Lewis does, and as it is elevated into something more than itself, then the vehicle is greater than the merely human; the range and wealth of meanings will be limitless provided we hold to the reality of what we read.[42] Given, for instance, the lack of discussion and planning between the disparate

---

39   Lewis, *The Problem of Pain*, see ch. 8.
40   Lewis, *Reflections on the Psalms*, 96.
41   Lewis, *Reflections on the Psalms*, 100.
42   Lewis, *Reflections on the Psalms*, 100–101.

5. The Hebrew Scriptures: Historicity and Humanity

authors of the Book of Isaiah, let alone the role played by an oral tradition spread over decades, the author is truly God. Only God knew the entire text, but it was not dictated to one person complete, it was put together by this disparate group. The full range of what is carried by the books (written, by-and-large, in unknowing) was beyond the authors. The total responsibility therefore lies with God. For Lewis there is another reason for accepting the scriptures of the Hebrews framed by these conclusions: we stand committed to what is recorded of Jesus's encounter on the road to Emmaus.[43] He upbraided the disciples for not believing what was recorded of the sayings of the prophets: "They ought to have known from their Bibles that the Anointed One, when He came, would enter his glory through suffering."[44] Jesus then explains from Moses and through the prophets what was predicted and the warnings that came with the prophecies (Luke 24:25–27). What is more, for Lewis, Jesus, the Anointed One, acknowledged his identity with these scriptural prophecies—and with the need for the Messiah! This all linked up with the prediction he had made to the disciples about what we now call his passion, but they skirted round it or sought its denial: "We do not know—or anyway I do not know—what all these passages were. We can be pretty sure about one of them. The Ethiopian eunuch who met Philip (Acts 8, 27–38) was reading Isaiah 53."[45] The fact, as Lewis terms it, is that "Isaiah is speaking of Jesus." This sets us a firm method and value for approaching and valuing the Hebrew scriptures.

4. HISTORICITY AND MYTH IN THE HEBREW BIBLE

In a letter to Clyde S. Kilby, that is, in many ways, a short academic paper, Lewis summarizes the questions and resulting doctrine that will emerge on scripture. In 1959 an American scholar, Clyde S. Kilby, wrote to Lewis asking his opinion of the Wheaton College Statement, Inspiration of the Bible. Wheaton College was at the time reputed to subscribe to a relatively strict evangelical, some would say fundamentalist, approach to scripture, believing the Bible to be inerrant, flawless, and without contradiction. Lewis's response, a letter dated May 7, 1959, is valuable because he deals head on with the issues that underpin fundamentalism, and he deals in a

---

43 Lewis, *Reflections on the Psalms*, 101.
44 Lewis, *Reflections on the Psalms*, 101.
45 Lewis, *Reflections on the Psalms*, 101.

small but systematic way with questions raised in relation to scripture, in particular the nature and value of the Bible.[46] Lewis gets right to the heart of the question: that is, the relationship between scriptural text and history, and between what is written—flaws and contradictions included—and the nature of scripture. Lewis notes how the question of inerrancy and flaw never holds much importance for him—whether in his religious life, as such, or in his studies—compared to the prominence such questions hold in what may be termed broadly conservative Protestant circles: "The difference between reading the story of Ruth and that of Antigone—both first class as literature—is to me unmistakable and even overwhelming. But the question 'Is Ruth historical?' (I've no reason to suppose it is not) doesn't really seem to arise till afterwards."[47] Therefore, the pertinent question is, what exactly is the function of the Bible and what is it that scripture teaches us? What are we supposed to be learning? Here Lewis asserts that some stories/events can—indeed must—be taken as non-historical, while others as historical. Not all of scripture is the same genre. The resurrection is fundamentally an historic event; the precise fate of Lot's wife is not. Lewis then goes on to cite several examples of questions/difficulties that mitigate a fundamentalist approach to inerrancy: the key being the genre or type of text—some texts, for example, are to be seen as sacred fiction. Therefore, Lewis cautiously rejected the concept of biblical inerrancy. Given the different genres and function, given the various writings in the Bible, given the aims of the authors, given that the books were often composed by different authors, sometimes many, many years apart, further that most were written in isolation without any knowledge of the others, then inerrancy—or systematic coherency, which is really what the fundamentalist mindset is talking about—for the whole is not possible. He comments that we should "rule out the view that every statement in scripture must be historical truth . . . [also] rule out the view that any one passage taken in isolation can be assumed to be inerrant in exactly the same sense as any other."[48] One is reminded here of Karl Barth. For Barth, biblical inerrancy seeks to provide a basis

46   "Lewis to Clyde S. Kilby, May 7, 1959." Lewis, *Collected Letters, Vol. III*, 1044–46. Clyde Samuel Kilby (1902–86) was writer and Professor of English at Wheaton College, and founder of the Marion E. Wade Centre at Wheaton; he met C. S. Lewis in 1953 and exchanged correspondence with him until Lewis's death ten years later.
47   "Lewis to Clyde S. Kilby, May 7, 1959," 1044–45.
48   "Lewis to Clyde S. Kilby, May 7, 1959," 1046.

5. The Hebrew Scriptures: Historicity and Humanity

or ground for belief other than Jesus Christ—but *Christ*, he insists, is the foundation of faith, *not* a perfect flawless Bible.[49] The Bible's primary value is as witness to the Word of God; that is, as testimony, witness, bystander, and onlooker, to Yeshua, the Nazarite, the second person of the Trinity, incarnate, crucified, and resurrected as atonement realized. *This* is what is important. Fundamentalism, on the other hand, sometimes leads to bibliolatry. What is important is how we understand what it is to give testimony.

Witnesses, Holocaust survivors, in the Nuremberg trials sometimes contradicted each other on small details. Do we expect the accounts of widely disparate genres in the Hebrew scriptures to be verbatim, word-for-word, courtroom transcribed and verified records of what happened and what was said? There is unquestionably a degree of what may be termed theological interpretation to these accounts, but the evidence is too great when it interlocks with other accounts for us to be dismissive of its historical value. How do we assess accounts of the Holocaust by Jewish survivors today? On television documentaries and in the newspapers men and women who were children or teenagers many decades earlier will recount what happened to them in the concentration camps, they will even recount what the SS guards said to them. How accurate are these accounts? Given the passage of years, decades, there will be an element of error, small details may be confused, apparent errors had crept in. Accounts will vary from one survivor to the other, even if they are recounting the same shared experience, the memory will now be more memory of memories, the tale will, subconsciously, be a recounting from memory of the telling to investigators in the 1950s of what happened, but this does not prove that the Holocaust did not happen, that they had not been there and saw what happened, that they created the memories. In law, in any courtroom trial, this human fallibility is taken into account. Apparent variances between testimonies given by two or more people are attributed to human frailty; a witness's recollection of another person's words may vary slightly from what happened, but the general drift and meaning is accepted as historical. This is especially so when the words and events witnessed to are from the accounts of hundreds of people whose testimony all point to the same conclusion: this is so with the accounts

---

49   Barth, *Der Römerbrief*, Zweite Fassung, 6.

on which the Gospels are based, but also with many accounts relating to salvation history amongst other aims in the Hebrew Bible.

In the context of inerrancy Lewis states that, "Whatever view we hold on the divine authority of scripture must make room for the following facts."[50] He then proceeds to outline six categories that must be considered.

Divine and Human Origin

First, Lewis distinguishes between divine word and human comment; for Lewis this is where the apostle Paul draws a distinction in 1 Corinthians between what he says is from the Lord, while other sayings are his and not from the Lord (1 Cor 7:10 and 12). This is the difference between the *Deus dixit* (God spoke), and *paulus dixit* (Paul spoke); therefore, some words in the Bible are, to a greater extent, of human origin.

Levels of Historicity

Second, that there are inconsistencies between the lineage and descent of Jesus listed in Matthew's Gospel and Luke's; likewise, there are historical discrepancies between the account of Judas's death in Matthew and Acts. Therefore, there are different levels of historicity even within the Gospels.

A Human Element

Third, that Luke, in the preface to his Gospel, acknowledges that *he* was instrumental in being the historian—gathering together records of events, personal accounts, and testimony from witnesses. Therefore, there is an important human element in what Luke has selected and compiled (Luke 1:1–4).

Mythological Narratives

Fourth, the, as Lewis terms it, "universally admitted unhistoricity (I do not say, of course, falsity) of at least some narratives in scripture (the parables), which may well extend also to Jonah and Job."[51] Whether they are historically true or false is not of primary importance. Specific stories in the Hebrew Bible are an important framework for how God generates a right understanding in our minds and draws humanity to *himself.*

---

50   "Lewis to Clyde S. Kilby, May 7, 1959," 1045.
51   "Lewis to Clyde S. Kilby, May 7, 1959," 1045.

5. The Hebrew Scriptures: Historicity and Humanity

In the same way that the characters within Jesus's parables have a profound effect on us whether they existed or not as real people, the stories and characters in the Hebrew Bible are a demonstration and a lesson to us. Historicity occurs when we understand that it is *true* that Moses authored and inspired an oral tradition eventually to be written down, recorded; we find the same thing happening in the same way, that is, with the sayings of Jesus, who composed the parables and spoke them essentially to his disciples among others: they were not made up by the disciples, though his followers heard and caused them to be written down.[52] Furthermore, there is *truth* in that Jesus observed humanity around him wherever he went and that these observations inspired and informed him in composing the parables.

Divinely Inspired Writings

Fifth, Lewis, quoting James, asserts that if every good and perfect gift comes from the Father of Lights then all scripture must be accorded the value of inspired. However, he then continues by asserting a proposition we will come across again and again in his work, that if this is so then all true and edifying writings, whether in scripture or not, must be in some sense inspired. God's action through the Holy Spirit may not stop at inspiring the writers of scripture. However, the Holy Spirit does not use humans as an amanuensis, the Bible was not dictated, and certainly not to only one person: inspiration leads to human interpretation and decision. Therefore, the Hebrew Bible and the Christian Testament are quantitatively different to the claims surrounding Muhammed's reception of the Qur'an, where he claims to have received the holy text *verbatim and unfiltered.*

Inspiration and the Purposes of God

Sixth, therefore, writes Lewis, "inspiration may operate in a wicked man without his knowing it, and he can then utter the untruth he intends (propriety of making an innocent man a political scapegoat) as well as the

---

[52] In early Anglo Saxon England, when conversion of the people was moving across the various kingdoms apace, and also of the invading Vikings, tribes who had never come across written documents often referred to books and scrolls as "words without sounds, ideas without people," documents were seen as having a life and authority of their own. We can fairly say that this was probably true in pre-literate societies in the Middle East, and that this points to the veracity of biblical books as witness.

truth he does not intend (the divine sacrifice)."[53] Lewis is here referring to John 11:49–53; Caiaphas's comment about how one man should die for the people was quite ironic, he stated truth but for the wrong reasons. Therefore, there is a human element in the writing of scripture as well as the events recorded: the humanity of scripture.

For Lewis, these examples serve to dismiss the claim that all statements in scripture must be seen as historical truth; also the view that inspiration is always of the same mode and to the same degree. The problem is compounded when a passage is taken in isolation, any contradictions are then ignored: we cannot assume that if one event written in the Bible is true, all events are without flaw—"that the numbers of Old Testament armies (which in view of the size of the country, if true, involves continuous miracle) are statistically correct because the story of the Resurrection is historically correct."[54] For Lewis, the aim of scripture is to convey the Word of God: therefore both writer and reader are inspired, but not necessarily to the same degree nor in the same mode.[55] Lewis concludes his comments to Clyde S. Kilby by pointing out that "the very kind of truth we are often demanding was, in my opinion, never even envisaged by the Ancients," that is, those who were inspired to write and to construct the Bible.[56]

5. THE HUMANITY OF SCRIPTURE

All of this that we have considered adds up to what Lewis refers to generally as the humanity of scripture. What is the historicity of the Hebrew Bible, of scripture, generally? Lewis lays great stress on humanity receiving infinite wisdom, which "comes down," is revealed by God, and is beyond complete human comprehension; this does not necessarily make certain elements of the Bible historically true. The Bible is ruled over by a divine presence which *inspires* but does *not dictate*: and this divine presence coheres with the evolving understanding—and naming—of God. This is especially true with the books that make up the Hebrew scriptures,

---

    53   "Lewis to Clyde S. Kilby, May 7, 1959," 1046.

    54   "Lewis to Clyde S. Kilby, May 7, 1959," 1046.

    55   In terms of the modes of scripture see: Brazier, *C. S. Lewis—The Work of Christ Revealed*, Ch. 2 Scripture, Revelation, and Reason II: Mediation and the Bible, §1. C. S. Lewis: A Doctrine of Scripture? 46–52.

    56   "Lewis to Clyde S. Kilby, May 7," 1959, 1046.

5. The Hebrew Scriptures: Historicity and Humanity

that originated in an oral tradition going back a thousand or more years. Therefore, Lewis, in the context specifically of the Book of the Psalms, speaks of the human qualities—naivety, error, contradiction, cursing, and wickedness. Such things are, for Lewis, not excluded by inspiration.[57] This, again, represents the humanity of scripture. Therefore, as we noted, Lewis argues that the Bible is disorderly and at times messy, permeable and unsecured by certainty: "To a human mind this working up (in a sense imperfectly), this sublimation (incomplete) of human material, seems, no doubt, an untidy and leaky vehicle."[58] Humanity would have preferred the psychological security of absolute truth systematically presented, unrefracted light that could be contained and quantified in an encyclopedic fashion. But this is not what God has given to us, and it is important to remember that there is a givenness about the Bible. Lewis does not approach the Judaea-Christian Bible with a fundamentalist mind-set: a humanity shines through, particularly in the ancient Hebrew scriptures.

A few years earlier Lewis had corresponded with Corbin Scott Carnell, an American academic.[59] In the letter Lewis offered a similar framework and comments on the nature, genres, and reliability of the Bible, but he sees the different genres as no less historic and important than historically factual accounts.

> The Hebrews, like other people, had mythology: but as they were the chosen people so their mythology was the chosen mythology—the mythology chosen by God to be the vehicle of the earliest sacred truths, the first step in that process which ends in the New Testament where truth has become completely historical.... I take it that the Memoirs of David's court come at one end of the scale and are scarcely less historical than St Mark or Acts; and that the Book of Jonah is at the opposite end.[60]

Lewis asserts that Hebrew history was a long preparation that culminated in God's becoming incarnated human, so truth first appears before humanity in what is termed, "mythical form." It is then a lengthy procedure, a progression of salvation, "condensing or focusing" to become incarnate

---

57   Lewis, *Reflections on the Psalms*, 96f.
58   Lewis, *Reflections on the Psalms*, 100.
59   Written from Magdalen College Oxford, April 5, 1953. See Lewis, *Collected Letters Vol. III*, 318–19.
60   "Lewis to Corbin Scott Carnel, April 5, 1953," FN 114. See Lewis, *Collected Letters Vol. III*, 318–19.

in history: so, the early forms are mythical forms of truth, where myth can and is often truer than seemingly simple scientific fact.

Generalizations aside, the mature Lewis dedicated an entire book to his understanding and interpretation of the Book of the Psalms, with consideration systematic theological reflections. It is to that book that we turn next.

6

The Psalms I:
Hebrew Theological Poetry

> "Surely goodness and mercy shall follow me
> all the days of my life,
> and I shall dwell in the house of the LORD
> for the length of my days."
>
> PSALM 23:6

"The most valuable thing the Psalms do for me is to express that same delight in God which made David dance. I am not saying that this is so pure or so profound a thing as the love of God.... I am comparing it with the merely dutiful "church-going" and laborious "saying our prayers" to which most of us are, thank God not always, but often, reduced. Against that it stands out as something astonishingly robust, virile, and spontaneous; something we may regard with an innocent envy and may hope to be infected by as we read."

C. S. LEWIS[1]

1. INTRODUCTION

Late on in life, and after decades spent praying the Psalmody—morning prayer and evening prayer—from the Book of Common Prayer, Lewis published an entire book on the Psalms of David: *Reflections on the Psalms* (1958). Not necessarily biblical studies, ancient history, or archaeology, Lewis admits that he is no Hebraist—neither scholar or linguist—but presents a personal theological survey in relation to salvation history amongst all peoples (therefore looking at how the Psalms compare with a

---

[1] Lewis, *Reflections on the Psalms*, 39

limited revelation even in North European pagan mythology). One of his last books, *Reflections on the Psalms*, reveals considerable maturity.

Hebraists can devote volumes to analysis and understanding the chronology of the Psalms, authorship, the deportation to Babylon, a myriad of approaches. On a multidisciplinary approach to the Psalms, Lewis writes, "In a book of this sort nothing more need, or can, be said about it."[2] The framework stands. What he looks at is the theological heart of the Psalms.

2. POETRY: MEANING

Professionally, from the mid-1920s, Lewis earned his daily bread as a teacher of English Literature at Oxford, then as a professor at Cambridge. He was an academic of some distinction, albeit within his primary expertise in literature. He was also fascinated by the big systems of Platonic philosophy, accounts of the nature of things that are astonishingly ambitious in their attempts to encompass the whole of reality in one closed system (which does not necessarily fit well with the Hebrew revelation and relationship with the one true God). Lewis's major academic contributions focused on the medieval allegorical poets and on sixteenth-century English writers (he wrote on English literature in the sixteenth century for the *Oxford History of English Literature*; published a *Preface to Paradise Lost*; and traced the development of the medieval traditions into Spencer's *Faerie Queene* in arguably his greatest work, *The Allegory of Love*); in these writers we find, fundamentally, a colossal endeavor to make sense of the world. Allegory is an exercise in linking together endless partial meanings into an encompassing whole. He is therefore a poet and an expert on poetry, his public persona today fails to acknowledge this, to an extent. Therefore, the one foundational love of his life was literature. It was both his passion and his profession. And the literature that he loved was not confined to the texts of medieval and Renaissance Europe, in which he was so deeply read, but included Homer and Sophocles, Virgil and Cicero, the literature of classical Greece and Rome, as well as the Norse sagas and the pre-Christian writings of Old English. On becoming a Christian, he could have abandoned the truth he had found in those works, replacing them with the Bible and the

---

2   Lewis, *Reflections on the Psalms*, 2.

6. The Psalms I: Hebrew Theological Poetry

teachings of the church. Instead, he looked at the Bible and looked at the pagan sources with fresh literary eyes.

Lewis knew poetry and literature (he was an acknowledged and published poet himself). When reading the Bible, he noted how the Hebrew Bible as literature is taken up to be the medium of something that is more than merely human; so, can we set any limit on the multiplicity of meanings, the gravity of the text, which is laid upon it by God? Lewis acknowledges the work of Bible scholars down the years and the consensus of opinion regarding dating, cultural background, etc. However, in such a work as *Reflections on the Psalms*, Lewis notes that nothing more need to be said on these issues.[3] What Lewis the *literatus* focuses on is the structure of the Psalms as poems and a literary theological analysis.

For Lewis, the Psalms are primarily poems—poems that are to be sung. Reading the Psalms as a form of literature does not mean, for Lewis, neutralizing them: removing their theological truth and religious context as worship and discussion with God.[4] The Psalms inform us about humanity's relationship with God, faith, the unfolding of salvation history, and the myriad of emotions and reasoning that the human can experience.

> Most emphatically the Psalms must be read as poems; as lyrics, with all the licences and all the formalities, the hyperboles, the emotional rather than logical connections, which are proper to lyric poetry. They must be read as poems if they are to be understood; no less than French must be read as French or English as English. Otherwise we shall miss what is in them and think we see what is not.[5]

The Psalms do have a unique poetic structure, grammar and syntax; this structure, the pattern, survives translation, the Psalms are relatively unique in this, which has allowed their uniqueness to be translated into dozens—hundreds—of world languages.

Parallelism

What can we learn from Lewis about this structure, what does it tell us about the Psalms, about the Bible, for that matter about the Hebrew

---

[3] Lewis, *Reflections on the Psalms*, 2.
[4] Lewis, *Reflections on the Psalms*, 2.
[5] Lewis, *Reflections on the Psalms*, 3.

A HEBRAIC INKLING

mindset: rhetoric and humor, grammar and language, vocabulary and technique, device and balance? This is a structure that is then characteristic of the sayings of Jesus, as recorded. Known as rhetorical parallelism, though found in many languages and cultures, it does have a uniquely Hebraic imprint, so to speak, and is used throughout most of the Bible, being richly displayed in Psalms, Proverbs, and the Book of Revelation:

In the way of righteousness is life,
And in its pathway there is no death
Prov 12:28

I am the rose of Sharon,
And the lily of the valleys
Song 2:1

For the LORD knows the way of the righteous,
But the way of the ungodly shall perish
Ps 1:6.

He who sits in the heavens laughs;
the LORD has them in derision.
Ps 2:1

The cords of death encompassed me;
the torrents of destruction assailed me
Ps 18:4

The LORD is my shepherd;
I shall not want
Ps 23:1

He will make your vindication shine like the light,
and the justice of your cause like the noonday.
Ps 37:6

As the deer pants for the water brooks,
So pants my soul for You, O God
Ps 42:1

Let the evildoer still do evil, and the filthy still be filthy,
And the righteous still do right, and the holy still be holy.
Rev 22:11

Lewis was only too familiar with this when, as a Christian convert, he began reading the Psalms on a daily basis. As a device that uses compounds words or phrases with equivalent, though divergent meanings, a clear pattern is created. This is effective when enumerating pairs and series, similar but dissimilar, therefore parallelism is a basic rhetorical grammatical principle.[6] Parallelisms is, to many, the chief rhetorical device of biblical—essentially Hebrew—poetry.[7] In the Hebraic

---

6 See, Connors and Corbett, *Style and Statement*.
7 See, Herbermann, ed. "Parallelism." *Catholic Encyclopedia*.

6. The Psalms I: Hebrew Theological Poetry

tradition, this is often in *tristich* and *distich* parallels.[8] Robert Lowth (eighteenth-century Anglican bishop, Hebraic scholar, and professor of poetry and grammarian at Oxford University) established the recognition of and study of the poetic structures in the Hebrew scriptures, inventing the term *parallelismus membrorum* to refer to parallelism of poetic lines, which would have influenced Lewis in his own professional capacity at Oxford.[9]

For Lewis this parallelism is not merely for aesthetics, or effect; it is inherent to the meaning. With synonymous parallelism the same idea is repeated twice: cord-death-encompassed/torrents-death-assailed (Ps 18:4), thus the danger, the suffering is stressed, underscored, highlighting the seriousness of what has been survived. Emblematic parallelism sees the first concept compared, or set against the second: compassion links, compares: "As a father has compassion for his children, so the LORD has compassion for those who fear him": Father-children/Lord-those who fear. Likewise this comparison may lead, whereby a figure of speech, a trope, in the first line of poetry exemplifies, illuminates, the concept in the second line (Ps 42:1; Prov 11:22). Incomplete parallelism, as Lewis notes in the Psalms, relates closely to emblematic, but this is where the parallelism is incomplete; likewise, formal parallelism is where the subsequent lines simply are usually balanced in length.[10] Antithetic parallelism juxtaposes two lines contrary to each thus creating a contrast (similar to a complementary paradox): "For the LORD knows the way of the righteous/But the way of the ungodly shall perish (Ps 1:6)." This type is parallel in form only; the two (or more) lines don't contrast, expand, or emphasize. Formal parallelism is merely two lines of poetry, expressing similarity: "Yet I have set My King/On My holy hill of Zion (Ps 2:6).

Lewis notes how in reality parallelism is an example of what all pattern and art involves: "the same in the other."[11] Likewise, Lewis notes that parallelism in the Psalms is intentionally partially concealed for emphasis, but also to add-in multifaceted patterns "crossways," and in

---

8   **Tristich**: three lines of poetry, forming a stanza or a complete poem. **Distich**, a couplet as a pair of successive lines of meter in poetry, two successive lines that rhyme and have the same meter: open, run-on, or closed.

9   See, Lowth, *Lectures on the Sacred Poetry of the Hebrew Nation*.

10 Lewis, *Reflections on the Psalms*, 3–7.

11 Lewis, *Reflections on the Psalms*, 4.

A HEBRAIC INKLING

"refrain, as in Psalm 107 and 119."[12] Lewis wonders whether the parallelism of the Psalms is "a wise provision of God's, that poetry which was to be turned into all languages should have as its chief formal characteristic one that does not disappear (as mere meter does) in translation."[13]

If ultimately the authorship of the Psalms lies with *YHWHs* inspiration then it is of no surprise that the parallelism we see in the Psalms occurs in the saying of Jesus in the Gospels, as they have come down to us.

> Parallelism is a central feature of Hebrew poetry. It permeates the words of biblical poets and prophets. The frequency with which parallelism occurs in the utterances of Jesus is surprising, and leads inevitably to the conclusion that the Greek source (or, sources) used by the authors of Matthew, Mark and Luke derive from Hebrew documents.[14]

Poetic Structure

Lewis well understood how The Sermon on the Mount is full of Hebraic parallelism redolent of Hebrew poetry, demonstrated essentially in the Beatitudes, but found throughout the sayings of Jesus.[15] This provides emphasis and contrast, stress and repetition, prominence enabling the message/meaning to be driven home. Therefore, asserts Lewis, "Our Lord, soaked in the poetic tradition of His country, delighted to use it. 'For with what judgement ye judge, ye shall be judged; and with what measure ye mete, it shall be measured to you again.'"[16] Lewis, quoting here Matthew 7:2, adds that the second half makes no necessary addition but echoes with variation: this is important in terms of emphasizing meaning and context, as, notes Lewis also in Matthew 7:7: "Ask, and it will be given to you; search, and you will find; knock, and the door will be opened for you."[17] Different images are used to achieve this: ask, seek, knock, receive, find, be opened. This is rhythmic and incantatory, didactic and memorable. The Word, notes Lewis, that formed and created all in the

---

12   Lewis, *Reflections on the Psalms*, 4.

13   Lewis, *Reflections on the Psalms*, 4.

14   Biven, "'Cataloguing the Gospels' Hebraisms: Part Five (Parallelism)."

15   See, Burney, *The Poetry of Our Lord*; also, Muilenburg, "Hebrew Poetry," *Encyclopaedia Judaica* 13:671–81. See also, Kierspel, *The Jews and the World in the Fourth*.

16   Lewis, *Reflections on the Psalms*, 4.

17   Lewis, *Reflections on the Psalms*, 4.

6. The Psalms I: Hebrew Theological Poetry

first place, when expressing itself through human speech, speaks using poetry, poetry that Lewis defines as a little incarnation—giving form to that which was not seen or heard.[18]

Lewis identifies the same Hebraic poetic structure in the Magnificat,[19] noting how there "is a fierceness, even a touch of Deborah,[20] mixed with the sweetness in the Magnificat to which most painted Madonnas do little justice," corresponding to the frequent severity of the sayings of Jesus, consistent with the grammatical nature of Hebraic parallelism.[21]

Azariah

Rabbi Azariah di Rossi established the linguistic framework for our, and Lewis's, understanding of Hebrew poetry over three hundred years ago.[22] Published in 1574, Azariah's *Me'or 'Enayim* (*Light of the Eyes*) advances and advocates the theory of Hebrew poetry that still holds sway today. Azariah postulate the thesis that

> There can be no doubt that the sacred songs possess measures and proportions; these, however, are not dependent upon the number of syllables, whether full or half syllables, according to the system of versification which is now in use among us, . . . but their proportions and measures are by the number of things and their parts, i.e. subject and predicate and their adjuncts in each written phrase and proposition.[23]

Thus, as in Lewis's own expertise in poetry, Azariah demonstrates how a phrase that consists of two measures joined with a second set become four (irrespective of syllables) or three measures, six complete measures: always.[24] Thus:

18 Lewis, *Reflections on the Psalms*, 5f.
19 Lewis, *Reflections on the Psalms*, 6.
20 Deborah (or Debbora), a prophet and judge, heroine of Israel, wife of Lapidoth, who served the ancient Hebrews (Judg 4 & 5), inspired the Israelites to a mighty victory over their Canaanites.
21 Lewis, *Reflections on the Psalms*, 6.
22 Rabbi Azariah di Rossi was an Italian-Jewish physician and scholar (1511–78); early in life he became exceptionally proficient in Hebrew, Latin, and Italian literature. He studied simultaneously medicine, archaeology, history, Greek and Roman antiquities, Jewish history, also Christian ecclesiastical history.
23 Azariah, Me'or 'Enayim (1574) quoted in Burney, *The Poetry of the Lord*, 69.
24 Azariah quoted in Burney, *The Poetry of the Lord*, 69.

A HEBRAIC INKLING

```
"Thy right-hand / O-LORD"      "is-glorious / in-strength"
  1st measure/2nd measure         1st measure/2nd measure
                                                   Exod 15:16
```

Unlike poetic systems in other languages and traditions, the number of words or syllables (half or full) is unimportant: balance is, especially balance of ideas.

Revd C. F. Burney noted in his seminal 1925 study of Hebraic poetry forms in the Hebrew Bible that

> Considerable portions of our Lord's recorded sayings and discourses are cast in the characteristic forms of Hebrew poetry. ... [T]he formal characteristics of Hebrew poetry, which, when we meet them in the Old Testament writings, [are] suffice to convince us that the writers are consciously employing poetry and not prose as the medium of their expression.[25]

This mode of expression in the Hebrew Bible is not scientific as we know the mode of thought today, yet it is in many ways scientific poetry, relating to the medieval Latin/scholastic concept of *scientia*: knowledge reasoning, skill, understanding, even wisdom, objective knowledge—reason, science. Hebraic poetry is used in various forms and types to convey God's dealings with humanity. This can be said to reach its height in the Psalms.

3. BEAUTY: HARMONY: SWEETNESS

David danced before the ark of the covenant—wildly—rejoicing in gratitude and love for the Lord God, notes Lewis.[26] Although Judaism is the worship of the one eternal and true God, it still exhibited elements of worship more associated with ancient pagan religions: excitement, exuberance, but then there is the smell of a sacred slaughterhouse: roast meat, sacrifices (as Lewis terms it). The Psalms were meant to be sung and to be sung with emotion! Later Judaism focused on the synagogue as a meeting house where law was studied: preaching, teaching, listening, but still the Psalms: "The most valuable thing the Psalms do for me is

---

25   Azariah quoted in Burney, *The Poetry of the Lord*, 69.
26   Lewis, *Reflections on the Psalms*, 38. Referring to 2 Sam 6:14–22.

6. The Psalms I: Hebrew Theological Poetry

to express that same delight in God which made David dance."[27] This is therefore "astonishingly robust, virile, and spontaneous; something we may regard with an innocent envy and may hope to be infected by as we read."[28]

This meeting with God is intrinsically related to sacrifice: a sacrificial offering, yes, but also—and perhaps underlined by the concept of sacrifice in the Psalms—personal conversion, giving-up, amendment of ways, honoring God with repentance, reparation, and a change of heart: "You do not delight in sacrifice, or I would bring it; you do not take pleasure in burnt offerings. The sacrifices of God, are a broken spirit; a broken and contrite heart you, O God, will not despise" (Ps 51:16–17). And yet, notes Lewis, somewhere in Hebrew history the unity between prayer repentance with scripture and law study becomes separate from the physical sacrificial offering.[29] Yet the Psalms, on numerous occasions, testify to this discontinuity:

> Not for your sacrifices do I rebuke you;
>> your burnt-offerings are continually before me.
> I will not accept a bull from your house,
>> or goats from your folds.
> For every wild animal of the forest is mine,
>> the cattle on a thousand hills.
> I know all the birds of the air,
>> and all that moves in the field is mine.
> 'If I were hungry, I would not tell you,
>> for the world and all that is in it is mine.
> Do I eat the flesh of bulls,
>> or drink the blood of goats?
> Offer to God a sacrifice of thanksgiving,
>> and pay your vows to the Most High.
> Call on me in the day of trouble;
>> I will deliver you, and you shall glorify me.'
>>> Ps 50:8–15

Lewis notes, somewhat controversially, perhaps, how the system of animal sacrifice had become an end in itself, a commercial transaction with a covetous and avaricious god, who required large amounts of

---

27   Lewis, *Reflections on the Psalms*, 39.
28   Lewis, *Reflections on the Psalms*, 39–40.
29   Lewis, *Reflections on the Psalms*, 41–42.

roasted flesh, dead cattle, sheep and birds for amendment, atonement: for the priesthood this can seem self-serving, maintaining their status as religious professionals.[30] And yet, the psalmists and prophets continually speak out, voicing God's self-sufficiency, YHWH has no need, of these sacrifices.[31]

The question of animal sacrifice apart, there is a longing in the Hebrew people for this meeting with God, going up to the temple, being in and with the presence, something that moderns can sometimes have little conception of (except where there is a sacramental spirit in some of the churches, though that is so often tolerated, perhaps even dismissed, by those of a particular persuasion). For Lewis, the Psalms speak of the Jews longing for the journey to the temple so they may spend their days contemplating "the fair beauty of the LORD,"[32] their longing is like an insatiable thirst to go up to Jerusalem and "appear before the presence of God."[33] and to behold "God's perfect beauty" (Ps 50:2) for their souls are parched (Ps 63:2); The craving they feel can only be satisfied with this presence (Ps 65:4):[34]

> For a day in your courts is better
>   than a thousand elsewhere.
> I would rather be a doorkeeper in the house of my God
>   than live in the tents of wickedness.
>   Ps 84:10 (cf. Ps 27:4; Isa 58:13)

This appetite is the love of God in the Jews. It is full of, for Lewis, cheerful spontaneity, a natural even physical desire.[35] This is gladness and rejoicing (Ps 9:2), cites Lewis; musical (Pss 43:4 and 57:9), a cheerful noise (Ps 81:1–2), excited, animated music (Ps 47:1), and loud, with dancing (Ps 150:5).[36] However, this does not all bode well. By comparison, Lewis states "There is thus a tragic depth in our worship which Judaism

---

30 Lewis, *Reflections on the Psalms*, 42.

31 For example: "obedience is better than sacrifice, and attentiveness is better than the fat of rams" (1 Sam 15:22); and "Sacrifice and offering You did not desire, but my ears . . ." (Ps 40:6). See also: Ps 69:31; Jer 7:22; Hos 14:2; Mic 6:6.

32 Ps 27:4. See, Lewis, *Reflections on the Psalms*, 44.

33 Ps 42:1–3. See, Lewis, *Reflections on the Psalms*, 44.

34 Ps 27:4. See, Lewis, *Reflections on the Psalms*, 44.

35 Ps 27:4. See, Lewis, *Reflections on the Psalms*, 44.

36 Ps 27:4. See, Lewis, *Reflections on the Psalms*, 44.

6. The Psalms I: Hebrew Theological Poetry

lacked"—why?—because so often our worship is founded in the cross—the broken body the shed blood.[37] But we still owe an enormous debt of gratitude to this Hebraic poetry, notes Lewis.

Lewis links the joy, desire, and gratitude, the beauty and harmony in the Psalms with not just God's mercies but also the Law. Lewis finds this bewildering (relating to his skepticism for the Law as a young apostate, and the criticism he exhibited to the, essentially, Mosaic Law in *The Pilgrim's Progress*).[38] Yet, obedience to and thanks for the Law is to be desired: sweeter than honey is the Law, or fine gold (Ps 19:10): "One can well understand this being said of God's mercies, God's visitations, His attributes. But what the poet is actually talking about is God's law, His commands."[39] However, Lewis concedes that the psalmists were referring to the contentment, the serenity, and the satisfaction the Hebrews felt from obedience to the Law. For Lewis, this is the "pleasures of a good conscience."[40] There is much digression on the Law and criticism by Lewis, which can appear, given his complaint about the character of the Hebrews and the corruption as he sees it of the Law, to be veiled anti-Semitism: regarding the autonomous nature of the laws as deadly, that this love of the Law leads to pride, a lack of abstract philosophical thinking, the danger of what he terms priggery.[41] Therefore, despite Lewis's concessions, there is much digression.

4. PRAISE

Lewis somewhat embarrassedly confesses to feeling a puzzlement in the weeks and months after his conversion over praising—particularly the Hebrew emphasis on praise being essential. This should not have been so, he writes, nearly thirty years after the event of his conversion.[42] Initially he found a mental block when adjured by Christians around him that he must praise God, even demand this in him. (His unspoken response was, it seemed at the time, characterized by more than a touch of Hebraic

---

37   Ps 27:4. Lewis, *Reflections on the Psalms*, 45.

38   Lewis, *The Pilgim's Regress: An Allegorical Apology for Christianity, Reason and Romanticism*, chs I.2, I.5, V.5, VIII.7, X.2.

39   See, Lewis, *Reflections on the Psalms*, 47.

40   Lewis, *Reflections on the Psalms*, 47.

41   See, Lewis, *Reflections on the Psalms*, 50–55.

42   See, Lewis, *Reflections on the Psalms*, ch. 9.

A HEBRAIC INKLING

humor.) We've seen how Lewis's conversion was protracted, and how there was so much that needed to change in his thinking. He found the Psalms especially troublesome. Apart from trying to put words into God's mouth (Ps 50:20) ordering whales and snowstorms, the sun and the moon, nature, to praise when they could not do otherwise (Ps 104, etc.), it was the number of times he found the multiple uses of phrases like "Praise the LORD" (Pss 22, 33, 102–6, 111–13, 115–17, 135, 146–50), "Praise Him" (Pss 22, 42–43, 69, 107–9, 148, 150) that concerned him. This was a sorry picture of Lewis, a North European pagan, wrestling with the nature of worship that had been trained into Hebrews for millennia. It took Lewis some time through his protracted conversions to arrive at not simply a full acceptance but to see this coming naturally to him.[43]

Lewis also questioned the motivation of the psalmists: if I do this and praise you, can I have this?—etc. How valid was he to identify a distinction between action and reward, demand and deserve? Eventually with maturity Lewis can see that this is what we the creature has been created for:

> God does not only "demand" praise as the supremely beautiful and all-satisfying Object. He does apparently command it as lawgiver. The Jews were told to sacrifice. We are under an obligation to go to church. . . . I did not see that it is in the process of being worshipped that God communicates His presence to men."[44]

God may love us; but as love, God does not need us, God does not need to love us—but we need God, the God of love, self-giving, self-denying love, *agápē*.

Lewis eventually realized that enjoyment overflows—spontaneously we may say—into natural unaffected, artless praise. Such extemporaneously motivated love for God exudes praise and glory, gratitude and a right religion: "The world rings with praise."[45]

---

43 See, Lewis, *Reflections on the Psalms*, ch. 9, 79.
44 Lewis, *Reflections on the Psalms*, 79.
45 Lewis, *Reflections on the Psalms*, 80.

7

The Psalms II: Judgements and Cursings— Imprecatory Poems

"Happy shall they be who take your little ones and dash them against the rock!"

PSALM 137:9

"We need not therefore be surprised if the Psalms, and the Prophets, are full of the longing for judgement, and regard the announcement that 'judgement' is coming as good news. Hundreds and thousands of people who have been stripped of all they possess and who have the right entirely on their side will at last be heard. Of course they are not afraid of judgement. They know their case is unanswerable—if only it could be heard. When God comes to judge, at last it will."

C. S. LEWIS[1]

1. INTRODUCTION

Lewis devotes separate chapters to the understanding of judgement in the Psalms and the cursings we find in the Psalms: of necessity these should be tackled together.

Going back to the Sayings of Yeshua, with emphasis for Lewis on the parable of the sheep and the goats (Matt 25:31–46), it is judgement that preoccupies Christians of a traditional "Catholic" and "Evangelical" persuasion. Such will "tremble" at the thought of God's judgement.[2] Such

---

1   Lewis, *Reflections on the Psalms*, 10.
2   Lewis, *Reflections on the Psalms*, 8f.

will pray for deliverance. Though the modern mind will dismiss this as a medieval fantasy.

> This can leave no conscience untouched, for in it the "Goats" are condemned entirely for their sins of omission; as if to make us fairly sure that the heaviest charge against each of us turns not upon the things he has done but on those he never did—perhaps never dreamed of doing.[3]

By contrast, for Lewis, the Psalmist greets judgement, yearns for it: judgement, he asserts, is an occasion for universal rejoicing:

> Let the nations be glad and sing for joy,
>   for you judge the peoples with equity
>   Ps 67:4a

> Then shall all the trees of the forest sing for joy
>   before the LORD; for he is coming,
> for he is coming to judge the earth.
>   He will judge the world with righteousness,
>   and the peoples with his truth
>   Ps 96:12–13

> Vindicate me, O LORD, my God,
>   according to your righteousness,
>   and do not let them rejoice over me.
>   Ps 35:24

These three Psalms Lewis quotes in relation to judgement: a reckoning, a vindication, because they are who they are, they are plaintiffs before *YHWH*, the LORD.[4] This is the language of a court of justice. For the Jews, notes Lewis, this is a civil case; for the Christian, this is a criminal case. The Jew seeks triumph, with damages awarded; the Christian seeks acquittal, pardon, mercy, exoneration—liberty:[5] hence, for the Jew it is "Wake up! Bestir yourself for my defense, for my cause, my God and my Lord!" (Ps 35:23). Lewis here makes the error of classifying the parable of the sheep and the goats as uniquely Christian, a "characteristically

---

3   Lewis, *Reflections on the Psalms*, 8.
4   Lewis, *Reflections on the Psalms*, 8.
5   Lewis, *Reflections on the Psalms*, 9.

7. The Psalms II:Judgements and Cursings—Imprecatory Poems

Christian picture,"[6] but as Yaakov Brown has noted it is deeply Hebraic imagery of the final judgement rooted in a distinctly pastoral context.[7] Furthermore, Jesus is here talking about animals, sheep and goats, that to all intents and purposes, today, are distinct and obviously different, but during the intertestamental period the distinctions between them were barely discernible, therefore telling the two apart is very difficult, as it is today between saints and sinners:[8]

> "Anyone who has seen a picture of wheat and tares growing together will agree that it is very difficult to determine one from the other. The same is true of the varieties of sheep and goats herded in the land of Israel and throughout the Middle East. The point is that it's the farmer or the shepherd who is best equipped to identify one from the other."[9]

Hence *God's* judgement, not ours.

Lewis digresses to write on Luke 18:1–5 as an illustration of the Psalmists' Hebraic cry for the plaintiff in a civil case: the poor woman deprived of justice, faced with a corrupt judiciary. Therefore, he writes about how we are surprised to find in the Book of the Psalms a deep longing—not fear!—for judgement, welcoming it as good news. Consider these people, stripped of all they possess and who are unequivocally in the right: they fear not to face God. They simply seek, waiting patiently to be heard.[10] Is Lewis correct to see this as quantitatively different to the concept of judgement in a Christian, Western, mindset? He lists

---

6   Lewis, *Reflections on the Psalms*, 134.

7   Yaakov Brown, Spiritual leader of Beth Melekh Community, Auckland, N.Z. See, Beth Melekh: "The Sheep and the Goats," §§. 32–46.

8   From a contemporary British viewpoint, sheep are very different in appearance to goats: fluffy balls of white cottonwool, grazers who would attack no one (the product of a thousand years of selective breeding in a mild wet climate), compared to mean-spirited, thin, wiry, grey animals that would eat anything and attack to defend and expand. In the intertestamental period, goats and sheep were mountain animals, barely domesticated, and looked virtually identical, as can be seen from Iberian and North African sheep today. Jesus's point in his parable is that judging by appearances no one can tell the difference (except for the shepherd, and some discerning livestock workers: the only clue is often in the tail: in most varieties one points up, the other down!); so the same is true with humans: merely looking at someone won't tell you if they are an eschatological sheep or a goat.

9   Yaakov Brown, Spiritual leader of Beth Melekh Community, Auckland, N.Z. See, Beth Melekh: "The Sheep and the Goats," §. 32.

10   Lewis, *Reflections on the Psalms*, 10.

many examples from the Psalms to demonstrate: "God will minister true judgement" (Ps 9:8), he "forgets not the grievance of the poor" (Ps 9:12), is "father to the fatherless, a protector of widows" (Ps 68:5), God will judge the people *rightly*, he will *defend* the poor (Ps 72:2), will *rise up* to *judge*, assist the meek (Ps 76:9); God *censures* false judges and *defends* the rights of the poor: "How long will you defend the unjust, and show partiality to the wicked? Defend the weak and the fatherless; uphold the cause of the poor and the oppressed!" (Ps 82:2-3). The plaintiff should be before a just judge, asserts Lewis. Often this is in relation to Israel's defense against the surrounding pagan nations seeking the destruction of God's chosen. Those who today champion the cause of right, the heroes of children's stories and of many myths and legends, are, writes Lewis, "acting almost as 'judges' in the old Hebrew sense: so is the modern solicitor (and I have known such) who does unpaid work for poor clients to save them from wrong."[11]

However, Lewis forces a distinction. He asserts that the Christian concept of God's judgement, one of unattainable purity, against which we fail, leads not to vindication but to mercy. Many civil actions may be based on wrong in the first place, so mercy and reconciliation must be the touchstone if we are to avoid self-righteousness. In seeking judicial justice against the other do we often forget our own faults? Lewis quite correctly seeks a balance between the Hebrew and the Christian concepts of judgement; that is, distinct to the model that the churches sought down the centuries to replace the Hebrew model with (a form of supersessionism?): "Our quarrels provide a very good example of the way in which the Christian and Jewish conceptions differ, while yet both should be kept in mind."[12]

Lewis seeks to closely compare the Jewish conception of a civil judgement with the Christian—but this is that of a defendant, not a plaintiff; Lewis is forced to stress how the writers of the Psalms never present this. This, what seems to Lewis to be constant appealing, may in certain circumstances lead to an accusation of self-righteousness.[13] But self-righteousness can be cancelled-out by humility. Lewis therefore argues that God is the accuser—Psalm 50—and how this can be juxtaposed with

---

11   Lewis, *Reflections on the Psalms*, 11.
12   Lewis, *Reflections on the Psalms*, 12.
13   Lewis, *Reflections on the Psalms*, 14.

7. The Psalms II:Judgements and Cursings—Imprecatory Poems

the plaintiff's genuine humility: "Do not enter into judgement with your servant, O LORD, for no one living is righteous before you" (Ps 143:2.) But, according to Lewis, there are protestations of innocence:

> O LORD my God, if I have done this,
>   if there is wrong in my hands,
> if I have repaid my ally with harm
>   or plundered my foe without cause,
> then let the enemy pursue and overtake me,
>   trample my life to the ground,
>   and lay my soul in the dust.
>   Ps 7:3–5 (Cf. Ps 35:12–14

Lewis, however, skirts dangerously close to a form of anti-Semitism by accusing: "All this of course has its spiritual danger. It leads into that typically Jewish prison of self-righteousness which Our Lord so often terribly rebuked."[14] However, he pulls back by claiming a distinction between the idea that one is *in the right* as compared to the conviction that petitioner is righteous. In the absence of genuine righteousness the second option is a delusion. In relation to other peoples, they often were in the right. But, notes Lewis, the desire for justice must not be equated with the demand for vengeance, and vengeance must not be allowed to turn over into cursings.[15]

In the end, all this talk about judgement is about righteousness, or to invoke the old Anglo-Saxon word used in early English translations of the New Testament around the sixth to tenth centuries: *Rihtwis, Rightwis*, or *rightwise*;[16] used especially in the translation of Paul's epistles.[17] To be

---

14   Lewis, *Reflections on the Psalms*, 15.

15   Lewis, *Reflections on the Psalms*, 16.

16   From the Anglo-Saxon (Old English), *Rihtwis*, "rightly," "correctly," "justly," hence "justified;" into the Middle English *rightwise, rightwis*, "righteous," "just;" "right," "justifiable."

17   Early, or Old English (essentially Anglo Saxon) was one of very few vernacular languages the Bible was translated into; that is, the Gospels and some other books from Jerome's Latin *Vulgate*, which at the time was the standard Bible in Western Europe. An English translation of the Psalms was in use prior to the Synod of Whitby (664AD). The Venerable Bede (c.673–c.735) translated the Gospel of John into Anglo Saxon English in his later years; however, apart from references to it, it remains lost. It is with the House of Wessex (875–999) that translations abound. In church circles, Jerome's Latin *Vulgate*

right with God, *Elohim*, is to be obedient to the Law, the commandments. Hence, the Hebraic injunction of being in the right as a plaintiff: "If we diligently observe this entire commandment before the LORD our God, as he has commanded us, we will be in the right."[18] Christians may be justified, *Rihtwis*, through faith in the anointed Yeshua because of his commandment of love, disinterested *agapē*, but is this not underpinned by the Mosaic Law, framed by the Torah? "For truly I tell you, until heaven and earth pass away, not one iota, not one stroke of a letter, will pass from the law until all is accomplished."[19]

2. CURSINGS . . . SELF-RIGHTEOUSNESS

Imprecatory psalms relate to judgement in that rather than submissively placing oneself before God and accepting the absolute perfect wisdom of God in judgement on oneself, the Psalmist, in imprecations and frustration (even hatred, vengeance) petitions—even demands—judgment, misfortune, and calamity: these poets even curse troublemakers, enemies, in particular those defined as God's enemies. Ironically, it can be warranted to assert that Lewis tackles these psalms from a typically disinterested, pietistically Anglican, approach redolent of establishment and civic religion.[20] He notes how many of these verses are redolent of hatred and heat: anger. They often demand vengeance. While invoking judgment, the Jews claim their status (often as outsiders and different from the gentile tribes) before God as justification.

Like so many people today in the West who are filled with horror at the ending of Psalm 137, Lewis almost automatically objects to the infanticide called for: "Happy shall they be who take your little ones and dash them against the rock!" (Ps 137:9). Is Lewis correct to criticize this sentiment? Writing having lived through World War Two, perhaps

---

was the standard; vernacular translations were made to complement, and for hearing and understanding by the laity! A complete Old English Bible was therefore rare, but the most popular books to be translated after the Gospels were those of the Pentateuch, and Paul's epistles: Alfred the Great (849–899) used this material to influence the foundations of English law: civil and criminal.

18   Deut 6:25.

19   Matt 5:18.

20   Significant imprecatory psalms are Psalm 69 and Psalm 109; expressing imprecatorial sentiment are generally considered to be Psalms 5, 6, 11, 12, 35, 37, 40, 52, 54, 56, 57, 58, 59, 79, 83, 94, 137, 139, and 143.

7. The Psalms II:Judgements and Cursings—Imprecatory Poems

the pietistic, mild-mannered Anglicans (Lewis's contemporaries) who would also have voiced objections to Psalm 137:9 might have stopped to consider how many babies were killed—burned alive—in the allied carpet bombing of German and Japanese cities? But somehow that was actual and hidden; Psalm 137 is open and an invitation to a blessing. And Lewis's concern is how this injunction jars in the flow of an otherwise beautiful poetic lament for enslavement and exodus: "Even more devilish in one verse is the, otherwise beautiful, psalm 137 where a blessing is pronounced on anyone who will snatch up a Babylonian baby and beat its brains out against the pavement."[21] Not the sort of sentiment for Lewis's polite, mild-mannered, pietistic Anglicans to endorse, yet, Lewis gave talks on basic theology to RAF bomber crews during the Second World War; the crews were then blessed by RAF Chaplains (ordained priests)—many of whom were prepared to bless the bombs and the aircraft, in their endeavors in carpet bombing of German cities, with incendiaries and high explosives: is it right to name Lewis a hypocrite on this point? The Hebrew psalmist and priest may have called for a blessing on those who were to kill the children of their enemies, but none, we may assume, were *actually* killed. It may be asserted that this represent a double-standard that is often invoked when the ancient Hebrews in the past, or Jews today, are criticized by gentiles/pagans/heathens, and is reminiscent of Jesus's question about sawdust as compared to a plank of wood in the eye! (Matt 7:3.)[22]

Lewis naturally brings up Psalm 109, filled with judgement and censorship against the ungodly man: but this invective seems to be addressed not to God in absolute terms but to an earthly judge. Therefore, one only has to remember how certain criminals were sentenced and subject to severe conditions in prison to see where the author of the psalm is coming from. Lewis notes in particular in five verses:[23]

---

21   Lewis, *Reflections on the Psalms*, 17–18.

22   The psalmists did not actually kill children—they did not take vengeance into their own hands, but surrendered it to God. The bomber crews, by contrast, actively killed children. That said, it is the seeming delight in the death of children that is so distasteful, something the bomber crews took no delight in.

23   Lewis, *Reflections on the Psalms*, 21.

A HEBRAIC INKLING

> When he is tried, let him be found guilty;
> let his prayer be counted as sin. (v. 6)
>
> May his days be few;
> may another seize his position. (v. 7)
>
> May his children wander about and beg;
> may they be driven out of the ruins they inhabit. (v. 9)
>
> May there be no one to do him a kindness,
> nor anyone to pity his orphaned children. (v. 11)
>
> May the iniquity of his father be remembered before the LORD,
> and do not let the sin of his mother be blotted out. (v. 13)

Despite the fact that this jars with a modern Western judiciary, this does, considers Lewis, sound like a plaintiff before a human judge, and we err if we forget that it is only with the age of Romanticism in Europe in the early nineteenth century that individuals are considered immune from the sins and crimes of their relatives.[24] The problem is that vengeance is often mistakenly taken to be a human prerogative.[25] So perhaps we must see this psalm as expressing anger and frustration.[26]

Lewis is often concerned where a psalm will develop with beauty, poetic wisdom, and then disquietingly voice vengeance. He notes how Psalm 143 proceeds "in a strain that brings tears to the eyes, adds in the twelfth, almost like an afterthought 'and of thy goodness slay mine enemies.'"[27] But why is this a problem? Did not God aid the ancient Hebrews when they were forced to defend themselves, vastly outnumbered, against the powerful pagan nations that surrounded and preyed upon them?

The honesty with which the Hebrews called for a blessing on those who were prepared to kill the babies of their enemies and oppressors was at least candid, truthful, and authentic, whereas Lewis's Christian West simply never made the connection between what they were doing and the honesty of Psalm 137. This was an example of how for Lewis the "common experience"

---

24   Lewis, *Reflections on the Psalms*, 17.

25   "... it is written, 'Vengeance is Mine, I will repay,' says the LORD." Deut 32:35; cf. Rom 12:17–19

26   Lewis, *Reflections on the Psalms*, 18f.

27   Lewis, *Reflections on the Psalms*, 18. Other examples of this discontinuity for Lewis can be found in Psalms 23 (v. 5), 139 (v. 19).

7. The Psalms II: Judgements and Cursings—Imprecatory Poems

in imprecatory psalms can be seen allegorically.[28] This is, for Lewis, an example of frustration, powerlessness, "resentment, expressing itself with perfect freedom, without disguise, without self-consciousness, without shame—as few but children would express it today." He notes how in ancient and oriental cultures hatred was not veiled for the sake of social propriety, politeness.[29] Also, warns Lewis, just because it is written in the Bible does not automatically make the comment good and pious; we must, he adds, face the hatred as "festering, gloating, undisguised."[30] Such sentiments and actions, if common to humanity in its fallen—postlapsarian—condition, should be in the Bible.[31]

Lewis shows concern: we cannot, he asserts, excuse the poets because they were not Christian. After all, criticism of imprecatory sentiments can be justified from the Mosaic Law itself: "You shall not hate in your heart anyone of your kin; you shall reprove your neighbor, or you will incur guilt yourself. You shall not take vengeance or bear a grudge against any of your people, but you shall love your neighbor as yourself: I am the LORD." (Lev 19:17–18; Lewis also cites Exod 23:4–5, Prov 24:17 and 25:21). It is here that Lewis notes how the New Testament is an echo and affirmation, in many ways, of the Hebrew Bible: The New Testament "repeated, reinforced, continued, refined, and sublimated, the Judaic ethics."[32] But then should not the righteous rejoice when justice is meted on perpetrators of evil, sinners, deluded fanatics who oppress, and echo the psalmist crying out "Surely there is a reward for the righteous; surely there is a God who judges on earth" (Ps 58:9–11)?

---

28   Lewis, *Reflections on the Psalms*, 19

29   Lewis, *Reflections on the Psalms*, 19f. By comparison, today in the West merely expressing an opinion, or a biblical truth, about another person's sexual behavior is legally classified as a hate crime!

30   Lewis, *Reflections on the Psalms*, 19.

31   And remember that there is an awful lot of political activities, sheer willfulness, in the Book of the Judges that is unacceptable before God, unacceptable, that is, to the Hebrew descendants and to the Jewish-Messiah-following Christian. For example the commonly cited sentence, "In those days Israel had no king; all the people did whatever seemed right in their own eyes" (Judg 21:25; see also: Judg 17:6; 18:1; 19:1; 20:27, 28; 21:25. See also related: Ezek 30:13; Hab 1:14; Hos 3:4; 10:3; Isa 3:7; Jer 13:18; 1 Kgs 22:17, 47; Mic 4:9; Prov 30:27), which is precisely the situation that has bedeviled the West, since Lewis's death, in its post-Christian, anti-Semitic, postmodern-societal-confusion: everyone does what s/he finds enjoyable with governments having to, post haste, a posteriori, sort out legislation to protect individual identity-politic groups who demand elite-status-preferential-treatment, often contrary to the Mosaic law and the Decalogue.

32   Lewis, *Reflections on the Psalms*, 23.

A HEBRAIC INKLING

It is important to note, when we consider Lewis trying to justify or repudiate imprecatorial sentiments in the Psalms, that we also find such severe statements in the New Testament: the Hebrew Bible is not alone in containing imprecations.[33] These are uttered by Jesus, but also by Paul and the other epistle writers: those who are accused, those subject to eternal damnation, those crying out for judgement, justice, and for the LORD to avenge them . . . .

Whilst studying at King's College London, I conversed over lunch with a traditional ultra-Orthodox Rabbi, the conversation moved onto a realized eschaton. He noted the Hebraic accuracy of Jesus's parables, if not a one-to-one correspondence with judgement illustrations in the Jewish Torah and Mishnah, and recounted a story from his father, also a Rabbi, who survived the Holocaust death camps:

> There were three groups of Jewish prisoners in the concentration camps awaiting extermination. The first group were those who sought to co-operate with the Germans, to deny, refute, their Jewish status—"We want to be good Germans, just like you," they said, free us and we will be obedient to you all, we will forget Israel: we are good Germans." This group died in the gas chambers and went to hell. A second group were obedient to the demands of the SS, but held to their faith and their status as God's chosen people and went as lambs to the slaughter. These went to heaven but some to a cleansing first.[34]

---

33   For example: "But woe to you, scribes and Pharisees, hypocrites! For you lock people out of the kingdom of heaven. For you do not go in yourselves, and when others are going in, you stop them" (Matt 23:13). "He answered, 'The one who has dipped his hand into the bowl with me will betray me. The Son of Man goes as it is written of him, but woe to that one by whom the Son of Man is betrayed! It would have been better for that one not to have been born" (Matt 26:23–24). "Let anyone be accursed who has no love for the Lord. Our Lord, come!" (1 Cor 16:22). "But even if we or an angel from heaven should proclaim to you a gospel contrary to what we proclaimed to you, let that one be accursed! As we have said before, so now I repeat, if anyone proclaims to you a gospel contrary to what you received, let that one be accursed!" (Gal 1:8–9). "I wish those who unsettle you would castrate themselves!" (Gal 5:12). "Alexander the coppersmith did me great harm; the Lord will pay him back for his deeds" (2 Tim 4:14). "[T]hey cried out with a loud voice, 'Sovereign Lord, holy and true, how long will it be before you judge and avenge our blood on the inhabitants of the earth?'" (Rev 6:10).

34   There appeared to be an un-acknowledged element of Roman Catholic/Orthodox Christian eschatological thinking here: i.e. purgatory/purgation. Although the Jewish beliefs about the afterlife are flexible and varied some do appear to exhibit some concept of change/cleansing. Then there is the Jewish joke: "There's no heaven or hell: we all go to the same place when we die, where Moses and Rabbi Akiva give constant and everlasting classes on the Bible and the Talmud. For the righteous this is eternal

7. The Psalms II:Judgements and Cursings—Imprecatory Poems

The third group did not co-operate, they decried the SS at every turn, even mocked them: your 1,000 year Reich will be over before the end of the year, your Fuhrer is an insane clown, history will wipe you out, you will burn in hell: for their truth-speaking they were summarily shot or bludgeoned to death by the SS and the Gestapo, as they stood. This group went straight to heaven.

Should the Jews being herded into cattle trucks to be shipped to the extermination camps not have spoken imprecatory satire to the guards and the SS commandant? Should they rather have spoken reconciling religious sentiment acknowledging a difference of lifestyle and identity politics? Who was right? Are we to reject Stephen's speech to the Jewish religious authorities (Acts 7) as imprecatorial intolerance, for that matter should it be condemned as a "hate" crime? Do Jews and Christians have a right, divinely bequeathed, which they must use to challenge wrong, even evil, providing they state recognizable facts and turn the other cheek if attacked for speaking out? Can truth ever be reconciled to falsehood?

3. MORTALITY: DEATH

Lewis moves on to death: mortality and life beyond the earthly, the corporeal. God's working with the Jews, forming them to be the chosen, did not involve the promise of eternal and everlasting paradisal life. No, any sense of this was withheld: get life on earth sorted out properly and salvation and eternal life will follow: but there are hints, promises, whispered on the breath of the prophets—individuals who prove, yet the actual is withheld till . . . the Messiah. The psalmists are preoccupied with these questions. Lewis notes how there is more than enough evidence for sifting, for judgement, for a separation of the dead—eventually. The psalmist urges this judgement upon those who deserve to be "cast down," "crushed," in this life (Ps 17); the cost of

---

bliss, while for the wicked this is eternal suffering." See Haaretz website: https://www.haaretz.com/jewish/.premium-what-is-the-jewish-afterlife-like-1.5362876. See also: II Macc 12:44–45. See also: "[T]he teaching of the Shammaites:* 'In the last judgment day there shall be three classes of souls: the righteous shall at once be written down for the life everlasting; the wicked, for Gehenna; but those whose virtues and sins counterbalance one another shall go down to Gehenna and float up and down until they rise purified; for of them it is said: 'I will bring the third part into the fire and refine them as silver is refined, and try them as gold is tried' (Zech. 13:9)." Jewish Encyclopaedia website, Kaufmann Kohler, "Purgatory," http://www.jewishencyclopedia.com/articles/12446-purgatory
* Jewish scholars, Schools of Thought, from the intertestamental period: *Beit Shammai*. (House of Shammai)

deliverance is too much for the merely human to pay: redeem, redemption is the language, we cannot ransom our souls, or pay the debt (Ps 49): "The price of salvation is one that only the Son of God could pay.... But apparently the Hebrew poets meant something quite different and much more ordinary. He means merely that death is inevitable."[35] Because none can buy, none can purchase from God life that shall never end. We are enslaved to personified evil through the fall, through original sin. Because of the place and role of evil that underpins our death, the psalmists speak in the language of economy, of money: ransom and remit, cost and debt. Therefore, as Lewis notes, there is little or no belief in a future life in the Hebrew Bible: "The word translated 'soul' in our version of the Psalms means simply 'life'; the word translated 'hell' means simply 'the land of the dead,' the state of all the dead, good and bad alike, Sheol."[36]

The Hebrew concept of death, often a place in the Psalms, is Sheol: a place of conscious existence after death; as with other religions in the surrounding nations, this existence is bereft of the intensity, joy, and fulfilment that the resurrection brings. The Greek *Hades* is, like *Sheol*, neither hell or heaven, but a thin, nihilistic, apparent existence to be endured, to be borne, suffered, the Sheol of the Psalms is filled with regret, vagueness, marginality. This pit of seemingly nothingness, for Lewis, is a living death. The thinness of life, this *fallen state* (though here Lewis is reviving, via Augustine, the ancient Hebrew story of the fall into original sin), leads to the grave, and speculation as to this persistent endurance. Lewis refers in support a number of psalms: see opposite

What we have in the Psalms is a temporal paradox: have we been saved yet or is salvation still to come?

Lewis notes how Judaism changes much as it moves and develops towards the intertestamental period, particularly following the Maccabees: "The Sadducees held to the old view. The Pharisees, and apparently many more, believed in the life of the world to come."[37] By contrast, Lewis notes how the many powerful nations that surrounded ancient Israel were to a degree obsessed with the afterlife and generating it, in many ways, themselves. In Egypt it appeared, to Lewis, that the main business of life was in controlling and ordering the afterlife. God, wrote Lewis, clearly did not want the chosen

---

35 Lewis, *Reflections on the Psalms*, 30.
36 Lewis, *Reflections on the Psalms*, 31.
37 Lewis, *Reflections on the Psalms*, 35.

7. The Psalms II: Judgements and Cursings—Imprecatory Poems

people to follow this path: they must focus on this life and prepare for the Messiah! But this had to be more than worldly hope.

Remember how short my time is— for what vanity you have created all mortals! Ps 89:46 LORD, let me know my end, and what is the measure of my days; let me know how fleeting my life is. You have made my days a few handbreadths, and my lifetime is as nothing in your sight. Surely everyone stands as a mere breath. Ps 39:4–5 When we look at the wise, they die; fool and dolt perish together and leave their wealth to others. Their graves are their homes for ever, their dwelling-places to all generations, Ps 49:10–11a	What profit is there in my death, if I go down to the Pit? Will the dust praise you? Will it tell of your faithfulness? Ps 30:9 For in death there is no remembrance of you; in Sheol who can give you praise? Ps 6:5 When their breath departs, they return to the earth; on that very day their plans perish. Ps 146:4 Do you work wonders for the dead? Do the shades rise up to praise you? Is your steadfast love declared in the grave, or your faithfulness in Abaddon?* Are your wonders known in the darkness, or your saving help in the land of forgetfulness? Ps 88:10–12 [*: *place of destruction, the realm of the dead*] [T]hey will go to the company of their ancestors, who will never again see the light. Ps 49:19	*And yet the psalmists appears to yearn for, what Lewis terms, "Christian salvation:* O LORD, you brought up my soul from Sheol, restored me to life from among those gone down to the Pit. Ps 30:3 The snares of death encompassed me; the pangs of Sheol laid hold on me; I suffered distress and anguish. Then I called on the name of the LORD: O LORD, I pray, save my life! Ps 116:3 *But is this to do with joy and health, life in our earthly existence?*

As Lewis commented:

> Century after century, by blows which seem to us merciless, by defeat, deportation, and massacre, it was hammered into the Jews that earthly prosperity is not in fact the certain, or even the probable, reward of seeing God. Every hope was disappointed. The

lesson taught in the Book of Job was grimly illustrated in practice. Such experience would surely have destroyed a religion which had no other center than the hope of peace and plenty with "every man under his own vine and his own fig tree."* And of course many did "fall off." But the astonishing thing is that the religion is not destroyed.[38]
[*: Micah 4:4]

4. CONDONE: CONNIVANCE

The psalmists' poems are, for Lewis, excellent at identifying the types of sin—explicit religious sins—that corrupt and separate the human from God. But Lewis considers that they are at fault in their criticism by committing the same sin: offering hate to those who are hateful enemies of God? They connive, they secretly allow, they conspire to do something unlawful or harmful. Is Lewis right? Or is he missing the point? Do they, as God's chosen, have warrant for such language and behavior while the enemies of God do not?[39] However, imprecatorial divine curses aimed at God's opponents do not sit well with a Christian mindset (or what is taken to be a Christian mindset?).

The risks here that Lewis sees in the psalms are related to vanity, falsehood, idolatry (Pss 31:7; 50:8; 41:4–6; 139:21–22), all of which raises the specter of Pharisaism.[40] How do we square these problems with the teaching of "our Lord"—Jesus, the anointed savior? True, writes Lewis, times have not really changed if one considers the state of the media, and gossip amongst people in his day (and today!).[41] Lewis does say that we must not see ourselves as superior to them when we voice criticisms, but that we should see ourselves as not good enough, and even as inferior gentiles:[42]

> We are not good enough to cope with all the temptations, nor clever enough to cope with all the problems, which an evening spent in such society produces. The temptation is to condone, to connive at; by our words, looks and laughter, to "consent."[43]

38   Lewis, *Reflections on the Psalms*, 36–37.
39   See, Pss 5:10; 10:15; 28:4; 31:17–18; 35:4–6; 40:14–15; 58:6–11; 69:22–28; 109:6–15; 140:9–10.
40   Lewis, *Reflections on the Psalms*, 56–57.
41   Lewis, *Reflections on the Psalms*, 58f.
42   Lewis, *Reflections on the Psalms*, 58f.
43   Lewis, *Reflections on the Psalms*, 61.

7. The Psalms II: Judgements and Cursings—Imprecatory Poems

Often the solution, if we are not to judge, however much we feel justified, is to avoid being complicit is silence. The psalmists were correct, for Lewis, if the "good man" seeks to avoid the scornful and the ungodly their concern should be ruled by lead us not into temptation.[44] Lewis therefore places emphasis and warning on "the sins of the tongue"[45] more than the sins of violence from an age of the sword: "Their throat is an open sepulcher, they flatter" (Ps 5:10); "under his tongue is ungodliness and vanity"; "deceitful lips" (Ps 12:3); "lying lips" (Ps 31:20); "words full of deceit" (36:3); "whispering(s)" (Ps 41:7); "lies that cut like razors" (Ps 52:3); "pitiless jeering" (Ps 102:8).[46] Do we not shut our eyes to our own sins?

5. THE PSALMS: INTERIM CONCLUSION

So, what can we conclude so far on Lewis's understanding of the Psalms and what does this tell us of his respect or criticism of Judaism?

In *Reflections in the Psalms* Lewis began by dealing, literally in the first half of the book, with critical problems in the Psalms: imprecatorial judgementalism, self-righteousness, cursings, death, and he finds these poems wanting. It is easy for a middle-aged Anglican, steeped in establishment piety, on a secure, publicly funded salary in a university at the heart of the establishment to criticize.[47] However, even if one is not completely sympathetic to Lewis's critique, there is still a form of redemption for it when he deals with connivance, whereby society can be blind to its own sins, only identifying them in others—in this case, the ancient Hebrews (and our criticisms of the Hebraic mindset). The problem for Lewis, as we have seen, is the statements in the Psalms confessing hatred for God's enemies because they are a clear contradiction of Jesus's teaching that we should love our enemies. Lewis notes how mid-twentieth-century British society approved of such a contradiction of God-given natural law. This moral free-for-all has become much worse in the sixty years since Lewis wrote, particularly in the now non-religious

---

44   Lewis, *Reflections on the Psalms*, 63.
45   Lewis, *Reflections on the Psalms*, 63f.
46   Lewis, *Reflections on the Psalms*, 64.
47   For many of Lewis's contemporaries the belief that appeared to dominate the British establishment was that they had arrived at the perfect society (the British pagan nation state, ruling an empire spanning the globe) and in most cases of dispute and difference, the end justified the means.

nature of British society. A multi-faith perspective is tolerated by the British establishment, but no religious person must offer criticism of this moral nihilism. Anyone who offers contradiction or criticism is then accused of speaking a "hate-crime," the accuser suffering from a form of politicized paranoia: which merely points to the encroaching mental health crisis in contemporary British society. (But this is post 1960s and post Lewis's death.) For Lewis, the psalmists hate for the haters of God is merely to condone the so-called hate: they are conniving. So what value is there for Lewis in connivance and the other psalmist sins he has been criticizing?

The Psalms were written by God's chosen people; a people forged by God, taken from one ordinary person (Abraham), warts and all, and given their centuries of oppression are they wrong to speak out? Are they wrong to speak truth about how they feel? The great weakness in Christendom has always been for any criticism of the Jews to slip over into anti-Semitism: the pagans are, as ever, un-reformed, unreconstructed, and never really understanding Hebraic justice, the demands of the plaintiff . . . and, for that matter, for Hebrew humor.

Is Lewis missing the point? Hating hate? "Do I not hate those who hate you, LORD, and abhor those who are in rebellion against you? I have nothing but hatred for them . . ." (Ps 139:21–23)—is this a nonsensical double negative of sorts! Can some of the psalmists' comments be interpreted as rhetorical? The Psalms do not actually encourage their users to take vengeance. They always surrender retribution to God, and do not encourage taking it oneself. The Psalmists are weak and need divine intervention: vengeance is mine, says the Lord.[48] So if anything, the Psalms encourage one to be honest about one's situation and to pass vengeance over to God, rather than to take it yourself.

---

48   "Vengeance is mine, and recompense, for the time when their foot shall slip; because the day of their calamity is at hand, their doom comes swiftly." Deut 32:35. See, also, "Do not avenge yourselves, beloved, but leave room for God's wrath. For it is written: "Vengeance is Mine; I will repay, says the Lord." Rom 12:17–19.

8

The Psalms III:
A Hebraic Doctrine of Creation

"You visit the earth and water it, you greatly enrich it; the river of God is full of water; you provide the people with grain, for so you have prepared it. You water its furrows abundantly, settling its ridges, softening it with showers, and blessing its growth. You crown the year with your bounty; your wagon tracks overflow with richness. The pastures of the wilderness overflow, the hills gird themselves with joy, the meadows clothe themselves with flocks, the valleys deck themselves with grain, they shout and sing together for joy."

PSALM 65:9–13

"Thus when the Psalmists speak of 'seeing' the Lord, or long to 'see' Him, most of them mean something that happened to them in the Temple. Thus in Psalm 68,

> 'It is well seen, O God, how thou goest:* how thou, my God and King, goest in the sanctuary. The singers go before, the minstrels follow after: in the midst are the damsels playing with the timbrels.' (vv. 24–25),

it is almost as if the poet said, 'Look, here He comes'. If I had been there I should have seen the musicians and the girls with the tambourines; in addition, as another thing, I might or might not have (as we say) 'felt' the presence of God. The ancient worshipper would have been aware of no such dualism."

C. S. LEWIS[1]

1. INTRODUCTION

Lewis understood that the Psalms can give us a sound doctrine of creation in terms of a model that complements the account in the Book of Genesis, that is in some circumstances comparable to the creation myths from surrounding gentile cultures and pagan nations—including Ancient Greece. What exactly is this understanding?

---

1   Lewis, *Reflections on the Psalms*, 41. * : Lewis notes how this was perhaps sung while the Ark itself was carried around.

2. A PSALMIC DOCTRINE OF CREATION: "AND GOD SAID..."

At the center of any doctrine of creation is the biblical account: the Book of Genesis, the prologue to John's Gospel, and, for example, Psalms 104 and 148. The Genesis account tells us that, as Francis Watson has demonstrated, the act of creation (if we acknowledge the centrality of the biblical account) is a speech-act.[2] This is quite different from many of the creation myths found in ancient religions: in Genesis God speaks and things happen. Watson shows how the speech-act is crucial to creation: God conceives and speaks, and creation is created. But not all in an instant. This is also a "fabrication model" for Watson: objects do not magically appear, complete, existence is not instantaneous, they are *constructed*, they *develop*, they *evolve*. Genesis shows how God does initially create *instantaneously* by the speech-act and then through this fabrication model, but God *employs* creatures as the womb out of which the others proceed. The Psalms speaks of "the womb of the day," "the womb of the morning" (Ps 110:3). Creation has a specific nature and it is not inherently divine, creation is separate and different from God: stars and planets—according to the Genesis account—are created objects, not "gods," as they were in many ancient Near Eastern religions.[3] What is more, the earth and the waters *bring forth*. Thus we find God's speech act creates heaven and earth—the speech is important—but then God also declares, "let the earth bring forth..." Therefore, at God's initiative creation creates: "And God said, 'Let the land produce living creatures according to their kinds: livestock, creatures that move along the ground, and wild animals, each according to its kind.' And it was so" (Gen 1:24). God enables the creation to form something new.[4] The opening of Genesis and the first chapter of John's Gospel illustrate the close link between creation, the creative act, and Christ: the Logos. Watson comments—from and in the revelatory context of Psalm 148, that,

> If the act of creation is accomplished through speech, then speech and act are identified, and this results in what we may call the speech-act model of divine creativity.... [T]he first and best known is the command, "Let there be light," which immediately

---

2 Watson, *Text, Church and World*, 137–53
3 And also in other parts of the Hebrew bible.
4 Watson, *Text, Church and World*, 137, 138.

8. The Psalms III: A Hebraic Doctrine of Creation

produces the desired effect—"and there was light" (Gen 1:3). In the second case, the utterance concerning the separation of sea and dry land is followed by the words, "and it was so." . . . In the third case, the same words announce the immediate fulfillment of the command that the earth should put forth vegetation (Gen 1:11). The specific speech-act implied in all three cases is that of the command, a strange command addressed to entities that do not yet exist and whose coming into being is their act of obedience to it: "For he commanded and they were created" (Ps 148:5).[5]

God has made known through scripture what is conceivable for the human mind to comprehend about the creation of reality. What is important about the creation of reality is the election of Israel and the incarnation, and the atonement: God allows us to know what is important for us to comprehend. There are limits, God-given limits: "the creator is known only insofar as he interacts with the creation."[6] The word of God in the speech-act is creation because it is the gift of God to humanity: "Ever since the creation of the world his eternal power and divine nature, invisible though they are, have been understood and seen through the things he has made" (Rom 1:19). Therefore, from the created order we can come to some knowledge of God, but not of the true nature of God or the necessity for our salvation: reality reveals a creator, but whether we can clearly and rightly perceive the creator is another matter, and given our state defined by original sin, we are left without excuse. Nonetheless, creation, as the Psalms assert, sings of God's glory because creation is a gracious act by the gracious God. To this extent there is a strong tradition that a doctrine of creation reflects a doctrine of universal grace: "It's the grace of creation: because the gracious God has created the world, the universe, simply reflects the marks of his creating grace."[7]

As Karl Barth noted, The world reveals God because reality is an actuality, and because of time's movement it is always a possibility: growth and change. This is at the heart of redemption: the incarnation and resurrection.[8] Therefore, one can't conceive of creation separate from Christ.[9] As Maximus the Confessor (c.580–662) wrote, "[t]he one who is

5	Watson, *Text, Church and World*, 137–53
6	Gunton, *Revelation and Reason*, 22.
7	Gunton, *Revelation and Reason*, 22.
8	See, Barth, *CD*, IV/3, §.72, 769
9	Brunner, *The Mediator*, 262. See also, Gunton, *Revelation and Reason*, 249f.

initiated into the infinite power of the resurrection knows the purpose for which God knowingly created all things and loves all things."[10] This is very much Lewis's approach to creation. However, as we will see, from the psalmic model of creation, it is important to get the right balance. If too much emphasis is placed on creation and not on soteriology—with the renewal of creation—the Hebraic economy and history of salvation (the incarnation, cross, and resurrection) becomes marginalized, rendering one's understanding of creation flawed. Likewise, if too great an emphasis is placed on salvation to the detriment of creation and the created order, then you will have a skewed understanding of humanity's importance over and above creation: "If you overweight the Incarnation and the cross at the expense of creation then you tend to have a conception of salvation out of the world, rather than in the world."[11] The resurrection and the anticipation of a new creation (Rev 21) bears witness to this, creation is ongoing and its fulfillment is in the future: "To say that something is created is to say that it is on its way to being made; full knowledge will be granted at the end—this will be full revelation."[12]

So, what understanding of creation did Lewis read from the Hebrew Bible generally and the Book of the Psalms specifically?

3. AN AGRARIAN PEOPLE: A RURAL ECONOMY

Like the surrounding nations and peoples, the ancient Hebrews were an agrarian economy with small villages and cities merging seamlessly with the land and its crops. The majority of people were rural, living off the land: livestock and crops. In the establishment of the ethical and religious structure of society under Moses for the Hebrew people, key festivals were a thanksgiving for the life and produce of the land: "Celebrate the Festival of Harvest with the first fruits of the crops you sow in your field. Celebrate the Festival of Ingathering at the end of the year, when you gather in your crops from the field." (Exod 23:16). How is this understanding of creation presented in the Psalms? How does it define worship? Given the importance to the ancient Hebrews of the Psalms, and singing, Lewis postulates that we can see something analogous in a contemporary picture of a farm-laborer attending services in the village church. That is, in key festivals

---

10   Maximus the Confessor, *Centuries*, 1108A–B. In Maximus, *The Ascetic Life*.
11   Gunton, *Revelation and Reason*, 29.
12   Gunton, *Revelation and Reason*, 66

8. The Psalms III: A Hebraic Doctrine of Creation

from Christmas, Easter, Pentecost, but especially Harvest Thanksgiving.[13] However, much of this church attendance was tied up with folk traditions (Plough Monday, Mummers Plays, Whit Monday, or the memory of such ceremonies and music, with traditions tied up with the land and its fertility), just as it was for the ancient Hebrews, for example, festivals and celebrations when the harvest was gathered in. Lewis saw this farm laborer not as an occasional visitor to church, going out of obligation, but as baptized and confirmed, a regular member: a committed Christian. Like the ancient Hebrew he was a peasant, very close to the soil. He had never heard of religious music and festivals as separate from tilling the soil, the fundamental activity of agriculture, crucially, giving thanks for the harvest without which lay famine and starvation. This rural life, this rural economy, was a single culture, notes Lewis.[14] Whether in the temple in Jerusalem or in an obscure part of Judea, the agricultural festivals of the ancient Hebrews were not simply "nice" religious ceremonies, social gatherings; they were meetings with the LORD, *YHWH*, observes Lewis.[15]

Lewis notes how when the poets write of seeing *YHWH*, indeed longing to see God, we would be in error to see this as only a desire to be religious in a "religious" social setting: they were meeting with the source and sustainer of their lives; and we should note how the rural economy is at the heart of this relationship (Gen 3:17–19). Lewis places emphasis on Psalm 68:

> Your procession, God, has come into view,
> the procession of my God and King into the sanctuary.

---

13   Though it is important to remember that the Church of England Harvest Thanksgiving service Lewis was familiar with was in many ways a Victorian invention, originally medieval, but lost, marginalized with the Reformation.

14   Lewis, *Reflections on the Psalms*, Ch. 5, 40–41. It is, however, important to remember that since Lewis wrote, British—indeed European, American, and generally global—agriculture has been subject to massive industrialization, staffed not by farm laborers living on the land but urban engineers who commute from the city to run and maintain the machinery of the chemicalized "pharms." The farm laborer cottages are now second homes for middle-class intellectuals, business leaders, etc.: these farm technicians are sitting in the cab of some giant environmentally destructive machine, insulated from a rural reality, and who in the majority would be secular-humanists, and consumers of popular music and culture, which represents and promotes an urban liberal fantasy world.

15   Lewis, *Reflections on the Psalms*, 41.

A HEBRAIC INKLING

> In front are the singers, after them the musicians;
>   with them are the young women playing the timbrels.
>
> Praise God in the great congregation;
>   praise the LORD in the assembly of Israel.
>
> Ps 68:24–26

It is, for Lewis, almost as though the poet asserts, "Look, here He comes!" The ancient Hebrew saw, and sensed the presence of God; there was for Lewis no dualism inherent in this, whereas the enlightened modern compartmentalizes the gods from "secular" life and relegates divinity to the so-called 'religious' zones of our lives, such as church gatherings. The ancient Hebrew desired above all to dwell in the house of the LORD all the days of life given, to "behold the fair beauty of the LORD" (Ps 27:4).[16]

Thus, we may assert that this would not be distinguishable from the sustenance of his life in a rural economy: there would have been frequent moments of spiritual vision and the love of God centered on communal acts of worship, radiating out into his rural joy, . . . and, yes, often hardship (Gen 3:17–19).

Lewis notes how for many at the time he was writing, the name Jew was associated, for better or for worse, stereotypically, with city finance, trade, shops and medieval money-lending (remembering that usury is a contradiction of the Mosaic Law and Christians were thus forbidden to lend money to other Christians at interest, so they asked Jews to be money lenders). However, from their creation through Abraham, though to the expulsion in 70AD and 135AD, the Jews were a rural nation, a rural people, an agrarian economy. The medieval stereotype reflects the diaspora: bereft of land they travelled, no longer the peasants or farmers of the Hebrew Bible, celebrated in the Psalms. Pre-70AD, the destruction of the temple, and 135 AD, the expulsion by the Romans from the promised land, the concept of the countryside, a rural, sylvan idyll, was yet to be invented.[17] Israel, Judaea, the promised land was approximately

---

16   Lewis, *Reflections on the Psalms*, 41.

17   It was through the late-eighteenth-century European Romantic movement (essentially in England and Germany, in poetry and painting, and to a lesser extent in music) that an idealized rural landscape was invented, almost worshipped, just as the countryside was being destroyed by the industrial revolution—as in William Blake's "dark satanic mills." At the beginning of the nineteenth century, 80 percent of the population in England lived in the countryside; by 1900, only 10 percent remained living outside of the sprawling urban development. For a general introduction, see, https://en.wikipedia.org/wiki/Romanticism

8. The Psalms III: A Hebraic Doctrine of Creation

95 percent a rural economy: towns were few and small, villages merged with the tilled land, but the Jews did not worship a rural idyll, they simply praised and thanked God for the soil, the landscape, the life on the land![18]

The Hebrew praise for the functional beauty of a landscape was also common in the ancient world: "Homer can enjoy a landscape," wrote Lewis, "but what he means by a beautiful landscape is one that is useful—good deep soil, plenty of fresh water, pasture that will make the cows really fat, and some nice timber."[19]

The psalmists, considers Lewis, are writing lyrics—songs of praise—not romantic escapism.[20] Perhaps a Western example was in much of the English folk song movement in the eighteenth through nineteenth centuries: songs were sung ceaselessly by those who had gone through a back-breaking day's work on the land, yet sang praise to the landscape, the animals and birds, the sun and the weather . . . to the glory and beauty of the God-given landscape, to their love, their families, and the rural life, and praised God in the village church on Sunday mornings:

> Lay still my fond shepherd and don't you rise yet
> It's a fine dewy morning and besides, my love, it is wet.
>
> Oh let it be wet my love and ever so cold
> I will rise my fond Floro and away to my fold.
>
> Oh no, my bright Floro, it is no such thing
> It's a bright sun a-shining and the lark is on the wing
>
> Oh the lark in the morning ariseth from her nest
> And mounts in the air with the dew on her breast,
>
> And like the pretty ploughboy she will whistle and sing
> And at night she will return to her nest again.[21]

---

18   Lewis, *Reflections on the Psalms*, 65f.

19   Lewis, *Reflections on the Psalms*, 66.

20   Lewis, *Reflections on the Psalms*, 66.

21   The earliest known version was published in a garland (a broadside containing a number of songs) called *Four Excellent New Songs*, printed in Edinburgh in 1778, though the song would have been in circulation in the oral folk tradition for at least three generations prior to publication. Many versions were collected from singers by composers and musicians, such as Cecil Sharp and Ralph Vaughan Williams (and with an earlier generation, for example, Francis James Child), in the early twentieth century, just as the folk tradition was dying out due to industrialization and urbanization, then lost with the carnage of the First World War.

A HEBRAIC INKLING

The song is not about an educated urban elite smiling at the countryside through rose-tinted lenses; like nature in the Psalms, it is about *living in* the landscape, *working* the land, *being one with* nature and the joy of rewarding hard work. Lewis notes in particular Psalm 65:

> You care for the land and water it;
>   you enrich it abundantly.
>
> The streams of God are filled with water
>   to provide the people with grain,
>   for so you have ordained it.
>
> You drench its furrows and level its ridges;
>   you soften it with showers and bless its crops.
>
> You crown the year with your bounty,
>   and your carts overflow with abundance.
>
> The grasslands of the wilderness overflow;
>   the hills are clothed with gladness.
>
> The meadows are covered with flocks
>   and the valleys are mantled with grain;
>   they shout for joy and sing.
>
>   Ps 65:9–13

Unlike the creation myths of many of the world's religions—pagan ones being favorites known by Lewis—the Hebraic revelation is clear: "Nature and God were distinct; the One had made the other; the One ruled and the other obeyed."[22] All is created by God out of nothing; nothing pre-exists. This is clearly read from the Psalms, writes Lewis, and the condition of creation (including man) is to honor the Lord in love and obedience. Creation can turn away and rebel, but it must live with the consequences.

Lewis the classicist notes the theological genius of Plato, who with no encouragement or revelation from *El Shaddai* formulated a clear "Theology of Creation in the Judaic and Christian sense" whereby the entire universe, and the conditions of temporality, time and space, does exist. This is the will of "a perfect, timeless, unconditioned God" above, outside, all made. The genius for Lewis is that Plato made this leap,

---

22   Lewis, *Reflections on the Psalms*, 66.

8. The Psalms III: A Hebraic Doctrine of Creation

perhaps with inspiration from "the Father of Lights" beyond the confines of his indigenous pagan religion.[23]

Lewis takes further this detail in his Hebraic doctrine of creation. Such a doctrine that empties nature of any sense of pagan divinity, allows creation to be a symbol of God-like action, an expression, even as an appearance from God. Lewis notes how in Psalm 19, "the searching and cleansing sun becomes an image of the searching and cleansing Law."[24] He compare this with Psalm 36:

> Your love, LORD, reaches to the heavens,
>   your faithfulness to the skies.
>
> Your righteousness is like the highest mountains,
>   your justice like the great deep.
>   You, LORD, preserve both people and animals.
>   Ps 36:5–6

Being freed from pagan notions of divinity, ordinary objects in creation can become "magnificent symbols of Divinity,"[25] without the risk of idolatry. Thus, although this can be seen as being close to the divine anthropomorphism of pagan religion (Lewis notes the Greek "gods," Zeus hurling thunderbolts, etc.), this does allow nature, as created, to manifest God's glory, and God's presence, and energy: light can be his garment; thunder can be God's voice, as he dwells in a thundercloud; God's touch may trigger an eruption, an answer, from a volcano. Thus, the created world is full of "emissaries and executors";[26] the psalmist's wind, God's messengers, flames his servants. Lewis demonstrates with reference:

> The LORD wraps himself in light as with a garment;
>   he stretches out the heavens like a tent
>   and lays the beams of his upper chambers on their waters.
> He makes the clouds his chariot
>   and rides on the wings of the wind.
> He makes winds his messengers,
>   flames of fire his servants.   Ps 104:2–4

---

23 Lewis, *Reflections on the Psalms*, 68.
24 Lewis, *Reflections on the Psalms*, 69.
25 Lewis, *Reflections on the Psalms*, 69.
26 Lewis, *Reflections on the Psalms*, 70.

> The voice of the LORD is over the waters;
>   the God of glory thunders,
>   the LORD thunders over the mighty waters.
> The voice of the LORD is powerful;
>   the voice of the LORD is majestic.
> The voice of the LORD breaks the cedars;
>   the LORD breaks in pieces the cedars of Lebanon.
>   Ps 29:3–5

> He parted the heavens and came down;
>   dark clouds were under his feet.
> He mounted the cherubim and flew;
>   he soared on the wings of the wind.
> He made darkness his covering, his canopy around him—
>   the dark rain clouds of the sky.
> Out of the brightness of his presence clouds advanced,
>   with hailstones and bolts of lightning.
> The LORD thundered from heaven;
>   the voice of the Most High resounded.
>   Ps 18:9–13

> He who looks at the earth, and it trembles,
>   who touches the mountains, and they smoke.
>   Ps 104:32

There is no immortality, no *ex nihilo*, in them, they are playing out a role *for* God. Scientists, thinks Lewis, regard creation as mere fact, data, but in a Hebraic doctrine of creation the natural world is an "achievement,"[27] to compliment and praise God, and reveal God's glory.

To the writers of the Psalms nature is *enchanted* (an appropriate word given that, while creation may not be God, or an extension, panentheistically, of God, the natural world is not simply dead, meaningless matter). The writers of the Psalms are enchanted with what appears to be the stability and endurance, for Lewis, the solidity, of creation. Lewis invokes the Hebrew concept of *emeth*: firmness, truth and faithfulness, sureness and reliability, not, he claims, nature as *vague* or *phantasmal*. Again, Lewis demonstrates with reference:

---

27 Lewis, *Reflections on the Psalms*, 71.

8. The Psalms III: A Hebraic Doctrine of Creation

By the word of the LORD were
  the heavens made,
  their starry host by the breath of his mouth.
For he spoke, and it came to be; he commanded, and it stood firm.
                      Ps 33: 6 & 9

[W]ho formed the mountains by your power,
  having armed yourself with strength,
who stilled the roaring of the seas,
  the roaring of their waves,
  and the turmoil of the nations.
            Ps 65:6–7

He set the earth on its foundations;
  it can never be moved.
You covered it with the watery depths as with a garment;
  the waters stood above the mountains.
But at your rebuke the waters fled,
  at the sound of your thunder they took to flight;
                Ps 104:5–7

Let them praise the name of the LORD,
  for at his command they were created,
and he established them for ever and ever—
  he issued a decree that will never pass away.
           Ps 148, 6

But this is not abstract creation theory, notes Lewis: "Notice how in Psalm 136 the poet passes from God's creation of Nature to the delivering of Israel out of Egypt: both are equally great deeds, great victories."[28]

Given this agrarian nature of the ancient Hebrews and the Jews of the intertestamental era, such an understanding formed metaphors for their religious language, and affected every aspect of their lives, concerned as they were with the weather and growth of their crops—to an almost neurotic state. (Talk to any arable farmer or market gardener today and the same is true, though now they have insurance and government subsidy to soften the blow of crop failure, and even famine.) There is one important difference, says Lewis, in this context between Israel and the surrounding pagan/gentile nations. Lewis notes how Israel exhibit a detachment of sorts, they express a pleasure and interest that is no utilitarian use to subsistence farming.

28   Lewis, *Reflections on the Psalms*, 71.

A HEBRAIC INKLING

Lewis notes how in Psalm 104—devoted to creation and the natural world—God is praised for the creatures useful to people: livestock, grape vines, cereals, but water courses where animals can drink, forests for birds to roost, wild expanses where fauna can live independent of man all have their place in creation. Lions have their place at night, away from field laborers in the day, and the seas and ocean have a life of their own.[29] What does this mean? There is a degree of detachment, disinterestedness, in this. Praise for the place of dangerous wild animals in creation is difficult for cattle herders to tolerate. This is unlike, considers Lewis, the kindness expressed to animals by an urban elite today, insulated from the dangers. The ancient Hebrews were acknowledging that creation was from God and all in creation had a right to exist and coexist, and God—*YHWH*—was to be wondered at and praised for the breathtaking nature of creation: Psalm 104 is therefore a hymn of praise.[30] Clean and unclean animals have their place in creation:

> The Jewish feeling, however, is vivid, fresh, and impartial. In Norse stories a pestilent creature such as a dragon tends to be conceived as the enemy not only of men but of gods. In classical stories, more disquietingly, it tends to be sent by a god for the destruction of men whom he has a grudge against. The Psalmist's clear objective view—noting the lions and whales side by side with men and men's cattle—is unusual. And I think it is certainly reached through the idea of God as Creator and sustainer of all.[31]

The Jews are the chosen people of God, and have a unique role in the midst of the world, but neither they nor the rest of humanity are the center of creation, and the rest of creation is not necessarily organized around humanity. All wait upon God for their sustenance, their livelihood, their very existence to be: "When you hide your face, they are terrified; when you take away their breath, they die and return to the dust. When you send your Spirit, they are created, and you renew the face of the earth" (Ps 104:29–30). Lewis's conclusion is that nature is a fellow dependent upon God, all wait upon God, all stand equally in creation. Is there not the genesis of the intellectual framework here of the environmental movement of the late twentieth century?

29 Lewis, *Reflections on the Psalms*, 71.
30 Lewis, *Reflections on the Psalms*, 72.
31 Lewis, *Reflections on the Psalms*, 72.

9

The Psalms IV:
Hebraic Prefigurement and Meaning

"He said to them, 'How foolish you are, and how slow to believe all that the prophets have spoken! Did not the Messiah have to suffer these things and then enter his glory?' And beginning with Moses and all the Prophets, he explained to them what was said in all the scriptures concerning himself.
    He said to them, 'This is what I told you while I was still with you: Everything must be fulfilled that is written about me in the Law of Moses, the Prophets and the Psalms.' Then he opened their minds so they could understand the [Hebrew] scriptures."

LUKE 24: 25–27, & 44–45

"It is conceivable that ideas derived from Akhenaten's system formed part of that Egyptian 'Wisdom' in which Moses was bred. There is nothing to disquiet us in such a possibility. Whatever was true in Akhenaten's creed came to him, in some mode or other, as all truth comes to all men, from God. There is no reason why traditions descending from Akhenaten should not have been among the instruments which God used in making Himself known to Moses. But we have no evidence that this is what actually happened."

C. S. LEWIS[1]

1. INTRODUCTION

An important question that relates pertinently to the Book of the Psalms is the relationship of the Hebrew Bible to other religions, but specifically, to other forms of God's revelation to humanity—specifically from the ancient pagan religions Lewis studied (North-West European, ancient Indian, Egyptian, *et al.*). This is not a question of a multi-faith confusion,

---

1   Lewis, *Reflections on the Psalms*, 74.

regarding all religions as equal, yet equally nothing, from a secular liberal humanist perspective. No. The obvious question to begin with is how is the revelation of God given through Yeshua Ha Mashiach—the incarnate second person of the Trinity? Also, how was he foreshadowed, prefigured, in the Hebrew Bible, and what did Lewis think about these anticipations?

If there are links of intimation between religions (for example, pagan models of the Christ), in the same way that there are intimations of God's purposes through salvation history, centered on the revelation in and through the ancient Hebrew people and their scriptures, then this raises questions about subsequent interpretations, or, as Lewis termed it, "second meanings."

If the apostle and disciples were right, that their eyewitness testimony is correct, that Yeshua Ha Mashiach was and is the long-awaited Hebrew savior—the universal Christ—at the center of all creation and God's dealings with *fallen* humanity, then at the heart of this chapter is a question: "To what extent are our readings of the Book of the Psalms, and the Hebrew scriptures generally, valid—from a Christian perspective?"

At the center of this question is a proposition that the locus of God's revelation and dealing with humanity—salvation history—is the Hebrew people and their scriptures, and that we can find intimations sown wide amongst peoples and cultures across the world, in various religions and religious mythologies (peoples that were isolated from each other and from the Jews, and where knowledge and understanding could only have been intimated by the Holy Spirit: God seeded intimations through dreams, through tiny moments of revelation, through story and song, through myth. *Deus dixit*: God said—look what I am to do for you, this may help lead you towards salvation.

2. CHRISTOLOGICAL PREFIGUREMENT

Because the ancient Hebrew society through to the intertestamental period, and to the Jewish-Roman wars and the diaspora[2] was agrarian, and at the heart of agrarian societies the world over were myths of death and resurrection, then a "god" who dies and is often raised up again, a "god" who through death brings life to people, bears an uncanny

---

2   Following the revolt against Roman rule in 66AD in the First Jewish-Roman War, which led to the destruction of Jerusalem and the razing of the Second Temple in 70AD, then again in 132AD, subsequent to the *Bar Kokhba* rebellion, Jews were forbidden from Jerusalem: the land of Israel was a no-go zone.

9. The Psalms IV: Hebraic Prefiguration and Meaning

relationship—intimation—of what happened to Jesus on the cross and in the tomb. An obvious one is in the English folk tradition: the story of John Barleycorn, the journey of the grain, killed, buried in death in the ground, only to be recreated, raised up to new life, a new barley plant: and to become life-giving ale!—though also to our daily bread.[3] Although the story of Yeshua—the Anointed One—has remarkable parallels with the principle of descending and re-ascending within nature myths, there is no suggestion in the Gospels of a self-awareness of this parallel in Jesus or his disciples. In the incarnation story God descends to reascend. This is a familiar pattern in nature—all life must die to grow again: descend (i.e., die as a seed) to reascend. Cultures all over the world have death and resurrection myths woven into their perception and understanding of the natural world, many such myths are elevated to the status of corn kings, the king must die in the ground as a seed to reascend, to grow again, to rule again. Lewis writes,

> The doctrine of the Incarnation, if accepted, puts this principle even more emphatically at the center. The pattern is there in Nature because it was first there in God. All the instances of it which I have mentioned turn out to be but transpositions of the Divine theme into a minor key.[4]

Lewis asserts that many could see Christ as simply another corn-king. Yet although Jesus was addressing an agrarian society, and although the metaphor of a seed falling and dying to rise again is used in his sayings, as well as in other parts of the New Testament,[5] there is no conscious parallel drawn between this observable fact of creation and the reality of God (Yeshua) descending to reascend, taking fallen creation with him. Lewis writes, "The records, in fact, show us a person who *enacts* [Lewis's emphasis] the part of the Dying God, but whose thoughts and words remain quite outside the circle of religious ideas to which the Dying God belongs.... It is as if you met the sea-serpent and found that it disbelieved

---

3 Barley was much more tolerant of changes in the weather, and other environmental factors than wheat, which is why it is often cited, as the "Barley Harvest" in the Hebrew Bible: see the Book of Ruth. Therefore, to ordinary Jews, living in a subsistence agrarian economy the barley harvest was crucial, as were the celebrations after the harvest, or the ash-soaked repentance when the crop failed, or beckoned a famine.

4 Lewis, *Miracles* (1st ed.), 118.

5 For example, Matt 13; 25; Mark 4; Luke 8; 13; 17; 1 Cor 15; 2 Cor 9:10; 1 Pet 1; 1 John 3.

in sea-serpents."⁶ Lewis addresses this problem by asserting that the Christians are not simply claiming that God was incarnate in Yeshua, but that the one true God whom the Hebrews worshipped as YHWH had descended. On the one hand, this is the God of creation—of nature. On the other hand, this is not a nature-god. This is the God for whom the earth is his footstool, not his vesture—"Yahweh is neither the soul of nature nor her enemy . . . ."⁷ We can therefore understand why Christ is at once so like the corn-king and so silent about him. He is like the corn-king because *the corn-king is a portrait of him*. Elements of nature-religion are strikingly absent from the teachings of Jesus and from Hebrew history; this is because of the unique calling of the Hebrew people to testify to the one true God, author and Lord of creation, not merely a part of creation. Why? Because, notes Lewis, in the incarnation–crucifixion–resurrection we have the truth behind so-called nature-religion, but more than that, the reality that grounded, was foundational to, nature itself: "Where the real God is present the shadows of that God do not appear, that which the shadows resembled does. The Hebrews throughout their history were being constantly headed off from the worship of nature-gods; not because the nature-gods were in all respects unlike the God of Nature but because, at best, they were merely like, and it was the destiny of that nation to be turned away from likenesses to the thing itself."⁸

Hence, there is no internal evidence within the Gospels of these echoes/prefigurements; likewise, there is no direct parallel between the incarnation-resurrection narrative and these echoes/prefigurements, which are merely shadows, because to Lewis the Christ-event is the reality beyond the shadows breaking in to redeem. This is Lewis at his most Platonic. Further, we find that the value he gives to prefigurement, and for that matter natural theology, natural or general revelation, is entirely subordinate to the reality of the Christ-event, which in many ways transcends religion.

3. A HEBRAIC-EGYPTIAN MODEL OF GOD

Lewis does consider a digression with reference to a form, as such, of prefigurement that relates to the evolution of the understanding and the

---

6   Lewis, *Miracles* (1st ed.), 119.
7   Lewis, *Miracles* (1st ed.), 14, 121.
8   Lewis, *Miracles* (1st ed.), 121.

9. The Psalms IV: Hebraic Prefigurement and Meaning

names for God amongst the ancient Hebrews. Lewis considers an ancient Egyptian poem, *The Hymn to the Sun*, by Akhenaten (circa fourteenth century BC).[9] Lewis here is dealing with a doctrine of God that issues from a revelation, a realization, to the Pharaoh Amenhetep—in this context, he referred to himself as Akhenaten. Lewis is referring to a "gentile" poem, which is not necessarily pagan, because it advances a monotheism (or henotheism?), a monotheism contradictory to all forms of polytheism, and echoing like an intimation a Hebraic doctrine/model of God, the one true living God, *El, Elohim*, the eternal self-existing One, entire, distinct, and disinterested from humanity, yet committed to humanity, to a people that he was forging, the Jews: God, that is creator of the earth, the heavens, and praised in a creation account/story similar to Psalm 104.[10] This concept of divinity radically changed in the early period of Hebrew religious development. The ambiguity of these changes—vertical translatability—is reasoned in that the Hebraic understanding of the one true living God evolves over their encounters:[11] from *El Shaddai* (God Almighty), to the relational intimacy of *YHWH*, the LORD, caring and chastising them. However, what Lewis speculatively identifies broadly as *Elohim*, the simply divine entity, the One, is seen as comparable to that which Akhenaten seemingly identifies in his poem—*The Hymn to the Sun* (properly, *The Great Hymn to the Aten*)[12]—and seeks to project as a monotheistic deity onto his people. The Egyptian people rejected this, they wanted to carry on possessing their multiple gods and goddesses. Akhenaten stood by his concept, his realization: the single divine entity—unknowable, yet perceivable.

---

9   Lewis, *Reflections on the Psalms*, 73–76

10   Lewis, *Reflections on the Psalms*, 73.

11   See: Smith, *God in Translation*. Smith notes how, in the Hebrew Bible the patriarchs, judges, and prophets condemn many foreign deities, while also, many passages display an early Hebraic acceptance of the deities other people worship. (This does not, however, promote what Smith considers to be the Western concept of universal religion.)

12   *The Great Hymn to the Aten* is a hymn-poem written to the sun-disk, a mono-deity: Aten, attributed to Akhenaten, written in the fourteenth century BC. Akhenaten was radical in banning the traditional Egyptian religion of multiple gods, eventually replacing the sun-disc image by spelling out the name phonetically. While seen as a precursor of monotheism, many see his doctrine as henotheistic (the worship of one "god" while not denying the possible existence of other "gods").

A HEBRAIC INKLING

Akhenaten is seen as a forerunner of monotheistic religion, as represented in the ancient Hebrews. However, there are as many different models of monotheism as there are religions or prophets to initiate. The psychoanalyst Freud was amongst the first to notice a possible connection between Moses in Egypt and Akhenaten. Lewis and Freud are of a shared mind: they take seriously the exodus story, that Moses was actually in Egypt with the Israelites. For Freud, Moses was an Atenist priest, who was forced to leave, with his people: both see Moses as a promoter of exclusive monotheism.[13] *The Great Hymn to the Aten* the sun-disc aligns the sun with a single God, creator, sustainer:

> How manifold it is, what thou hast made!
> They are hidden from the face (of man).
> O sole god, like whom there is no other!
> Thou didst create the world according to thy desire,

Lewis notes the comparison with much of the creation doctrine in Psalm 104

> When you have dawned they live.
> When you set they die;
> You yourself are lifetime, one lives by you.
> All eyes are on [your] beauty until you set.[14]

While some see Akhenaten as a precursor of Christ, in the Pharaoh's relationship with Aten, other find the relationship either wrong, or something of a precursor to Christ, or considering Lewis's respect for intimations in ancient pagan religion, something of a prefigurement. However, not all agree and some are dismissive of such claims:

> Before much of the archaeological evidence from Thebes and from Tell el-Amarna became available, wishful thinking sometimes turned Akhenaten into a humane teacher of the true God, a mentor of Moses, a Christlike figure, a philosopher before his time. But these imaginary creatures are now fading away one by one as the historical reality gradually emerges. There is little or no evidence to support the notion that Akhenaten was a progenitor of the full-blown monotheism that we find in the Bible. The monotheism of

---

13 Freud, *Moses and Monotheism* (1939).
14 Lichtheim, *Ancient Egyptian Literature: Volume II: The New Kingdom*, 99.

9. The Psalms IV: Hebraic Prefigurement and Meaning

the Hebrew Bible and the New Testament had its own separate development—one that began more than half a millennium after the pharaoh's death.[15]

But what has Lewis to say on the relationship between Moses and Akhenaten's theology—and in relation to the Book of the Psalms? Akhenaten's monotheism is described by Lewis as of an extremely pure and conceptual type; this deity was not simplistically identified as the Sun:

> The visible disc was only His manifestation. It is an astonishing leap, more astonishing in some ways than Plato's, and, like Plato's, in sharp contrast to ordinary Paganism. And as far as we can see, it was a total failure. Akhenaten's religion died with him. Nothing, apparently, came of it.[16]

It is at this point that Lewis attempts to connect Akhenaten with the evolving Hebraic understanding—a proto-doctrine—of God. Lewis asks the question, Did Judaism partly emerge from the identification and worship of Aten? Were elements of this single creator-God religion foundational in the "Egyptian wisdom" that formed Moses' evolving religious understanding? Lewis then cautiously identifies a form of prefigurement:

> Whatever was true in Akhenaten's creed came to him, in some mode or other, as all truth comes to all men, from God. There is no reason why traditions descending from Akhenaten should not have been among the instruments which God used in making Himself known to Moses.[17]

But there is no concrete evidence for this. Besides, the model of God held fast by the Hebrews in their 430-year captivity went back to Abraham, and while patriarchal religion was about the God above all gods (henotheism?) it was always moving towards actual monotheism. Paradoxically, it seemed to take something akin to a triune form: for example, Abraham's encounter with the LORD, the Oaks of Mamre,

---

15 Redford, "The Monotheism of the Heretic Pharoah. Precursor of Mosiac Monotheism or Egyptian Anomaly?" Redford notes in the introduction, "Others have even gone so far as to find in Akhenaten a harbinger of Jesus. After all, Akhenaten did call himself the son of the sole god, 'thine only son that came forth from thy body.'"
16 Lewis, *Reflections on the Psalms*, 73.
17 Lewis, *Reflections on the Psalms*, 73.

A HEBRAIC INKLING

the three persons (Gen 18).[18] The three visitors to Abraham are not a pagan distant unknowable god, a philosophical-cerebral apophatic deity. They are real and relate to Abraham and Moses, they know and rule in an authoritative manner. Given the evidence for Christological prefigurement (though in this case Hebraic-Theos prefigurement), this—if there is an influence from Akhenaten and Egyptian wisdom theology—should not alarm us. It does not, writes Lewis, diminish the relevance of Moses' mission: "There is nothing to disquiet us in such a possibility. . . . There is no reason why traditions descending from Akhenaten should not have been among the instruments which God used in making Himself known to Moses."[19] It is at this point that Lewis skirts into a form of anti-Semitism, arguing that the cerebral apophatic God, the almost Grecian-philosophical deity of Akhenaten, can be seen as more viable and valued to religious development "than those earliest documents of Judaism in which *Jahveh* seems little more than a tribal deity."[20]

But, writes Lewis, if humanity is to know God, the one true God, the non-corporeal, eternal and enduring ground of all that is, and not as a mere, abstract, romantic philosophical speculation—even projection—but as personal lord, for some as *YHWH*, as an utterly concrete being and more real than we believe ourselves to be, then perhaps God in wisdom started with the stone tribal altars, traditions, and feasts, with the memory of God's judgements, with a reminder of God-given natural law specific to a chosen people: with promises, and mercies. Lewis muses, what if God had revealed as something akin to ethereal philosophical enlightenment at this time:

> At that early stage it may not be fruitful to typify God by anything so remote, so neutral, so international and (as it were) interdenominational, so featureless, as the solar disc. . . . Since in the end we are to come to baptism and the Eucharist, to the stable

---

18   It is salutary to note that many modern biblical critics will believe—presume—that these patriarchal stories, in the form we have them in the Book of Genesis, are the produce of much later Jewish theology. However it can also be argued that generations of Jews deliberately preserved Abraham's stories in relative pristine form, and that they are not a later transformation of whatever ancient oral sources underpinned them. In addition they are the product of divine inspiration and divine preservation, regardless of when they were actually written down! This hinges on what sort of doctrine of scripture we are dealing with.

19   Lewis, *Reflections on the Psalms*, 74.

20   Lewis, *Reflections on the Psalms*, 74.

9. The Psalms IV: Hebraic Prefigurement and Meaning

at Bethlehem, the hill of Calvary, and the emptied rock-tomb, perhaps it is better to begin with circumcision, the Passover, the Ark, and the Temple.[21]

Therefore, Lewis conceded that Akhenaten's monotheism was not an anticipation of the Hebraic understanding, and evolving model, of God, but it does leave Akhenaten free, according to Lewis, to write theological nature poetry. *The Great Hymn to the Aten*, is, we are advised, similar to, and yet different to Psalm 104. It praises God for creation, even in the most tiny and intimate moments of creation (the embryonic human in the womb; also that Akhenaten's God creates out of desire—even love?—and pleasure). But, notes Lewis, in Psalm 104, lions are seen as an equal creation, deserving of life and place in the created order. This is not so to Akhenaten, who compared them to the Serpent's sting: they are enemies not allotted their place in creation.[22]

4. THE HEBREW SLAVES TAUGHT AKHENATEN . . . ?

Of course, the influence (if there was one) between Akhenaten's monotheism and the ancient Hebrews—the Israelite slaves of over 400 years—could have been the other way round. Akhenaten may have heard, via the religious authorities, of a Hebrew song praising the creator God, and his lordship over creation, he was intrigued by their stern monotheism going back centuries, which was sustaining them in their enslaved captivity, and came to value it: so this early proto-"psalm," later to be developed, changed (such is how an oral sung tradition can work, yes, over hundreds of years!),[23] and it could have been a trigger in his realization of the one true living God, a God that he then encouraged people to see in corporal form represented by the disc of the sun in the sky, the life-giving disc without which there is nothing, which died in the

---

21   Lewis, *Reflections on the Psalms*, 75. The solar disc (the sun) was taken to be the manifestation of this one God and was not, to Akhenaten's thinking, to be identified with God. But it does raise the problem of such a model of God being corrupted into pagan idolatry.

22   Lewis, *Reflections on the Psalms*, 76.

23   This can be seen in studying the English folk tradition (or any oral tradition), or the origin and development of the English and Scottish Ballads, as collected by Prof. Francis James Child in the early nineteenth century. Many of these great long ballads, epic stories, going back centuries, show stylistic roots and iconography reminiscent of Anglo-Saxon myths. See, Child, *The English and Scottish Popular Ballads* (1884–98).

evening to be resurrected the next morn. (In Hebrew tradition, as the sun tips below the horizon, this moment is the start of the next day.) So perhaps all these religious academics got it the wrong way round? Maybe the Hebrew slaves introduced Akhenaten to a monotheistic doctrine of God!

5. HEBREW SALVATION: SECOND MEANINGS

If there are parallels in other world religions and myths, parallels with the central link between the Hebrew world and the Christian world, that is, the incarnation–crucifixion–resurrection, then are we asserting that many texts in the Hebrew Bible, especially the Book of Psalms, can be interpreted with second or subsequent meanings? There is nothing new in this, such has been asserted for virtually all of the time of Christian history. But is it coherent and how does it work? The answer was Lewis's fascination; the answer, for Lewis, came through analysis, not through mere Christian propaganda. The answer is that many of these prefigurements are prophetic.

Some may consider there to be a problem with such prefigurement because it appears to do an injustice to the original aims and intentions of the author of the myth in asserting a second, a subsequent, level of meaning? Lewis thought not, and could defend such an interpretation. Is it possible for anyone today to view such myths without considering what has happened in the intervening time? Regardless of concerns over purity, there is an indelible connection that must be explained. (For example, the apparent connection between ancient writings—Plato, Socrates, etc.—and what happened to the Christ in his passion.) Lewis therefore posits an alternative option to either prediction, or chance coincidence: to previse may be the result of wisdom. Questions are raised as to what extent these prefigurements may be considered idolatrous? Again, Lewis could refute accusations of idolatry. Through his understanding of natural theology, revelation, and human imagination (proximately to that of Augustine, but also to the English Romantics, especially the poet, theologian, and philosopher Samuel Taylor Coleridge) Lewis's esteem, prior to his conversion, for pagan myths relating to the appearing (incarnation?) and reviving from death (resurrection?) of pagan gods, avatars, and spirits, led him after his conversion to analyze why and how these religious myths/stories related to the actual Christ-event. Lewis's understanding in this is contiguous with the Romantic movement English poet Samuel Taylor Coleridge and the Scottish Presbyterian minister George MacDonald, but also fellow Inkling J. R. R. Tolkien (from whom he learns and uses many concepts—for example, sub-creation, mythopoeic/mythopoeia, refractions and splinters of the true light). His cautious respect for these intimations of prefigurement were as a mode of revelation rooted in Augustine's doctrine of illumination and the proposition that there is no un-aided true knowledge of God. Knowledge and understanding are given through prevenient grace and imbued through the faculty of the imagination.

Intention and Subsequent Meanings

According to Lewis's understanding of God's self-revelation, intimations of the Christ-event (the incarnation-cross-resurrection) were given, often in the form of myth, to people geographically and cognitively remote (with no opportunity for cross-fertilization of ideas) from the revelation given to the ancient Hebrews, and specifically the Jews in the intertestamental period: God's chosen people. These intimations, in narrative form, story, myth—often dreams—were also imparted, *a posteriori*, to people isolated for various reasons from the efforts of the church to attest to God's salvific actions through the Yeshua, the Anointed One. These intimations we have termed Christological prefigurement, that is, part of a doctrine of Christology and pneumatology. As a working hypothesis, we may say that such intimations are eschatological, in that they draw people closer to Christ's forgiving judgement.[24] Lewis saw many of the pagan myths amongst, for instance, North European peoples as manifestations of the universal Christ—hints and intimations of the Christ-event in stories of an incarnate "god" come to save his people, dying and raised up again. Therefore pagans, for Lewis, were (at least potentially) people moving towards Christ without *explicit* knowledge of Christ. Is there a potential problem with a doctrine of Christological prefigurement, in that it appears to do an injustice to the original aims and intentions of the authors?[25]

---

24 This is a foreshadowing of forgiving judgement rather than the over-realized eschatology that Barth is sometimes accused of.

25 These poets as such were not just a pagan Shaman, a myth-teller, in a non-literate culture, their ideas transmitted through an oral tradition, but they also include Hebrew psalmists, and those who wrote down the Pentateuch, and the Book of the prophet Isaiah.

Lewis's justification is in the form of a philosophical interpretation of the pneumatological element of the economic Trinity.[26]

Intention and Validity

Lewis was not alone in subscribing second or subsequent meanings to religious myths. Sir James George Frazer and other academics recognized the coincidences in these of stories of incarnate gods/idols, and dying and reviving gods.[27] Frazer, a late nineteenth-century colonial religionist and social anthropologist, provided a catalogue of these ancient pagan myths, and the similarities both among them and to the incarnation-resurrection narrative; however, his conclusions grounded the myths

---

26   There is much here which has been analyzed in depth elsewhere, which does not need repeating. For example, what does a critical evaluation of Lewis's proposition that the incarnation-resurrection narrative is both myth and history disclose? What did Lewis mean by myth, and how does myth become reality in the Christ-event? What exactly did Lewis classify as ideas of prefigurement in relation to the incarnation-resurrection narrative, and how do these intimations relate to natural theology, revelation and imagination? What doctrine of Christ as the light of the world in reality and in mythopoeic intimations was Lewis working with—and did Tolkien's proposition of splintered fragments of the true light give Lewis a particular understanding of how these prefigured ideas came to be in pagan myths? We may also ask, how does the incarnation-resurrection narrative act/operate on us as a myth, whether spoken or read? And what internal evidence for a mythopoeic interpretation is there within the incarnation-resurrection narrative? Finally, how do our conclusions measure up to Lewis's "supposal": Aslan, Lewis's own mythopoeic sub-creation? See, Brazier, "C. S. Lewis & Christological Prefigurement." This work is part of a much larger project: Brazier, *C. S. Lewis: Revelation and the Christ* (7 Vols. 2012–18). See specifically, Vol. 1: Revelation, Conversion and Apologetics: see: chapter 9 Apologist and Defender of the Faith I: Revelation and Christology, 1931–44—The Early Works, 4. The Broadcast Talks: A Summa?, The Christ of Salvation History, 149, 164–65. Also: chapter 10 Apologist and Defender of the Faith II: Revelation and Christology, 1941–47—The Middle Works, 2. The Revelatory "I Am," and "The Grand Miracle," 177–78, vii. Three Paradigms: "Descent/Re-ascent," "Christological Prefigurement," and "Selectiveness and Vicariousness," "Descent/Re-Ascent," and "Christological Prefigurement," 186–87.

See specifically, Vol. 2: *The Work of Christ, Revealed*: Part Three Christ Prefigured—Intimations to the Pagans, chs 9, 10 & 11 inclusive, 89–267

27   Frazer, *The Golden Bough* (1911–15). Initially published in two volumes in 1890, the work grew to the final twelve-volume third edition published 1911–15: Vol 1–2, part I, *The Magic Art* ; Vol 3, part II, Taboo and the Perils of the Soul ; Vol 4, part III, *The Dying God* ; Vol 5–6, part IV, *Adonis, Attis, Osiris Studies in the History of Oriental Religion* ; Vol 7–8, part V, *Spirits of the Corn and of the Wild* ; Vol 9, part VI, *The Scapegoat* ; Vol 10–11, part VII, *Balder the Beautiful the Fire-Festivals of Europe and the Doctrine of the External Soul* ; Vol 12, *Bibliography and General Index*. See also: Frazer, *The Golden Bough* (abridged ed.; 1922).

9. The Psalms IV: Hebraic Prefigurement and Meaning

in the human psyche. For many of his followers they were rooted in a Feuerbachian-Freudian interpretation of a Darwinian model of human evolution, which classified religion as a tribal human construct within a hostile world. Frazer's supporters used these conclusions as ammunition against Christianity and the church. The young apostate and atheist Lewis read Frazer and concluded that the Gospel account was simply one amongst many similar stories. On the evening of his conversion from theism to Christianity, C. S. Lewis is recorded as having described myths as beautiful and moving, though they were lies, falsehoods, and of no consequence or worth, even though they appeared to have been breathed through silver.[28] At the point of his conversion Lewis is dismissive of the Frazer-Feuerbachian position he had subscribed to in his youth. Gradually, however, Lewis came to regard these prefigurements as the work of the Holy Spirit—intimations of God's salvific action in Christ. Indeed, in his maturity he was to comment that we should *expect* the similarities to be there, given the global inclusive nature of the Christ-event and the fact that God in freedom seeks the redemption of all creation. Lewis's understanding of myth was to change radically during his life as a result of his adoption and championing of an orthodox Christian faith. Myth was, and continued to be, very important to him—primarily the Northern European myths, Greek mythology, and Asiatic-Indian (Hindu) religion and myth.

But how do these myths and dreams intimating the possibility of atonement and redemption relate to the thousands of years of Hebrew salvation history, and the key point of this atonement and redemption in Yeshua, son of David, crucified and resurrected—not simply slain in hatred as the myths purport—for our redemption? Perhaps the most significant Christological myth, for Lewis, was the myth of Balder the Beautiful.[29] But can Balder be said to be the Christ? Certainly, Balder's

---

28 Quoted by Tolkien in his poem "Mythopoeia," reflecting Lewis's position up to the point of his conversion: see Tolkien, "Mythopoeia," in *Tree and Leaf*. See also "Lewis writing to Arthur Greeves, Oct. 18, 1931," in Lewis, *Collected Letters* Vol. I, 1969–72.

29 The "god" of light and joy in Norse mythology (son of Odin and Frigga, king and queen of the gods) Balder—or Baldhr—was regarded as beautiful, compassionate, and graceful compared to the other gods. An oath was extracted from the forces and objects in nature that they would not harm him, but the mistletoe was overlooked. The "gods," thinking Balder safe, rained blows and objects at him; Loki maliciously placed a twig of mistletoe in the hands of the blind Hoder, god of darkness, and directed his aim against Balder. Balder fell, mortally wounded, pierced to the heart. After his death

characteristics are in many ways similar to those of Christ—love, joy, light, beauty, compassion—and there are also similarities with the Logos, the Word. [30] Moreover, the Norse word notably used of Balder, *tivor*, is unquestioningly taken to mean divine, god-like: Balder is the *blaupom tivor*, the bloody victim, the slain god. Similarities can now be seen with the suffering Christ: Jesus's temptation in the wilderness, the passion in the Garden of Gethsemane, through to the scourging, the trial, and the violent humility of the *via Delarosa*, and to death through pagan crucifixion. Balder's sacrifice can be seen as a prefiguration of Christ, but more with the Hebrew concept of the scapegoat, where through taking the sins of the people, especially a Hebrew monarch, onto the animal, and sacrificing it, atonement is achieved for the Hebrews.[31] In the ancient rite of *Yom Kippur* (the Day of Atonement), one goat was killed, the other released into the wilderness taking with it the sins and impurities of the Jews.

> Then Aaron shall lay both his hands on the head of the live goat, and confess over it all the iniquities of the people of Israel, and all their transgressions, all their sins, putting them on the head of the goat, and sending it away into the wilderness by means of someone designated for the task. The goat shall bear on itself all their iniquities to a barren region; and the goat shall be set free in the wilderness.
>
> Lev 16:21-22

Balder does not take on death voluntarily as Jesus (*Angus Dei*, the sacrificial lamb) did; from the prophetic dream he fears death, yet the action taken to defend him causes his death. His death is caused by the

---

Odin sent another son the messenger Hermod to the underworld to plead for his return. Balder's release was conditional on everything in the world weeping for him. Everything wept except one old woman in a cave, and so Balder could not return to life.

30   See, Frazer, *The Golden Bough*, part VII: Balder The Beautiful, Vol I and Vol II (1913) specifically, ch. 3, "The Myth of Balder," 101.

31   This relates to Azazel, in Jewish mythology, a demon or evil spirit to whom, in the ancient rite of Yom Kippur (Day of Atonement), a scapegoat was sent, bearing the sins of the Jewish people: two male goats were chosen for the ritual, one designated by lot "for the LORD," the other "for Azazel" (Lev 16:8). The ritual was carried out by the high priest in the Second Temple (see the *Mishna*). After the high priest symbolically transferred all the sins of the Jewish people to the scapegoat, the goat destined "for Azazel" (the personification of uncleanness, oftimes a fallen angel) was driven out into the wilderness and hurled over a precipice to death.

9. The Psalms IV: Hebraic Prefigurement and Meaning

trickery of Loki; Jesus wrestled with his fate in the Garden of Gethsemane but accepted what was to befall him. What is more, there is the potential for Balder being revived or restored, but this falls short of resurrection: it does not happen in our reality. There is a similar potentiality with the Egyptian god Osiris here, who is tricked into death, like Balder. Scapegoating was common in ancient cultures the world over. But these were to do with protecting the tribe from bad weather, failed crops, invasion, success in battle, they were to do with worldly success and worldly preservation, to a degree, not a realization of sin before the one true God, and the necessity for atonement to salvation. These pagan sacrifices lacked the eschatological dimension of *Yom Kippur*, Baldur, and "the lamb of God that takes away the sins of the world" (John 1:29). The multiple references to the sacrificial lamb of God in the Book of Revelation, and the wedding feast of the lamb, can be seen as prefigured in Jewish eschatology, whereby the Messiah will hold a wedding feast with the righteous of every nation, a *Seudat Chiyat HaMatim*, wherein the Messiah and his wedding guests will feast.[32]

But what did the original composers and audiences of the Myth of Balder believe? The myth leaves open the possibility of a righteous one being brought back to life, but this does not happen because of sin and objection amongst the people. In claiming prefigurement is not Lewis working against the original setting of the myth, ignoring the intentions of the authors and audiences, that is, how it was conceived to be read and heard?—or is he right? Balder is not utterly innocent and righteous; and human attempts to generate not so much resurrection but *renovatio* (rebirth) fail because of a lack of agreement: all must agree (but, in the story, one elderly person objects). But this is not so with God, because the righteous one is God-descended! Lewis's second or hidden meaning actually is the completion of the story, the myth; humanity could not provide the conclusion because it is demonically possessed by original sin. Such a subsequent interpretation and context, Lewis claims, generates suspicion: it "arouses deep distrust in a modern mind, because, as we know, almost anything can be read into any book."[33] With the Hebrew scriptures it is different: prefigurement and intimation are woven throughout. The

---

32   See: *The Jewish Encyclopaedia* (12 Vols. 1901–6), online: http://www.jewishencyclopedia.com/articles/5849-eschatology

33   Lewis, *Reflections on the Psalms*, 85.

question is, was Yeshua the Messiah, or not? Was Jesus the longed-for promise?

There is always scope for self-deception because we are human, fallible and fallen. Are we guilty of reassigning meaning and intention? Lewis recounts several examples of prophetic prefigurement, and although he concedes that in some instances these can be explained simply as coincidence, and although it is easily possible for someone to make a comment that can be applied to subsequent events, there is, Lewis asserts, something more than a chance happening.

Lewis concurs that it is feasible that someone can say or write what is true and relevant, vital, without fully understanding or realizing the significance of what has been stated.[34] Was this chance? If not prophecy, then what? As we noted earlier, Lewis posits an alternative to both prophecy and coincidence: to *previse* (Lewis's term) or *preview* may be the result of wisdom, pneumatologically authored wisdom. Foreseeing, even unselfconsciously, may be caused by wisdom, where wisdom is insight and knowledge, an understanding of how the world works, of what constitutes human existence, which leads to a mature reflection on what is and what is possible.

Plato and the Christ

Apart from the examples of scapegoating in ancient Greece, Lewis as a classicist places great emphasis on examples that confirm a doctrine of prefigurement from Graeco-Roman sources. There are cases where the later truth, which the earlier author/teller was unaware of, is, however, closely related to the truth, a truth that had in many ways underpinned and motivated the composition. Examples of prefigured truths which can be seen after the event they foretell are manifold in relation to the incarnation-resurrection. The sheer number must, Lewis asserts, deny a theory of chance coincidence (here the Victorian atheistic anthropologists are in agreement with Lewis in claiming a unifying cause, though he dismisses their citing of atheism and psychology as a common denominator). Lewis's preferences are for North European pagan myths, but in defending a doctrine of prefigurement he draws on Graeco-Roman examples.

---

34 Lewis, *Reflections on the Psalms*, 87.

9. The Psalms IV: Hebraic Prefigurement and Meaning

Perception, insight, and knowledge will lead to wisdom. This is grounded in reason, but, as Lewis notes, something more than scientific knowledge is in evidence.[35] Lewis here draws on Plato's *Republic*. Plato argues that righteousness is often praised for its benefits, honor and popularity, but that if we are truly to understand righteousness, we must see it without these popular worldly attributes and rewards. Lewis notes how Plato imagines a perfectly righteous man treated by all around him as unwanted, wrong, even evil, such a man is then bound, scourged, and finally impaled (the Persian equivalent of crucifixion). Lewis comments how at this passage a Christian is taken aback and should query what is happening: this he argues is more than mere coincidence, or "luck."[36] This is not a case of someone who is talking about something else that coincidentally resonates with a subsequent event or person. Lewis correctly asserts that Plato is consciously extrapolating about what happens to goodness in this world, a wicked and misunderstanding world. This understanding is not separate or independent from what happened to Yeshua Ha Mashiach, the only true and good and sinless person: the passion, for Lewis, is the supreme example of goodness destroyed by fallen humanity. Was Plato writing of the untimely death of his master Socrates? Not necessarily, considers Lewis. Plato, starting perhaps from Socrates, then moves to the nature of goodness in this world. He then extrapolates to the possibility of a perfect example, and something like Christ's passion, though he was outside of the knowledge of the Christ-event in both time and space. Lewis believed that Plato arrived at this understanding not out of coincidence or luck, but from wisdom.[37] But what exactly did Plato write?

> Now, if we are to form a real judgment of the life of the just and unjust, we must isolate them; there is no other way; and how is the isolation to be effected? I answer: Let the unjust man be entirely unjust, and the just man entirely just; nothing is to be taken away from either of them, and both are to be perfectly furnished for the work of their respective lives. . . . They will tell you that the just man who is thought unjust will be scourged, racked, bound—will have his eyes burnt out; and, at last, after suffering every kind of

---

35   Lewis, *Reflections on the Psalms*, 89.
36   Lewis, *Reflections on the Psalms*, 89.
37   Lewis, *Reflections on the Psalms*, 90.

A HEBRAIC INKLING

evil, he will be impaled: then he will understand that he ought to seem only, and not to be, just.[38]

Lewis concludes that Plato's insight is not simply a *prevision* or *preview*, a *prophecy*. For Christians to recognize something here that resonates with the passion is not simply retro-projection. Plato's insight issues from wisdom. There is a universal truth. But not all examples of prevision are rooted in wisdom. There may be a parallel or comparable perception that resonates with the ultimate sacrifice of goodness that is the passion, but still rooted in wisdom. For example, Lewis cites the instance of a poem by the Roman poet Virgil, written not long before the birth of Christ, which extols the new age where the Virgin returns, the reign of Saturn is renewed, and the new child is sent down from high heaven. The poem goes on to describe the paradisal age, which this nativity ushers in. Throughout Christian history, Virgil's comments were taken to have been prophetic. The question is, is this resemblance to the birth of Christ simply an accident? It may be argued that knowledge from the Hebrew prophets might have reached Virgil (though whether there is evidence for this is another matter); however, there is a resemblance that, as with Plato, can be explained through a common consciousness grounded in knowledge and understanding of humanity, leading to wisdom. Virgil may well have recognized, through wisdom, what the world needed: Virgil may well have recognized in his wisdom that these were the things the world needed, and trusting in his own gods, believed that they would come. Rooting or grounding prefigurement in a common consciousness leading to wisdom also applies to the numerous examples of prefigurement in pagan myths—whether North European, Asiatic-Indian, Egyptian, or Oceanic.

Wisdom

Lewis therefore concludes that wisdom is at the heart of prefigurement. But this is not just human cleverness and ingenuity. Wisdom involves inspiration, imagination, and reason—it is a bridge between the divine and the human. Wisdom, in the Bible, is often personified to suggest that it is external to the human, proceeding from the Holy Spirit. Lewis commented on several occasions that no good work is done anywhere

---

38   Plato, *The Republic*, Bk II (tr. Jowett).

9. The Psalms IV: Hebraic Prefigurement and Meaning

without the aid of the Father of Lights.[39] This raises once again the question of inspiration and illumination. Lewis writes, "In other words, when we examine things said which take on, in the light of later knowledge, a meaning they could not have had for those who said them, they turn out to be of different sorts."[40] This implies a conception of meaning as, like truth, existing outside of the human, where the original intentions and aims of the author of the myth, the teller of the tale, are only relative and contribute to a wider meaning and truth that reflects Christ as the way, the truth, and the life. This is, to a degree, Platonic, reflecting Lewis's beliefs as a Christian Platonist. So, we may ask, if wisdom is to be equated with light, divine illumination, how does this wisdom relate to revelation?

Wisdom and the Hebrew Bible

Wisdom raises the question of prefigurement in the Hebrew Bible in relation to the sayings of Jesus, and the second meanings applied to ancient Hebrew events and stories in the Acts of the Apostles: for example, Stephen's speech before the Sanhedrin and the High Priest, reinterpreting Jewish events and history in the light of the incarnation-cross-resurrection (Acts 7). This is potentially a large area of study; suffice it briefly to see what Lewis made of it. Lewis read and studied the Psalms and was aware of the subtle references that could be seen as applying to Jesus of Nazareth and his passion.[41] Further, from what is recorded both in his ministry and in his words from the cross, Jesus aligned himself with the suffering servant in Isaiah 53.[42] The resurrection narratives—for example, the encounter on the road to Emmaus—have Jesus looking back over the history of the Jews, and the Hebrew Bible, to interpret his own story in their light.[43] Isaiah 53—referred to explicitly in the Acts of the Apostles—is probably the clearest example of the full meaning of an ancient passage coming

---

39   Lewis, *Reflections on the Psalms*, 95.

40   Lewis, *Reflections on the Psalms*, 95.

41   Lewis in particular notes Mark 15:34, linked to Psalm 22. See, *Reflections on the Psalms*, 102.

42   Lewis in particular notes Acts 8:26–39, Phillip's encounter with the Ethiopian Eunuch over the interpretation of Isaiah 53. See, *Reflections on the Psalms*, 101–2.

43   Lewis in particular notes Jesus's identity as David's Lord (Mark 12:35–36); the use of words from Psalm 91:11–12 in Matthew 4:6; the explicit appropriation of Psalm 118:22 in Mark 12:10; and the linking of Psalm 16:11 to the resurrection. See, *Reflections on the Psalms*, ch. 11 "Scripture."

out only after an event subsequent to it composition. On the question of second meanings and validity Lewis concludes that

> [When] I read that poem of Virgil's . . . such a reading may after all be a mere coincidence (though I am not sure that it is). I may be reading into Virgil what is wholly irrelevant to all he was, and did, and intended. . . . But when I meditate on the Passion while reading Plato's picture of the Righteous One, or on the Resurrection while reading about Adonis or Balder, the case is altered. There is a real connection between what Plato and the myth-makers most deeply were and meant and what I believe to be the truth.[44]

Second meanings are therefore valid precisely because there is a God, and this God seeks to impart to humanity some knowledge of God and his salvific actions for humanity: hence, Christological prefigurement—prevision relating to Yeshua Ha Mashiach. This is revelation both in the imparting of understanding, which is relational, and the event or action of the atonement-redemption of humanity. This single event moves ever and onward towards the final fulfilment in the eschaton. Therefore, revelation unfolds. Meaning will therefore become fuller, or be augmented. It is a contemporary Western concept that protects and holds sacrosanct the aims, objectives, and intentions of the author, leading to the idea that the author is immutable, whilst other contemporary literary scholarship rejects intention as a fallacy. What was known in part and led to the inspiration of myths hundreds or even thousands of years ago will inevitably develop *in the fullness* of the revelatory event of Jesus of Nazareth, the Christ. Or is it the *significance* of the myth, rather than what underlies it, that changes, develops? Meaning is therefore teleological and our *grasp* on revelation is tentative, and unfolds towards the final completion in the eschaton: only with death and the last judgement will we know as completely as we are known (1 Cor 13).

---

44   See, *Reflections on the Psalms*, 92.

10

The Psalms V:
Yeshua, Mashiach:
Second Meanings in the Psalms

> "Sing to God, sing in praise of his name,
>   extol him who rides on the clouds;
>   rejoice before him—his name is the LORD.
>
> A father to the fatherless, a defender of widows,
>   is God in his holy dwelling.
>
> God sets the lonely in families,
>   he leads out the prisoners with singing;
>   but the rebellious live in a sun-scorched land.
>
> When you, God, went out before your people,
>   when you marched through the wilderness,
>   the earth shook, the heavens poured down rain,
>   before God, the One of Sinai,
>   before God, the God of Israel."
>
> PSALM 68:4–8

"There is nothing in it about peace and good-will, nothing remotely suggestive of the stable at Bethlehem. It seems to have been originally either a coronation ode for a new king, promising conquest and empire, or a poem addressed to some king on the eve of a war, promising victory. It is full of threats. The "rod" of the king's power is to go forth from Jerusalem, foreign kings are to be wounded, battlefields to be covered with carnage, skulls cracked. The note is not "Peace and goodwill" but "Beware He's coming."

C. S. LEWIS (ON PSALM 8)[1]

---

1   Lewis, *Reflections on the Psalms*, 106.

A HEBRAIC INKLING

1. INTRODUCTION

It is easy to cite examples from the Hebrew Bible where Christians can now see how a particular set of verses appears to refer prophetically to what happened in the incarnation-crucifixion-resurrection, but does the detail and the theology bear this out. Lewis, ever the philosopher and academic, analyzed these instances, often using the deconstructive techniques associated with linguistic philosophy, and criticizing the contemporary culturally conditioned ideas about the Christ-event (especially Christmas), as compared to a Hebraic mindset.

2. THE PSALMS: PREFIGUREMENT AND MEANING

The greatest evidence of prefigurement in the Hebrew Bible is of course the promise of the Messiah. As Augustine noted, the sacraments of the New Testament give salvation; the sacraments of the Hebrew Bible promise a savior.[2]

So what can we read of Jesus Christ from the Book of the Psalms' prophetic previsions, at the heart of the Hebrew Bible? And what did Lewis note? It can fairly be asserted that the Book of the Psalms has a unique place in Hebrew Bible; as revelation, it is in many ways a concise introduction to the Bible, even a summary of the evolving Hebrew understanding and relationship with and of the one God. Most of the component doctrines of a systematic theology can be discerned—some in embryonic form—in the Psalms. The authors of the New Testament generally interpret the Psalms as evidence of messianic fulfilment.

The analytical study of the representation of the Messiah in the Psalms is in itself a field of theological study; however, to frame Lewis's interpretation, study, and understanding, we need to at least see what identification and categorization he respected.[3] First, there are typical

---

[2] Augustine, *On Baptism, Against the Donatists* (Book I), Ch. 15. written c. 400AD.

[3] Lewis is outside of the academic tradition here. Most Old Testament scholars would reject them. For instance, there is no "kind" of psalms that is known as a directly predictive prophetic psalm; they would be skeptical of the phrase, "mystically messianic psalms" as a category. The categories scholars use are genre categories, e.g., psalms of lament, royal psalms, psalms of thanksgiving, etc. Some psalms were subsequently given messianic interpretations (esp. royal psalms), but those are not genre classifications. A possible source for Lewis is in, Binnie, *A Pathway into the Psalter* (1886), see 178–96.

10. The Psalms V: Yeshua, Mashiach: Second Meanings in the Psalms

messianic psalms;[4] second, directly predictive (prophetic) psalms;[5] third, mystically messianic psalms;[6] fourth, psalms of trust in Christ;[7] fifth, creation–new creation messianic psalms.[8]

The expectation of deliverance for Israel can be gleaned—explicitly and implicitly, in varying degrees—from the majority of the Psalms. The fulfilment of this hope and anticipation lay with Yeshua the Anointed One (to be recognized, *subsequently*, as the universal second person of the Trinity). However, it is necessary to be clear about the word "Messiah," in relation to the Psalms. The term messianic psalms can be seen in a narrow sense, "having no direct message of significance to the Old Testament period, they only predict the coming Messiah"; but then there are also in a general sense: "Psalms that anticipate the Messiah but also have meaning in a contemporary context of the writer."[9] Ralph F. Wilson notes,

> True prophets—Old Testament, New Testament, or today—don't necessarily understand all that they are saying to the degree that they could expound on their prophecies and interpret them accurately in advance. They may not even know that they are speaking in prophecy. They are given the words from the Holy Spirit and speak or write those words. The fulfilment and interpretation are usually far beyond them, to be revealed by God in his own good time.[10]

Thus, we find a brief confirmation of Lewis's doctrine of Christological prefigurement, from a different perspective, and, we may say, different churchmanship: prophetic prevision, where a psalm writer, or a myth maker in the Indian sub-continent, or in North West Europe, for example, is merely a vehicle for God's, to a degree, veiled revelation. The myth-maker does not necessarily understand the full implications of what is composed.

---

4   For example, Pss 26:6; 43:4; 51:19; 84:3; and 118:27. See also, Ezek 34:23, 24; 37:24, 25; 2 Sam 7; Heb 9:10.

5   For example, Ps 22. See also, Heb 2.

6   For example, Pss 16 & 40. See also, Acts 2:23–33.

7   For example, Pss 9; 13; 20; 25; 33; 34; 37; 56; 119; 143. See also, Acts 2:30–31.

8   For example, Pss 8; 102 & 104. See also, Heb 1:2, 10–12; 2:5–9; John 1:1–3; Col 1:15–16.

9   Longman III, *How to Read the Psalms*, 67–68.

10   Wilson, *Understanding the Gift of Prophecy. I. Is Prophecy Preaching?* http://www.joyfulheart.com/scholar/preach.htm. See, Wilson, "The Holy Spirit as the Agent of Renewal." See also: www.joyfulheart.com/scholar/.

3. THE MESSIANIC PSALMS

For many, the purpose of the Hebrew Bible is teleological: to record and demonstrate the ongoing revelation of, and leading to, salvation history, to be achieved through the Anointed One. In the fullness of time, this was clear to the early church. But these moments of revelation and foretelling, prevision, were not necessarily as obvious as they are now with hindsight. The nineteenth-century Scottish systematic theologian William Binnie (1823–86) highlights this:

> The Old Testament is full of prefigurations of this kind—precursive representations of the truth respecting Christ by means of analogous personages and dispensations. The types, then, were events, institutions, persons, so ordered by the providence of God as to bring out, clearly and impressively, the leading features of the eternal purpose which was one day to be realized in the person and work of the incarnate Son. It was by means of these types, quite as much as by the more direct and explicit medium of verbal revelations, that the mind of God was made known.[11]

For Binnie this comes to a head, so to speak, in the messianic Davidian psalms, because David is the psalmist of Israel, he was also typologically of Christ (and therefore representative, to a degree, of the relationship between the Hebrew Bible and the New Testament). Binnie argues that David was seen as the image of a just and wise prince: raised in obscurity, full of the spirit of wisdom and kingship, counsel and strength, although anointed by Samuel the prophet to be king of Israel, was in humiliation, an outsider, before ascending to the throne and then delivering his people from their enemies. David is taken to prefigure Christ, and Christ's kingdom: this generated "and awoke presentiments regarding them in the hearts of God's people, no reader of the Bible needs to be told. His history, from first to last, was a kind of rehearsal of the sufferings and glory of Christ."[12] As David is in the Psalter, the Psalms are, we may say, therefore full with previsions of Christ. Did not David know that one day the Anointed One was to be born of his line, to be a king after him, as crucially to be a priest in the order of Melchizedek? How did Lewis see this?

---

11   Binnie, *A Pathway into the Psalter* (1886), 178
12   Binnie, *A Pathway into the Psalter* (1886), 178

10. The Psalms V: Yeshua, Mashiach: Second Meanings in the Psalms

4. THE PSALMS: VICTOR AND SUFFERER

Jesus and the Psalms—Lewis's Interpretation

That scripture has to be subject to ongoing understanding and interpretation is, for Lewis, a given. We need a guide, a trained guide. Writing of the Ethiopian eunuch in Acts of the Apostles (Acts 8:27–38), Lewis comments: "Even a gentile 'God-fearer' like the Ethiopian eunuch knew that the sacred books of Israel could not be understood without a guide, trained in the Judaic tradition, who could open the hidden meanings."[13] Most Jews in the intertestamental period who heard the Hebrew Bible read in synagogues would have perceived references to the Messiah in the same way that Jesus did when reading the Book of Isaiah (Luke 4:16f.) publicly, but, notes Lewis, this was different and radical: "[w]hat was controversial was His identification of the Messianic King with another Old Testament figure and of both with Himself."[14]

Lewis identifies two figures that emerge from and meet us in the Psalms: the conquering, liberating king on the one hand, and the sufferer on the other.

The Sufferer

> How long, LORD? Will you forget me forever?
>   How long will you hide your face from me?
> How long must I wrestle with my thoughts
>   and day after day have sorrow in my heart?
>   How long will my enemy triumph over me?
>   Ps 13:1–2

> To you, LORD, I call;
>   you are my Rock,
>   do not turn a deaf ear to me.
> For if you remain silent,
>   I will be like those who go down to the pit.
> Hear my cry for mercy
>   as I call to you for help,
> as I lift up my hands
>   toward your Most Holy Place.
>   Ps 28:1–2

---

13 Lewis, *Reflections on the Psalms*, 104.

14 Lewis, *Reflections on the Psalms*, 104.

Listen to my prayer, O God,
> do not ignore my plea;
hear me and answer me.
> My thoughts trouble me and I am distraught
because of what my enemy is saying,
> because of the threats of the wicked;
for they bring down suffering on me
> and assail me in their anger.
>> Ps 55:1–2

Hear my prayer, LORD;
> let my cry for help come to you.
Do not hide your face from me
> when I am in distress.
Turn your ear to me;
> when I call, answer me quickly.
>> Ps 102:1–2

The King

The One enthroned in heaven laughs;
> the LORD scoffs at them.
He rebukes them in his anger
> and terrifies them in his wrath, saying,
"I have installed my king
> on Zion, my holy mountain."
>> Ps 2:4–6

Endow the king with your justice, O God,
> the royal son with your righteousness.
May he judge your people in righteousness,
> your afflicted ones with justice.
>> Ps 72:1–2

We may look back with hindsight—subject to prevision, prefigurement—and identify the sufferer as Yeshua, but, Lewis argues, at the time the psalms were written the sufferer was generally identified to be the whole nation of Israel. The King was taken by Israel to be a Davidite, the successor of David—*Mashiach*. In his preaching Jesus does identify himself typologically with both of the archetypes.[15]

---

15   Lewis, *Reflections on the Psalms*, 105.

10. The Psalms V: Yeshua, Mashiach: Second Meanings in the Psalms

Psalm 110: Victor and King (Christmas)

It is of worth to note that Lewis, at this point, issues a cautious criticism of allegory and projectionism when reading back new or second meanings into the Psalms, though this caution does not invalidate all such interpretations. Established second meanings may be more valid than today's, which may be culturally conditioned by a post-Enlightenment contemporary perspective, though this modernist danger has established itself to a much greater extent since Lewis's death in 1963. An example of this is Lewis respect for the use in the Church of England's Book of Common Prayer (1549 edition) of the use of Psalm 110, appointed to be read on Christmas Day. The content of this psalm, Cranmer implicitly asserted, bears witness as what we now call prefiguration to the events of the incarnation and birth of Jesus, but, importantly, to the nature, mission, and model of the Christ. This is nothing that relates to a school nativity play today, but a deep theological truism—which can be found throughout the Hebrew Bible—regarding the nature of the coming Messiah. For example, Lewis notes how Psalm 110 offers none of the peace and good will, or the picture of manger and stable (which has become heavily romanticized) at Bethlehem; much that we've come to associate with a Western Christmas, created many would say, by the Victorians, is wide of the mark. Psalm 110 appears like a coronation ode for a new king, a conqueror, a poem offering the monarch a blessing on the eve of a war: a blessing of victory. That is, for Lewis, the rod of the monarchically divine power from Jerusalem leading to battlefields, carnage, broken bones. Perhaps Christmas cards should be blazoned with the injunction "Beware He's coming," writes Lewis, rather than "Peace and Goodwill."[16]

But beyond Cranmer's liturgical reformation, this psalm, for Lewis, is pertinent to Yeshua Ha Mashiach, for two reasons. Christ in his own words stated that he is the "Lord" that King David refers to "my Lord" in the psalm. There is then the association with Melchizedek the mysterious person as a symbol or prophecy of Christ made in of Hebrews 7. (We are not concerned, neither was Lewis, with the use and meaning of this ancient priest by the writer of Hebrews but rather with why this Psalm 110 is theologically relevant to prevision and to Christmas.) But Melchizedek is a mysterious figure, he is unrelated, unaccounted for, and apart from the nature of the surrounding narrative, he comes from

---

16   Lewis, *Reflections on the Psalms*, 106.

nowhere, blesses in the name of the highest God, possessor of heaven and earth (Gen 14:18–20) and, for Lewis, utterly disappears: this gives him the effect of belonging, to heaven; or to another world, other than the world of Abraham. The association with the second person of the Trinity comes in the fullness of time:

> The LORD has sworn
> and will not change his mind:
> "You are a priest forever,
> in the order of Melchizedek."
>
> The LORD is at your right hand;
> he will crush kings on the day of his wrath.
>
> He will judge the nations, heaping up the dead
> and crushing the rulers of the whole earth.
>
> He will drink from a brook along the way,
> and so he will lift his head high.
> Ps 110:4–7

The writers of Genesis and Hebrews assumed a superiority of Melchizedek over Abraham (which Lewis notes Abraham accepts) as a majestic, imposing, and regal figure—mystical, numinous, supernatural. Lewis takes it further. Lewis displays his doctrine of scripture: how a sway from God lay upon these "tellings and re-tellings"[17] (the construction and multiple authors of Genesis) to give us the text we have today, independent to a degree from a single human author, or ego. What is important for Lewis is the model of priesthood: impressive, deeply supernatural, yet of this world, "not Pagan but a priesthood to the one God, far earlier than the Jewish Priesthood which descends from Aaron, independent of the call to Abraham, somehow superior to Abraham's vocation. And this older, pre-Judaic, priesthood is united with royalty; Melchizedek 'is a priest-king.'"[18] Priest-kings were not normal in Israel. It is thus simply a fact that Melchizedek resembles Christ (the only actual figure in the Hebrew Bible to do so). Melchizedek points to Christ and so does the hero of Psalm 110: priest and king: whom the Book of Common Prayer draws us to on Christmas Day.

---

17   Lewis, *Reflections on the Psalms*, 107.
18   Lewis, *Reflections on the Psalms*, 107.

10. The Psalms V: Yeshua, Mashiach: Second Meanings in the Psalms

Lewis is then inspired and is light-years ahead of the average Anglican intellectual religious professional, the cleric in the bishop's palace, or the average member of the Church of England laity. Influenced, it is fair to assert, by his Jewish wife, Joy Davidman, Lewis notes how helpful placing Psalm 110 to be read on Christmas Day would be for a Jewish convert: extremely important, providing a profound explanation. That is, to such a seeker, it would help them to understand how Yeshua was indeed the Messiah, because he was the inheritor and heir, successor—in a legal sense—of King David, more than the inheritor of Aaron. This belief in his priestly ontology is justified if we see a form of priesthood different from and higher than Aaron's: Melchizedek is referenced so as to imbue the scripture with authority, asserts Lewis.[19]

By comparison, we are "gentile Christians."[20] What Lewis is saying is that our approach is distinct, with a different emphasis, from a Hebraic model or interpretation of the role of the Christ. That is, the gentile model is divergent from the Hebrew, for Lewis. More than that, it is dissimilar as compared to the standard, or what Lewis asserts is a generalized, normal or usual, approach by Western Christians to Christmas. For us, our emphasis at Christmas, he writes, is a contrast. "We" may start by focusing on the priestly sacrifice, the intercessory nature of Jesus, and as a result thereby marginalize the King and conqueror, the supernatural battle. However, we forget that *Jesus is Victor*.[21] Such forgetfulness began to repudiate the eschatological victory of Christ over evil supernatural forces and thereby is a marginalizing of a traditional theology, originating with the ultra-early—Hebraic—church. This traditional theology is Cranmer's emphasis (as distinct from something of a contemporary approach). This traditional approach can be read from the Jewish early church as it developed into the patristic church. Cranmer's reason for including Psalm 110 on Christmas day reflects a distinctly Hebraic model. This Lewis identifies, and values: as evidenced in Psalm 110, read during the service of Evening Prayer on Christmas Day (though it is fair to suspect he has been introduced to it by his wife, Joy Davidman, reflecting on her

---

19   Lewis, *Reflections on the Psalms*, 107.

20   Lewis, *Reflections on the Psalms*, 107.

21   The phrase *Jesus is Victor* comes from German nineteenth-century eschatological ministry of the two German pastors, the father-and-son team of Johann Christoph Blumhardt (1805–80) and Christoph Friedrich Blumhardt (1842–1919), who found miracles happening amongst the people they were ministering to.

Jewish heritage and upbringing). This charismatic Lewis was also clearly evident from *The Screwtape Letters*.[22]

Lewis's Christmastide perception then extends to identifying Yeshua as the victor, reading from Psalm 45 and 89, and how perhaps most of Oxford's Anglican establishment had yet again missed this Hebraic model and mission of the Lord:

> In your majesty ride forth victoriously
> > in the cause of truth, humility and justice;
> > let your right hand achieve awesome deeds.
>
> Let your sharp arrows pierce the hearts of the king's enemies;
> > let the nations fall beneath your feet.
>
> Your throne, O God, will last for ever and ever;
> > a scepter of justice will be the scepter of your kingdom.
>
> > > Ps 45:4–6

And in Psalm 89 the promises to David's line that he will be first-born, the eldest son, heir, and be given the whole world; and in Psalm 32, continues Lewis, his enemies will be defeated.

> Here I will make a horn grow for David
> > and set up a lamp for my Anointed One.
>
> I will clothe his enemies with shame,
> > but his head will be adorned with a radiant crown.
>
> > > Ps 132:17–18

Along with the Magnificat, Lewis's perception demonstrates how those in the early Jewish church saw the arrival of the Messiah as confrontational and radical and entirely in keeping with the two-thousand-year-old Hebrew witness and expectation (but not as a military leader against Roman occupation!). This understanding, central to the Hebraic origins of the church, continues as the post-apostolic church develops, but changes, perhaps, with the Constantinian church:

> All this emphasizes an aspect of the Nativity to which our later sentiment about Christmas (excellent in itself) does less than justice. For those who first read these Psalms as poems about the birth of Christ, that birth primarily meant something very militant; the hero, the "judge" or champion or giant killer, who

---

22   Lewis, *The Screwtape Letters*.

10. The Psalms V: Yeshua, Mashiach: Second Meanings in the Psalms

was to fight and beat death, hell and the devils, had at last arrived, and the evidence suggests that Our Lord also thought of Himself in those terms. (Milton's poem on the Nativity well recaptures this side of Christmas.)[23]

Pentecost, Psalm 68: God's Victory

The picture of God the Victor as evident in Psalm 68 is assigned in The Book of Common Prayer to Whit Sunday (i.e. Pentecost).[24] But how was victory to be achieved. Contrary to the understanding amongst many intertestamental Jews, this was not a military victory against the Romans, the expulsion of a colonizing force. Psalm 68, for Lewis, indicates a far more supernatural, eschatological victory. Lewis notes in particular:

> The earth shook, the heavens poured down rain,
>   before God, the One of Sinai,
>   before God, the God of Israel.
>   Ps 68:8

So the miracles of exodus are aligned with the descent of the Holy Spirit in the form of tongues of fire. How so?—"The LORD announces the word, and the women who proclaim it are a mighty throng. Kings and armies flee in haste!" (Ps 68:11). So much for a violent macho-male military revolution and junta! But, notes Lewis, the real reason for Psalm 68 being assigned to Pentecost lies later:

> When you ascended on high,
>   you took many captives;
>   you received gifts from people,

---

23   Lewis, *Reflections on the Psalms*, 108.

24   Pentecost named "Whitsunday," or "White Sunday" (Whit Monday, following, with Whitsuntide, for the week) originally derived from the wearing of white vestments on Pentecost in the pre-Reformation churches on the Sunday feast of Pentecost, and earlier, in the Anglo-Saxon church, *hwitmonedei*, for the day after Whit Sunday, a holy day, from the early English *wit*, or, understanding.

Later, post-Reformation, there was the English folk tradition of wearing white clothes—men, women, and children!—on Whit Monday (a public holiday)—with dancing (reminiscent of the exodus—the Hebrew slaves having crossed the Red Sea) to celebrate: May Pole, Morris for the men, with Country Dancing for the maidens, all outdoors. A tradition that died in the carnage of the First World War: the May Poles all over the country being replaced by war memorials.

> even from the rebellious—
> that you, LORD God, might dwell there.
>
> Ps 68:18

So what does Lewis make of this? Lewis digresses on the translation and meaning of verse 18. The classic Hebrew translation as compared to the standard Pauline text (Eph 4:8) demonstrates that God, with the Israelite armies took huge masses of prisoners, and received tribute and booty. Paul in Ephesians 4:8 has a different interpretation or reading: "When he ascended on high, he took many captives and gave gifts to his people."[25] Lewis considers that this interpretation first inspired the association with the coming of the Holy Spirit, therefore Lewis sees the gifts of the Spirit referred to here, the importance of this coming after the ascension cannot be understated, writes Lewis. Following the ascension, the resurrected Yeshua instills gifts to the inner core of the disciples: "the Christ gives these gifts to men, or receives these gifts (notice how the Prayer Book version will now do well enough) from His Father 'for men,' for the use of men, in order to transmit them to men."[26] Lewis identifies a deep relationship between the ascension and the coming of the Spirit quoting John's Gospel: "It is expedient for you that I go away, for if I go not away the comforter will not come unto you" (John 16:7). The ascension is the withdrawal from the space-time in which our present senses operate, so as to allow the full presence of the Holy Spirit, the comforter (in a different mode from the manifestations of the Holy Spirit amongst the ancient Hebrews?). Lewis does note that there is a mystery here that attempting to explicate is beyond him.[27]

Psalm 22 and 68: Victim and Sufferer

Lewis continues with Psalm 68: Christ is the archetypal sufferer.[28] This is then a second complimentary layer of meaning: Jesus, as the epitome of those afflicted and suffering in their Hebraic status as *YHWH*'s chosen, is ultimately crucified; this is the expression of all who have ever suffered, and their afflictions are intimately related to his: starting with the Jew and moving out like radiating circles out into all humanity.

---

25   Lewis, *Reflections on the Psalms*, 108–9.
26   Lewis, *Reflections on the Psalms*, 109.
27   Lewis, *Reflections on the Psalms*, 109.
28   Lewis, *Reflections on the Psalms*, 109–10.

10. The Psalms V: Yeshua, Mashiach: Second Meanings in the Psalms

As with Psalm 22, for Lewis, the emergence of a second level of meaning requires no special, secret, gnostic knowledge, in the light of the crucifixion-resurrection, it is clear, in the fullness of time what the psalm is about. Furthermore, writes Lewis, Christ quoted this psalm as he endured the torture of being crucified. For Lewis, the sufferings on the cross evoke a depth of connection with afflicted humanity that the Psalms, even the Book of Job, scarcely begin to comprehend, but it is the meaning and prediction from the Hebrew Bible that gives us the connection.

> It is the union of total privation with total adherence to God, to a God who makes no response, simply because of what God is: "and thou continuest holy" (v. 3). All the sufferings of the righteous speak here . . . . But this too is for us the voice of Christ, for we have been taught that He who was without sin became sin for our sakes, plumbed the depth of that worst suffering which comes to evil men who at last know their own evil. Notice how this, in the original or literal sense, is hardly consistent with verses 8 and 9, and what counterpoint of truth this apparent contradiction takes on once the speaker is understood to be Christ.[29]

And yet in verses 7 and 9 Lewis notes a counterpoint to drive home how anyone—even the Jews, and of course Christians—may not realize what they say and do:

> All who see me mock me;
>   they hurl insults, shaking their heads.
> "He trusts in the LORD," they say,
>   "let the LORD rescue him.
> Let him deliver him,
>   since he delights in him."
> Yet you brought me out of the womb;
>   you made me trust in you,
>   even at my mother's breast.
>   Ps 22:7–9

In many ways the second-meaning prefigured interpretations are the Christological movement of the entire Hebrew scriptures. The disciples' ignorance during the days in Jerusalem leading to the cross are testimony to not just the blindness of the Jewish religious authorities (the Western churches' obsession with the splinter in the Jewish eye) but also

---

29   Lewis, *Reflections on the Psalms*, 110.

the myopia of fallen humanity's religious obsession with self-justification (the plank of self-righteousness in the eye of the Western churches). It is as if Jesus says, all of you, my disciples, will be spared, but I, Yeshua, will be sacrificed, and even when you witness a miracle it will be outside of all of your expectations: being taken and tried, tortured and spat on, humiliated and executed, slowly, horribly: crucified—it is all there in the Hebrew Bible—and then raised up, defeating death. All this together will be miraculous! By his wounds we are healed (1 Pet 2:24; cf. Isa 53) as the sins of the world are cleansed and forgiven. Atonement without the need of animal sacrifice: God saves—follow, and we will know God.

Psalm 45: Light on the Incarnation (Christmas)

Lewis does note that to say more about suffering would be to labor the point, as this is in many ways all too obvious to Christians; but these ideas—an afflicted, rejected, suffering Messiah—are a puzzle to many Jews who claim that Yeshua was not the long-awaited Messiah, but a sinner and heretic, worse, they appear foolishness to the pagans and gentiles even today (1 Cor 1:23). However, the importance of Christmas psalms is still relatively new in comparison with the movement over the last 150 years into what many see as a romantic, sentimental—populist—doctrine of the incarnation. The Christmas psalms, as Lewis names them, previse the incarnation in a Hebrew context, and they can give us "so many aspects of the Nativity we could never get from carols or even (easily) from the gospels."[30]

Because Psalm 45 was in all probability written as a poem for a royal wedding, or as Lewis terms it an "ode," then we have an almost secular poem that leads us towards the concept of the church as the bride, with Christ-Yeshua as the bridegroom, and aligns it with the incarnation and therefore with Christmas:[31] thus, we have humanity wedded into the chosen people of God.[32] How so, for Lewis: first, because, according to mystics in many religions, sexual union is a metaphor for the union

---

30   Lewis, *Reflections on the Psalms*, 110–11.

31   The psalm on its own does not bring us that concept. It simply gives the royal wedding. To see that concept, one must bring a much fuller (and later) understanding to the text.

32   Though, again, we cannot read this directly from the psalm. Only in reading through a later Christian understanding of the *ekklēsia* can we see this because the psalm says nothing about humanity in general united to the (coming) Messiah.

10. The Psalms V: Yeshua, Mashiach: Second Meanings in the Psalms

between God and humanity; second, this is a recurring theme and a recurring ritual" in many forms of paganism.

> [T]he god as bridegroom, his "holy marriage" with the goddess, is a recurrent theme and a recurrent ritual in many forms of Paganism—Paganism not at what we should call its purest or most enlightened, but perhaps at its most religious, at its most serious and convinced. And if, as I believe, Christ, in transcending and thus abrogating, also fulfils, both Paganism and Judaism, then we may expect that he fulfils this side of it too.[33]

Therefore, the pagan concept of divine marriage, unity with the gods, can be seen as a prefigurement of this. And as with all else in humanity, it can be seen even as a summed-up in him who is incarnated as Yeshua, the Hebrew Anointed One. Once the concept of Messiah is translated into Greek and Latin—*Christos*, the Christ—it takes on a different, possibly, more universal character, but it is still rooted in and is an ontological salvific unity with the Hebrews and with Jewish history: we worship a Jewish Messiah! Then; and as it is now?

Therefore, read with Hebraic insight, Psalm 45 restores Christmas to what Lewis terms its proper complexity: Christ-Yeshua, his arrival, sees a great warrior king, but also the bridegroom, the lover, and we must see the bride as the church, an ecclesial gathering that is called out of the world into a supernatural life. (Though perhaps we should see this as the *ecclesial invisibilis* rather than the earthly compromise that is the *ecclesial visibilis*.) This is a terrible calling, for Lewis: being church should be seen as "a costly honor,"[34] which brings us back to the place of suffering for the afflicted.

5. IMAGINATION AND THE THEOLOGICAL TRADITION

If, in addition to the Hebrew Bible, pagan Christs—that is, ideas, intimations, myths, and stories, pneumatologically generated in the mind of people isolated in space and time from God's chosen people— are a foreshadowing or allusion, relating figuratively to the incarnation-resurrection, and if they are rooted in genuine wisdom, then how do we

---

33 Lewis, *Reflections on the Psalms*, 112. See also, notes Lewis, the imagery and unity, the troubles of *YHWH's* relationship with Israel, in chapter 16 of Ezekiel.

34 Lewis, *Reflections on the Psalms*, 112–36.

assess and judge one interpretation from another? Lewis' mature beliefs about inspiration and imagination must be examined to ascertain what *value* he placed on prefigurement. It is Lewis' doctrine of the imagination that is fundamental to prefigurement and the developing understanding of the meaning and truth that we can learn from such myths, crucially, in relation to Hebraic revelation, as it inched slowly through generations across hundreds of years, to arrive at the incarnation-cross-resurrection . . . and ascension.[35]

An important source for Lewis of a doctrine of the imagination is the Scottish author, poet, and Christian minister George MacDonald (1824–1905)—Lewis' acknowledged master and teacher.[36] According to MacDonald, it is not necessarily our cognitive faculties that identify truth, but our imagination: God uses people's imagination to get through to them. Through MacDonald, Lewis viewed imagination and the intellect as given by the Holy Spirit; however, the reception of intimations, and our subsequent actions are governed by free will, and consequently also by the effects of original sin: humanity is free to reject or accept God on a conscious level, even though God may be pressing on each and every one, to some degree, in their sub-conscious minds. What is important here is the concept of a baptized imagination: "It is not surprising that for MacDonald the closer one is to Christ the Creator, the more faithful and vibrant the imagination will be."[37]

If, to summarize, the imagination is the capacity (or, in many ways, the gift) to create mental images, the ability to generate, spontaneously, illustrations, pictures, or images in the mind, which give meaning to our experience of reality, then the imagination helps us to understand and make sense of the world. The imagination is therefore of fundamental importance if we are going to learn, particularly if we accept the idea of revelation as unfolding. Storytelling is the key to both imaginative creating and to listening and learning: storytelling is fundamental to the ancient Hebrews, particularly in societies reliant upon an oral tradition.[38]

35   For Lewis on imagination see Schakel, *Reason and Imagination in C. S. Lewis*, as well as Lewis, "Psycho-Analysis and Literary Criticism," in *They Asked for a Paper*. See also Swinburne, *The Concept of Miracle*, and Swinburne, *Revelation*.

36   See, Lewis, *The Great Divorce*, 66–67. See also Lewis, "Introduction," in MacDonald, *Phantastes*, v–xii.

37   Dearborn, *Baptized Imagination*, 81.

38   This is, of course, distinct from the manner in which our cognitive mental

10. The Psalms V: Yeshua, Mashiach: Second Meanings in the Psalms

Walter Hooper[39] notes the importance for Lewis of a distinction between fantasy and imagination: Lewis argued that Freud was incorrect in asserting that all creative art issues from day-dreams, fantasies, and wish-fulfilments generated by the sub-conscious mind. (There are quite simply instances where a scientist can intimate, "guess," [second-guess?] what the truth will be, then to find that the evidence and experiments, the theorizing, does lead inadvertently to the intimated truth.) Instead, Lewis the literary critic asserted that there are two modes or activities of the imagination: one free, and the other enslaved to the will. What makes the Hebrew scriptures superior to the pagan intimations, we may assert, is not just in the character and strength of the freedom of the baptism of the mind, but also in the Hebrews' status as God's chosen people in their chosen land.[40]

Lewis absorbed MacDonald and Coleridge's theorizing about the imagination (grounded essentially in the philosophical idealism of Schelling, Kant's categorical imperative, and aesthetic idealism) in relation to God's revelation, and therefore in relation to the manner in which theology is formulated. This allowed him to justify re-interpreting the ancient pagan myths Christologically, identifying a second, fuller, subsequent, meaning a posteriori—after the Christ-event, particularly by looking at the subsequent understanding of so much in the Hebrew Bible that pointed to the actuality of the Christ-event. Lewis wrote, "I think that all things reflect heavenly truth, the imagination not least." [41]

---

processes work: thoughts appear to arise from an often unidentifiable source, and are therefore creative. Lewis and MacDonald therefore, in this context, saw how the imagination should, must, be pneumatologically governed—i.e., under the influence and persuasion of the Holy Spirit.

39   Hooper, *C. S. Lewis, a Companion and Guide*, 565.

40   See, Lewis, "Psycho-Analysis and Literary Criticism," first delivered at Westfield College in 1941 to a Literary Society, in Lewis, *They Asked for a Paper* (quotation 125). Lewis saw much to support this place for a baptized imagination—whether in the North European pagan religions and myths or in the Hebrew—as a vehicle for God's revelations of salvation history, in the work of the English Romantic poets. For example, Samuel Taylor Coleridge in *Biographia Literaria* (1817), 77. The *Biographia Literaria* is a discursive philosophical and literary autobiography with important essays on philosophy and aesthetics, and as such draws on continental philosophy in the form of Kant and Schelling. See, Brazier, *C. S. Lewis & the Christ*, Vol. 2 *The Work of Christ Revealed*, see: ch. 11 Christ as the Light of the World III: Refractions—Splintered Fragments of the True Light, 245–57; see specifically, v. A Baptized Imagination, 253.

41   Lewis, *Surprised by Joy*, 167.

A HEBRAIC INKLING

He acknowledged that the mind is illuminated by the divine, and that this leads to a degree of understanding—theological activity is not solely the result of human striving and searching. The imagination can, under certain circumstances, be an oracle of truth where general cognitive activities fail. Therefore, for Lewis, there is still the possibility of prevenient grace engendering inspiration and intimation, although such revelatory reception is still subject to the effects of the fall. Lewis asserted that God has used this fallen human imagination, images and mental pictures/models, to communicate some sort of intimation of God's salvific actions: the prefiguring images/myths were for Lewis pneumatologically given, gifted by the Holy Spirit, not humanly invented.

> The Divine light, we are told, "lighteneth every man." We should, therefore, expect to find in the imagination of great Pagan teachers and myth-makers some glimpse of that theme which we believe to be the very plot of the whole cosmic story—the theme of incarnation, death and rebirth. And the differences between the Pagan Christs (Balder, Osiris, etc.) and the Christ Himself is much what we should expect to find.[42]

Therefore, there will be second, or subsequent, meanings to identify and interpret. Given that meaning and truth relate to that which is of most importance to humanity—our salvation—and given that such meaning is communicated in stories and images, through the faculty of the imagination, the relationship between any given individual and the Holy Spirit is to be paramount: a baptized imagination is the litmus test of any "author" or "hearer" of such Christological prefigurements—intimations will be subject to second and subsequent meanings. And the measure of these pagan prefigurements must be the Hebrew Bible and how its intimations and revelation lead to the Christ-event. Truth and meaning are therefore, as we have established, teleological: all meaning and truth relates to a greater or lesser degree to the central event in cosmic human history—the Hebrew incarnation-cross-resurrection.[43]

---

42   Lewis, "Is Theology Poetry?" a paper read to the Socratic Club in Oxford.

43   This was Lewis' view; and neither modernism nor postmodernism—which question such a doctrine of Christological prefigurement—can accommodate such a proposition.

10. The Psalms V: Yeshua, Mashiach: Second Meanings in the Psalms

6. CONCLUSION

Did the Hebrew scriptures ever exist by and for themselves, separate from the rest of humanity? Were they not, along with the election of Abraham and therefore the Jews, always for the rest of humanity? Therefore, there would be hints and intimations, dreams and inklings of God's relationship with humanity, allusions, suggestion of salvation history, humanity's redemption? There are, it can be argued, countless examples of deification of an individual, or possession either wholly or partly, temporarily or permanently, by spirits or divine powers or "gods," but is this the same as the Hebraic-Christian incarnation? Is there anything resembling the incarnation in form or typology?[44] Avatars in Hinduism represent the descent of a "god" to earth in apparent incarnate form.[45] This is often an incarnation or embodiment, or a manifestation (but not the incarnation). For example, Krishna was the eighth avatar of Vishnu, incarnated to help the five brothers regain their kingdom. Sometimes these "gods" appear in human form; but they can escape the world at a moment's will. Avatar (meaning descent in Hinduism) was usually to counteract some evil in this world. However, "descending," "appearing," or "abiding" are not ontologically synonymous with the nature of incarnate being in Yeshua of Nazareth: Mary's flesh. There are similarities, but the two are not synonymous: being made flesh with all that is implied in being human is a different concept altogether, ontologically speaking. And these intimations do not in themselves save; indeed, they fail from a soteriological perspective. Furthermore, Baldur is not revived, restored, "resurrected": the truly good person does die. Many pagan tribes appeared to respond to these dreams by inventing new forms of human sacrifice for their own self-justification! (Which is, of course, what the Jewish religious authorities—the Sanhedrin, the High Priest, *et al.*—and the Roman authorities did by sacrificing Jesus.) However, God's love and sacrifice is spread wide, generously, and all people should be able to perceive some hints of the truth: the promise of forgiving judgement and the fullness of real resurrected life to come. The value of dream is

---

44   See, Scott and Selvanayagam, *Re-visioning India's Religious Traditions*, xix, 233. See, ch. 9, Julius Lipner, "Avatara and Incarnation?" specifically 124ff.

45   From Sanskrit for "descent," and chiefly found in Hinduism, avatars are "gods" in apparent incarnate form, the term is therefore used for a manifestation of a deity or released soul in bodily form on earth, the term also applies to an incarnation or embodiment of a person or idea. (OED).

clear from the Hebrew scriptures (Joseph the dreamer, sold into Egyptian slavery: the preservation of Israel!) and the New Testament (Gabriel's intimations and warning to Joseph for the survival of the infant Yeshua), as it is in North-West European pagan myths.

Yeshua Ha Mashiach, conceived by the Holy Spirit, born of Mary's flesh, this man is a Jew; Lewis notes how God for Jesus the Jew is not a pantheistic Indian or Oceanic "god":[46] this is the God of the Jews, the one true living God outside and beyond all other gods—the Being outside the world, the creator, the God who was and is infinitely different from anything else.[47] Different from Asiatic-Indian-Oceanic myths—in particular ancient Hindu—and yet propagated, disseminated, intimated of a truth within these ancient religions. And he was resurrected; pagan intimations point to failure: they don't deserve death yet they die, and attempts to revive, to wind back death, fail. The prefigured intimations, previsions, merely point to the true center for humanity, in Jerusalem two thousand years ago.

---

[46] Lewis, *Broadcast Talks*, 3. "The Shocking Alternative," BBC Home Service, London, Feb. 1, 1942, 4:45 to 5:00 pm, see 50–51.

[47] Lewis, *Mere Christianity*, 51.

PART III

FAMILY

"Children's children are a crown to the aged,
and parents are the pride of their children."

"A wise son brings joy to his father,
but a foolish son brings grief to his mother."
PROVERBS 17:6 & 10:1

11

Sarai-Sarah:
Identity . . . in the LORD

"When I had tea with C. S. Lewis and told him my favorite book of his was probably *The Great Divorce*, he beamed with approval and called it his Cinderella. What I didn't realize then was that hidden in his Cinderella was an attack on anti-Semitism."

KATHRYN LINDSKOOG[1]

"God also said to Abraham, 'As for Sarai your wife, you are no longer to call her Sarai; her name will be Sarah. I will bless her and will surely give you a son by her. I will bless her so that she will be the mother of nations; kings of peoples will come from her.' Abraham fell facedown; he laughed and said to himself, 'Will a son be born to a man a hundred years old? Will Sarah bear a child at the age of ninety?' And Abraham said to God, 'If only Ishmael might live under your blessing!' Then God said, 'Yes, but your wife Sarah will bear you a son, and you will call him Isaac. I will establish my covenant with him as an everlasting covenant for his descendants after him. And as for Ishmael, I have heard you: I will surely bless him; I will make him fruitful and will greatly increase his numbers. He will be the father of twelve rulers, and I will make him into a great nation. But my covenant I will establish with Isaac, whom Sarah will bear to you by this time next year.' When he had finished speaking with Abraham, God went up from him."

GENESIS 17:15–22

1. THE MOTHER OF ALL . . .

Sarai is the wife of Abraham, the founding father of the covenant of the pieces:[2] the special relationship between the Hebrews and God.

---

1   Lindskoog, "C. S. Lewis's Anti-Anti-Semitism in *The Great Divorce*," 33.

2   The covenant between the parts (Hebrew: *berith bein hebĕtarim*) is an event whereby God revealed himself to Abraham establishing a covenant, in which God announced that his descendants would eventually inherit the Land of Israel. It is

Sarai is the mother of Isaac, and thus the matriarch, the forebear, of all Israel, and—through the Jewish Messiah—of all humanity, in potentia: her descendants, as with her husband and patriarch Abraham, will outnumber the grains of sand in the desert and on the beaches (Gen 22:17, c.f. Ps 139:18). Sarai doubts the messengers of God that she will bear a son, but relents and is convinced in her faith when she receives an annunciation of the birth of Isaac (Gen 17:15): thus, in her faith she is renamed Sarah. Together Abraham and Sarah had come to the promised land as part of God's assurance of children, descendants, in the land (Gen 12:1-5). Sarai saw her barrenness as endangering the promise and gives her handmaiden Hagar to Abraham as a surrogate womb (Gen 16:1-2). But despite her lack of faith, she does conceive with her husband, giving birth to Isaac, the beloved. She then urges Abraham to send Hagar and Ishmael away. Abraham, reluctant at first, does. Therefore, Sarah, for some modern Bible scholars, is the mother of emancipation: she frees the slaves Hagar and Ishmael, sending them away.[3]

2. SARAH SMITH OF GOLDER'S GREEN

Much of Lewis's work is in the form of analogical and symbolic narratives: theologically charged stories that reflect reality, often a biblical reality. We may call this method analogical narrative.[4] These analogical narratives are usually considered to be four works: *The Space Trilogy* (1938, 1943, 1945), *The Screwtape Letters* (1942), *The Great Divorce* (1945), and *The Chronicles of Narnia* (1950-56). The characters invented are often biblically inspired; and the stories really could have happened (Lewis's concept of the "supposal");[5] there is an inner logic to them that complements the source material. For example, the person and name of Sarah Smith in

---

important to note that the Bible speaks of a single covenant with the patriarchs, repeated to Isaac and Jacob. Critical scholars see Gen 15 and Gen 17 as originating in two different stories that have been merged into a single narrative; however, in context, Gen 17 can be seen as a ratification of an already-existing covenant.

3   However, that is putting a very positive spin on the story. Sarah has no interest in liberating slaves. Her only concern is not to have a threat to her son inheriting the family inheritance. So she insists on banishing Hagar and Israel to the wilderness. It was rather brutal.

4   See, Brazier, *C. S. Lewis—On the Christ of a Religious Economy. I*, ch. 5 Analogical and Symbolic Narratives I: Narrative Theology, Supposition and Genre, Mythopoeic Theorizing—Imagining The Christ, 123-40.

5   Brazier, *C. S. Lewis—On the Christ of a Religious Economy. I.*, 123-40.

The Great Divorce.[6] Names don't happen by accident in Lewis's work. For instance, Peter in *The Chronicles of Narnia*, named after Peter the apostle (remembering that religion is veiled in Narnia). A pertinent character in *The Great Divorce* is Sarah Smith. So who is Sarah Smith?—and how is she connected to Sarai/Sarah the Hebrew matriarch? It is fair to assume that Lewis invokes the name Sarah because of where the character lived: a Jewish district of London. Smith is a very common English family name.[7] Sarah Smith is dead, she is visiting the fringes of heaven to try to persuade her dead husband who languishes in hell to renounce his pagan rebellion and return with her to heaven.

When alive on earth they lived in Golder's Green.

Golder's Green is a middle-class and professional suburb in North London where the majority of the population is Jewish; the suburb has been a prominent Jewish community since the early twentieth century.[8] So Sarah Smith—named after Abraham's wife, with a stereotypical English family name—lived in the Jewish district of Golder's Green, when she was alive. For Lewis, she is the archetypal Jew, close to God yet exuding the selfless, unconditional love that is *agápē*, which characterized the Jewish Messiah—Yeshua, Ha Mashiach—and (should characterize) his followers.

3. RELIGIOUS IDENTITY?

Sarah Smith is an ordinary obscure woman. She is married—but it is not a good marriage. The fault lies with her husband. She had a very large family, but she was childless; without any feign or pretense or exhibiting herself, she loved everyone she met. She knew just what was right to help

6 Lewis, *The Great Divorce* (1945).

7 Derived from the old English *smið*, meaning one who works in metal. At the turn of the twentieth century, the surname was sufficiently prevalent in England to have prompted the statement: "Common to every village in England, north, south, east, and west"; and sufficiently common on the (European) continent (in various forms) to be "common in most countries of Europe." Wikipedia: "Smith," accessed Dec 21, 2020.

8 The Jewish community took root after Hitler's rise to power, with the first German Jewish immigrants forming the Golder's Green *Beth Hamedrash*. Soon after, Galician Jewish immigrants formed other synagogues. With it came the formation of Jewish schools such as Menorah before the onset of World War II. Today there are close to fifty Kosher restaurants and eateries under rabbinical supervision in Golder's Green, and more than forty synagogues dotted throughout the area continuing into neighboring Hendon, as well as thirty schools (some in outlying areas due to space restriction), many of them private. Wikipedia; accessed Dec 21, 2020. In recent years East Asian and South Asian migrants as well as second and third generation British have moved into the area.

them, complement them, love them, even if it was veiled love, or tough love, selfless love: *agápē*. If, because of the *fall*, love can become defective, corrupt, poisoned, then what is left of pure love? Pure love—God-generated love, *agápē*, preveniently initiated through the Holy Spirit—this should be the default position; pure love is prelapsarian, but humanity fell, and tainted by original sin all our loves can be defective, corrupt, poisoned, to a greater or lesser degree. But the more we deny ourselves the greater the possibility of a real purity in our loves. The weakness is obvious with *érōs*, but even *agápē* can be selfishly motivated: are we ever charitable for self-interest, to enhance our credibility and standing, or generous for misguided purposes? Pure love can be regained, rekindled, in the human, but only by the human surrendering to the one example of uncontaminated, unadulterated, pure love: Jesus, who is love and is logos and is reason, and is the ultimate self-denying sacrificial love. Human love without God is by default tainted and fallen.[9] It is only by allowing the love of God that is love itself to flow and work through us that we can begin to love as God intended for the human. This is at the heart of the soteriology Lewis presented in *The Great Divorce*: the damned visiting the fringes of heaven are locked into themselves. But the redeemed meet with them and invite them to come out of themselves and meet with love itself. This will be painful at first, even when taking tiny steps out of themselves, but the pain will gradually subside and if they but continue—with the benefit of the Holy Spirit—then they will begin to perceive love itself and move into love itself. But they don't: those who remain in hell were in hell all along, those who do move, however painfully at first, into *love itself* were in heaven all along.

This is best presented by Lewis in the meeting between Sarah Smith and her husband. Sarah, though an ordinary, obscure woman, a housewife, and certainly not a religious professional or great church figure, is presented as one of the greatest, purest, and most Christlike of saints.[10] Her husband is presented in *The Great Divorce* as a tragedian, who complains that she is misusing the sacred word love if it does not conform to or pander to his selfish pretense, and if everyone is not obedient, hanging on his every word, in loving him. The husband is self-centered and

    9   See, Brazier, *C. S. Lewis—On the Christ of a Religious Economy. I.*, ch. 7, §§. 1., specifically i. "God is Triune," ii. "Immanence and Economic Action," and, iii. "God is Love."
    10   Lewis, *Great Divorce*, chs. 12–13.

11. Sarai-Sarah: Identity... in the LORD

cannot begin to conceive how to love altruistically. We may ask, to what degree does the tragedian, Sarah's husband from this life, represents the European Enlightenment: modernism and liberalism, progress, the arts, humanity without God? Sarah is defined and accompanied by love—the visible manifestation of those she helped and loved for no other purpose than their benefit, even if it cost her, even if it diminished her in terms of human status, human power, human influence and authority. Those who are closest to Christ become more and more like this Jewish Messiah: the Christlike are by default obscure and often not noticeable. Sarah Smith puts to shame many Christians who understand about this love and think they are so marvelous at loving (and tell others how marvelous they are at loving). To her husband she comments, "'I cannot love a lie,' said the Lady. 'I cannot love the thing which is not. I am in Love [Christ], and out of it I will not go.'" As her husband vanishes (represented by both the dwarfish figure, and the tragedian; something of a split personality?), she turns to walk away, she is accompanied, by a song, inspired by Dante.

Lewis is deliberately writing from a Jewish-Christian perspective. He has very carefully crafted this song of love, having already established that she is not in love with her husband but is *in love himself*—the Christ. Lewis has very carefully drawn on scripture—both Hebrew and Christian Testaments. The analogy with the gospel of love needs no elucidation, however, the imagery is also drawn from the Book of Isaiah and from the Psalms. Lewis is intentionally echoing their style and adapting content from ancient Hebrew scripture, with some detail clearly from Dante's presentation of Beatrice in *The Divine Comedy*. Try as hard as he can, Frank, the husband, even using emotional blackmail (which he used effectively in their marriage when alive), fails to corrupt her, to destroy Sarah Smith.

4. ENCOUNTER

In *The Great Divorce* there are a number of characters—dead, languishing in hell—who are invited to visit the fringes of heaven. Greeted by friends or relatives who try to persuade them to desist from their rebellion against God, the damned become so embroiled in constantly repeating the conditions of their rebellion that there is nothing more to define them. The last elements of their humanity gone they disappear, they are drawn into (apparent) nothingness.[11] Either the charade is left, which is a mere echo, a parody, of what was once the human, or they disappear and cease to exist. For example, using graphic analogical narrative, Lewis presents Frank—Sarah's husband—who, though human, is a wizened and misshapen dwarf, held by a chain to a tall and pretentious man: a tragedian, an actor, a charade, who is constantly focused on the sad, the distressing, the tragic (both the dwarf and this artiste are Frank Smith!).[12] (Frank may have been Jewish, having adopted an English family name, or he may have been English and nominally Christian, Sarah being wedded to the gentile, the pagan, the heathen, just as the gospel is moved into the gentile by the apostle Paul.) The encounter and dialogue is spread across two chapters.[13] Frank the tragedian, the actor, speaks in an affected false

---

[11] Does Lewis veer close to a doctrine of annihilationism here? "In Christianity, annihilationism (also known as extinctionism or destructionism) is the belief that those who are wicked will perish or be no more. It states that after the final judgment, all unsaved human beings, all fallen angels (all of the damned) and Satan himself will be totally destroyed so as to not exist, or that their consciousness will be extinguished rather than suffer everlasting torment in hell (often synonymized with the lake of fire). Annihilationism is directly related to the doctrine of conditional immortality, the idea that a human soul is not immortal unless it is given eternal life. Annihilationism asserts that God will eventually destroy the wicked, leaving only the righteous to live on in immortality." Wikipedia: "Annihilationism." (accessed Dec 30, 2020).

While many scriptural references can be quoted to support annihilationism, an equal number can deny such a doctrine. The question, which Lewis demonstrates admirably in *The Great Divorce*, is, what is left of the human, the person as it subsists in hell and perhaps merely ceases to be itself, which—as Tolkien demonstrated in *The Lord of the Rings* with the character/person of Sauron—nothing but unadulterated hating and domineering evil exists where the person has gone, ceased . . . in the end. (Is this a variation of *post-mortem* Buddhist self-annihilation?)

[12] "Frank's character is a complicated metaphor for the way humans use pity and self-loathing to manipulate other people, though he only appears toward the end of the novel. In life Frank knew and was loved by Sarah Smith, and would take advantage of her love by pretending that she'd hurt his feelings. Indeed, Frank has a long history of pretending to be sad in order to make other people feel guilty—even as a child he would do so. In the afterlife, Frank appears as two different ghosts, one small (the Dwarf), the other tall (the Tragedian). The Dwarf represents Frank's inner life: his self-hatred, and his manipulative tendencies. The Tragedian, on the other hand, represents the "image" of pain and sadness that Frank tries to project in order to make other people feel guilty. Thus, in the afterlife Frank takes on a form that externalizes the psychological processes by which Frank would try to "blackmail" Sarah into feeling sorry for him." *Lit Charts*: https://www.litcharts.com/lit/the-great-divorce/characters/frank-dwarf-tragedian.

[13] Lewis, *Great Divorce*, Chps 12 & 13, 89–100.

and pretentious manner; Frank the dwarf rarely speaks. The actor's speech is full of constant self-pity and self-glorification, a demand, unending, for everyone—including his wife who has descended from the joys of heaven to meet him. Frank expects everyone to conform to his expectations, to hover round him to wait on his every demand. This not being so, his speech is a constant soliloquy of complaint and regret, *ennui*, at his marginalization. Initially this complaint was spoken in unison by the dwarf and by the actor, but gradually—even though his wife was speaking to Frank the dwarf, the actor takes over. His rhetoric opposes his wife's pleading for him to stop the pretense, accept his wrong, and repent—and to move into heaven. The dwarf gradually shrinks, getting smaller and smaller, he eventually disappears leaving the actor, the Tragedian, holding a hanging chain:

> "Love? How dare you use that sacred word?" said the Tragedian. At the same moment he gathered up the chain which had now for some time been swinging uselessly at his side, and somehow disposed of it. I am not quite sure, but I think he swallowed it. Then for the first time it became clear that the Lady saw and addressed him only.
> "Where is Frank?" she said. "And who are you, Sir? I never knew you. Perhaps you had better leave me. Or stay, if you prefer. If it would help you and if it were possible I would go down with you into hell: but you cannot bring hell into me."
> "You do not love me," said the Tragedian in a thin bat-like voice: and he was now very difficult to see.
> "I cannot love a lie," said the Lady. "I cannot love the thing which is not. I am in Love, and out of it I will not go."[14]

There was no answer. The Tragedian had vanished. The Lady was alone.[15] Frank has become nothing more than the artificial pretense of his rhetorical complaint, like a tragedian, an actor, who can no longer break out of the role it plays: there is nothing left but the pretense, which then dissolves into *nothingness*. Sarah is a saint of heaven, she loves selflessly, she is love: on earth she is presented as a Jewish Christian (that is, she is implicitly Christian, i.e. of the "Anointed One," because she is anointed in love, and is therefore possessed by the Christ—we know not what formal religious practice she indulged in when alive. Lewis tells us not).

14 Lewis, *Great Divorce*, 99.
15 Lewis, *Great Divorce*, 100.

So Sarah epitomizes the Hebrew as one of God's chosen. She is not consciously or outwardly either Jewish or Christian (she wears no badge of identity politics used to assert herself over others), yet she is both, while simultaneously being beyond formal religion: the unity, the connection, is with and in Yeshua Ha Mashiach, we may say, whether she knows him or not.

Lewis placed her living in the North London suburb of Golder's Green, so we were not mistaken in the Hebraic analogy!

5. DENOUNCING ANTI-SEMITISM

Kathryn Lindskoog, in 2001, published a brief article, which broached the subject of Sarah Smith's identity in relation to Lewis's attack on anti-Semitism: or what constitutes "anti- anti-Semitism," as she terms it, and in the context of European politics in the 1940s: Hitler and National Socialism, the Holocaust, and the Second World War.[16] Lindskoog notes how there is veiled, almost hidden, in *The Great Divorce*, an attack on anti-Semitism, centered on Sarah Smith.[17] Lindskoog notes how throughout the 1930s Lewis and Tolkien spared no embarrassment at denouncing the National Socialists and their attitude towards the Jews (Tolkien intentionally offended his German publisher for even asking about his racial purity as an author, confessing, "I regret that I appear to have no ancestors of that gifted people"). At the Fall of Western Europe in 1940 they both realized during an evening discussion[18] that there were statements in their works that would have marked them as sympathetic to the Jews but also as anti-Nazi!—they were prepared to face the onslaught of the tyrant Hitler and his legions if England fell to invasion. To Lewis, an anti-Semite was "an obnoxious and violent bully."[19] In *The Pilgrim's Regress*, Lewis had referred to "a tribe of black-shirted dwarfs named the Swastici, who were vassals to a bloodthirsty northern tyrant named Savage," notes Lindskoog.[20] She also notes how many people miss Lewis's dismissal of the stereotypical picture of Jews common to the British people (this was also true of Lewis's educators at public school, and to a

---

16 Lindskoog, "C. S. Lewis's Anti- Anti-Semitism," 33–37.
17 Lindskoog, "C. S. Lewis's Anti- Anti-Semitism," 33.
18 Lindskoog, "C. S. Lewis's Anti- Anti-Semitism," 33.
19 Lindskoog, "C. S. Lewis's Anti- Anti-Semitism," 33–34.
20 Lindskoog, "C. S. Lewis's Anti- Anti-Semitism," 33.

11. Sarai-Sarah: Identity . . . in the LORD

limited degree at Oxford) as evidenced by business characters (medieval-type money lenders) in *The Great Divorce*.[21]

The great strength of Lewis's portrait of Sarah Smith is in the analogy with Dante's Beatrice; *The Great Divorce* being Lewis's compliment to *The Divine Comedy*. Lindskoog then deals with the name Sarah Smith, and her location, Golder's Green, detailing the Hebrew heritage of both.[22] Lindskoog raises the question of whether she is a Jewish convert, i.e., a Messianic Jew, or Jewish Christian. "How is it that a Jewish woman is celebrated in heaven in a paraphrase of Psalm 91 that incorporates the Christian Trinity? I assumed that her felicity there might simply echo that of Pipheus in Dante's *Divine Comedy* and foreshadow Emeth's in Lewis's *The Last Battle*."[23]

6. EPHESIANS: UNITY

A key biblical text that epitomizes Lewis as a Hebraic Inkling and his developing relationship with Judaism is in Paul's letter to the church at Ephesus.

> Therefore, remember that formerly you who are gentiles by birth and called "uncircumcised" by those who call themselves "the circumcision" (which is done in the body by human hands)—remember that at that time you were separate from Christ, excluded from citizenship in Israel and foreigners to the covenants of the promise, without hope and without God in the world. But now in Christ Jesus you who once were far away have been brought near by the blood of Christ. For he himself is our peace, who has made the two groups one and has destroyed the barrier, the dividing wall of hostility, by setting aside in his flesh the law with its commands and regulations. His purpose was to create in himself one new humanity out of the two, thus making peace . . . .
> Eph 2:11–15

---

21   Lindskoog, "C. S. Lewis's Anti- Anti-Semitism," 35.

22   Lindskoog notes the pertinence with which Lewis preached his sermon "Miracles" at St Jude on the Hill Church in Golder's Green: Nov 26, 1942.

23   Lindskoog, "C. S. Lewis's Anti- Anti-Semitism," 36.

It is important to remember that Paul here is addressing gentiles, not Jews.[24] Gentile Christians are still gentiles—in the flesh, by birth. God has dealt differently with Jews from gentiles, but such believers are enfolded into God's chosen people. As gentiles, our belonging, enfolding, in Israel is not to be seen only as a gain—a matter of rights and privileges. No; we are obliged to observe a godly way of life that has its origin in God's relationship with Abraham, and with the chosen people. Further, we are obliged to relate as family to the Jewish community to whom our faith has combined us, fused, us (Eph 2:11–12; Rom 11:17–24; and 15:27).

Paul's comments are part of the *raison d'etre* for a Jewish Christian perspective, at the very least, a justification for a form of Messianic Judaism for many: Paul's perception is fundamental to understanding both the nature of the Torah, which is still considered valid and relevant, and is thus binding on those of faith in Yeshua, and sets out the relationship between Jews and gentiles from a messianic perspective.

This is what is developing in Lewis's thinking—a unity beyond distinction (Jews are still by birth Jews, gentile believers are still gentile in the flesh, but no longer pagan, heathen). There may be differences, but both Messianic Jew and gentile Christian are one in Jesus, the Jewish Messiah. As Barth noted, it is not a question of the Jews rejecting the Messiah, though some have, temporarily, not acknowledged him—yet.[25] Furthermore, the Jewish person is (from a Christian perspective) implicitly in Yeshua, *the second person of the Trinity*, because for thousands of years they have listened to *him* as God, *YHWH: HaShem*—by no other name. But this does not make self-confessed Christians any better; no, in many instances far worse because Christians so often deny their belonging to the Jewish family. This leads, as Paul notes, to a new humanity with difference but no division (thus does not denominational separatism become a demonic sin?). To deny this is to diminish us as we are all made in him. Lewis's work develops more and more along these lines in the 1950s. Furthermore, there is his marriage to a Jewish Christian: Joy Davidman. Lewis's life and career becomes defined more and more by this relationship between Judaism and Christianity, by millennia of Hebrew

---

24 On the word "gentiles," Greek *ethnē*, equivalent to Hebrew *goyim*; see Matt 5:46; 1 Cor 10:32; Rom 11:13.

25 "He was by necessity a Jew.... The man who is ashamed of Israel is ashamed of Jesus Christ and therefore of his own existence." Karl Barth, *Dogmatik im Grundriß*, 67. My translation.

revelation and its fulfillment in the Jewish Messiah, thus—through study, faith, and marriage—does he not become implicitly somewhat Jewish in his Christian faith, while still respecting and valuing Greek philosophy as a foundation of reason? Sarah Smith shows us how to love and how to be in love.

7. GLORY

If, through Sarah Smith we can begin to glimpse how we should love, such a perception does not redeem us. It merely points to how we should be, which without Christ's atoning sacrifice would lead to despair. No. We are on the outside, we are without love, we are where we do not belong, we love as we should not (yet we are obsessed with the wrong sort of love); we are not where we truly belong. We believe we know about God when we should really listen to what he knows and how he regards us. The warning is there in scripture, for some will come before him in judgment and will hear the terrible words, "You that are accursed, depart from me into the eternal fire prepared for the devil and his angels" (Matt 25:41). Our predicament outside becomes permanent and potentially utterly destructive in annihilation. Lewis has Sarah Smith deliberately echo Jesus's warning about eschatological judgement when she utters to Frank, "And who are you, Sir? I never knew you." (cf. Matt 7:23). We must accept the desire of God to delight in us, to change us, to draw us up: Christ descended for to draw us up.

When we have become as perfect as possible in voluntary obedience, and through our flawed attempts to love, then God will confer that glory that, Lewis notes, is delight and that issues from *love itself*. And this is a love that infiltrates and permeates the Hebrew Bible. But, Lewis continues and warns, the cross comes before the crown, and our neighbor now becomes a holy object presented to our senses, we must love our neighbor because Christ is hidden in our neighbor, the true glory is hidden: "for in him also Christ *vere latitat*—the glorifier and the glorified, Glory himself, is truly hidden."[26] If we can deny ourselves we can love our neighbor. If we

---

26 Lewis, "The Weight of Glory," 31. *Vere latitat*, literally "truly hides himself, lurks." Lewis is quoting from Thomas Aquinas' Eucharistic hymn *Adoro Te Devote*, (Thee We Adore, O Hidden Savior): therefore, Christ is "truly present, but concealed." Lewis is paraphrasing the second line "*Quæ sub his figuris vere latitas.*"

can deny our own self-glorification, exercised through our own corrupted loves, we will be glorified by God, *love itself* will glorify us.[27]

Sarah Smith is a template for what we find later in Lewis's work in the 1950s, especially in the context of the *analogia fidei*:[28] his study of the Psalms, his marriage to Joy Davidman, and an increasing respect for the Hebraic heritage of Christianity.

---

[27] If Christ is hidden in our neighbor does this therefore imply the judgment outlined in Matt 25:31–46, whether we claim to be Christian or live in ignorance of the Christ-event?—but what happens when anti-Semitism becomes the sin against the Holy Spirit (Matt 12:31)?

[28] In the context of the *analogia fidei*, see: Brazier, "C. S. Lewis and the Anscombe Debate."

12

The Incarnation Nation: the People and the Savior

> "Surely the nations are like a drop in a bucket;
>   they are regarded as dust on the scales;
>   he weighs the islands as though they were fine dust.
> Lebanon is not sufficient for altar fires,
>   nor its animals enough for burnt offerings.
> Before him all the nations are as nothing;
>   they are regarded by him as worthless
>   and less than nothing."
>
> ISAIAH 40:15-17

> "Love having become a god, becomes a demon. . . . I turn now to the love of one's country. Here there is no need to labour M. de Rougemont's maxim; we all know now that this love becomes a demon when it becomes a god. Some begin to suspect that it is never anything but a demon. But then they have to reject half the high poetry and half the heroic action our race has achieved. We cannot keep even Christ's lament over Jerusalem. He too exhibits love for His country."
>
> C. S. LEWIS [1]

1. INTRODUCTION

We are beginning to focus more and more on the heart of Judaea-Christianity: Jesus of Nazareth, the Christ—properly *Yeshua ben Yoseph, Ha Mashiach*. But this is more than merely one person; this is a man who has a cataclysmic role for the nation of Israel, and for humanity beyond. This is why God chose—more pertinently, forged and created—such

---

[1] Lewis, *The Four Loves*, 21-22 & 53

a people: from Abraham. And beyond Abraham and Yeshua: people, nations: humanity. But what value and what criticism of nations states before God is there when the chosen people should form a model for humanity, an ideal? What does the Hebrew witness tell us of nations? Babylon, Egypt Persia, Assyria, ... the Philistines, and a host of tribal identity politic groups (!): they are the enemies of Israel. They are the contradiction. These great pagan nations, gentiles, are before God, judged by God—*El Shaddai*. The prophet Isaiah asserts that they are dust on the scales, they are weighed in the balance and are less than nothing; and worse was to come: Greece and Rome, from Alexander the so-called Great, through to Caesar, Tiberius, Nero, the cult of personality—idolatry—raises up a single person to epitomize the nation state, but they are regarded as worthless, less than naught, a nonentity.

But what of Israel as a nation? Ancient Israel consistently fails. It struggles through mistakes as to what it should do and be; it keeps reverting to pagan religious practices, and when it does appear to get the temple worship right, it becomes a fixed civic religion that sacrifices the prophets and refutes their warnings. Yet it endures and bears witness, testimony, against, the surrounding pagan gentiles in all their demonic worldly success. The eternal Israel is not of this world. The value to this tiny (relative to the great nations and empires) nation state is in its status as God's chosen. And this witness is, as the Letter to the Hebrews offers, eschatological: righteousness through faith, witness through endurance. This is how a nation is to be defined. It is the future breaking into the present, and conflicting—jarring, declared incompatible—with the powers of this world. Again, the Israelite witness:

> All these people were still living by faith when they died. They did not receive the things promised; they only saw them and welcomed them from a distance, admitting that they were foreigners and strangers on earth; ... they were longing for a better country—a heavenly one. Therefore God is not ashamed to be called their God, for he has prepared a city for them.
>
> By faith Abraham, when God tested him, offered Isaac as a sacrifice. He who had embraced the promises was about to sacrifice his one and only son.... And what more shall I say? I do not have time to tell about Gideon, Barak, Samson and Jephthah, about David and Samuel and the prophets, who through faith conquered kingdoms, administered justice, and gained what was

12. The Incarnation Nation: the People and the Savior

promised; who shut the mouths of lions, quenched the fury of the flames, and escaped the edge of the sword; whose weakness was turned to strength; and who became powerful in battle and routed foreign armies. Women received back their dead, raised to life again. There were others who were tortured, refusing to be released so that they might gain an even better resurrection. Some faced jeers and flogging, and even chains and imprisonment. They were put to death by stoning; they were sawed in two; they were killed by the sword. They went about in sheepskins and goatskins, destitute, persecuted and mistreated—*the world was not worthy of them*. They wandered in deserts and mountains, living in caves and in holes in the ground. These were all commended for their faith, yet none of them received what had been promised, since God had planned something better for us so that only together with us would they be made perfect.

Heb 11:13, 16b–17, 32–40

The nation is replaced by a city (*polis*), within a kingdom—the kingdom of God—not a republic. The Hebrew nation leads to a city, the new Jerusalem, in the kingdom, but this is not of this earth. The nations of this world (often underpinned by patriotism)[2] will always fail: the history of nations, countries, even of ancient tribes, is a history, for Lewis, characterized by money and poverty, war and ambition, prostitution, the class struggle, empires, and slavery. Lewis takes this further: original sin is the key to history. Civilizations and cultures grow up, often founded on sound principles; good laws are formulated, but something always goes wrong: "some fatal flaw always brings the selfish and cruel people to the top and it all slides back into misery and ruin."[3]

In general terms, Lewis warns of the dangers of nationalism and the religious confusion and nihilism that gentile nations produce: "That is why horrible nations have horrible religions: they have been looking at God through a dirty lens."[4]

---

2 For Lewis on patriotism see: Lewis, *The Four Loves*, 18, 21–22, 39, 42–46, 47–48, & 53. Lewis, *Transposition and Other Addresses*, 21f. Lewis, *Collected Letters, Vol. I*, 88, 97, 102, 330, 341, 351, 424, 441, 448, 730, 744, 899, 1040, 1049. Lewis, *Collected Letters, Vol. II*, 42 & 699. Lewis, *Collected Letters, Vol. III*, 1390 & 1495.

3 Lewis, *Broadcast Talks*, 49.

4 Lewis, *Mere Christianity*, 165.

2. THE PEOPLE OF ISRAEL: THE NATION AND THE INCARNATION

Lewis notes how our modern democratic concepts (often driven by statistical/mathematical assumptions—some would say even by political rights) lead to expectations that all religious intent in humanity should be equivalent, so as to give all an equal opportunity to find God. This ignores the reality that any valid search for God is not on the part of *fallen* humanity, but it is God who searches for us, seeks out our salvation. As such is not God's search eschatological? Furthermore, there will be a single moment in every individual's life (John 3:1-10) when God offers them a clean, simple, open, unhindered choice. We noted this in Lewis's conversion account, but he also cites it in *The Screwtape Letters* (only, in this instance, a man rejects the sway of God on his mind, and does not convert).[5] Furthermore Lewis imagines a theory of multi-faith religious equality, a "picture of great centripetal roads coming from all directions, with well-disposed people, all meaning the same thing, and getting closer and closer together."[6] But this is a false picture, generated by, we might suggest, sublimated guilt from fallen humanity desperate to solve the eschatological crisis it finds itself in. But, notes Lewis, if we take seriously the thousands of years of Hebrew witness, the truth is polar opposite. God selects and forges one people out of all:

> Purged and proved again and again. Some are lost in the desert before they reach Palestine; some stay in Babylon; some becoming indifferent. The whole thing narrows and narrows, until at last it comes down to a little point, small as the point of a spear—a Jewish girl at her prayers. That is what the whole of human nature has narrowed down to before the Incarnation takes place.[7]

This is not what humanity expects, or demands (as the history of the Jews, of anti-Semitism, and the persecution by the churches demonstrates). But this is clearly God's way of working. Lewis lapses into the scientific and biological: the universe is astonishingly selective

---

5   See, Lewis, *The Screwtape Letters*, 2-4.

6   Lewis, "The Grand Miracle," (1945), in, *Undeceptions*, 71. See, (Pt. I, Ch. 9; London: 1971), 60.

7   Lewis, "The Grand Miracle," (1945), 60.

12. The Incarnation Nation: the People and the Savior

(some might say unpardonably) and undemocratic. Consider, notes Lewis, out of apparently infinite space, a relatively tiny proportion appears to be occupied by matter, furthermore an even tinier amount can sustain organic life, let alone intelligent, rational, beings. Selection and evolutionary waste appear, so Lewis asserts, to be unjust . . . by human standards.[8] There is also selectiveness in the Christian story, but not necessarily comparable with nature: "The people who are selected are, in a sense, unfairly selected for a supreme honor; but it is also a supreme burden. The People of Israel come to realize that it is their woes which are saving the world."[9] This may lead to injustice and tyranny, but it endows opportunity for grace: humility and kindness, love and wonder, awe and veneration. How would a world appear, where it was not possible for there to be difference: Lewis notes, the monotony and boredom of never meeting anyone of greater intelligence, or of different beliefs and life, never more or less beautiful, or stronger or weaker. Equality would then appear to be nihilistic. The criticism of orthodoxy is that the incarnation is, in its ontology, undemocratic, wildly inequitable and exclusive, and unfair on other religions. This critique usually comes from left-leaning secular liberals, or self-identifying religious atheists, in clerical positions in the churches, or in professional positions in the academy. Or to coin a phrase from modern academic philosophy, it represents *the scandal of particularity*.[10]

---

8   Lewis, "The Grand Miracle," (1945), 60
9   Lewis, "The Grand Miracle," (1945), 60
10   Lewis, "The Grand Miracle," (1945), 60–61. The concept goes back to Duns Scotus, that the truth is particular/concrete and moves to a wider universal understanding. Theologians call the principle of concrete-to-universal knowing "the scandal of particularity." John Duns Scotus asserted that God only created particulars and individuals, a quality he named "thisness" (*haecceity*). Thisness grounds the principle of incarnation in the concrete and the specific. You can't really love universals. It's hard to love concepts, forces, or ideas. A criticism is that ideology is just the ego wrapping itself around such abstractions. However, philosophers dismiss the incarnation as a particularity when they assert we can only know truth through the universal. For a salutary introduction, see: https://cac.org/the-scandal-of-the-particular-2018-03-19/

3. SKEPTICISM AND THE SCANDAL OF PARTICULARITY

Intellectual Arrogance and Disbelief

Hermann Samuel Reimarus (1694–1768), a German New Testament scholar and critic, and a philosopher, a proponent of the Enlightenment and of deism, claimed that the human mind can, through reason alone, know of God. Therefore, revelation was unnecessary. Reimarus, along with Gotthold Ephraim Lessing (1729–81), a German writer, philosopher, publicist, and art critic, and representative of the German Enlightenment and spokesperson of the bourgeoisie, together formulated and established much of a new doctrine of scripture that was adopted by many skeptics in the eighteenth century through to today. In Britain, contributing to this skepticism, Thomas Woolston (1668–1733), theologian, cleric, and English deist, asserted that all Hebrew and Christian scripture was unreliable, and that the resurrection narratives were a fabrication. In keeping with the deistic belief that denied miracles as an interference with the self-governing nature of the universe, Woolston had published a work in 1727 entitled, *A Discourse on the Miracles of Our Saviour, in View of the Present Controversy between Infidels and Apostates*, which effectively dismissed the miraculous in the Gospels, arguing for an allegorical interpretation, as a way to retain some contemporary value in a scientific age (if we can no longer take the stories literally, such skeptics will argue, then we can read them as symbolic stories with a moral point). By contrast, the bishop of Bangor, the Right Revd Thomas Sherlock, in 1729 published an apologetic defense of the Gospels entitled, *The Trial of the Witnesses of the Resurrection of Jesus*. This work was a defense of the apostles, those who witnessed Jesus's resurrection. Sherlock sets the powerful arguments of the apostles against the skepticism of Thomas Woolston among others. A characteristic of the Enlightenment that followed, and the modernism that Lewis was so critical of, was the principle that a respectable intellectual must be suspicious, skeptical of any religious truth-claims, especially when dealing with, in this case, the Bible (the incarnation-resurrection narrative, but especially the miracles of the exodus, and the miracles of the prophet Elijah), and only allow to count as truth that which could be measured, quantified, and controlled in principle by the human

12. The Incarnation Nation: the People and the Savior

intellect. That is, whatever is commonly available to all human intellect (assuming that Western intellectuals were a perfect representation of all humanity—past, present, and future—and not just an arrogant colonial elite). Thus, the argument championed by Reimarus and Lessing that it all happened too long ago for there to be any reliability in the scriptural accounts.[11] Lessing coined the phrase the "ugly broad ditch," which was applied to the gap between ourselves and the New Testament era. Lessing argued that we could not trust the contingency of history because there was this ugly broad ditch between then and now; therefore, we could not accept the New Testament accounts as fact or truth; further, this ditch lay between the contingent truth of history and what Lessing claimed to be the universal truth of reason. Lessing was convinced that rationalism was the universal mode of understanding available to humanity for comprehending the world.[12]

The Scandal of Particularity

Therefore, the Hebrew Bible and the New Testament could not be considered to be an acceptable source of truth: the church's account of Jesus was flawed with what was called the scandal of particularity. For the rationalists, only the universal was true, the universal available to all (Western) humanity through reason, not the particular enacted in the contingency of history. God's forging of one people, a chosen people, is—to this mindset—an unacceptable particularity; the incarnation, one person, from one people, is also to this Enlightenment-led religious perspective, an unacceptable particularity The argument from the skeptics was that if God was to come and reveal God's-self to humanity it would be through the universal—everybody would "know"—not through a particular event such as a chosen people, a nation, the incarnation. However, such a universal principle was in itself a particularity: the understanding of

---

11   Ironically, the "ugly broad ditch," the relativistic truth of history which invalidated scripture, did not nullify or invalidate the truth of Greco-Roman literature (which they had a particular love of and formed a foundational basis for their worldview): here there was no contamination of the universal truth of reason by an invented historical muddy ditch. Greco-Roman myths are not historical and any truth they have does not depend on their having happened. Lessing wants to treat the Gospels in the same way: detaching their "truth" from historical claims.

12   See, Brazier, *C. S. Lewis—Revelation, Conversion and Apologetics*, 194ff; Brazier, *C. S. Lewis—The Work of Christ Revealed*, 34, 151, 159; Brazier, *C. S. Lewis—An Annotated Bibliography and Resource*, 160–61.

Lessing, Reimarus, and their skeptical followers, especially in the so-called Quest for the Historic Jesus, was itself a *particularity*: that is, it issued from a white-European-male-patriarchal-bourgeois-liberal mindset, which was not universal, it had not been generated by all equally, but reflected European colonial attitudes.

By the mid-twentieth century the approach initiated by Reimarus and Lessing dominated debate in certain quarters of the church. Lessing valued the concept of the contingency of history (as a "broad ugly ditch") as a means to repudiate the church's story of Jesus; however, for two centuries the followers of Lessing have ignored this contingency of history in attempting to proclaim their watered-down story of Jesus as the one true version, though not *by necessity*, claiming it is the most likely version of what happened (for example, the so-called "quest" for the one true Jesus, outside of the church's account), grounded in an overinflated concept of reason and universalism, which postmodernism has done away with. In addition, this whole approach—with its prioritizing of the universal over the particular—is deeply anti-Semitic, rejecting the idea of the election and witness of the Jews for millennia, and the whole idea of "choseness."

4. WHY THE HEBREW?

But why the Hebrew? Why did God spend thousands of years forging and creating, honing and refining, at times seeming to brutalize, a people into the right character, the right religion, the right belief and obedience when so many are keen to believe that all religions are equally valid? Pagan religion is the default for *fallen* people, a humanity that will hold a mirror up to itself and invent the truth so as to compliment and complement. If the Messiah had just appeared out of the blue then there he would have no credibility. Having forged over thousands of years the people of God, then focusing down onto one seemingly small and irrelevant teenage girl, an obscure nobody in the wider, particularly religious, scheme of things, then there should be enough of a difference to shake humanity out of its self-indulgent malaise. Did it? With mixed results. But now humanity cannot shift the blame. All individuals are responsible for how they react to what the God above all gods has done for them. Hence, the Hebrews. One small obscure Hebrew girl at her prayers leading to the actual and real incarnation of God: the still small voice, the gently quivering breath,

12. The Incarnation Nation: the People and the Savior

the sound of a barely discernable fine breeze.[13] This is incarnation as a newborn baby: Yeshua Ha Mashiach—ontologically God, the Word made Jewish flesh, of the Jewish nation.

Most religions have as a focus some form of a "god," or may acknowledge and invoke God (or they answer the question of God with puzzling seemingly nonsensical sayings). The later, mature, monotheistic religions may lay claim to have identified such a God amongst the "gods," but without revelation the exponents of these monotheistic religions can say little about God. Peter Kreeft notes a particular objection that has developed in the later twentieth century. This is, the ability to "Orientalize" Yeshua. Here the argument is that Jesus was a mystic or guru who realized his own inner divinity as a Hindu mystic would. In this context, everyone is potentially divine: holiness, or intense religiosity, is equated with divinity. In Jesus's case he then went around believing he was the God of Israel, which, of course, is completely different from the Hindu "gods" or the Hindu sense of divinity, or higher consciousness (though it is perhaps important to remember that a Hindu doctrine of the divine should prepare people and point to the reality of an incarnation as distinct from an avatar).

> The problem with that theory is simply that Jesus was not a Hindu but a Jew! When he said "God," neither he nor his hearers meant Brahman, the impersonal, pantheistic, immanent all; he meant Yahweh, the personal, theistic, transcendent Creator. It is utterly unhistorical to see Jesus as a mystic, a Jewish guru. He taught prayer, not meditation. His God is a person, not a pudding. He said he was God but not that everyone was. He taught sin and forgiveness, as no guru does. He said nothing about the "illusion" of individuality, as the mystics do.[14]

Lewis was clear on this question. God for Jesus, raised in an orthodox Jewish culture, is the God of the Jews, the creator, *YHWH* the righteous Lord, the one true God outside of the world and beyond all other "gods." Jesus did not claim to be super religious; he was clearly not referring to being divine in the sense that anyone and everyone has the potential for such holiness or divinity: in eschatological reality, this intense human-generated divine holiness amongst religiously obsessed individuals the

---

13 1 Kgs 19:11–13
14 Kreeft, *Fundamentals of the Faith*, 63. See also, Kreeft, Between Heaven and Hell, 84–100.

world over was merely delusional religious emotionalism (comparable in some ways to Lucifer's *fall* from grace?). Lewis best understood this: "And when you've grasped that, you will see that what this man [Jesus] said was, quite simply, the most shocking thing that has ever been uttered by human lips."[15] Furthermore, Lewis comments that making such a claim in front of and to other Jews has to be different from any claim to divinity amongst all the world's religions; this is, different "to anything that happened with Plato, Confucius, Buddha, Mohammed."[16]

Perhaps the most Hebraic element in Jesus's life is the Passover. This practice roots him in the Jewish tradition, culture, and history, and presents the life and ministry of the Anointed One as the fulfilment of the Passover. (Hence, in all probability, no lamb at the actual Last Supper, only the bread (body) and wine (blood): Jesus is to take the place of the sacrificial lamb—crucified the next day, the divine and holy Jewish blood poured out onto the soil of the promised Hebrew land.) The Passover celebrates God's actions in Egypt, the freeing of the Hebrew slaves, this prefigures later demonstrations of God's saving power in the land of Israel. Likewise, the Passover points to the development of Hebraic and Christian traditions that inform and promote God's truth through history. The Passover meal, fulfilled on Calvary, demonstrates how God keeps his promises and remains faithful; it is forgiveness, love, and salvation. In Egypt and in Jesus's sacrifice it is deliverance.[17] It is important to see the Last Supper as higher, clearer, ascending above nature and the political (the exodus). The Passover is a precursor, an overture, which leads to the Last Supper and the moment of the death of Jesus on the cross. This is the moment of the fulfilment of all human history:

> Since in the end we are to come to baptism and the Eucharist, to the stable at Bethlehem, the hill of Calvary, and the emptied rock-tomb, perhaps it is better to begin with circumcision, the Passover, the Ark, and the Temple.[18]

15   Lewis, *Broadcast Talks*, 50.

16   Lewis, "Christian Apologetics." Paper read at the Carmarthen Conference for Youth Leaders and Junior Priests, Church of Wales, at Carmarthen, Easter 1945. See also, Allen, *Jesus Among Giants*. Allen discusses Mahavira, Buddha, Krishna, Confucius, Laozi, Moses, Muhammad, the finally with Jesus.

17   For more information on this approach, see, Bock and Glaser, eds., *Messiah in the Passover*.

18   Lewis, *Reflections on the Psalms*, 76.

12. The Incarnation Nation: the People and the Savior

Overall Lewis is surprisingly thin on the place of the Last Supper/Holy Communion, and rarely appears to make the connection with the Passover.[19] He says very little and even defers to better theologians to speak and write on the subject.[20] Lewis notes the paradox of how the most joyous Christian festival centers on the broken body and the shed blood;[21] how this is central to spreading the life of Christ to people far removed from Jerusalem and Golgotha.[22] Furthermore, we are commanded to partake[23] in a rite that was founded by Jesus himself, and cannot be altered or watered down, or re-packaged as humanist religion.[24] We are not necessarily directed to analyze or deconstruct, philosophize and understand, we are commanded, "Take, eat: not Take, understand," he says.[25] Make no mistake, notes Lewis, this is a supernatural event,[26] yet it also affirms the ordinary, the natural with the extraordinary: the senses and matter, flesh.[27] In the Eucharist, we are united into the chosen people of God, with all that Hebrew history and religion implies, yet we must be careful not to hive-off the Eucharist to ourselves. For example, Lewis notes how he can easily prefer private communions away from the congregation of a parish.[28]

---

19 Lewis, writing to Sr. Penelope CSMV, April 1, 1953. In, Lewis, *Collected Letters Vol 3*, 316–18.

20 Lewis, *Letters to Malcolm*, 93.

21 Lewis, *Reflections on the Psalms*, 45.

22 Lewis, *Mere Christianity*, 348f.

23 Lewis, *Undeceptions*, 57f.

24 Lewis writing to "an American lady" Dec 7, 1950. In Lewis, *Letters to an American Lady*, 68. (Note the recipient's name in this series of correspondence—for over a decade—was withheld at her request.)

25 Lewis, *Letters to Malcom*, Lt. 19, 7f.

26 Lewis, *Letters: to Malcom*, Lt. 2, 101f.

27 Lewis, *Miracles* (2nd ed.), 172–73.

28 Lewis writing to "an American lady" Mar 19, 1963, 114–15. In this context Lewis notes how Screwtape relished the arguments between Holy Communion and the Roman Catholic Mass: demonic division encouraged over labels.

5. HEBREW BLOOD, HEMORRHAGED

A Hebrew Concept

Lewis may, as we have asserted, be surprisingly thin on the place of the Last Supper/Holy Communion, and rarely appears to make the connection with the Hebrew Passover, but we must ask, in this context, a pertinent question: Why blood? Simple; because the ancient Hebrews conceptualized the very life-force of an individual as being in, with, contained by, but essentially part of the blood; people *bled to death*. Cain murdered Abel in a passion of religious self-righteousness, thus he spilled blood; this was sin: "The LORD said, 'What have you done? Listen! Your brother's blood cries out to me from the ground. Now you are under a curse and driven from the ground, which opened its mouth to receive your brother's blood from your hand'" (Gen 4:10–11). It is important to remember that blood is key to the apparent validity of sacrifice in the Old Testament. For the ancient Hebrews, blood sacrifices were in three groups—*Olah* sacrifices (burnt offerings, the whole animal burnt—today classified by the word *Holocaust*), guilt offerings (part burnt), and peace offerings (part burnt). However, often sacrifice is considered of lesser value as compared to prayer and contrition (as often exampled in the Book of the Psalms). The blood of the lamb does not deny the need for or negate the cross, but it does, certainly for Lewis, marginalize the *sole* need for punishment. The mechanism of blood spilt, the lifeblood of the one perfect, does make sense, though not as a punishment in the place of the guilty but rather as a debt repaid on behalf of the many who cannot repay. Also, it negates the need for absolute punishment because the debt is cleared. However, secondarily, the means of death (crucifixion) assuages the righteous anger (evident in the Hebrew Bible where God's love is turned to anger by humanity's sinfulness). Jesus therefore literally *bled to death*—the life-force left him, was extinguished—poured out onto the ground for the atonement of humanity.

To understand this, and Lewis's presentation, we need to consider not the general religious ideas about life after death across world religions but the true reality revealed from the Hebrew tradition. It is this tradition that paints a true picture of the human predicament, the situation Jesus was born into. This is not a picture of disembodied souls wafting around in some sort of spiritual afterlife where everybody is happy and ethereal.

12. The Incarnation Nation: the People and the Savior

The true reality was revealed by the beliefs about death the ancient Hebrews held.

- Both religious and secular people hide from the truth of the reality of the condition humanity is in.
- Eternal life, immortality, is a gift from God, a promise to all humanity; to the ancient Hebrews, an as yet-to-be-fulfilled promise.
- The situation we are in issues from the fall, humanity is infected with death due to original sin.
- Death follows on from the fall; it is our innate reward for rebellion (Gen 3).
- Death led to a diminished existence; this was the thin near-to-nothingness of the person's continued life after death in the Hebrew Sheol, or the Greek Hades.
- Resurrection restores the unity of body and soul; we are not a disembodied soul in the *post-mortem* state.

This true reality is attested to in the Letter to the Hebrews, as we established earlier.

The apostle Paul, in his Letter to the Colossians, asserts the new life that replaces this perilous situation of the human condition: completeness of life issues from the supremacy of Christ—"For in him all the fullness of God was pleased to dwell, and through him God was pleased to reconcile to himself all things, whether on earth or in heaven, by making peace through the blood of his cross" (Col 1:19–20). Therefore, together all humanity now has the potential for the fullness of real resurrection through the blood of the Lamb, shed on the cross.

Essentially, a theology of the blood of the lamb can be read from Hebrews chapters 9–13. The High Priest enters the inner sanctuary annually so as to offer a blood sacrifice on behalf of the sins the people had committed in ignorance (Heb 9:7); because without the shedding of blood there is no forgiveness (Heb 9:22); but without Christ's sacrifice this will not atone. Therefore, Jesus suffered outside of the city walls to make the people holy, through the shedding of his own lifeblood (Heb 13:12).

A HEBRAIC INKLING

Any earthly sacrifice is at best an imitation, a copy (Heb 9:24), and it is impossible for human-generated sacrifice to remove the stain of sin (Heb 10:3).[29]

Ultimately, what does the phrase, or idiom, "the blood of the lamb" mean contextually? The context must be that used by the writers of the Hebrew Bible, but pertinently, by the writers of the New Testament who, importantly, were raised in a Jewish religio-cultural context. They are not talking about a young sheep, whose throat was slit so it bled to death (though the phrase bled to death is important in a literal context). If Jesus willingly submitted himself to the atoning sacrifice of scourging, humiliation, crucifixion, and death, then we are talking about the will to submit to the will of God: the meaning and value of this was prefigured in the spotless lamb sacrificed on the Hebrew altar. Therefore, this submission of will means, in a Judeo-religio-cultural context, the "will to do the will of God."[30] Consider Jesus's mental wrestling prior to his arrest: "Father, if you are willing, take this cup from me; yet not my will, but yours be done" (Luke 22:42; also Mark 14:36; 26:39).

We can begin to understand how and why Lewis objected so strongly as a boy and as a young apostate man to the concept of blood, partly considering his childhood experience in his schooling and from his mother's death, and then upon the period of his conversion where it was this whole question of propitiation that puzzled him and held him back from a sound doctrine of atonement, how he was puzzled with the doctrine of redemption and in what sense the life and death of another person saved humanity or "opened salvation to the world."[31]

---

29   In general terms see Heb 2:14; 9:7–12, 18–25; 11:28. In terms of the impossibility of human-generated sacrifice, see, Heb 10:4, 19–29. In terms of the value of the blood for humanity see, Heb 12:4, 24; 13:11–12.

30   "Hebrew Idioms and Blood of Lamb." www.ccel.org/node/4938, para. 6.

31   ". . . right in the centre of Christianity, in the Gospels and St Paul, you keep on getting something quite different . . . 'propitiation'—'sacrifice'—'the blood of the Lamb'" wrote Lewis to his childhood friend at the time of his protracted conversion: Lewis writing to Arthur Greeves, Oct. 18, 1931. Lewis, *Collected Letters Vol. I.*, 975–77. Specifically, 974.

12. The Incarnation Nation: the People and the Savior

6. WHY THE NATION?

The Incarnation Nation[32]

Lewis has no intellectual qualms about naming the Hebrews as the chosen people.[33] Furthermore, as the Messiah was the ultimate chosen one amongst them, Yeshua represented and carried all with him. The people are the nation. Through their history they were—and are— vouchsafed by *YHWH* in their identity and security: they will endure. But their safekeeping and sanctuary lies in obedience and service and witness, promised secure from foreign invasion, from death and destruction, as the annals of the Hebrew Bible bear witness. How did Israel fare? How did it appear to the peoples of the world? And how does Lewis understand this? He notes that if we were looking at the peoples in the fifteenth century BC, we may be surprised to have seen the Hebrews as the ones who were to be entrusted with, as he terms it, the consciousness of God, entrusted with the transmission of God, incarnated in Hebrew flesh.[34]

Lewis notes how a special illumination was given to the Jews, and subsequently to Christians, but (in the context of prefigurement) there is also some divine light—fragments of the true light—that was given, and is still being offered, to other people, irrespective of how flawed their own religious scheme of things was or is.[35] However, this elevated Hebraic illumination informed the Jews' responsibility as a nation: century after century it was hammered into the Jews that earthly prosperity is not the reward of seeing God, neither success and immunity, protection and worldly power, particularly in the face of willful disobedience as the Jews wandered off after false "gods."[36] As a nation, the Hebrews were not chosen for their own sake but for the sake of the unchosen.[37] This was implicit in the thousand or more years prior to the incarnation; then explicit after

---

32   Lewis deals with this concept in several places: Lewis, "The Grand Miracle," (1945); "Miracles" (1942).

33   Lewis, "The Psalms," in *Christian Reflections*, 116–17.

34   Lewis, *Christian Reflections*, 116–17.

35   Lewis, "Is Theology Poetry?" A paper presented to the Socratic Club in Oxford in 1944.

36   Lewis, *Reflections on the Psalms*, 33ff..

37   Lewis, *Miracles* (1st ed.), ch. 14 "The Grand Miracle," 122f, specifically, 123–24. See also, Lewis, *Undeceptions*, 59–60.

A HEBRAIC INKLING

the crucifixion-resurrection: thus, what Lewis terms the centuries-old hammering process played out on the nation's public stage—which acted as a revelation.[38]

Jesus' earliest followers were all Jews. Lewis notes that if the story of Jesus the God-man were a legend, it would be very odd for it to grow up among the pre-eminent monotheistic people out of all the religious confusion of humanity:

> His followers were all Jews; that is, they belonged to that Nation which of all others was most convinced that there was only one God—that there could not possibly be another. It is very odd that this horrible invention about a religious leader should grow up among the one people in the whole earth least likely to make such a mistake. On the contrary we get the impression that none of His immediate followers or even of the New Testament writers embraced the doctrine at all easily.[39]

Furthermore, the disciples stood to be killed ceremonious by the Jewish religious leaders, and as enemies of the state by the Roman occupiers for asserting what they did, that the crucified Yeshua was the Christ, the Son of *YHWH*. We may ask, were not suffering and affliction, marginalization and martyrdom the price they paid for their testimony? This supports confidence in their honesty—why choose to suffer for what one knows is untrue?.

We look to the cross, but, notes Lewis, we often fail to make the connection with the pain and suffering of the Jews; our religion may have started among the Jews, but the links continue—we are still at one with them in our election: as a people they were defeated time and time again, led captive—"the tragic story of the conquered."[40] It is of paramount importance, he writes, that we understand that as Christians God chose and created the Hebrews for salvation history, a history that is still being played out eschatologically:

> If we are not Christians we shall dismiss this with the old gibe "How odd of God to choose the Jews." That is impossible for us who believe that God chose that race for the vehicle of His own

---

38   Lewis, *Mere Christianity*, 54.
39   Lewis, *Undeceptions*, 125.
40   Lewis, *The Problem of Pain*, 4.

12. The Incarnation Nation: the People and the Savior

Incarnation, and who are indebted to Israel beyond all possible repayment.[41]

Lewis emphasizes just how far we have come from a Hebraic mindset—certainly in the Anglo-Catholic approach he had aligned with post-conversion—when he asserts how a Jewish convert will seek to see Ha Mashiach as king and conqueror, as distinct to the sometimes "gentile" approach that will often focus on intercessor, priesthood.[42] Jesus in effect bypassed the national apparatus of a religious state—the Sanhedrin, the temple and priestly caste, the wealthy elite living in luxurious houses on the side of the temple precinct, even the Roman occupiers—by focusing his ministry on a relatively obscure rural backwater. God demonstrates that the true Hebrew nation—exemplified by Mary, bearer of the incarnate God—"are examples of God's undemocratic way of working," asserts Lewis: this is essentially, God's selectiveness.[43] What we see is the true eternal Israel, quite distinct from a worldly nation state.[44] Lewis relentlessly repeated and reinforced the Judaic ethics and how this fitted in with the Jesus event; representative of the Hebrew nation and law. Jesus did not introduce novelties:

> Every good teacher, within Judaism as without, has anticipated Him. The whole religious history of the pre-Christian world, on its better side, anticipates Him. It could not be otherwise. The Light which has lightened every man from the beginning may shine more clearly but cannot change. The Origin cannot suddenly start being, in the popular sense of the word, "original."[45]

Therefore, we emphasize Lewis's often repeated aphorism that all that was best in Judaism survives in Christianity.[46] Therefore, Christ, in

---

41   Lewis, *Reflections on the Psalms*, 24. See also, related, Lewis, *Mere Christianity*, 74, 83, 128 and 156.

42   Lewis, *Reflections on the Psalms*, 124.

43   Lewis, "The Grand Miracle" in *Undeceptions*, 60–61. See also, Lewis, "The Grand Miracle," in *Miracles* (1st ed.), 121f.

44   This is where Lewis's Platonism comes to the fore: Israel is an ideal, a very real ideal in the mind of God; Israel on earth is a shadow of the real Israel: Greek-Platonic philosophy, which Lewis majored in, comes to the fore, which the Hebrew prophets and patriarchs were either oblivious to or repudiated.

45   Lewis, *Reflections on the Psalms*, 23. See also, Lewis, "On Ethics," 47; Lewis, *Mere Christianity*, 78; and, Lewis, *Problem of Pain*, 63.

46   See, Lewis, "Religion without Dogma" in *Undeceptions*, 99–114.

transcending and moving on from Judaism, fulfils both paganism and Judaism.[47] But what is then appealed to is the Eternal Israel.[48] Both must stand: Christ's church and the Eternal Israel; both are community at its best.

---

47 Lewis, *Reflections on the Psalms*, 115–16.
48 See, for example, Horner, *Eternal Israel*; See, also, Horner, *Future Israel*.

13

Joy Davidman and the Mature C. S. Lewis: Race, Semitism, . . . and Family

"For I am not ashamed of the gospel, because it is the power of God that brings salvation to everyone who believes: first to the Jew, then to the gentile. For in the gospel the righteousness of God is revealed—a righteousness that is by faith from first to last, just as it is written: 'The righteous will live by faith.' What does scripture say? 'Abraham believed God, and it was credited to him as righteousness.'"

ROMANS 1:16-17 & 4:3[1]

". . . the righteous person will live by faith."

HABAKKUK 2:4c

"Their prophets told them that defeat and exile and slavery were Jehovah's punishment for disobeying the Commandments—and they drew the materialist inference that his reward for obedience would be worldly success. If they placated the Spirit properly, it would shower them with gifts of matter. How could they placate that angry God? Perhaps it was then that the bitter Jewish saying, still current today, originated: "Chosen for what? Chosen for trouble!""

JOY DAVIDMAN, ON THE DECALOGUE, AND THE PENTATEUCH[2]

". . . What prayers have Red men, and Black, and Brown and Yellow, sent up against us to their gods or sometimes to God Himself? All over the earth the White Man's offence 'smells to heaven': massacres, broken treaties, theft, kidnappings, enslavement, deportation, floggings, beatings-up, rape, insult, mockery, and odious hypocrisy make up that smell."

C. S. LEWIS[3]

1   C.f. Gen 15:6; Ps 106:31; Rom 4:9 & 22; Gal 3:6; Jas 2:23.
2   Davidman, *Smoke on the Mountain*, 133.
3   Lewis, "The Psalms," in *Christian Reflections*, 119. c. 1952–57.

1. RACE AND THE EMPIRE-MENTALITY

C. S. Lewis's view on race and culture as a boy was predictably of its time. The Edwardian public-school system, which had evolved over the previous two centuries, appeared superficially Christian, but was deeply grounded in the pagan religion of Freemasonry.[4] This system schooled and trained an elite to run a global empire based on supposed English racial superiority: peoples were classified as different races, and most were considered innately inferior: Britain ruled the waves. The fault lines in this *Weltanschauung* were exposed during two world wars with the collapse coming in the latter half of the twentieth century. Lewis, when he returned from the trench-war carnage of the First World War, was something of an isolated, even nihilistic, individual. His views on the Jews, we noted earlier, were predictably anti-Semitic and were in keeping with this supposedly racially superior ruling elite of early twentieth-century Britain.

Anti-Anti-Semitism . . . and Anti-Racism?

By the time of his sixtieth year he not only raises the Jews up as the model and template for humanity but warns of the cost of the racism he had witness as a privileged member of a public-school educated elite:

> I am inclined to think that we had better look unflinchingly at the work we have done.... For the same reason we ought to read the Psalms that curse the oppressor; read them with fear. Who knows what imprecations of the same sort have been uttered against ourselves? What prayers have Red men, and Black, and Brown and Yellow, sent up against us to their gods or sometimes to God Himself? All over the earth the White Man's offence "smells to heaven": massacres, broken treaties, theft, kidnappings, enslavement, deportation, floggings, beatings-up, rape, insult, mockery, and odious hypocrisy make up that smell.[5]

---

4   Which despite claims of antiquity was founded in the early eighteenth century in, reputedly, Brussels.

5   Lewis, "The Psalms," in *Christian Reflections*, 119. From the preface: Walter Hooper, "Judging by the handwriting (Lewis wrote all his works by hand), it roughly corresponds in time with the publication of the book Reflections on the Palms (1958)," xiii. Personally, in terms of the content and the style of writing I would adjust this timeframe to the period of study leading up to the writing of *Reflections on the Psalms* . . . , therefore c. 1952–55.

13. Joy Davidman ... and the Mature C. S. Lewis

Lewis's view of the Jews—and associated anti-Semitism—was, as we have seen so far, turned on its head initially by his conversion in the early 1930s, but then with his marriage to Joy Davidman in the 1950s:

> Another point of interest in Joy Davidman's work comes from her race. In a sense the converted Jew is the only normal human being in the world. To him, in the first instance, the promises were made, and he has availed himself of them. He calls Abraham his father by hereditary right as well as by divine courtesy. He has taken the whole syllabus in order, as it was set; eaten the dinner according to the menu. . . . And we ourselves, we christened gentiles, are after all the graft, the wild vine, possessing "joys not promised to our birth"; though perhaps we do not think of this so often as we might. And when the Jew does come in, he brings with him into the fold dispositions different from, and complementary of ours; as St. Paul envisages in Ephesians chapter 2.[6]

If Lewis can be excused the use of inaccurate racist stereotypes (black-white-red-yellow), his criticism of the endemic and institutionalized racism of the British Empire is highly pertinent and way ahead of any understanding both within the establishment that schooled him or the fledgling anti-racism movement among liberal-socialists, which has geared-up over the generations since Lewis's death in 1963. Lewis also notes how he witnessed a shop keeper in Oxford refusing "to serve a Chinese,"[7] noting how he has long known how talk of brotherhood is hypocrisy. Further, he notes how the one who talks of brotherhood actually means s/he has no superiors, but will delight in claiming others as inferior to him.[8] Brotherhood in the English establishment was often meant to refer to the closed-shop mentality of trade unions or religious sects such as Freemasonry, both of which Lewis eschewed. Racism and anti-Semitism breeds on this. Christianity should forbid this closed-shop superiority mentality (Rome does forbid it; but Protestant churches and congregations vary),[9] including the extreme patriotism that breeds

---

6   Lewis, "Foreword" in, Davidman, *Smoke on the Mountain*, 7–11; referring to Eph 2:14–19.

7   Lewis writing to "an American lady" June 7, 1955. In Lewis, *Letters to an American Lady*, 43. This was written not long after Lewis's meeting with Joy Davidman.

8   Lewis writing to "an American lady" June 7, 1955. In Lewis, *Letters to an American Lady*, 43..

9   It is important to remember that slavery, racism, and the cultural superiority that led to world empires during the Reformation was at the heart of Western humanity

national superiority,[10] but also the hatred and vindictiveness that can be expressed in prayers.[11]

So, what do we make of Lewis's conclusion in *Surprised by Joy* where he is talking about how he regarded the Jews back in his youth? Was there still an element of anti-Semitism in the following passage:

> I was by now too experienced in literary criticism to regard the Gospels as myths. They had not the mythical taste. And yet the very matter which they set down in their artless, historical fashion—those narrow, unattractive Jews, too blind to the mythical wealth of the Pagan world around them—was precisely the matter of the great myths. If ever a myth had become fact, had been incarnated, it would be just like this. And nothing else in all literature was just like this. Myths were like it in one way. Histories were like it in another. But nothing was simply like it. And no person was like the Person it depicted . . . .[12]

Lewis is perhaps justified in his comparison between the North-West European pagan myths he praises and the documentary style, as some would assert of some scripture, but what need is there to label the Gospel writers artless, narrow, unattractive, blind? Perhaps none that can be justified. The pertinent question is, Was Lewis speaking in the voice of

---

specifically, though it is a deep flaw in all humanity and was supported by Protestant governments and many Protestant congregations. Rome, two generations after Columbus discovered the Americas (1492), issued *sublimis Dei* (1537), a Papal bull that explicitly forbade enslavement of humans or the belief in the racial superiority of the European. Until the discovery of the Americas and Australasia humanity from the time of the ancient Greeks saw the human in three groups: African, Asian, and European. The assumption by the explorers following on from Columbus was that any new peoples were to be considered sub- or non-human. *Sublimis Dei* stated that if a newly discovered people could make a decision to either reject of accept the gospel, then they were equal to European humans and should not be enslaved or racially abused: ". . . [they] are fully rational human beings who have rights to freedom and private property, even if they are heathen." Many of the explorers were excommunicated for enslaving. (However, often governments in both nominally Catholic and Protestant countries and colonies/empires approved of the enslavements.)

10   Lewis recounts a conversation with an elderly clergyman who criticized the belief, across various countries and nations, in racial and national superiority, with the exception that the English were superior. See, Lewis, *The Four Loves*, 25f.

11   "We may have repented of our wrong: we do not always know if he has repented of his hatred. How do accounts now stand between us if he has not?" See, Lewis, "The Psalms." In *Christian Reflections*, 118–19. See also, Lewis, *Reflections on the Psalms*, 20–21.

12   Lewis, *Surprised by Joy*, 195, 228.

13. Joy Davidman ... and the Mature C. S. Lewis

his younger self here, offering the thoughts he had as a young apostate: this was how he used to regard and enjoy the pagan myths? This was not necessarily how he considered the nature of scripture as literature in his mature years, but how he used to think. Even if this is so, perhaps such sentiments are unhelpful and perhaps he should not have written them down (unless he was to repudiate them; which he does not).

Ethnicity and Racism

So if it is clear that in his mature years Lewis eschewed the colonial racist and anti-semitic mentality of his education and his youth, how does this sit with the liberal establishment, particularly those academics and religious professionals, writers and opinion formers today: Lewis is condemned by them as racist. Why? For example, both the children's story writer Philip Pullman and the former Archbishop of Wales and of England Rowan Williams pick on details in *The Chronicles of Narnia*, for example, a bad character in *The Last Battle* comments derogatively on the "dark skin" of one of the Calorman soldiers whose army has invaded and is laying waste to Narnia; also in *The Horse and His Boy* both Calormen characters and Narnians exchange comments about skin tone. However, neither are speaking racism but establishing ethnicity and parentage (Arsheesh the fisherman claims Shasta is his biological son—but the child is clearly Caucasian: his skin tone along with facial features proves the truth, when Arsheesh drives and works the boy as a slave).[13] Such scripted comments—like hundreds of stories and characters in films and books about war and conflict—were entirely in keeping with the characters portrayed, and it is clear from what we have examined so far that Lewis was no racist.[14] The problem for Pullman and Williams is that Lewis represents what for many is an old English culture, seemingly diametric to that which has evolved since the "world-turned-upside-down" revolution in the West since the 1960s with regard to sex and culture, religion and society, liberal

---

13   C. S. Lewis, *The Chronicles of Narnia: The Last Battle*, 17, 26, 31, 31, *et al.*; *The Horse and his Boy*, 11–15. (One of the critcisms is about a character with a long dark skinny finger: but this is not a human, but an ape!). See: https://www.theguardian.com/books/2013/nov/19/cs-lewis-literary-legacy; also, https://www.narniaweb.com/resources-links/are-the-chronicles-of-narnia-sexist-and-racist/.

14   To give but two examples, no one from the liberal establishment (including religious professionals and children's writers), objects to the appalling racism and anti-Semitism embedded in such excellent films as *Schindler's List* (1993), or *Downfall* (2004), but they contain comments a hundred times worse than the Narnia books!

neo-colonialism, and politics. Though there does remain the question for some, that in Narnia, the baddies are like central Asian nomads—particularly Genghis Kahn's invading army—(though the liberal cultural establishment sees them as "dark-skinned" Arab-looking people), while the goodies are seemingly "white" European people: is this a picture of unintentional racial superiority by Lewis? The only problem here is that it is the Colorman's (baddies) who are the colonialists (stressing the comparison with Genghis Khan, or the cold war Soviet army which was at its height when Lewis was writing!

2. HELEN JOY DAVIDMAN

A confirmed bachelor, Lewis got married in 1956, late-on in life—at the age of fifty-eight years—to Helen Joy Davidman. Academic colleagues at Oxford were astounded, and despite the fact that she died of cancer four years later they were a happy couple and were in many ways soul mates. Lewis commented that—

> She was my daughter and my mother, my pupil and my teacher, my subject and my sovereign; and always, holding all these in solution, my trusty comrade, friend, shipmate, fellow-soldier. My mistress; but at the same time all that any man friend (and I have good ones) has ever been to me. Perhaps more.[15]

A crucial fact that has a deep effect on Lewis is that Joy was born and raised an American Jew, further that she comes to him with two sons from her first marriage.

Cultural Judaism: New York

Helen Joy Davidman's parents were, she asserts, self-confessed Jewish atheists. Immigrants from Poland and the Ukraine, Joy's grandparents were orthodox Jews; her grandfather is reputed to have died through contracting pneumonia whilst preaching to the gentiles of Manhattan's Lower East Side.[16] Joy's parents, Joseph Davidman and Jeanette Spivack, subscribed to a form of humanism

---

15   Lewis, *A Grief Observed*, 39. (Published initially under the pseudonym of N. W. Clerk.)

16   Davidman, "The Longest Way Round," in *These Found the Way*, 13–26. See also, Dorsett, *And God Came In*. See also, Sibley, *Shadowlands*, 64–77 and 79–94. Davidman also examined something of this in her novel, *Anya* (1940); that is the existential crisis of Eastern European Jews in relation to their religious heritage and culture, pre-WW2, hemmed in by Russia and Germany. See King, *Yet One more Spring*, 114–35.

that acknowledged Judaism as a cultural religion that offered morality and a way to live, but they firmly subscribed to materialism and atheism. Joy wrote how her parents came to America as children from

> small villages in Eastern Europe where for a thousand years the Jews had held desperately to their faith against fire and terror and murder. Cut off, hemmed in, embittered, the Judaism of such villages resembled the taboo systems of savages more than it resembled the prophetic Judaism of the Old Testament or the philosophic and scholarly Judaism of medieval Western Europe. Six hundred and more ritual taboos governed daily conduct; striking a match or stacking the dishes carelessly could be an offence against a very jealous God.[17]

In New York many of these immigrant Jews abandoned this form of Judaism as a religion, but retained belief in a vague, ill-defined "god" of human progress, which Joy refers to as a form of Unitarianism; however, her parents rejected this cultural "god." "My father declared proudly that he had retained the ethics of Judaism, the only 'real' part of it, and got rid of the theology—rather as if he had kept the top floor of our house but torn down first floor and foundation. When I came along, I noticed that there was nothing supporting the ethics; down it crashed. It's not true that an atheist cannot have any morality; what he cannot have is a rational morality" [Joy's emphasis].[18] Therefore, for Joy, her parents' rigid morality, derived to a greater or lesser degree from the survival-Judaism of Poland and the Ukraine, became habit and sentiment. Joy noted how her parents believed in temperance and justice, fortitude and prudence; however, she writes that her father never appreciated how these virtues were meaningless in an atheistic universe:

> Moral ideas could only be something men had put together for their own convenience, like the horse and buggy; something you could scrap as soon as an automobile morality came along. And he tried his level best to pass his virtues on to me. Atheist virtues, however, don't keep very well. My parents had never been taught that faith and hope and charity were virtues at all. With no revealed law, no conviction of sin, no weekly reminder of shortcomings, no humility before God, no wonder at mystery, no hope of heaven, no help of grace—what can the best atheist do but turn Pharisee?[19]

17 Davidman, "The Longest Way Round," 14.
18 Davidman, "The Longest Way Round," 14–15.
19 Davidman, "The Longest Way Round," 15.

Joy's razor-sharp intellect could see that if there was no God then there was also no morality, nothing was inherently wrong—people would invent morals and ethics to suit a given situation, and such morality was movable, it was redefined according to the needs of the moment, according to whichever group in society shouted the loudest. She could also see that her parents' belief in justice and temperance, fortitude and prudence, was really only self-interest, thinly disguised—such morality had suited them, given them social and cultural advancement and wealth to go with it.

Cultural Judaism: Childhood

Helen Joy Davidman was born on the 18th April 1915 in the Jewish ghetto in Manhattan. She had a comfortable childhood, a good education, private music lessons, and holidays to New England and the West Coast. The Davidmans moved to the Bronx, and then to Grand Concourse, which was characterized by bourgeois respectability, as their wealth and standing increased. Joy's father was a very strict disciplinarian who regularly subjected Joy and her brother Howard to corporal punishment. She had a very high IQ of over 150 and after graduation from Hunter College (BA, 1934, aged nineteen years) and Columbia University (MA, in English, 1935, aged twenty years), she taught English in high schools in New York from 1936 to 1938, but then took to writing. She became a radical card-carrying communist, a famous American poet, novelist, and writer, and a scriptwriter for Hollywood. Then in 1946, in her thirties, she underwent a profound conversion to Christianity. At the time she was married to the writer William Lindsay Gresham and had two children—David (b.1944) and Douglas (b.1945). William Gresham, however, had become an alcoholic; he was unfaithful and violent, and the marriage was collapsing. This is the background to her conversion. She came to England and met C. S. Lewis. The story is well-known and has been the topic of a TV docu-drama, a Hollywood film, and a stage play: they married after her divorce, initially as a formality to naturalize her as a British citizen; however, when Joy was diagnosed with terminal cancer they were married before God in a Christian ceremony. She recovered, remission lasted a few years, then she died. Her death devastated Lewis and formed the trigger of another stage of conversion for him, perhaps the most profound of his conversions. So what was Joy's spiritual pilgrimage and how does it compare to Lewis's? What was her hidden, implicit, relationship with the Christ who sought her, courted her, approached and even hunted her, as he had done with Lewis? What was Joy's conversion? What was it *to* and *from*? What was it characterized by?

3. CHRIST HAUNTED ME

"The Sacrament at the Heart of all Beauty"

Joy had declared her atheism to her parents when she was eight years old; by her teenage years she had rejected all morality as a human construct, setting her own standards according to pleasure. She recalls that when she was fourteen years old she experienced a profound aesthetic sense, which relates to *Sehnsucht* (though she does not use the German word or concept). This was an encounter in many ways, like Lewis's:

> I went walking in the park on a Sunday afternoon, in clean, cold, luminous air. The trees tinkled with sleet; the city noises were muffled by the snow. Winter sunset, with a line of young maples sheathed in ice between me and the sun—as I looked up they burned unimaginably golden—burned and were not consumed. I heard the voice in the burning tree; the meaning of all things was revealed and the sacrament at the heart of all beauty lay bare; time and space fell away, and for a moment the world was only a door swinging ajar. Then the light faded, the cold stung my toes, and I went home, reflecting that I had had another aesthetic experience. I had them fairly often. That was what beautiful things did to you, I recognized, probably because of some visceral or glandular reaction that hadn't been fully explored by science just yet. For I was a well-brought-up, right-thinking child of materialism. Beauty, I knew, existed; but God, of course, did not.[20]

Joy initially categorized this as aesthetic—that is, it was concerned with or relating to beauty. But did she see this appreciation of beauty as within her mind only? Was the perception or awareness only inside her head? The Holy Spirit affected Joy's mind, triggered the perception. But is actual beauty something outside of her mind that exists in created reality? Joy realized, in retrospect, years later, that this was an *encounter*, but we may also assert that this was not just in her mind, for she perceived *beauty*, and beauty is not just in the eye of the beholder. More than that, she perceived that beauty was a sacrament at the heart of all things. Why? God created and sustains and is at the heart of all things. Beauty was from God; beauty lay at the heart of all things because all created things are mysteriously imbued with God's sacramental grace. Grace was in a moment imparted to Joy *from* the sacramental beauty at the heart of all creation. The Holy

---

20 Davidman, "The Longest Way Round," 13.

Spirit simultaneously touched Joy's mind from within the sacramental beauty of sun, mist, ice, and trees, the created natural world. To worship this spirit in the natural world, excluding God, would be wrong, it would be pantheism. However, it is important to remember that God declared that creation was good (Gen 1:31), and we will see, perceive, moments when we can almost grasp the goodness, the rightness, the wonder, and the beauty at the heart of creation, particularly the natural world: Lewis on Leatherhead station (to name but one occasion) and Joy in Central Park, New York. There are people whose brains are simply not wired (through nature or nurture) in such a way as to be receptive to such intimations from the Holy Spirit. There are others who are. Ironically, despite her atheism, Joy was more open to God than Lewis, and had a sounder understanding of the theology behind these moments related to *Sehnsucht*; this was a theological understanding, despite her lack of synagogue attendance. She writes about how she sensed the voice in the burning tree as the bright winter sun burned through the bare frost-laden branches, how she had in a single moment an intimation of the meaning of all things—this was a revelation, it was not a human construct, this was revealed; but if so, by whom or by what? She writes in terms of sacramental theology, she perceived, as a fourteen-year-old atheistic cultural Jew, the sacramentality in all things, all creation! David and the prophets would have rejoiced at her perception, a perception we find in the Psalms, that creation actually sings praise joyously, beauteously, to the Lord.[21] She comments that she perceived that sacrament lay at the heart of all beauty, that this sacrament was laid bare, open for all to perceive. She notes how this realization was a moment of temporal paradox when her mental cognitive awareness of time's relentless movement, of the physicality of space and distance (and hence separation and aloneness even), were gone: "time and space fell away, and for a moment the world was only a door swinging ajar."[22] Joy's perception is not conditioned by her religious or cultural heritage or background because she had been raised by moralistic atheists. The imagery, the mental categories she invokes to try to make sense of what had happened were, we may assert, more the result of revelation than the religious upbringing her parents gave her (though she is clearly aware of the image of Moses and the burning bush). This was a vision. But a vision

21 For example, "Let the floods clap their hands; let the hills sing together for joy" (Ps 98:8); see also Pss 65:12 and 114:4–6.
22 Davidman, "The Longest Way Round," 13.

of what? That beauty is real; beauty is *actual*. It is not subjective; it is not a question of personal taste; it is not a human construct: beauty is *real*; it is sacramental; it issues from God and is, to one degree or another, in all created things. Therefore, Joy begins to believe in God, who despite all our human confusion, wills to communicate to us in love, often through the good creation that is imbued sacramentally with *his* beauty, *his* Spirit; a God who can touch our conscious minds and in that moment we will taste eternity and our lives thereafter will not be the same. Behind this encounter for Joy, as she came to realize in her adult years, was something that was trinitarian: Christ, the second person of the Trinity. This was about incarnation—Yeshua, the anointed Hebrew of God's chosen people.

Joy's experience in Central Park, New York was, yes, similar in many ways to Lewis's experiences, yet subtly different. Joy's experience certainly lacked the intense guilt-laden longing that Lewis recalled with such encounters with the Holy Spirit, probably because she had never known and therefore never rejected the living God behind and in creation. However, it is fair to assert that as with Lewis's experience of *Sehnsucht* on Leatherhead Station, this was the instant, the point where heaven and earth met in a moment, when Joy Davidman's imagination was baptized. In both cases, this is perhaps also the point of commission for both of them, of their vocation before the Lord. Both examples are of a conscious realization, regardless of what their personal religious egos would believe (or more pertinently not believe!), that God communicated to them through the innate beauty of the natural world, his creation.

Poetry and Imagination

How did Joy respond to this encounter as an intellectual atheist? First, I think it is fair to say she was not a skeptic, as Lewis was, for there was not the element of piercing guilt-ridden longing (Lewis's "joy"—what he took for *Sehnsucht*?) in her experience of the Spirit. She was an intellectual atheist and although she had decided that the only meaning in life was self-defined pleasure this did not mean sexual libertarianism, alcohol, drugs, etc., for her; the ultimate pleasure for Joy was in reading and writing poetry (!), therefore her school and college friends nicknamed her "forbidden joy," partly because of her parents' repressiveness.[23] Joy therefore exhibited a caution and celibacy in her young life but was not

---

23   Sibley, *Shadowlands*, 69.

afraid to love. Lewis was in many ways afraid to love and had created intellectual barriers against loving: he, Lewis, was quite a loner, much of which can be attributed to the trauma following his mother's death. So how did Joy respond? She comments that following this experience-encounter when she was fourteen years of age: "A young poet like myself could be seized and shaken by spiritual powers a dozen times a day, and still take it for granted that there was no such thing as spirit. What happened to me was easily explained away; it was 'only nerves' or 'only glands.' As soon as I discovered Freud, it became 'only sex.' And yet if ever a human life was haunted, Christ haunted me."[24]

Christ haunted me, she writes. She is writing a few years after her eventual conversion, but can clearly see how religious experience, if it is genuine, is only valid in the context of the Holy Spirit of the resurrected and ascended Yeshua Ha Mashiach, whom she justifiably expands into the universal Christ, of which, at the time, she had very little knowledge. (At this time she writes in the full flush of her conversion, and her language is not so much informed by her Jewish heritage but beginning to be effected by Western Protestant idioms, tropes, and culture.) But this did not stop the Holy Ghost—to invoke more traditional language, particularly as Joy claims that she was *haunted* by Christ—acting on her, reassuring her in many ways, preparing her for the moment when he would fully reveal *himself* to her, give her the choice where she could turn and say yes, to follow God, or not. For Joy, anything resembling the religious impulse was channeled into her life, her education, and her parents' growing prosperity. Therefore, by the time she was fifteen years of age she recalls that: "I believed in nothing but American prosperity; in 1930 I believed in nothing. Men, I said, are only apes. Virtue is only custom. Life is only an electrochemical reaction. Mind is only a set of conditioned reflexes, and anyway most people aren't rational like *me*. Love, art, and altruism are only sex. The universe is only matter. Matter is only energy. I forget what I said energy was only. Portrait of the happy materialist" [Joy's emphasis].[25]

But, buried under all this brash assertive materialism was a girl who wrote poetry, who recognized and followed the creative impulse and lived a life contrary to these nihilistic materialistic beliefs. For Joy, her, "Inner

---

24   Davidman, "The Longest Way Round," 13–14.
25   Davidman, "The Longest Way Round," 15–16.

13. Joy Davidman ... and the Mature C. S. Lewis

personality was deeply interested in Christ, and didn't know it."[26] Like her parents and many of her Jewish relatives and family friends she had been taught to feel what she describes as a cold chill at the mention of the name of Jesus Christ. This was her religio-cultural conditioning. But did this mean she was antagonistic to the genuine Christ? Probably not, for two reasons: first, her openness to Christ's Spirit as evidenced from what we have seen already; second, as she notes, for hundreds of years European Jews lived among people who interpreted Christ's will to mean Jews were flogged and burnt as heretics and were regarded as the anti-Christ, they were excluded by gentleman's agreements and closed universities. If, she writes, "nominal Christians so confuse their Master's teaching, surely a poor Jew may be pardoned a little confusion."[27] Despite her religio-cultural prejudices, triggered by and ingrained through centuries of persecution, racism, and disenfranchisement by Christians, she had nevertheless read the Bible. Why? She argues she read the Bible for its literary beauty, simply as a work of literature. However, she found herself unconsciously quoting Jesus, not only in her poetry and writings, but in conversations, particularly when she was fighting her parents' bourgeois moralistic hypocrisy: "My first published poem was called 'Resurrection'—a sort of private argument with Jesus, attempting to convince him (and myself) that he had never risen. I wrote it at Easter, of all possible seasons, and never guessed why. The Cross recurs through most of my early poems, and I seem to remember explaining that Jesus was 'a valuable literary convention.'"[28] And it never occurred to her to invoke his Hebrew name, but despite claiming to be cultural Jews, her parents embraced everything they could from the West!

Despite her self-proclaimed atheism from the age of eight years, as a child and teenager she had loved reading fantasy works—in particular the work of George MacDonald, which we have encountered already through Lewis. So, in many ways she had exposed herself to implicit Christian ideas. To paraphrase Lewis's comment we came across earlier, as a young atheist she could not guard her faith too carefully.[29] Joy did not believe in

---

26   Davidman, "The Longest Way Round," 16.
27   Davidman, "The Longest Way Round," 16.
28   Davidman, "The Longest Way Round."
29   "... a young atheist cannot guard his faith too carefully." See, Lewis, *Surprised by Joy*, 219.

the supernatural, yet her cultural interests and reading generated a love of heaven, though she did not see it as such.

Communism and Intellect

By the mid-1930s, and in the American Depression, Joy espoused communism, further, she sought involvement with and membership of the Communist Party; paid her dues and became a card-carrying communist. She admits she would have killed for the Party had it asked her to. Ironically, she writes that "I think I was moved by the same unseen power that had directed my reading and my dreaming—I became a Communist because, later on, I was going to become a Christian."[30] With hardly any background—apart from having read Marx's *Communist Manifesto*, which she comments few of her colleagues in the party had— she was employed as journalist and critic for the Party's semi-official magazine, *New Masses*. She learned to lie for the Party, that claiming love for the people, the proletariat, would justify any action: that the end justifies the means. This time working for the Party was interrupted by six months working as a scriptwriter in Hollywood. However, on return, her interest in the Party was waning. She met and married a Spanish Civil War veteran, writer, and fellow poet, William Lindsay Gresham. The birth of her first son finally put paid to her involvement with the Party and with any communist activities. Whatever false gods influenced her had fallen aside to be replaced by communism, which in turn was being exposed as an incoherent false "god" or "idol," which itself was falling by the wayside. Marriage and a young family now took her time and energies and focus, in addition she was a successful, published poet and novelist.

4. AND GOD CAME IN

In 1945 Joy's childlike interest in what she called fantasy had led her to read C. S. Lewis's *The Screwtape Letters* and *The Great Divorce* (interest in Lewis's Christian books was at that time sweeping America). She was still a card-carrying atheist—or so she believed—but, she writes, "I hadn't given quite enough attention to developing the proof of it."[31] Joy's involvement with the Party was waning; she notes how in the 1930s, during the Depression, a sincere rage at injustice and misery had led to many being

30   Davidman, "The Longest Way Round," 19.
31   Davidman, "The Longest Way Round," 22.

13. Joy Davidman ... and the Mature C. S. Lewis

involved in Party activities. America, or the American economic system, was seen to have failed. By the early- to mid-1940s, with the Second World War at its height, a renewed faith in America and dismay at the antics of the Soviet Union had led to patriotism and a repudiation of Marxism amongst many who had been stalwart Party activists.[32] Joy saw those that remained as embittered failures more interested in revenge on the existing society than in building a better one. Joy's involvement grew less and less: "By 1946 I had two babies; I had no time for Party activity, and was glad of it; I hardly mentioned the Party except with impatience. And yet, out of sheer habit, I went on believing that Marxism was true.... For I had no knowledge of divine help."[33]

Joy notes with poignancy that, as Francis Thompson symbolized God as the "Hound of Heaven" pursuing on relentless feet, with her God was acting more like a cat in that he had been stalking her for many years. Christ had been courting her patiently, judging when to reveal his Lordship: "He crept nearer so silently that I never knew he was there. Then, all at once, he sprang."[34] In early spring 1946 there came a morning where Bill, her husband, phoned from she knew not where to announce he was having a nervous breakdown, his mind going. He did not return home. Bill had become an alcoholic and an adulterer, and his work as a novelist and poet was failing. Hours later Joy was desperate. She writes that she felt helpless for the first time in her life, that she was forced to acknowledge that she was no longer in charge of her fate, that she was certainly not, as she puts it, the captain of her soul.

> All my defences—the walls of arrogance and cocksureness and self-love behind which I had hid from God went down momentarily. And God came in. How can one describe the direct perception of God? It is infinite, unique; there are no words, there are no comparisons. Those who have known God will understand me; the others, I find, can neither listen nor understand. There was a Person with me in the room, directly present to my consciousness—a Person so real that all my previous life was by comparison mere shadow play. And I myself was more alive than I had ever been; it was like waking from sleep. My perception of God lasted perhaps half a minute. In that time, however, many

---

32 For example, see, Schama, *The American Future*. See, ch. 12.
33 Davidman, "The Longest Way Round," 22.
34 Davidman, "The Longest Way Round," 23.

things happened. I forgave some of my enemies. I understood that God had always been there and that since childhood I had been pouring half my energy into the task of keeping him out. When it was over I found myself on my knees, praying. I think I must have been the world's most astonished atheist.[35]

Was this awareness of God? Was it no more than a comforting illusion? asks Joy. She answers that in terms of her and Bill's life-crisis nothing had changed: afterwards she was just as worried and helpless as before. If it was an illusion, the awareness of God had not helped on a practical level. No, within this was the moment of choice for Joy, if anything was offered that could help her situation it was reassurance, an assurance of God's love. But this was not an assurance that was self-generated, sentimental, cosseting, like a cuddly soft toy; for Joy this was characterized by "Terror and ecstasy, repentance and rebirth."[36] In essence, this is comparable to the presence encountered by many ancient Hebrews as codified in the Bible culminating in Saul's conversion.[37] Christianity is true not because it meets a human need. Joy's experience was not simply a psychological projection produced as the mind's response to the desperate state she was in; on the contrary, the experience was sparked by a perception of that which came from outside of her mind. It met a human need precisely because it is true (the Word of God, the person of Christ Jesus resurrected and ascended, pressed on her at this the most desperate time in her life precisely because it was the most beneficial moment *from Christ's perspective*). What happened to her was eternal, external, true, and beautiful, and occurred at precisely the right moment. As with Lewis in his rooms in Magdalen in 1929, she had sensed the approach of God and had given in and admitted, realized, that God was indeed God. So is all religious experience valid? It is easy for Bible scholars to dismiss the experience of individuals as recorded in the Hebrew Bible claiming they have been re-written and politically spun out of all recognition, but look to what underpins the experiences, the relationship with YHWH, God. Are all conversion experiences from the Holy Spirit? Most Christian and Jewish are. But not all: we are the object, not the subject; we are not the author of valid conversion experiences, we are the object. And as Christian

---

35   Davidman, "The Longest Way Round," 23.
36   Davidman, "The Longest Way Round," 24.
37   See Brazier, "Saul, Epilepsy, & Conversion."

salvation demonstrates, this all comes down to and is grounded in *HaShem* "*The name*": from *El*, to *Elohim*, from *El Shaddai*, to *YHWH/HaShem* to *Yeshua*: At the name of Jesus . . . .[38] Because of our fallen status we may delude ourselves to believe that it is God who has initiated the experience, who is courting us, seeking us, but, it might just well be a demonic or evil force acting, inviting, us. The measure of all religious experience has to be the self-revelation of God, which is in Christ Jesus. The question is, how does a religious experience measure up against the gospel? From a Christian perspective, the conversions of Lewis and Davidman are seen as valid in retrospect; first, because in each case the Spirit drew each of them to the knowledge of God's self-revelation in Christ; second, the way they lived their lives after the encounter is testimony to the truth of God's revelation. In the case of people who were born outside of the knowledge of the incarnation-cross-resurrection, the ultimate test of the validity of a conversion experience is *postmortem*, after death, before the judgment seat of Christ where—as laid out in Matthew 25—the way they lived their lives after a conversion experience/encounter is testimony to the truth of God's revelation. There are a lot of issues here in the context of how God gave intimations to pagans (i.e., people outside of the Judaic-Christian revelation) and how Lewis valued such intimations Christologically.

5. THE HOUND OF HEAVEN

When Bill eventually returned home, Joy writes that he accepted what had happened to her, commenting that he was, "on the way to something of the kind himself."[39] Both knew that they needed to change, to reorder their life together. "If my knowledge of God was true, the thinking of my whole life had been false. I could not doubt the truth of my experience. It was so much the realest thing that had ever happened to me!"[40] In a gentle manner, in a less overwhelming manner, this encounter with the Holy Spirit continued as Joy reordered her mind, her ideas, her beliefs, her whole life: "I snatched at books I had despised before; re-read *The*

---

38   "At the name of Jesus ev'ry knee shall bow, / ev'ry tongue confess him King of glory now. / 'Tis the Father's pleasure we should call him Lord, / who from the beginning was the mighty Word." *At the Name of Jesus Every Knee shall Bow*: Caroline Marie Noel (1817–70), her poems were collected in *Noel, The Name of Jesus and Other Verses for the Sick and Lonely*.

39   Davidman, "The Longest Way Round," 24.

40   Davidman, "The Longest Way Round," 24.

A HEBRAIC INKLING

Hound of Heaven, which I had ridiculed as a piece of phoney rhetoric—and, understanding it suddenly, burst into tears. (Also a new thing; I had seldom previously cried except with rage.) I went back to C. S. Lewis and learned from him, slowly, how I had gone wrong. Without his works, I wonder if I and many others might not still be infants 'crying in the night.'"[41]

The Still Small Point of Contact

Joy refers to Francis Thompson's (1859–1907) poem, "The Hound of Heaven," first published in 1900, which charts the slow, gradual, at first imperceptible, progress of the God that courts, and awaits a response whilst the human seeks ever to escape. Who is this God?—it is not the self-righteous political "god" of communism, it is not the literary "god" of a successful writer and poet who basks in the limelight of publicity, it is Jesus—Yeshua—who had died for her on the cross and awaits her response: and behind the Christ-event is approaching two thousand years of Hebrew witness from the patriarchs to the prophets, to Israel and its kings coming down to the tiny narrow point of an obscure young Jewish teenager, faced with the visitation of an angel and a decision that took over her life and turned everything for her upside down: the moment the world changed. The initiative lay with Yeshua-Christ, but the response had to come from Joy. The Lion of Judah became for Francis Thompson the Hound of Heaven (for Joy he had a more feline, stealth-like, quality):

> I fled Him, down the nights and down the days;
> I fled Him, down the arches of the years;
> I fled Him, down the labyrinthine ways
> Of my own mind; and in the mist of tears
> I hid from Him,[42]

A Hebrew seeking Reality

Strangely, one of the first acts of faith, as Joy puts it, was a renewed interest in the Communist Party because she still considered that Marxist economic theory was relevant because she asserts that once she recognized God she also recognized the need for moral responsibility.

41 Davidman, "The Longest Way Round," 25.
42 Davidman, "The Longest Way Round," 25.

13. Joy Davidman ... and the Mature C. S. Lewis

Joy felt she had a duty to show the Party that it did not need atheism. Like Lewis following his crossing of the spiritual Rubicon in 1929, Joy was not necessarily a Christian following her conversion encounter. Throughout all her atheist life she had regarded the apostate Jesus with traditional Jewish horror. So, initially what Joy desired was to develop into a good Jew, of the "comfortable Reformed type. . . . I had the usual delusion that all religions mean the same thing."[43] In studying religions she found them shot through with difference and contradiction. Some were characterized for her by wisdom, some by strong ethical intentions, some were characterized by insight:

> But only one of them had complete understanding of the grace and repentance and charity that had come to me from God. And the Redeemer who had made himself known, whose personality I would have recognized among ten thousand—well, when I read the New Testament, I recognized him. He was Jesus. The rest was fairly simple. I could not doubt the divinity of Jesus, and, step by step, orthodox Christian theology followed logically from it. My modernist objections to the miraculous proved to be mere superstition, unsupported by logic . . . I am a writer of fiction; I have made up stories myself, and I think I can tell a made-up story from a true one. The men who told of the resurrection told of something they had seen. Not Shakespeare himself could have invented the Synoptic Gospels. My beliefs took shape . . .[44]

There are two important points here: first, Joy recognized through a degree of comparative religious study that what had touched her was a person, not some inanimate abstract spiritual force, and that through simple comparative deduction that person was Jesus Christ; second, that she had no doubt about the divinity of this Jesus Christ—unlike C. S. Lewis, who struggled to accept the fact of Christ's divinity, even after being preached to by Dyson and Tolkien.

Joy and Bill and the children were baptized in Pleasant Plains Presbyterian Church in 1948; and there she thought she would remain. Leastwise, that is how she finishes her spiritual autobiography written in 1949, and published two years later. Despite his apparent conversion William Gresham's alcoholism, his adultery, his abusive violence did not change. The marriage was on the rocks. He had an affair with Joy's cousin,

43 Davidman, "The Longest Way Round," 25.
44 Davidman, "The Longest Way Round," 25.

Renee Rodriguez. Joy left him and took the children to England, eventually to divorce Bill, and to marry C. S. Lewis. She would contract cancer, recover, see the cancer to reassert itself, then die aged forty-five years on July 13, 1960—in the faith. Bill's conversion was most probably genuine, but he still—like all Christians—had free will, a will he exercised. Joy and Bill are examples of the parable of the sower and the seed:[45] in the case of Joy the seed of conversion bore good fruit, a hundred fold, in the case of Bill, the seed of conversion fell on barren ground and was choked by the weeds of this world. Joy knew that following her conversion encounter/experience she had to change. That change was analogous to the growth of the seeds in the parable of the sower and the seed.

After years of substance abuse and transitory relationships William Gresham on the September 14, 1962, committed suicide in a run-down hotel room in New York by taking an overdose of sleeping pills.[46]

6. HEBRAIC LAW: THE DECALOGUE

If Joy had marginalized at best her Jewish heritage in her earlier life, once she settled from the first flush of conversion into thinking about her faith as a Christian (as a Yeshuaite?), she turned to the heart of the Hebrew Bible, the patriarchs and prophets, to analyze the foundation, some would say, of her Christian faith, as she saw it: the Decalogue. She is studying and writing not so much as a Messianic Jew (for she had rejected the legal and cultural framework of Judaism as a child, from her parents' influence) but as a Hebraic Christian.

This reading and thought goes into her book *Smoke on the Mountain*[47] about the Ten Commandments; the work is written in what appears to be a journalistic style; Davidman has a sound understanding of the theological and biblical academic *status quo* of the time regarding the Decalogue, but offers nothing new in terms of an advancement in understanding, save for what is in effect a general eschatological approach: what does it mean today to value and attempt to follow the Decalogue, how essential is it for people's well-being, and ultimately, salvation?[48]

---

45   Matt 13; Mark 4; Luke 8.

46   See Douglas Gresham in Wikipedia: http://en.wikipedia.org/wiki/William_Gresham.

47   Davidman, *Smoke on the Mountain*, 9.

48   Don King has analyzed Davidman's *corpus* and has produced an understanding

13. Joy Davidman ... and the Mature C. S. Lewis

Joy Davidman's *Smoke on the Mountain* (Lewis wrote the foreword at Joy's invitation) is not strictly academic Bible studies, but is—as the subtitle states—"An Interpretation of the Ten Commandments." The book is academically informed, but it is very much the opinion of a Jewish convert seeking to understand what most people fail to consider: what is the function of the Decalogue and why did God give it to the ancient Hebrews? And if she is now a believer, how does she reassess this heritage? As Lewis notes in the foreword, what should a "Jewish Christian" focus on in such depth, but the Law.[49] But, warns Lewis, this is not a regression into legalism. Furthermore, he notes that the converted Jew is the only real (i.e., normal) human in the human race, because God's promises were made to the Hebrew initially—by a form of divine courtesy—the rest of humanity (pagan, gentile, all other religious including Christians) are a "special case" subject to emergency regulations. We as Christians are the wild vine, grafted into God's elect, the chosen. Lewis warns that we think of this hardly ever, yet we should have it at the top of our minds, regarding the Jews, in whatever religious condition they are before the Lord as innately superior—"we do not think of this as often as we might."[50] Lewis notes in this context Paul's comments about the Jews and the gentiles as one body subject to dispensation in his letter to the church in Ephesus:

> For he himself is our peace, who has made the two groups one and has destroyed the barrier, the dividing wall of hostility, by setting aside in his flesh the law with its commands and regulations. His purpose was to create in himself one new humanity out of the two, thus making peace, and in one body to reconcile both of them to God through the cross, by which he put to death their hostility. He came and preached peace to you who were far away and peace to those who were near. For through him we both have access to the Father by one Spirit. Consequently, you are no longer foreigners and strangers, but fellow citizens with God's people and also members of his household....
>
> Eph 2:14–19

---

of her work in the context of American theology in the mid-twentieth century: King, *Yet One More Spring*; see also, King, *Out of My Bone: The Letters of Joy Davidman*.

49   Lewis, "Foreword." In Davidman, *Smoke on the Mountain*, 9.
50   Lewis, "Foreword." In Davidman, *Smoke on the Mountain*, 7–8.

Lewis notes how despite her parents' Jewish cultural religious atheism, and her own disbelief, both feeding into her communist allegiance, Joy was deeply aware of a distinction, that he puts down to blood, that is, between her as a racial/tribal Jew and the rest of humanity. He notes how one of her early poems saw the Aryan ethos like a clinging fog, northern mists that shrouded and obscured any clarity before God (which, though they were unknown to each other in the decade after the First World War, was quite a good picture of the state of Lewis's mind and soul). Lewis can see a Hebraic quality of clarity in her writing despite her repudiation of Judaism as a young woman (a contradiction of this Northern European "fog"?). Writing on the nature and style of her work, Lewis notes how the book is distinctly American, how Joy's use of language is markedly her own, and exhibits what he terms a "Jewish fierceness," which is also "modern and feminine."[51] Such fierceness is justifiably critical of both Western nominal Christians and many of the Jews of her day: such is the clarity of a Jewish-Christian. Therefore, Lewis raises the question, "What should a Jewish-Christian write on if not the Law?"[52] Does this imply a relapse into "mere" Judaism? She knew the Law from growing up with her own people, she had rejected moralism early on in adulthood and now as a Christian she understands that legalism will never bring us to heaven: "She knows that only love can fulfill the law." And if love is the cure to the human condition, the true cure, that true love is a person. So, despite the chapters of her book analyzing the appalling state of humanity as represented by the human contradiction of the Decalogue (the diagnosis), love is not expressed in a set of instructions,[53] thus we read Davidman pointing us to the central act of forgiveness, the submission to torture and slaughter of Yeshua Ha Mashiach.

It is, therefore, after analyzing and illustrating the range and depth of her own people (here she is writing as an American and a Jew) as sinners and a contradiction of the Law that the final chapter, a conclusion, presents Christ as the only way forward

> And perhaps Christianity, if we ever embrace it not for our own worldly advantage but through surrender to God, will not only enable us to obey the Ten Commandments but enable us to enjoy

---

51   Lewis, "Foreword." In Davidman, *Smoke on the Mountain*, 9.
52   Lewis, "Foreword." In Davidman, *Smoke on the Mountain*, 9.
53   Lewis, "Foreword." In Davidman, *Smoke on the Mountain*, 9.

it; not only save this transitory world for the few perplexed years we spend in it, but bring us out of this noise and darkness and helplessness and terror that we call the world into the full Light: Light we remember from our childhood dreams, and from glimpses through music and art and the ecstasy of first love; Light we have known through a brief glow in our few moments of really selfless charity; Light which, in our secret hearts, we desire more than money and sex and power and the pride of the self. We men are all thieves who have stolen the self which was meant as a part of God and tried to keep it for ourselves alone. But if we give it up again, we might hear the words he spoke to a penitent thief once: "To-day shalt thou be with me in paradise."[54]

Davidman notes in criticism that, throughout Jewish history, Hebrew prophets told them that suffering and affliction, military defeat, eventually exile into slavery were punishment for failing to live up to the Decalogue as well as the numerous judicial details in the Mosaic laws. The opposite was that fame and wealth, success and children, livestock and land, were a "materialist" incentive and recompense for obedience: the world's acknowledgement was everything. More, the Spirit that the numerous names of God pointed to was to be placated. If so, if this was done correctly *YHWH* would reward: material gifts. God was either angry, or over-generous. Like a puzzled school child who did not know which way to turn to get it right (when it knew not how to enact rightness), a common saying amongst Davidman's Jewish ancestors in Eastern Europe questioned what they had been chosen for: "Perhaps it was then that the bitter Jewish saying, still current today, originated: 'Chosen for what? Chosen for trouble!'"[55]

Joy exhibits the sort of criticism—some of which might appear to those who expect her to be accommodating from a multi-faith perspective—that could be considered to be anti-Semitic. But then the same criticism has been levelled by the Gospel writers towards the Jewish religious authorities, in particular John's Gospel, which refer to the Sanhedrin, the Pharisees, the Sadducees, and the High Priest and his council in Herod's Temple, as "the Jews," forgetting that the writers themselves were Jews who were all too readily oppressed by this Jewish

---

54   Davidman, *Smoke on the Mountain*, 139.

55   Davidman, *Smoke on the Mountain*, 133.

religious elite.[56] Joy's criticisms were not levelled at a Jewish religious elite but the remnant of Eastern European Jews who, according to Davidman, had all but lost their Hebrew heritage and were mired in folk religion and superstitions.

What is perhaps pertinent is to try to assess what the relationship is for Davidman between Judaism and Christianity *in her day*: in some ways the relationship between Moses and Christ. Explicitly invoking John's Gospel in reference to Yeshua the Anointed One, the Christ:

> Light we remember from our childhood dreams, and from glimpses through music and art and the ecstasy of first love; Light we have known through a brief glow in our few moments of really selfless charity; Light which, in our secret hearts, we desire more than money and sex and power and the pride of the self.[57]

But are we not obsessed and possessed by our desire for power and control even in the privacy of our personal religious life?—

> We men are all thieves who have stolen the self which was meant as a part of God and tried to keep it for ourselves alone. But if we give it up again, we might hear the words he spoke to a penitent thief once: "To-day shalt thou be with me in paradise."[58]

Like many Jewish converts who simply accept and embrace the Anointed One, Joy is prepared to be critical to her own people and their religious heritage. (Though it is important to highlight that it is not simply converts to Jesus who do this. Judaism has always been self-critical and from biblical times to today Jews have criticized aspects of their faith and their fellow Jews; there is nothing new in Joy doing this, it is, we may assert, at the heart of her birth-faith as a Jew.)

Prior to her conversion to Christian faith Joy was only superficially interested in Judaism, and actively, cynically, against Judaism in her communist phase. With conversion she takes her faith heritage seriously, as the heritage and roots of the Jewish Messiah she now believes in and acknowledges as Lord. Therefore, there are two communities (Israel and the gentiles), as the apostle Paul asserts, but they are one community in

---

56   There are fifty-eight references to "the Jews" in John's Gospel, the majority are to be seen as critical.
57   Davidman, *Smoke on the Mountain*, 139.
58   Davidman, *Smoke on the Mountain*, 139.

13. Joy Davidman ... and the Mature C. S. Lewis

the sense that they are both in different ways called and elected. Joy's marriage to Lewis represented these two communities.

7. MARRIAGE ... AND FAMILY

Marriage

Lewis, the confirmed bachelor married Joy Davidman in a secular ceremony in a registry office to formalize her citizenship.[59] However, when Joy was diagnosed with terminal cancer they were married before God in a Christian ceremony by an Anglo-Catholic priest. It is important to remember that many of the churches, though not all, rejected Lewis's marriage to Joy Davidman because she was a divorcee. Though ironically from a strict interpretation of the Bible, her first marriage did not count against them because her first husband himself had been married and divorced; also, William Gresham's marriage was a secular marriage: a legal contract sanctioned by governmental authorities. All this would not have counted against them marrying in the eyes of Rome, if they had been Roman Catholics (ironically the approach to divorce by the Henrician Church of England was an early example of liberal freedom causing confusion through the piecemeal approach to marriage and divorce laws by the Church of England). So Lewis knew what it meant to be abandoned by the Church (of England). The marriage of Joy and Lewis was before God in Christ, the first true—*sacramental*—marriage *before and in God* (that is true according to biblical revelation)[60] either had entered into—

---

59   The story is well known from the Hollywood film, *Shadowlands* (1993), but also from a British Broadcasting Corporation (BBC) docudrama from 1985, as well as literary accounts of the story.

60   Remarriage after divorce is impossible: there are certain universal ethical truths that hold beyond religion and reflect the very nature of the human as created by God (with the truth revealed to the ancient Hebrews and reiterated in the Gospels: Gen 2:24, Matt 19:5, Mark 10:8, Eph 5:31, 1 Cor 6:16). Because Gresham had been previously married he could not truly marry Joy before and in God: remarriage in this instance would have been adultery (Matt 5:32b). A Roman Catholic would argue that way (there is also something of the purity of this doctrine of marriage in Hinduism—imparted by God as revelation?). If Jews took seriously the one-flesh statement in Genesis, and therefore the impossibility of divorce, and listened to Jesus on the Mosaic compromise where he, and not God, permitted, tolerated, not gave, the Jews divorce, "because your hearts were hard" (Matt 19:8), then surely Jews would have agreed with Roman Catholics on this count? But would Lewis and Joy have seen it that way as Episcopalian/Anglican? Probably not. Or did they simply consider that remarriage after divorce was permissible?

that is, a genuine ontological marriage where the two become one flesh, *in the Spirit*, (Gen 2:24; reiterated by Jesus: Matt 19:5, Mark 10:8, Eph 5:31),[61] where divorce is an ontic impossibility; thus Joy's first "marriage" to a divorced man was a legal contract to live together: yes, a secular marriage.[62] Following her marriage to Lewis, Joy recovered from cancer, remission lasted a few years; then she died.[63] Her death devastated Lewis and formed the trigger of another stage of conversion for him, perhaps the most profound of his conversions.

Lewis was faced with a paradox when his wife Joy died, and he failed to see the immediacy of the paradox of Christlikeness in her Job-like suffering; he rebelled and rejected his long-held sound doctrine of sufferance. He did not lose his faith, but he was severely critical of God for allowing Joy to suffer and die, he even began to consider God as innately cruel and behaving like a vivisectionist.[64] What Christlike comfort and consolation did Lewis gain in his late years from the love of God? In *The Four Loves* (1960), he exhibits a sound orthodox understanding of the love of God as compared to human love in its manifold forms, but in his grief he was as confused as Job before his inquisitors.

Marriage inevitably caused Joy to influence Lewis, and refresh his understanding of Judaism, but particularly his understanding of the place of suffering before God the Lord.[65]

---

61   Paul (1 Cor 6:16) says that a man who sleeps with a prostitute becomes "one flesh" with her. But this does not constitute the pure marriage between one man and one women, chaste before marriage, who form a deeply spiritual link in their flesh. It is perhaps impossible for people in the West today to appreciate this since the sex-crazed cultural revolution of the 1960s.

62   Yes, the concerns that come out of an ecclesial context (Roman Catholic) were alien to Joy's twentieth century Jewish background, and Lewis's Anglican background. Lewis and Joy probably thought that remarriage after a civil divorce was permissable. At the time mainstream Western Christian tradition has not considered remarriage after divorce to be acceptable (on the basis of an interpretation of Jesus' teaching in the Gospels); the Catholic Church today maintains that tradition.

63   When Joy was initially recovering from cancer, and the leg bone was rebuilding itself in a miraculous manner, she needed massive amounts of calcium, which were not, could not, be administered, at the time, medically: Lewis found he was suffering from brittle bone disease (normally associated with post-menapausal women) as he was in effect "leaking" calcium to his sacramental wife, in one flesh.

64   His rebellion is recorded with honesty in, *A Grief Observed*, published initially under the pseudonym N. W. Clerk.

65   See King, *Yet One More Spring*. In particular, 200f.

13. Joy Davidman ... and the Mature C. S. Lewis

David and Douglas Gresham

Upon Joy's death, Lewis, with help from Warnie, had two teenage boys to bring-up. Douglas Gresham went into farming, married, and has five children. Douglas is today well known as a Christian, and a defender of his stepfather's work. A British-American stage and voice-over actor, biographer, film producer, and executive producer of films of Lewis's work, he has written personally about his life, particularly in relation to his mother's marriage to Lewis. He has also spoken of his relationship with his brother and how this brought out a side of Jack and Warnie in raising the two boys after Joy's death that few know about. David was something of an enigmatic and secret character. Little has been said of him, or known, or published. Douglas, his younger brother, is the one person who knew David well, and is prepared to speak of him since his death. While Douglas appeared as a character in both versions of the Shadowlands story, David was air-brushed out of the second—Hollywood—film (1993); while the BBC docudrama (1985), gave equal presentation to both boys. David has also, by and large, been left out of the scholarly picture of Lewis's marriage and family. In his own biographical memoir of Lewis, Douglas writes of his own upbringing, and his adult years, but is quiet about David. Why? Following David's death, Douglas has now spoken of his brother. In an interview, published online, conducted by Jonathon Van Maren a new picture emerges:[66]

> David died several years ago in a secure Swiss mental hospital, and Douglas has finally broken his silence about a hitherto unknown aspect of life at The Kilns. His earliest memories, he told me, were of his brother, who was later diagnosed as schizophrenic. "When I was a small child," Douglas said, "he was continually trying to get rid of me. This went on into our teen years." Douglas said he recalls "running like crazy or defending myself from my rather insane brother.... I would never have said anything to harm him or upset him while he was alive, because oddly enough I still loved him as a brother. In fact, I wept when he died."[67]

---

[66] First Things website. Interview conducted on Sept 3, 2020. See: https://www.firstthings.com/web-exclusives/2020/09/c-s-lewis-and-his-stepsons. Accessed Oct 2. 2020

[67] See: First Things https://www.firstthings.com/web-exclusives/2020/09/c-s-lewis-and-his-stepsons

Aged eleven and twelve respectively at the time of Lewis and Joy's marriage, Lewis dedicated *The Horse and His Boy* (*The Chronicles of Narnia*) to the boys. Douglas has now spoken of life with a mentally ill brother, who once doused Douglas in petrol and attempted to strike a match and burn him. "We didn't tell anybody. The only reason I'm releasing it now is because people should know what Jack put up with and what Warnie put up with and how heroic they were to do it at all. It is time that people understand what Jack and Warnie went through . . . ."[68]

Lewis struggled to dedicate himself to David's well-being, facing difficulties in educating both of the boys. In religious terms, David decided to become Jewish rather than Christian (Douglas notes how David had already attempted Islam and Buddhism). As David settled into Judaism, Lewis "went out of his way to get special pots and pans for him so he could cook his own kosher food and get kosher food from the Jewish shop in the middle of the covered market in Oxford."[69] Lewis's attempts at accommodating David's faith, and seeking to see David grow, met with mixed results: "Well, it was accepted, but he was never grateful about it. He was just very badly damaged mentally and emotionally, and he stayed that way."[70] With Lewis's death David attempted to forge a life, at least staying committed to Judaism, eventually living for some time as a Chasidic Jew in *Meah Shearim* in Israel.[71] However, "his mental illness plagued him for his entire life."[72] David was effectively air-brushed out of studies and biographies on Lewis, ending his days in a secure mental hospital in Switzerland.

8. LEWIS' AND DAVIDMAN'S LIFE AND DEATH

Lewis's theology grew out of his personal experience of God in Christ: the death of his mother and of his wife, Joy Davidman, both from cancer, and his conversion experiences. These events point not to a single Damascus Road epiphany but to a process with identifiable moments. Lewis's

---

68   First Things https://www.firstthings.com/web-exclusives/2020/09/c-s-lewis-and-his-stepsons. It is important to remember that both Lewis brothers had been life-long bachelors, and now around the age of sixty years had to cope with these two boys!

69   Ibid; See also https://forums.catholic.com/t/c-s-lewis-stepson-david-gresham/113316

70   Ibid

71   Ibid

72   Ibid

13. Joy Davidman ... and the Mature C. S. Lewis

invocation of the shadows of eternity, intimations through the veil of this world of the life to come revealed through Christ, which characterize and define his theology, grew out of his personal experience of God in Christ: the death from cancer of his mother (in 1908), which contributed to his loss of faith (the clearing out, perhaps, of a false "god"?), his conversion back to faith (to theism in 1929), and then to Christ (in 1931), and then the death of his wife Joy Davidman, again from cancer (1960), are all staging posts in the process of *conversion* and *reorientation*, driven by serious changes in his thinking and the ideas that formed his life and character. The conversion he underwent to a deeper level of possession in/by Christ after Joy's death is to be seen as reflecting an understanding of reconciliation in Christ—the psychology of atonement?[73]—built upon the cross.

Lewis's conversion as a young man was protracted and drawn out over a number of years.[74] Joy Davidman's, as we also saw, was something of the opposite in many ways. She accepted and valued the moments of epiphany—even as a self-confessed Marxist atheist—and underwent a single, clear conversion (with epiphanic moments leading up to it; for example, the afternoon in Central Park).[75] This implies that there was something Lewis had to come to in his mind, his heart, his very being; that God was not satisfied until he had reached that point. Is this what a *conversion* is about in many ways? Lewis's mind, his beliefs and prejudices, prevented in some ways the single immediacy of a Damascus Road conversion.[76] Joy, having exhausted the manifold delusions of Marxism, had abandoned the false "gods," her event has the immediacy and single purity of Saul's. So what aim was there in her suffering from cancer? Or is suffering sometimes without meaning? Does God use the natural existence of suffering for God's purposes? We perhaps need to examine the final point of conversion near the end of his life where, following

73 See, Nicholi, *The Question of God*.

74 See, Brazier, *C. S. Lewis—Revelation, Conversion, and Apologetics*, Pt. 1, chs. 1–2, specifically, ch. 2, §. 2.i–ii, and, §. 4.i–iv.

75 Brazier, *C. S. Lewis—Revelation, Conversion, and Apologetics*. See, Pt. 1, ch. 3, specifically, §. 3.i–iii, and, §§4–5.

76 Christians may refer to the Damascus Road event in Paul's life as a "Christian" event, but it was in fact distinctively Hebraic: to Saul the Jew, the Pharisee! And are not all subsequent conversion events, even those experienced by gentiles, Hebraic? If valid before the Lord God, such events are drawing the individual into the chosen people of God. To the Jew first, and then to the rest of humanity—as Lewis demonstrated.

the death of his wife Joy from cancer, he struggled and wrestled with his faith, accusing God of being a cosmic vivisectionist, of doubting the goodness and mercy of God.[77] In other words, he wrestled and struggled with the doctrine of God he held to in his mind. Twenty years earlier Lewis had stated in *The Problem of Pain* how God might use pain and suffering to turn us from our selfish desires to a right judgment of God and God's purposes. Ironically, Lewis did not realize that he did not have a right judgment of his own or Joy's suffering. He assumed that Joy was being punished or that the cancer had been foisted directly onto her by God. His assumption was that the genesis of the cancer was at the time of the breakdown of her first marriage and her coming to Oxford as a middle-aged woman with two young children. There was a miraculous healing from the cancer—bone eaten away was rebuilt with no natural explanation; they had four years married together, but the cancer returned, and she died. The actual genesis of the cancer was twenty-five years earlier. As a teenage young woman Joy had been diagnosed with an overactive thyroid—and prescribed a radium belt to wear. At the time, in the early twentieth century, medical and scientific opinion was that radioactivity was good for you(!); what was not realized was that this belt gave Joy a dangerous dose of radiation, engendering the cancer, which when it appeared was multiple tumors all over her, including bone cancer that had eaten away to nothing some bones.[78] The miracle is that she did not die in her twenties of cancer. The miracle—unknown to either her or Lewis—is that she lived for several decades: long enough to have two children and to meet and marry Lewis, for there to be a miraculous cure of the cancer when it did erupt, and for God to use the illness in minute detail *to God's purposes*, which by definition are *God's loving purposes*: the Hebraic God of the Book of Job. Lewis had to wrestle with this, eventually to realize the error of his ways in judging God as wrong in how God handled Joy's disease and death. Joy's cancer was not *caused* by a violent and distant "deity," by a vindictive and cruel "god," toying with Joy like a cat playing with a mouse, to tenderize it before eating it; this was not the "god" of vivisection who had played with and experimented on the human. God was not a cruel "demi-god," who had visited cancer onto

---

77 See, Lewis, *Grief Observed*, published initially under the pseudonym N. W. Clerk.

78 See, Sibley, *Shadowlands*, ch. 4, also, Davidman, *Out of My Bone*, xxvii.

her. The cancer issued from medical scientific ignorance, which, often is merely an example of original sin.[79]

All these events in Lewis's and Joy's lives are significant pointers that afford evidence of Lewis's appropriation of Christ's redemption. We may term this element, the sufferance of salvation: without Christ, suffering is meaningless. God may, or may not, have willed the suffering and pain (including mental hurts from relationships, not solely physical pain), but God in Christ may *use* the suffering and pain. Christ's love beckons us to endure our suffering for *his* sake. This is, as we have seen and established, the *imago Christi* (the image of Christ). But this is not an attempt at mere imitation. Only when the demands of Christ impinge on us, challenge us, yes, hurt us in manifold ways (disfavor or disadvantage, sometimes disenfranchisement at work; being a Christian is the reawakening of the imago Christi in the human as much as it is suffering, pain, even martyrdom). Lewis knew only too well the wrestling hurt of this reawakening. Therefore, we must acknowledge this distinction between precisely what the *imago Christi* (the likeness, the image, the echo of Christ in, and to us) and the *imitatio Christi* (the imitation of Christ, our faltering attempts at Christlikeness, initiated and driven preveniently by the Holy Spirit) were in Lewis's writings; this is something that is often implicit in his work but underpins his entire *corpus*: humans must indeed *endure* their going, must *endure* these things, must *endure* as they go hence from this life to be re-born in humility from holy poverty.

---

79 Deliberate use of radon and radium in medicine commenced in the early twentieth century, based on the flawed logic—supported and endorsed by many doctors—that the power of these newly discovered radioactive "scientific" elements could be used to cure illness. Drinking radium or radon dissolved in water, or placing the elements inside a belt worn next to the skin, was popular and fashionable in the 1920s and 1930s, this at a time when smoking was considered good for one's health. Even a low dose from these "treatments" caused radiation poisoning and many deaths. Radiation poisoning, and the full implication of exposure, were not fully comprehended until after the two atomic bombs were dropped on Japan in 1945.

Conclusion

> "Then the LORD spoke to Job out of the storm. He said . . .
>
> Where were you when I laid the earth's foundation?
> Tell me, if you understand.
>
> Who marked off its dimensions? Surely you know!
> Who stretched a measuring line across it?
>
> On what were its footings set,
> or who laid its cornerstone—
>
> While the morning stars sang together
> and all the angels shouted for joy?"
>
> THE BOOK OF JOB 38:1, 4–7

"Once more, it may be madness—a madness congenital to man and oddly fortunate in its results—or it may be revelation. And if revelation, then it is most really and truly in Abraham that all people shall be blessed, for it was the Jews who fully and unambiguously identified the awful Presence haunting black mountain-tops and thunderclouds with 'the righteous Lord' who 'loveth righteousness.'"

C. S. LEWIS[1]

1. INTRODUCTION

From what we may term the Edwardian establishment standard anti-Semitic, even racist, remarks of his youth to the slow even painful conversions as a young don, to the mature Lewis who reflected more and more a complementary Hebraic perspective in his works and to his marriage to an American Jewish Christian, Lewis covered practically all the positions he could during his life in relation to the Hebrews, God's chosen for the unchosen.

---

1 Lewis, *The Problem of Pain*, 10–11.

A HEBRAIC INKLING

2. THE HEBRAIC GOD OF JOB

C. S. Lewis is at his most Hebraic after the death of his wife, Joy Davidman. His grief, his loss, his confusion and rebellion before and against God are Jobian.[2] Lewis felt betrayed by God, abandoned and assaulted by *YHWH*: where was God! Where was Christ! His understanding of the cross became confused. But in the end, like Job, he held on through the existential nihilism. But this apparent dark night of the soul was not for Lewis a confrontation with evil—but Lewis seemingly oppressed by God with no rational way out: his suffering induced by rebellion, but was ironically creative. Lewis had written about the Psalms, analyzed them, but when the crunch came, he rebelled in his selfish confusion against the rack of his struggle—wresting with God—his suffering, his loss played out as theodicial rants? And he would have had no idea of the role played in his wife's suffering and death by the radium belt worn in her teenage years. If he had, surely he would have been thankful for the life he had with Joy, thankful that she had not died in her mid-twenties: "Who is this that obscures my plans, with words without knowledge?" (Job 38:2).

Was Job (*'Iyyov*)[3] a Hebrew? Well, that one of three friends who sought to console Job and placate his rebellion is said to be Temanite—Eliphaz the Temanite[4]—probably indicates that he was an Edomite, or a Palestinian descended from Esau (who had sold his birthright). Job, like Lewis, is therefore related to the Jews, yet struggles to comprehend his theodicial state and search for the answers to such difficulties: why, God, oh, why. Both Job and Lewis are bereft of the full facts surrounding their situation. His wrestling with God over Joy's death contrasts sharply with his refusal to engage with God over the death of his mother.

In some ways the relationship between Christians and Jews might be seen in the parable of the two sons.[5] Many Christians say "I will," but

2   Jobian as in the sufferings and puzzlement of the protagonist in the Book of Job in the Hebrew Bible. Not to be confused with the modern usage referring to the beliefs and actions of Steve Jobs, chief executive and concept designer of Apple Computers.

3   Persecuted, hated, He who weeps.

4   Job 2:11; 4:1; 15:1; 22:1; 42:7, 9.

5   "What do you think? There was a man who had two sons. He went to the first and said, 'Son, go and work today in the vineyard.' 'I will not,' he answered, but later he changed his mind and went. Then the father went to the other son and said the same thing. He answered, 'I will, sir,' but he did not go. 'Which of the two did what his father wanted?' 'The first,' they answered. Jesus said to them, 'Truly I tell you, the tax collectors and the prostitutes are entering the kingdom of God ahead of you. 'For John came to you

either don't, or redefine the will of the Father according to their desire; while many Jews deny the divine nature of the Son, Yeshua, saying, "I won't" but are obedient to the Father, where the Father and the Son are one. Israel says no to Christ, but many Jews conform to the will of God in Christ. And in both cases the answer is not final till the *eschaton* (hence, Barth's comment, echoed implicitly by Lewis, regarding the Jews not believing—*yet*). Despite their erroneous denial of who and what Yeshua was, perhaps, today, many Jews and Muslims are more right with God than many Christians when measured by the will of God in Christ.

3. THE FINAL LEWIS

We have clearly demonstrated that Lewis's approach to and valuation of Judaism changed dramatically over the course of his life. So what was the influence of Joy Davidman on Lewis? As a Jewish Christian, Davidman influenced C. S. Lewis; throughout the 1950s even before she came to Oxford, "Lewis began to ask for Davidman's opinion and criticism when he was writing."[6] Hence, her teaching Lewis about the concept and use of humor in the Hebrew Bible—also evidenced in the sayings of Jesus—as one example. But, as we have seen, also generally to elevate the value and importance of the Hebrew Bible, and to see the Jewish covenant on a par with the redemption bought by Jesus, where both stand alongside each other under the Abrahamic promise and dispensation, reigned over by the resurrected and ascended Christ. She also taught Lewis not to shy from seeing faults in the history of the Jews (are we not our brother's keeper, and our sister's too?), but she taught him to eschew anti-Semitism and fear pride taking hold over the new covenanters. And we can see something of this Hebraic character in his works from circa 1955 on. Inevitably this generated distance between Lewis and the Anglican establishment's presence in Oxford, particularly in the common rooms. Yes, there was an element of anti-Semitism towards Joy, knowing what they thought they knew of Lewis, but also an almost tribal dislike for her American citizenship.

---

to show you the way of righteousness, and you did not believe him, but the tax collectors and the prostitutes did. And even after you saw this, you did not repent and believe him." Matthew 21:28–32

6 See "Joy Davidman," Wikipedia: https://en.wikipedia.org/wiki/Joy_Davidman

A HEBRAIC INKLING

In April 1959 Lewis declared that the only living Judaism was Christianity: Lewis in effect was repeating a view he had read in Joy Davidman's *Smoke on the Mountain*.[7] And yet Lewis's view was that without Judaism we are nothing for gentiles are enfolded into the Chosen People of Israel. Anti-Semites merely bite the hand that feeds them salvation! And, as we noted earlier from Barth, such people deny their own humanity.

Writing on the ancient Hebrews, Lewis notes, perhaps only a single people, as a people, took the step with perfect decisive originality, away from what Lewis terms "the obscenities and barbarities of the unmoralised worship or the cold, sad self-righteousness of sheer moralism."[8] With both Judaism and Christianity, he notes, paganism and pantheism—particularly in the form of morals and ethics—is always breaking in, attempting to corrupt; but we find this with most religions. Even free-wheeling Western liberals can be surprisingly judgmental, ever seeking to impose its own personal moral order on everyone. Lewis notes that even Stoicism finds itself hide-bound to its own moral dictates. But this is religion: human-centered religion, before which the true God-given revelation may seem a madness, congenital to the human condition, for we ever seek God but find ourselves lost in blind alleys. We must face the selectiveness of revelation in the chosenness of the ancient Hebrews through to today's Jews. Therefore, as existential revelation, all people, *in potentia*, are blessed by and in Abraham, for it was the ancient Hebrews who, through revelation, without ambiguity, free from abstruseness came to know the awesome divine presence, which courted them, praised them, chastised them, held to them for the sake of the unchosen: this was the righteous Lord of and for all.[9]

Lewis did not know or use the terminology of "Messianic Jew" or "Hebraic Christian," but he is prepared to use the term "Jewish Christian," particularly in the context of his wife, Joy Davidman. In addition, his work demonstrates more-and-more, as the years go by, a respect for Judaism, and an increasing place within Christian theology for the foundational roots of the Hebraic. But he was well beyond the unbalanced establishment anti-Semitism indicative of many Western nation states of

---

7   "Lewis writing to Dom Bede Griffiths, April 30, 1959." *Letters of C. S. Lewis*, 285–86

8   Lewis, *The Problem of Pain*, 10–11.

9   Lewis, *The Problem of Pain*, Ch. 1 "Introductory," 10–11

Conclusion

his day, especially as compared to the early twenty-first century where so many Western supposedly enlightened modern liberals—implicitly or explicitly—are. It is fair to say that he was, in effect, a Hebraic Inkling!

In some ways Lewis's life, religion, and worldview move from the British Empire anti-Semitism racist[10] of his youth to coming to espouse a deep surprisingly post-modern approach to race and racism, and to understand the spiritual seniority[11] of the ancient Hebrews and the Jewish Messiah: the chosen for the unchosen, while being for better or for worse deeply Anglican.[12]

---

10   "Lewis to his brother Warren (Warnie) Lewis, c. 20 April 1921." In Lewis, *Collected Letters Vol I*, 536–38.

11   Though it is imperative to remember that the Bible is clear, that the Jews are not better than gentiles; indeed, in the Hebrew Bible specifically they are often accused by God of behaving even worse.

12   "Lewis writing to Mrs Johnson, May 14, 1955." In Lewis, *Collected Letters, Vol. III*, 607–8.

Select Bibliography

Alexander, Samuel. *Space, Time and Deity—The Gifford Lectures 1910-1918. Volumes I and II*. London: Macmillan, 1920.
Allen, Leslie C. *The Psalms 101-151*. Rev. ed. Word Biblical Commentary, Vol. 21. Zondervan, 2016.
Allen, William Cully. *Jesus among Giants: Religious Biographies in Comparative Context*. New York: Peter Lang, 2019.
Anselm of Canterbury. *The Proslogion*. In *Anselm of Canterbury—The Major Works*, edited by Brian Davies, and G. R. Evans, 82-104. Oxford World Classics. Oxford: Oxford University Press, 1998.
Ariel, Yaakov. "Chosen People Ministries and Its Place within the Larger Context of Evangelical Missions to the Jews." *Journal of Messianic Jewish Studies* 3 (2020) 153-70.
Ariel, Yaakov. "Messianic Judaism." In *The Jewish Annotated New Testament*, edited by Amy-Jill Levine and Marc Zvi Brettler, 756-59. 2nd ed. Oxford: Oxford University Press, 2017.
Ariel, Yaakov. *Evangelizing the Chosen People: Missions to the Jews in America, 1880-2000*. H. Eugene and Lillian Youngs Lehman Series. Chapel Hill, NC: University of North Carolina Press, 2000.
Augustine of Hippo. *On Baptism, Against the Donatists (Book I)*. New Advent website: https://www.newadvent.org/fathers/14081.htm.
Auret, Adrian. "The Theological Intent of the Use of the Names of God in the Eighth-Century Memoir of Isaiah." *Old Testament Essays* 5.2 (1992) 272-91.
Baines, John. "The Dawn of the Amarna Age." In *Amenhotep III: Perspectives on His Reign*, edited by David Bourke O'Connor, Eric Cline, 371-89. Ann Arbor, MI: University of Michigan Press, 1998.
Barth, Karl. "Die alten Hebr[äer] sollen keine Deutschen warden, aber Sie alten Hebräer." *Karl Barth, Konfirmandenunterricht 1909-1921*. Zurich: Theologischer Verlag Zürich, 1987.
———. *The Church Dogmatics*. Translated and edited G. W. Bromiley and T. F. Torrance. 14 vols. Edinburgh: T. & T. Clark, 1936-77.
———. *Dogmatik im Grundriß*. München: Kaiser, 1947.
———. "Evangelische Theologie im 19. Jahrhundert." In *Evangelische Theologie im 19. Jahrhundert*, 1-24. Zollikon-Zurich: Evangelischer Verlag A. G., 1960.
———. "Die Gerechtigkeit Gottes." An address delivered in the Town Church of Aarau on 16th January, 1916. Published in *Neue Wege X* (1916); later reprinted in, Karl Barth, *Das Wort Gottes und die Theologie*, 5-17. München: Kaiser, 1925.

———. *Konfirmandenunterricht 1909-1921*. Zurich: TVZ, 1987.
———. "Nachwort." In *Schleiermacher-Auswahl*, 113–14. Siebenstern Taschenbuch. München: Siebenstern Taschenbuch, 1968.
———. *Der Römerbrief. Zweite Fassung 1922*. Zürich: Theologischer Verlag Zürich, 1999.
Bauckham, Richard. *Who Is God? Key Moments of Biblical Revelation*. Grand Rapids: Baker, 2020.
Belcher, Richard P. *Finding Favor in the Sight of God: A Theology of Wisdom Literature*. Downers Grove, IL: IVP Academic, 2018.
Bergman, Alexander F., and Joy Davidman. *They Look Like Men*. New York: Ackerman, 1944.
Berlin, Adele, and Marc Zvi Brettler, eds. *The Jewish Study Bible*. Oxford: Oxford University Press. 2014
Biddle, Mark E. "The 'Endangered Ancestress' and Blessing for the Nations." *Journal of Biblical Literature* 109 (1990) 599–611.
Binnie, William. *A Pathway into the Psalter: The Psalms: Their History, Teachings and Use*. 1886. Reprint, Birmingham, AL: Solid Ground Christian Books, 2005.
Biven, David N. "'Cataloguing the Gospels' Hebraisms: Part Five (Parallelism)." *Jerusalem Perspective*. See https://www.jerusalemperspective.com/6628/
Bledstein, Adrien J. "The Trials of Sarah." *Judaism* 30 (Fall 1981) 411–17.
Blocher, Henri. "The Fear of the Lord as the 'Principle' of Wisdom." *Tyndale Bulletin* 28.1 (1977) 3–28.
Blue, Lionel. *A Backdoor to Heaven*. London: Darton, Longman & Todd, 1979.
———. *Hitchhiking to Heaven: An Autobiography*. London: Hodder & Stoughton, 2005.
Bock, Darrell L., and Mitch Glaser, eds. *Gospel According to Isaiah 53, The: Encountering the Suffering Servant in Jewish and Christian Theology*. Grand Rapids, MI: Kregel Academic, 2012.
———. *To the Jew First: The Case for Jewish Evangelism in Scripture and History*. Grand Rapids, MI: Kregel Academic, 2008
——— *Messiah in the Passover*. Grand Rapids, MI: Kregel, 2017.
———. *The People, the Land, and the Future of Israel: Israel and the Jewish People in the Plan of God*. Grand Rapids, MI: Kregel, 2014.
Boyarin, Daniel. "Logos, a Jewish Word: John's Prologue as Midrash." In *The Jewish Annotated New Testament*, edited by Amy-Jill Levine and Marc Zvi Brettler, 688–91. 2nd ed. Oxford: Oxford University Press, 2017.
Brackmann, Rebecca. "'Dwarves Are Not Heroes': Antisemitism and the Dwarves in J. R. R. Tolkien's writing." *Mythlore: A Journal of J. R. R. Tolkien, C. S. Lewis, Charles Williams, and Mythopoeic Literature* 28.3–4 (2010). Available at: https://go.gale.com/ps/anonymous?id=GALE%7CA227196960&sid=googleScholar&v=2.1&it=r&linkaccess=abs&issn=01469339&p=LitRC&sw=w
Brazier, P. H. *C. S. Lewis—An Annotated Bibliography and Resource. C. S. Lewis: Revelation and the Christ, Book 4*. Eugene, OR: Pickwick, 2012.
———. "C. S. Lewis and the Anscombe Debate: From *Analogia Entis* to *Analogia Fidei*." *The Journal of Inklings Studies* 1.2 (2011) 69–123.
———. "C. S. Lewis and Christological Prefigurement." *The Heythrop Journal* 48.5 (2007) 742–75.
———. "C. S. Lewis's and Karl Barth's Conversions: Reason and Imagination, a Realization—*fides quaerens intellectum*." In *C. S. Lewis and the Inklings Reflections*

Bibliography

on *Faith, Imagination, and Modern Technology*, edited by Salwa Khoddam, Mark R. Hall, and Jason Fisher, 6-45. Newcastle upon Tyne, UK: Cambridge Scholars, 2015.

———. "C. S. Lewis's Conversion and Karl Barth's *Retraktation*—'God is God,' a Realization." Paper presented to the Research Institute in Systematic Theology, King's College London, on July 27, 2004.

———. "C. S. Lewis: A Doctrine of Transposition." *The Heythrop Journal* 50.4 (2009) 669-88.

———. C. S. Lewis—*On the Christ of a Religious Economy. I. Creation and Sub-Creation. C. S. Lewis: Revelation and the Christ, Book 3.1*. Eugene, OR: Pickwick, 2013.

———. *C .S. Lewis—On the Christ of a Religious Economy. II. Knowing Salvation. C. S. Lewis: Revelation and the Christ, Book 3.2*. Eugene, OR: Pickwick, 2014.

———. "C. S. Lewis on Revelation & Second Meanings: A Philosophical & Pneumatological Justification." *The Chronicle of the Oxford University C. S. Lewis Society* 7.1 (2010) 18-35.

———. "C. S. Lewis on Scripture and the Christ, the Word of God: Convergence and Divergence with Karl Barth." *Sehnsucht*, 4 (2010) 89-109.

———. *C. S. Lewis—Revelation, Conversion and Apologetics. C. S. Lewis: Revelation and the Christ, Book 1*. Eugene, OR: Pickwick, 2012.

———. *C. S. Lewis—The Work of Christ Revealed. C. S. Lewis: Revelation and the Christ, Book 2*. Eugene, OR: Pickwick, 2012.

———. "'God . . . or a Bad, or Mad, Man:' C. S. Lewis's Argument for Christ—A Systematic Theological, Historical and Philosophical Analysis of aut Deus aut malus homo." *The Heythrop Journal* 55.1 (2014) 1-30.

——— *In the Highest Degree Vol I. Essays on C. S. Lewis's Philosophical Theology—Method, Content, & Reason. C. S. Lewis: Revelation and the Christ*. Eugene, OR: Pickwick, 2018.

——— *In the Highest Degree Vol II. Essays on C. S. Lewis's Philosophical Theology—Method, Content, & Reason. C. S. Lewis: Revelation and the Christ*. Eugene, OR: Pickwick, 2018.

———. "The Pittenger-Lewis Debate: Fundamentals of an Ontological Christology." *The Chronicle of the Oxford University C. S. Lewis Society* 6.1 (2009) 7-23.

———. "Saul, Epilepsy, & Conversion." *The Evangelical Review* 8 (2020) A29-46. Online Journal: www.evangelicalreview.net, 1 June 2020.

Brewer, Douglas J., and Emily Teeter. *Egypt and the Egyptians*. 2nd ed. Cambridge: Cambridge University Press, 2007.

Bricker, Daniel P. "The Doctrine of the 'Two Ways' in Proverbs I: The Constraints of Hebrew Poetry." *Journal of the Evangelical Theological Society* 38.4 (1995) 501-17.

Broadie, Alexander. "Maimonides and Aquinas on the Names of God." *Religious Studies* 23 (1987) 157-70.

Brown, J; N. Perrin; J. B. Green, eds. *Dictionary of Jesus and the Gospels*. Downers Grove, IL: IVP, 1992.

Brown, Michael L. *Our Hands Are Stained with Blood: The Tragic Story of the Church and the Jewish People*. Shippensburg, PA: Destiny Image, 2019.

Brown, Yaakov. *Spiritual leader of Beth Melekh Community*. Auckland, NZ. See: Beth Melekh: https://www.bethmelekh.com/

Brueggemann Walter. Psalms. *New Cambridge Bible Commentary*. Cambridge: Cambridge University Press, 2014

Brunner, Emil. *The Mediator: A Study of the Central Doctrine of the Christian Faith.* Philadelphia: Westminster, 1947.

Burney, C. F. *The Poetry of Our Lord: An Examination of the Formal Elements of Hebrew Poetry in the Discourses of Jesus Christ.* Oxford: Clarendon, 1925.

Busch, Eberhard. "God Is God: The Meaning of a Controversial Formula and the Fundamental Problem of Speaking about God." *Princeton Seminary Bulletin* 7.2 (1986) 101–13.

Byargeon, Rick W. "The Structure and Significance of Prov 9:7–12." *Journal of the Evangelical Theological Society* 40.3 (1997) 367–75.

Campbell, Constantine R. *Paul and Union with Christ: An Exegetical and Theological Study.* Grand Rapids: Zondervan, 2015.

Carpenter, Humphrey. *The Inklings: C. S. Lewis, J. R. R. Tolkien, Charles Williams and Their Friends.* London: Allen & Unwin, 1978.

Child, Francis James. *The English and Scottish Popular Ballads, Vol. I–IX.* New York: Houghton Mifflin & Co. 1884–98. Unabridged reprint of the full original in 5 volumes by Dover Publications, 1965. See, also, online edition, Project Gutenberg: http://www.gutenberg.org/.

Clements, Ronald. *God's Chosen People: A Theological Interpretation of the Book of Deuteronomy.* Religious Book Club 182. London: SCM, 1968.

Clerk, N. W. (C. S. Lewis pseudonym). *A Grief Observed.* London: Faber & Faber, 1961.

Coleridge, Samuel Taylor. *Biographia Literaria: or, Biographical Sketches of My Literary Life and Opinions.* 1817. Edited with an introduction by George Watson. Everyman's Library 11. London: Dent, 1997.

Connors, Robert J., and Edward P. J. Corbett. *Style and Statement.* Oxford: Oxford University Press, 1999.

Craigie, Peter C., Marvin E. Tate, et al. *The Psalms 1–50. Word Biblical Commentary 19.* Rev. ed. Grand Rapids: Zondervan, 2016.

Crawford, John S. "Multiculturalism at Sardis: Jews and Christians Live, Work and Worship Side by Side." *Biblical Archaeology Review*, 22.5 (1996) 38–47.

Darnell, John. *Tutankhamun's Armies: Battle and Conquest During Ancient Egypt's Late Eighteenth Dynasty.* Hoboken, NJ: Wiley & Sons, 2007.

Davidman, Helen Joy. *Anya.* New York: Macmillan, 1940.

———. *Letter to a Comrade.* New Haven, CT: Yale University Press, 1938.

———. "The Longest Way Round." In *These Found the Way: Thirteen Converts to Protestant Christianity*, edited by David Soper, 13–26. Philadelphia: Westminster, 1951.

———. *A Naked Tree: Love Sonnets to C. S. Lewis and Other Poems.* Edited by Don W. King. Grand Rapids: Eerdmans, 2015.

———. *Smoke on the Mountain: An Interpretation of the Ten Commandments in Terms of Today.* Foreword by C. S. Lewis. Philadelphia: Westminster, 1954.

———, ed. *War Poems of the United Nations: The Songs and Battle Cries of a World at War, Three Hundred Poems, One Hundred and Fifty Poets from Twenty Countries.* New York: Dial, 1943.

———. *Weeping Bay.* New York: Macmillan, 1950.

de Blois, Kees F. "Translating the Names of God: Tryggve Mettinger's Analyses Applied to Bible Translation." *Bible Translator* 43 (1992) 406–14.

Dearborn, Kerry. *Baptized Imagination: The Theology of George MacDonald.* Ashgate Studies in Theology, Imagination and the Arts. Aldershot, UK: Ashgate, 2006.

Bibliography

Dempster, Stephen G. *Dominion and Dynasty: A Biblical Theology of the Hebrew Bible.* Leicester, UK: Apollos, 2003.

Donaldson, Terence L. "Paul within Judaism: A Critical Evaluation from a 'New Perspective' Perspective." In *Paul within Judaism: Restoring the First-Century Context to the Apostle,* edited by Mark D. Nanos and Magnus Zetterholm, 277–302. Philadelphia: Fortress, 2015.

Dorsett, Lyle W. *And God Came In: The Extraordinary Story of Joy Davidman, Her Life and Marriage to C. S. Lewis.* New York: Macmillan, 1983.

———. *Eine andere Art von Hunger: Joy Davidman—ihr Leben u. ihre Ehe mit C. S. Lewis.* Basel: Brunnen-Verlag, 1985.

———. *A Love Observed: Joy Davidman's Life and Marriage to C. S. Lewis.* 2nd ed. Reprint, Colorado Springs, CO: Harold Shaw, 1998.

Ehrensperger, Kathy. "The Question(s) of Gender: Relocating Paul in Relation to Judaism." In *Paul within Judaism Restoring the First-Century Context to the Apostle,* edited by Mark D. Nanos and Magnus Zetterholm, 245–76. Philadelphia: Fortress, 2015.

Eichler, Barry. "On Reading Genesis 12:10–20." In *Biblical and Judaic Studies in Honor of Moshe Greenberg,* edited by Tehillah Le-Moshe, 23–38. State College, PA: Eisenbrauns imprint, Penn State University Press, 1997.

Elliott, Neil. "The Question of Politics: Paul as a Diaspora Jew under Roman Rule." In *Paul within Judaism Restoring the First-Century Context to the Apostle,* edited by Mark D. Nanos and Magnus Zetterholm, 204–44. Philadelphia: Fortress, 2015.

Evans, Craig A., and David Mishkin, eds. *A Handbook on the Jewish Roots of the Christian Faith.* Peabody, MA: Handbook on Jewish Roots (Hendrikson), 2019.

Evans, Craig A., and Stanley E. Porter, eds. *Dictionary of New Testament Background.* Downers Grove IL: IVP, 2000.

Exum, J. Cheryl. "Who's Afraid of 'the Endangered Ancestress'?" In *The New Literary Criticism and the Hebrew Bible,* edited by J. Cheryl Exum and David J. A. Clines, 91–113. Sheffield, UK: Sheffield Academic Press, 1993.

Fagenblat, Michael. "The Concept of Neighbour in Jewish and Christian Ethics." In *The Jewish Annotated New Testament,* 2nd ed., edited by Amy-Jill Levine, and Marc Zvi Brettler, 645–50. Oxford: Oxford University Press, 2017.

Finto, Don. *Your People Shall Be My People: How Israel, the Jews and the Christian Church Will Come Together in the Last Days.* Ada, MI: Chosen Books (Baker Books), 2016.

Firestone, Reuven. *Who Are the Real Chosen People? The Meaning of Chosenness in Judaism, Christianity and Islam.* Center for Religious Inquiry. Nashville, TN: Skylight Paths, 2011

Fleischer, Leonore, and William Nicholson. *Shadowlands: A Novel.* New York: Signet, 1993.

Fonrobert, Charlotte Elisheva. "Judaizer, Jewish Christians, and Others." In *The Jewish Annotated New Testament,* 2nd ed., edited by Amy-Jill Levine and Marc Zvi Brettler, 637–40. Oxford: Oxford University Press, 2017.

Frazer, James George. *The Golden Bough.* Abridged ed. London: Macmillan, 1922.

———. *The Golden Bough: A Study in Magic and Religion.* 12 vols. London: Macmillan, 1911–15.

Fredriksen, Paula. "The Question of Worship: Gods, Pagans, and the Redemption of Israel." In *Paul within Judaism Restoring the First-Century Context to the Apostle,* edited by Mark D. Nanos and Magnus Zetterholm, 175–203. Philadelphia: Fortress, 2015.

Freud, Sigmund. *Moses and Monotheism*. New York: Knopf, 1939.

Gentry, Peter, and Stephen Wellum. *Kingdom through Covenant: A Biblical-Theological Understanding of the Covenants*. Wheaton, IL: Crossway, 2018.

Gitlin, Todd. *Chosen Peoples: America, Israel, and the Ordeals of Divine Election*. New York: Simon & Schuster, 2013.

Glaser, Mitch. *Isaiah 53 Explained*. New York, NY: Chosen People, 2010.

Goldsworthy, Graeme. *Gospel and Wisdom: Israel's Wisdom Literature in the Christian Life*. Carlisle, UK: Paternoster, 1995.

———. *Gospel and Kingdom*. Milton Keynes, UK: Paternoster, 2012.

———. "Wisdom and Its Literature in Biblical-Theological Context." *Southern Baptist Journal of Theology* 15 (2011) 42–55.

Gordis, Robert. *Emet Ve-Emunah,* Statement of Principles of Conservative Judaism*. The Jewish Theological Seminary. New York: United Synagogue Book Service, 1988. (*Emet Ve-Emunah* : "True and faithful")

Green, Roger Lancelyn, and Walter Hooper. *C. S. Lewis: A Biography*. 2nd ed. London: Harper Collins, 2002.

Gresham, Douglas H. *Jack's Life: The Life Story of C. S. Lewis*. Nashville, TN: Boadman & Holman, 2005.

———. *Lenten Lands: My Childhood with Joy Davidman and C. S. Lewis*. New York: Macmillan, 1988.

———. *A Life Observed: A Spiritual Biography of C. S. Lewis*. Grand Rapids: Brazos, 2013.

Gresham, Douglas H., and Jonathon Van Maren (interviewer). "C. S. Lewis and His Stepsons." *First Things*, 9/3/2020: https://www.firstthings.com/web-exclusives/2020/09/c-s-lewis-and-his-stepsons.

Guillebaud, Revd Maggie. "Letter." *The Church Times*, 13 August 2008.

Gunton, Colin E. *The Barth Lectures*. Transcribed and edited P. H. Brazier. New York: Continuum, 2007.

———. *Revelation and Reason: Prolegomena to Systematic Theology*. Transcribed and edited by P. H. Brazier. London: T. & T. Clark, 2008.

Gurkan, S. Leyla. *The Jews as a Chosen People: Tradition and Transformation*. Routledge Jewish Studies Series. London: Routledge, 2008.

Guyénot, Laurent. *From Yahweh to Zion: Jealous God, Chosen People, Promised Land . . . Clash of Civilizations*. Translated by Kevin J Barrett. Madison, WI: University of Wisconsin Press, Sifting & Winnowing Books, 2018.

Hagg, Gregory. "Passover Controversies in Church History." In *Messiah in the Passover*, edited by Darrell L. Bock and Mitch Glaser, 131–40. Grand Rapids: Kregel, 2017.

Harwood, Laurence. *C. S. Lewis, My Godfather: Letters, Photos, and Recollections*. Downers Grove, IL: IVP, 2007.

Hatfield, Jamie Elisa. *Suppressed by Jack: The Discovery of Lewis's Views on Women*. Milligan College, TN: Milligan College, 1996.

Hennekes, Mary. *C. S. Lewis: An In-Depth Study. The Pilgrim's Regress Analysis*. Available at: http://apbritlithennekesm.blogspot.com/2013/02/the-pilgrims-regress-analysis.html.

Herbermann, Charles, ed. "Parallelism." In *Catholic Encyclopedia*. New York: Robert Appleton Company, 1913.

Heschel, Susannah. "Jesus in Modern Jewish Thought." In *The Jewish Annotated New Testament*, 2nd ed., edited by Amy-Jill Levine and Marc Zvi Brettler, 736–41. Oxford: Oxford University Press, 2017.

Bibliography

Hodge, Caroline Johnson. "The Question of Identity: Gentiles as Gentiles—but also Not—in Pauline Communities." In *Paul within Judaism Restoring the First-Century Context to the Apostle*, edited by Mark D. Nanos and Magnus Zetterholm, 153–74. Philadelphia: Fortress, 2015.

Hoffman, Matthew. "Jesus and the New Testament in Modrn Yiddish and Hebrew Culture." In *The Jewish Annotated New Testament*, 2nd ed., edited by Amy-Jill Levine and Marc Zvi Brettler, 747–49. Oxford: Oxford University Press, 2017.

Hooper, Walter. *C. S. Lewis: A Companion and Guide*. London: Harper & Collins, 1996.

Horner, Barry E. *Eternal Israel: Biblical, Theological, and Historical Studies That Uphold the Eternal, Distinctive Destiny of Israel*. Nashville, TN: Wordsearch Academic, 2018

Horner, Barry E. *Future Israel: Why Christian Anti-Judaism Must Be Challenged*. New American Commentary Studies in Bible and Theology. Nashville, TN: B&H Academic, 2007.

Karesh, Sara E., and Mitchell M. Hurvitz. *Encyclopedia of Judaism*. Encyclopedia of World Religions. New York: Infobase, 2005.

Keren, Mendi. "Jewish? Christian? Why Not Both?—Leopold Cohn and the Introduction of Messianic Judaism to America." *Journal of Messianic Jewish Studies* 3 (2020) 31–56.

Kesler, Ed. "The New Testament and Jewish-Christian Relations." In *The Jewish Annotated New Testament*, 2nd ed., edited by Amy-Jill Levine and Marc Zvi Brettler, 763–67. Oxford: Oxford University Press, 2017.

Kierspel, Lars. *The Jews and the World in the Fourth Gospel: Parallelism, Function, and Context*. Wissenschaftliche Untersuchungen Zum Neuen Testament No. 2. Reihe. Tübingen: Mohr Siebeck, 2006.

King, Don W. *C. S. Lewis, Poet: The Legacy of his Poetic Impulse*. Kent, OH: Kent State University Press, 2001.

———. "Joy Davidman and the New Masses: Communist Poet and Reviewer." *The Chronicle of the Oxford University C. S. Lewis Society* 4.1 (2007) 18–44.

———. *Out of My Bone. The Letters of Joy Davidman*. Grand Rapids: Eerdmans, 2009.

———. *Yet One More Spring. A Critical Study of Joy Davidman*. Grand Rapids: Eerdmans, 2015.

Kinzer, Mark S. *Searching Her Own Mystery. Nostra Aetate, the Jewish People, and the Identity of the Church*. Eugene:OR, Wipf & Stock, Cascade, 2015.

Kreeft, Peter, ed. *Between Heaven and Hell: A Dialog Somewhere beyond Death with John F. Kennedy, C. S. Lewis and Aldous Huxley*. 2nd ed. Downers Grove, IL: IVP, 2008.

———. *Fundamentals of the Faith: Essays in Christian Apologetics*. San Francisco: Ignatius, 1990.

Langer, Ruth. "Birkat ha-Minim: A Jewish Curse of Christians." In *The Jewish Annotated New Testament*, 2nd ed., edited by Amy-Jill Levine and Marc Zvi Brettler, 653–55. Oxford: Oxford University Press, 2017.

Langton, Daniel R. "Paul in Jewish Thought." In *The Jewish Annotated New Testament*, 2nd ed., edited by Amy-Jill Levine and Marc Zvi Brettler, 741–44. Oxford: Oxford University Press, 2017.

Levine, Amy-Jill, and Marc Zvi Brettler, eds. *The Jewish Annotated New Testament*. 2nd ed. Oxford: Oxford University Press, 2017.

Lewis, C. S. "Answers to Questions on Christianity [1944]." In *C. S. Lewis, Undeceptions: Essays on Theology and Ethics*, edited by Walter Hooper, 27, 30–31, & 54. London: Bles, 1971.

A HEBRAIC INKLING

———. *Broadcast Talks. Reprinted with some alterations from two series of Broadcast Talks "Right and Wrong: A Clue to the Meaning of the Universe" and "What Christians Believe" given in 1941 and 1942*. London: Bles, The Centenary Press, 1942.

———. "Christian Apologetics." Paper read at the Carmarthen Conference for Youth Leaders and Junior Priests, Church of Wales, at Carmarthen, Easter 1945. In C. S. Lewis, *Undeceptions: Essays on Theology and Ethics*, edited by Walter Hooper, 64–76. London: Bles, 1971.

———. "A Christian Reply to Professor Price." *The Phoenix Quarterly* 1.1 (1946) 31–44. Reprinted under the title, "Religion without Dogma," in *The Socratic Digest* 4 (1948) 82–94. Published with related material in, C. S. Lewis, *Undeceptions: Essays on Theology and Ethics*, edited by Walter Hooper, 99–114. London: Bles, 1971.

———. *Christian Reflections*. Edited by Walter Hooper. London: Bles, 1967.

———. *Collected Letters, Vol. I: Family Letters 1905–1931*. Edited by Walter Hooper. San Francisco: Harper San Francisco, 2004.

———. *Collected Letters, Vol. II: Books, Broadcasts and War 1931–1949*. Edited by Walter Hooper. San Francisco: Harper San Francisco, 2004.

———. *Collected Letters, Vol. III: Narnia, Cambridge and Joy 1950–1963*. Edited by Walter Hooper. San Francisco: Harper San Francisco, 2007.

———. "De Futilitate." In C. S. Lewis, *Christian Reflections*, edited by Walter Hooper, 57–71. London: Bles, 1967.

———. "Foreword." In Helen Joy Davidman, *Smoke on the Mountain*, 7–11. Philadelphia: Westminster, 1954.

———. *The Four Loves*. London: Bles, 1960.

———. "The Grand Miracle." A sermon, published in *The Guardian*, April 27, 1945, 161 and 165. Reprinted in C. S. Lewis, *Undeceptions: Essays on Theology and Ethics*, edited by Walter Hooper, 56–63. London: Bles, 1971.

———. *The Great Divorce: A Dream*. London: Macmillan, 1945.

———. "Introduction." In George McDonald, *Phantastes* [1858], v–x. Grand Rapids: Eerdmans, 2000.

———. "Is Theology Poetry?" A paper presented to the Socratic Club in Oxford in 1944. Published in *The Socratic Digest* 3 (1945) 25–35. Reprinted in C. S. Lewis, *The Weight of Glory*, 116–40. London: Bles, 1949; and in C. S. Lewis, *They Asked for a Paper: Papers and Addresses*, 150–65. 1944. Reprint, London: Bles, 1962.

———. *Letters to an American Lady*. Edited by Clyde S. Kilby. Grand Rapids: Eerdmans, 1967.

———. *Letters to Malcolm: Chiefly on Prayer*. London: Bles, 1964.

———. "Lewis to Arthur Greeves, Nov 5, 1933." In C. S. Lewis, *They Stand Together. The Letters of C. S. Lewis to Arthur Greeves (1914–1963)* 466–687. London: Collins, 1979.

———. "Lewis to Clyde S. Kilby, May 7, 1959." In C. S. Lewis, *Collected Letters, Vol. III: Narnia, Cambridge and Joy 1950–1963*, edited by Walter Hooper, 1044–46. San Francisco: Harper San Francisco, 2007.

———. "Lewis to Corbin Scott Carnel, April 5, 1953," FN 114. In C. S. Lewis, *Collected Letters, Vol. III: Narnia, Cambridge and Joy 1950–1963*, edited by Walter Hooper, 318–19. San Francisco: Harper San Francisco, 2007.

———. "Lewis to his brother Warren ('Warnie') Lewis, c. 20 April 1921." In C. S. Lewis, *Collected Letters, Volume One: Family Letters 1905–1931*, edited by Walter Hooper, 536–38. San Francisco: Harper San Francisco, 2004.

Bibliography

———. "Lewis to Mrs Johnson, May 14, 1955." In C. S. Lewis, *Collected Letters, Vol. III: Narnia, Cambridge and Joy 1950-1963*, edited by Walter Hooper, 607-8. San Francisco: Harper San Francisco, 2007.

———. "Lewis writing to 'an American lady' Dec 7, 1950." In C. S. Lewis, *Letters to an American Lady*, 68. Grand Rapids: Eerdmans, 1967. (Note the recipient's name in this series of correspondence—for over a decade—was withheld at her request.)

———. "Lewis writing to 'an American lady' June 7, 1955." In C. S. Lewis, *Letters to an American Lady*, 43. Grand Rapids: Eerdmans, 1967.

———. "Lewis writing to 'an American lady' Mar 19, 1963." In C. S. Lewis, *Letters to an American Lady*, 114-15. Grand Rapids: Eerdmans, 1967.

———. "Lewis writing to Arthur Greeves, Oct. 18, 1931." In C. S. Lewis, *Collected Letters, Vol. I: Family Letters 1905-1931*, edited by Walter Hooper, 975-77. San Francisco: Harper San Francisco, 2004.

———. "Lewis writing to Arthur Greeves, Oct. 18, 1931." In C. S. Lewis, *Collected Letters, Vol. I: Family Letters 1905-1931*, edited by Walter Hooper, 975-77. San Francisco: Harper San Francisco, 2004.

———. "Lewis writing to Arthur Greeves, Oct. 18, 1931." In C. S. Lewis, *Collected Letters, Vol. I: Family Letters 1905-1931*, edited by Walter Hooper, 969-72. San Francisco: Harper San Francisco, 2004.

———. "Lewis writing to Arthur Greeves, Sept. 22, 1931." In C. S. Lewis, *Collected Letters, Vol. I: Family Letters 1905-1931*, edited by Walter Hooper, 969-72. San Francisco: Harper San Francisco, 2004.

———. "Lewis writing to Dom Bede Griffiths, April 30, 1959." In C. S. Lewis, Letters of C. S. Lewis, 2nd ed., 479-80. New York: Harcourt Brace, 1968.

———. "Lewis writing to Mr Lucas, Dec 6, 1956." In C. S. Lewis, *Collected Letters, Vol. III: Narnia, Cambridge and Joy 1950-1963*, edited by Walter Hooper, 814-15. San Francisco: Harper San Francisco, 2007.

———. "Lewis writing to Mrs Ashton, May 14, 1955." In C. S. Lewis, *Letters of C. S. Lewis*, 2nd ed., 448-49. New York: Harcourt Brace, 1968.

———. "Lewis writing to Mrs Green, Jun. 18, 1962." In C. S. Lewis, *Collected Letters, Vol. III: Narnia, Cambridge and Joy 1950-1963*, edited by Walter Hooper, 1353. San Francisco: Harper San Francisco, 2007.

———. "Lewis writing to Mrs Sonia Graham, 15 May 1952." In C. S. Lewis, *Letters of C. S. Lewis*, 2nd ed., 421-22. New York: Harcourt Brace, 1968.

———. "Lewis, writing to Sr. Penelope CSMV, April 1, 1953." In C. S. Lewis, *Collected Letters, Vol. III: Narnia, Cambridge and Joy 1950-1963*, edited by Walter Hooper, 316-18. San Francisco: Harper San Francisco, 2007.

———. "Lewis writing to Vera Gebbert, Oct. 16, 1960." In C. S. Lewis, *Collected Letters, Vol. III: Narnia, Cambridge and Joy 1950-1963*, edited by Walter Hooper, 1198. San Francisco: Harper San Francisco, 2007.

———. "Lewis writing to Wayne Schumaker, 21 March 1962." In C. S. Lewis, *Letters of C. S. Lewis*. 2nd ed., 303. New York: Harcourt Brace, 1968.

———. *Mere Christianity—A Revised and Amplified Edition, with a New Introduction, of the Three Books Broadcast Talks, Christian Behaviour and Beyond Personality*. London: Bles, 1952.

———. *Miracles*. 1st ed. London: Bless, 1947.

———. *Miracles*. 2nd ed. London: Bless, 1960.

———. "Miracles" (1942). A sermon preached in St Jude on the Hill Church, London. Published in *St Jude's Gazette*, 73 (Oct. 1942) 4–7. A shorter version was published in *The Guardian*, Oct. 2, 1942. Re-printed in C. S. Lewis, *Undeceptions: Essays on Theology and Ethics*, edited by Walter Hooper, 5–16. London: Bles, 1971.

———. "Modern Theology and Biblical Criticism." In *Christian Reflections*, 152–66. Bles: London, 1967.

———. "Myth Became Fact." In C. S. Lewis, *Undeceptions: Essays on Theology and Ethics*, edited by Walter Hooper, 39–43. London: Bles, 1971.

———. "On Ethics," in C. S. Lewis, *Christian Reflections*, edited by Walter Hooper, 44–56. London: Bles, 1967.

———. *Out of the Silent Planet*. London: Bodley Head, 1938.

———. *Perelandra*. London: Bodley Head, 1943.

———. *The Pilgrim's Regress: An Allegorical Apology for Christianity, Reason and Romanticism*. London: Dent and Sons, 1933.

———. "Poem to Joy Davidman." Memorial Plaque in the Garden of Remembrance at Oxford Crematorium, Bayswater Road, Headington, Oxford, OX3 9RZ, 1960.

———. "Preface to Third Edition." *The Pilgrim's Regress: An Allegorical Apology for Christianity, Reason and Romanticism*, xiv. London: Dent and Sons, 1933.

———. The Problem of Pain. London: Centenary, 1940.

———. "The Psalms" (1957–58). In C. S. Lewis, *Christian Reflections*, edited by Walter Hooper, 114–28. London: Bles, 1967.

———. "Psycho-Analysis and Literary Criticism." In C. S. Lewis, *They Asked for a Paper: Papers and Addresses*, 120–38. London: Bles, 1962.

———. *Reflections on the Psalms*. London: Bles, 1958.

———. "Religion without Dogma." In C. S. Lewis, *Undeceptions: Essays on Theology and Ethics*, edited by Walter Hooper, 99–114. London: Bles, 1971.

———. *The Screwtape Letters: Letters from a Senior to a Junior Devil*. London: Bles, 1942.

———. *Surprised by Joy: The Shape of My Early Life*. London: Bles, 1955.

———. *Transposition and Other Addresses*. London: Bless, 1949.

———. *Undeceptions: Essays on Theology and Ethics*. Edited by Walter Hooper. London: Bles, 1971.

———. "The Weight of Glory" (1949). In *Transposition and Other Addresses*, 21–33. London: Bless, 1949.

———. *The World's Last Night*. New York: Harcourt, Brace and World, 1960.

Lichtheim, Miriam. *Ancient Egyptian Literature: Volume II: The New Kingdom*. 2nd ed. Oakland, CA: University of California Press, 2006.

Lindskoog, Kathryn Ann. "C. S. Lewis's Anti-Anti-Semitism in the Great Divorce." In *Surprised by C. S. Lewis, George MacDonald and Dante: An Array of Original Discoveries*, 33–37. Macon, GA: Mercer University Press, 2001.

Locke, John. *Essay concerning Human Understanding*. 1690. Reprint, Harmondsworth, UK: Penguin Classics, 1997.

Loewenstein, Andrea Freud. *Loathsome Jews and Engulfing Women: Metaphors of Protection in the Works of Wyndham Lewis, Charles Williams and Graham Greene*. Literature and Psychoanalysis 4. New York: New York University Press, 1993.

Longman III, Tremper. *How to Read the Psalms*. How to Read series. Downers Grove, IL: IVP, 1988.

Lowth, Robert. *Lectures on the Sacred Poetry of the Hebrew Nation*. Oxford: Crocker & Brewster, 1829.

Bibliography

Maimonides. *Mishneh Torah, Yesodei ha-Torah* §6:2. See, http://www.mechon-mamre.org/i/1106.htm.

Marmorstein, Arthur. *The Old Rabbinic Doctrine of God: The Names and Attributes of God.* Oxford: Oxford University Press, 1927.

Martin, Dan. "Let the Simple Learn Wisdom: Difficulties in Constructing a Biblical Theology of the Proverbs." *The Evangelical Review* 9 (2021). Online only journal: wwwevangelicalreview.net.

Martin, Ralph P., and Peter H. Davids, eds. *Dictionary of the Later New Testament and Its Developments.* Downers Grove IL: IVP, 1998.

Maximus the Confessor. *The Ascetic Life, The Four Centuries on Charity.* Edited by Polycarp Sherwood. Ancient Christian Writers. Mahwah, NJ: Paulist, 1955.

Moberly, R. W. L (Walter). *The Old Testament of the Old Testament: Patriarchal Narratives and Mosaic Yahwism.* Philadelphia, PA: Fortress, 1992.

———. *Old Testament Theology: Reading the Hebrew Bible as Christian Scripture.* Grand Rapids, MI: Baker Academic, 2013.

Montserrat, Dominic. *Akhenaten: History, Fantasy and Ancient Egypt.* London: Routledge 2002.

Muilenburg, James. "Hebrew Poetry." In *Encyclopaedia Judaica, Vol. 13*, edited by Cecil Roth, 671–81. 1972. Reprint, London: Coronet, 1994.

Nanos, Mark D. "The Question of Conceptualization: Qualifying Paul's Position on Circumcision in Dialogue with Josephus's Advisors to King Izates." In *Paul within Judaism: Restoring the First-Century Context to the Apostle*, edited by Mark D. Nanos and Magnus Zetterholm, 105–52. Philadelphia: Fortress, 2015.

———. *Reading Paul within Judaism: Collected Essays of Mark D. Nanos, Vol. 1.* Eugene, OR: Cascade, 2017.

———. *Reading Romans within Judaism: Collected Essays of Mark D. Nanos, Vol 2.* Eugene, OR: Cascade, 2018.

Nanos, Mark D., and Magnus Zetterholm, eds. Paul within Judaism. *Restoring the First-Century Context to the Apostle.* Philadelphia: Fortress, 2015.

Najovits, Simson. *Egypt, the Trunk of the Tree: A Modern Survey of an Ancient Land, II.* New York: Algora, 2004.

Nassau, Scott P. "Passover, Temple and the Early Church." In *Messiah in the Passover*, edited by Darrell L. Bock and Mitch Glaser, 113–30. Grand Rapids: Kregel, 2017.

Nelson, Cary. *Anthology of Modern American Poetry.* Oxford: Oxford University Press, 2000.

Nicholi, Armand M. Jn. *The Question of God: C. S. Lewis and Sigmund Freud Debate God, Love, Sex and the Meaning of Life.* New York: Simon & Schuster, 2003.

Noel, Caroline Marie. *The Name of Jesus and Other Verses for the Sick and Lonely.* London: Wertheim, Mackintosh & Hunt, 1861, expanded 1870. See, for a facsimile of the 1861 first edition, Norderstedt, Germany: Hansebooks, 2015.

Patterson, Nancy-Lou. "The Jewels of Messias: Images of Judaism and Antisemitism in the Novels of Charles Williams." *Mythlore: A Journal of J. R. R. Tolkien, C. S. Lewis, Charles Williams, and Mythopoeic Literature*, 6.2, Article 8. Available at: https://dc.swosu.edu/mythlore/vol6/iss2/8.

Parry, Robin A. *The Biblical Cosmos: A Pilgrim's Guide to the Weird and Wonderful World of the Bible.* Eugene, OR: Cascade, 2014.

Pilat, Oliver. "Girl Communist: An Intimate Story of Eight Years in the Party." Serialized in *The New York Post*, 1949.

Plato. *The Republic*. Translated by Benjamin Jowett. The Internet Classics Archive: http://classics.mit.edu/Plato/republic.html.

Pritchard, James B., ed. *The Ancient Near East—Volume 1: An Anthology of Texts and Pictures*, Princeton, NJ: Princeton University Press, 1958.

Ramelli, Ilaria, and Judith Perkins, eds. *Early Christian and Jewish Narrative: The Role of Religion in Shaping Narrative Forms*. Wissenschaftliche Untersuchungen zum Neuen Testament No. 348. Tübingen: Mohr Siebeck, 2015.

Redford, Donald B. "The Monotheism of the Heretic Pharaoh. Precursor of Mosiac Monotheism or Egyptian Anomaly?" *Biblical Archaeology Review* 13.3 (1987) 16–32.

Reid, Daniel, Gerald F. Hawthorne, Ralph P. Martin, eds. *Dictionary of Paul and His Letters*. Downers Grove IL: IVP, 1994.

Runesson, Anders. "The Question of Terminology: The Architecture of Contemporary Discussions on Paul." In *Paul within Judaism: Restoring the First-Century Context to the Apostle*, edited by Mark D. Nanos and Magnus Zetterholm, 53–78. Philadelphia: Fortress, 2015.

Salzman, Jack, and Leo Zanderer. *Social Poetry of the 1930s: A Selection*. New York: Burt Franklin, 1978.

Santamaria, Abigail. *Joy: Poet, Seeker, and the Woman Who Captivated C. S. Lewis*. London: SPCK, 2015.

Schakel, Peter J. *Reason and Imagination in C. S. Lewis: A Study of "Till We Have Faces."* Grand Rapids: Eerdmans, 1984.

Schama, Simon. *The American Future: A History from the Founding Fathers to Barack Obama*. New York: Vintage, 2009.

Schreiner, Patrick. *The Kingdom of God and the Glory of the Cross*. Wheaton, IL: Crossway, 2018.

Scott, David, and Israel Selvanayagam. *Re-visioning India's Religious Traditions: Essays in Honour of Eric Lott*. Delhi: ISPCK, 1996.

Setzer, Claudia. "Jewish Responses to Believers in Jesus." In *The Jewish Annotated New Testament*, 2nd ed., edited by Amy-Jill Levine and Marc Zvi Brettler, 730–33. Oxford: Oxford University Press, 2017.

Shakespeare, William. *The RSC Shakespeare: The Complete Works*. London: Palgrave Macmillan, 2007.

Sibley, Brian. *Shadowlands: The True Story of C. S. Lewis and Joy Davidman*. London: Hodder & Stoughton, 1985.

———. *Shadowlands—eine späte Liebe: die Geschichte von C. S. Lewis und Joy Davidman*. Basel: Brunnen-Verlag, 1987.

Smith, Calvin L. *The Jews, Modern Israel and the New Supersessionism*. Kent, UK: King's Divinity Press, 2013.

Smith, Mark S. *God in Translation: Deities in Cross-Cultural Discourse in the Biblical World*. Grand Rapids: Eerdmans, 2010.

Soulen, R. Kendall. *The Divine Name(s) and the Holy Trinity, Vol. 1: Distinguishing the Voices*. Louisville, KY: Westminster/John Knox, 2011

Stern, David. "Midrash and Parables in the New Testament" In *The Jewish Annotated New Testament*, 2nd ed., edited by Amy-Jill Levine and Marc Zvi Brettler, 707–10. Oxford: Oxford University Press, 2017.

Storm, Hans Otto. *American Writing*. Prairie City, IL: Decker, 1940.

Swinburne, Richard. *The Concept of Miracle*. London: Macmillan, 1970.

———. *Revelation: From Metaphor to Analogy*. Oxford: Oxford University Press, 1992.

Bibliography

Tate, Marvin. *The Psalms 51–100*. Word Biblical Commentary 20. Rev. ed. Nashville: Thomas Nelson, 2010.

The Jewish Encyclopaedia. 12 vols. 1901–6. online: http://www.jewishencyclopedia.com/

Thornhill, A. Chadwick. *The Chosen People: Election, Paul and Second Temple Judaism*. Downers Grove, IL: IVP, 2015.

Tolkien, J. R. R. "Mythopoeia." In *Tree and Leaf*, edited by Christopher Tolkien, 85–90. London: Allen and Unwin, 1978.

Trible, Phyllis. "Genesis 22: The Sacrifice of Sarah." In *Not in Heaven: Coherence and Complexity in Biblical Narratives*, edited by J. P. Rosenblatt, 92–116. Hoboken, NJ: Wiley & Sons, 1991.

Tucker, Brian J. *Reading Romans after Supersessionism: The Continuation of Jewish Covenantal Identity*. 6 New Testament after Supersessionism. Eugene, OR: Wipf & Stock, Cascade Books, 2018.

Wakefield, Andrew. "Letter." *The Church Times*, 21 July 2006.

Watson, Francis. *Text, Church and World: Biblical Interpretation in Theological Perspective*. Edinburgh: T. & T. Clark, 1994.

Werblowsky, R. J. Zwi, and Geoffrey Wigoder, eds. *The Oxford Dictionary of the Jewish Religion*. Oxford: Oxford University Press, 1997.

Wilkinson, Toby. *The Rise and Fall of Ancient Egypt*. London: Bloomsbury, 2011.

Williams, Donald T. "An Apologist's Evening Prayer: Reflecting on C. S. Lewis's Reflections on the Psalms." In *C. S. Lewis Life, Works, and Legacy, Vol. 3: Apologist Philosopher and Theologian*, edited by Bruce L. Edwards, 237–56. Santa Barbara, CA: Praeger, 2007.

Wilson, Ralph F. "The Holy Spirit as the Agent of Renewal." PhD, Fuller Theological Seminary, 1984. See also: www.joyfulheart.com/scholar/

———. *Understanding the Gift of Prophecy. I. Is Prophecy Preaching?* http://www.joyfulheart.com/scholar/preach.htm.

Yoseloff, Thomas, ed. *Seven Poets in Search of an Answer: Maxwell Bodenheim, Joy Davidman, Langston Hughes, Aaron Kramer, Alfred Kreymborg, Martha Millet, Norman Rosten*. Introduction by Shaemas O'Sheel. New York: Ackerman, 1944.

Zetterholm, Karin Hedner. "The Question of Assumptions: Torah Observance in the First Century." In *Paul within Judaism: Restoring the First-Century Context to the Apostle*, edited by Mark D. Nanos and Magnus Zetterholm, 79–104. Philadelphia: Fortress, 2015.

———. "Paul within Judaism: The State of the Questions." In *Paul within Judaism: Restoring the First-Century Context to the Apostle*, edited by Mark D. Nanos and Magnus Zetterholm, 31–52. Philadelphia: Fortress, 2015.

Index of Names

Aaron 158, 172–73, 267
Abraham 3, 6, 12, 15, 20, 26, 50, 55, 5–61, 65, 72–73, 77, 79, 81, 83, 132, 138, 151–52, 172, 183, 187–89, 196, 200, 217–19, 249, 252
Akhenaten (14th century, BC) 19, 145, 149–50, 151–54, 265
    Amenhetep, Pharaoh 149
Akiva, Rabbi Akiva ben Yosef (b. 53 AD) 126
Anselm of Canterbury (1033/4–1109) 56, 255
Augustine of Hippo (354–430) 39, 128, 154–55, 166, 255
Azariah, Rabbi Azariah di Rossi 111–12
Azazel 158

Balder 29, 156–59, 164, 182–83
    Baldhr 157
Barth, Karl (1886–1968) 14, 52–56, 59, 61–69, 72–73, 76, 90, 98–99, 135, 155, 196, 251–52, 255–57, 260
Beatrice (*The Divine Comedy*) 191, 195
Bethlehem 153, 165, 171, 208
Binnie, William 166–68, 256
Brown, Yaakov 119, 217–18, 257
Brunner, Heinrich Emil (1889–1966) 136, 258
Bunyan, John (1628–168) 74
Burney, C. F. (1868–1925) 110–12, 258
Busch, Eberhard (1937) 52–53, 54–55, 258

Caiaphas 102
Calvary 153, 208
Cambridge 16, 106, 257, 262–63

Carnell, Corbin Scott (1929) 103
Chesterton, Gilbert Keith (1874–1936) 42–43
Cicero, Marcus Tullius (106BC–43 AD) 106
Coleridge, Samuel Taylor (1772–1834) 154–55) 181, 258
Columbus, Christopher (1451–1506) 220

Dante Alighieri (d. 1321) 43, 191, 195, 264
David 8, 22, 26, 33, 66, 81, 95, 103, 105, 112–13, 157, 163, 168, 170–71, 173–74, 200, 224, 226, 242–43, 244, 255–56, 258–59, 266
Davidman, Joy (1915–1960) 4, 12, 21–22, 55, 69, 173, 196, 198, 217, 219, 222–41, 244–47, 250–52, 256, 258–62, 264, 266–67 (See, Gresham)
Dearborn, Kerry 180, 258
Deborah 91, 111
Duns Scotus (1266–1308) 203
Dyson, Hugo (Henry Victor Dyson, 1896–1975) 43, 46, 48–49, 53, 70, 235

Elijah 204
Ezekiel 91, 179

Feuerbach, Ludwig (1804–1872) 157
Frazer, Sir James George (1854–1941) 156–58, 259
Freud, Sigmund (1856–1939) 150, 157, 181, 228, 260, 264–65

269

Frigga 157

Germany 5, 15, 51, 62-63, 69, 72, 74, 138, 222, 265
Gideon 200
God 1-4, 6-21, 22, 25-32, 33, 35-40, 42-45, 46, 47-62, 64-68, 69, 72-87, 89-99, 100-108, 110, 112-45, 146, 147, 148-57, 159, 164-70, 172, 174-84, 187-92, 194, 195, 196-98, 200-205, 206-10, 211-15, 217, 218, 222-28, 231-35, 237, 238-42, 244-47, 250-53, 255, 256, 257, 258-59, 260, 265-266 (See Christ)
  Deus 54, 64, 100, 146, 257
  El 33, 45-46, 48, 52, 57-59, 62, 74, 90, 140, 149, 200, 233
  Elohim 45-46, 48, 52, 57-59, 62, 74, 90, 122, 149, 233
  El Shaddai 33, 45-46, 48, 58-59, 74, 140, 149, 200, 233
  Godhead 40
  HaShem 58, 74, 196, 233
  Yahweh 148, 207, 260
  YHWH 14, 17, 21, 29, 33, 45-46, 48, 52, 57-60, 74, 75, 80, 114, 118, 137, 143, 148-49, 152, 176, 179, 196, 207, 213-14, 232-33, 239, 250
Golder's Green 189, 194-95
Greece 48, 106, 133, 160, 200
Greeves, Arthur (1895-1966) 34, 47, 48-49, 51, 71, 73, 74, 91-92, 157, 212, 262-63
Gresham, David (1944-2014) 224, 230, 235-36, 241-42, 260
Gresham, Douglas (b. 1945) 224, 236, 242-44
Gresham, William Lindsay (1909-1962) 224, 230, 235, 236. 241 (See Davidman)
Gunton, Colin E. (1941-2003) 64-68, 76, 135-36, 260

Habakkuk 217
Hagar 188
Hegel, Wilhelm Friedrich (1770-1831) 10, 27, 42, 52, 64, 67

Hitler, Adolf (1889-1945) 20, 47, 51, 61, 67-68, 69, 74, 189, 194
Holy Spirit 10, 28, 37-38, 40, 42-43, 46, 50, 54-55, 57, 101, 146, 157, 162, 167, 175-76, 180-82, 184, 190, 198, 225-28, 232-33, 247, 267 (See God)
Homer (b. 8th century BC ?) 106, 139
Hooper, Walter McGehee (1931-2020) 32, 181, 218, 260-64

Isaac 59, 61, 73, 77, 187, 188, 200
Isaiah 3, 33, 50, 59, 77, 79, 89, 96-97, 155, 163, 169, 191, 200, 255-56, 260
Ishmael 187, 188
Israel 1-3, 5-8, 10, 15, 20, 37, 52, 57-58, 59-61, 63-64, 65-68, 72-73, 78, 79, 81-82, 83-84, 111, 119-20, 125-26, 128, 135, 138, 143, 146, 158, 165-70, 172, 175, 179, 184, 187-88, 195-96, 199-200, 203, 207-8, 213, 215-16, 234, 240, 244, 251-52, 256, 259-61, 266

Jacob 53, 59, 61, 73, 77, 188
Jephthah 200
Jerusalem 9, 26, 76, 82-83, 91, 114, 137, 146, 165, 171, 177, 184, 199, 201, 209, 256
Yeshua, bar Yosef 2, 7, 9-10, 12, 18,-22, 26, 48, 60, 65-69, 72, 79, 82, 99, 117, 122, 146-48, 155, 157, 160-61, 164-67, 170-71, 173-74, 176, 178-79, 183-84, 189, 194, 196, 199-200, 207, 213-14, 227-28, 233-34, 238, 240, 251 (See God)
  Christ 1-2, 7-12, 18-20, 22, 26-27, 29, 37, 46, 48-50, 55, 61-68, 72-73, 76, 81-82, 89-90, 94, 98, 102, 134-36, 146-48, 150, 154-58, 160-64, 166-68, 171-74, 176-82, 188, 190-91, 194-99, 205, 209, 211, 214, 216, 224, 227-29, 23-35, 238, 240-41, 244-45, 247, 250-51, 256-58
  Christos 7, 8, 66, 179
  Jesus 2, 3, 5-12, 14, 17-21, 26-27, 46, 50, 55, 60-62, 64, 66-68, 72-73, 81-83, 89, 97-98, 100-101, 108,

110-11, 119, 123, 126, 130-31, 147-48, 151, 158-60, 163-64, 166, 169-71, 173, 176, 178, 183-84, 190, 195-97, 199, 204-12, 214-15, 229, 232-35, 240, 242, 250-51, 255, 257-58, 260-61, 265-66
Job 22, 91, 95-96, 100, 130, 177, 242, 246, 249-50
Jonah 91, 95, 100, 103
Joy 4, 12, 14, 21-22, 25, 28-32, 34-45, 50-52, 55, 69, 74, 173-74, 181, 196, 198, 217, 219-20, 222-47, 250-52, 256, 258-64, 266-67 (See also *Sehnsucht*, subject index)

Kant, Immanuel (1724-1804) 181
Kilby, Clyde Samuel (1902-86) 97-102, 262
Kirkpatrick, William Thompson (1848-1921) 31-32, 39
Kreeft, Peter John (b. 1937) 207, 261
Krishna 183, 208

Leatherhead 41, 226-27
Lessing, Gotthold Ephraim (1729-1781) 204-6
Lewis, Warren Hamilton ("Warnie, 1895-1975) 25-27, 30-31, 38, 50-51, 242-44, 253, 262
Lindskoog, Kathryn Ann "Kay" (1934-2003) 19, 20, 187, 194, 195, 264
Loki 157, 159
Lowth, Robert (1710-1787) 109, 264
Luke 5, 17, 26, 50, 97, 100, 110, 119, 147, 169, 212, 236

MacDonald, George (1824-1905) 41-42, 136, 155, 180-81, 229, 258, 264-65
Maimonides 57, 59, 257, 265
Mark 5, 77, 80-84, 103, 110, 147, 163, 212, 236, 241-42, 256-57, 259, 261, 265-67
Marx, Karl Heinrich (1818-1883) 5, 230
Matthew 81, 100, 110, 163, 233, 251, 261
Maximus , 265
Melchizedek 50, 168, 171-73

Milton, John (1608-1884) 28, 42, 92, 106, 175, 260
Moses 33, 52, 55, 59, 61, 83, 89, 97, 101, 126, 136, 145, 150-52, 208, 226, 240, 260

Odin 157, 158
Oxford 3, 4, 12, 16, 26-28, 38, 42, 48, 50, 52, 62, 69-73, 83, 90, 93, 103, 106, 109, 174, 182, 195, 213, 219, 222, 244, 246, 247, 251, 255-56, 257-62, 264, 265-67

Paul 6, 12, 15, 49, 65, 82-84, 100, 121, 122, 126, 176, 192, 195-96, 211, 212, 219, 237, 240, 242, 245, 258-59, 261, 265-67
Peter 50, 66, 178, 189, 207, 255, 258, 260-61, 265-66
Plato (428/427 or 424/423-348/347 BC) 43-45, 106, 140-41, 151, 154, 160-62, 164, 208, 266

Reimarus, Hermann Samuel (1694-1768) 204-6
Ruth 98, 147, 261

Samson 200
Samuel 43, 98, 154-55, 168, 181, 200, 204, 255, 258
Sarai 19, 187-89
Satan 192
    satanic 138
    devil 35, 85, 197
    Lucifer 85, 208
Saul 65, 232, 245, 257
Schelling, Friedrich Wilhelm Joseph Schelling (1775-1854) 181
Schleiermacher, Friedrich Daniel Ernst (1768-1834) 63-64, 67, 256
Shakespeare, William (1564-1616) 7, 10, 235, 266
Sharp, Cecil (1859-1924) 139
Sherlock, Right Revd Thomas (1678-1761) 204

Sisera 91
Smith, Frank (The Great Divorce) 191–93, 197
Smith, Sarah (*The Great Divorce*) 20, 188–95, 197
Socrates (c.470BC–399BC) 154, 161
Sophocles (497/496 BC–406/405 BC) 106
Spencer, Edmund (1552/3–1599) 106
Stephen 127, 163
Swinburne, Richard Granville (b. 1934) 180, 266

Thompson, Francis (1859–1907) 231, 234
Tolkien, J. R. R. (Ronald Reuel Tolkien, 1892–1973) 14, 20, 41, 43, 46, 48–49, 53, 70–71, 155–57, 192, 194, 235, 256–58, 265, 267

Valhalla 40, 79
Vienna 27
Virgil (70–19 BC) 106, 162, 164
Vishnu 183

Wagner, Richard (1813–1883) 34
Watson, Francis 134–35, 258, 267
Williams, Charles (1886–1945) 71, 256–58, 264–65
Williams, Ralph Vaughan (1872–1958) 139
Williams, Rowan (b. 1950) 221
Wilson, Ralph F. 167, 267
Woolston, Thomas (1668–1733) 204
Wright, N. T. (Nicholas Thomas, or "Tom", b. 1948) 9

Index of Subjects

absolute 4, 10, 45, 52, 54, 56, 72, 103, 122–23, 210
academy 11, 56, 69–70, 203
adultery 231, 235, 241
agápē 20, 91, 116, 189, 190 (See love)
agriculture 17, 137
    agrarian 17–18, 58, 136–38, 143, 146–47
allegory 16, 95, 171
America 26, 222, 230–31, 255, 260–61
    American 4, 21, 26, 34, 55, 64, 69, 85–86, 97, 103, 137, 209, 219, 222–24, 228, 230–31, 237–38, 243, 249, 251, 261–63, 265–66
'*am qadosh* 15, 78
analogy 5, 19, 32, 83, 191, 194–95
    analogical 19, 188, 192
    analogia fidei 64, 198

angel(s) 7, 41, 126, 158, 234
annihilationism 192 (See universalism)
a/Anoint(ed) 7–8, 11, 33, 50, 66–67, 72, 83, 97, 122, 130, 147, 155, 166–68, 174, 179, 193, 208, 227, 240
    anointing 7
    anoints 9
anthropology 13
    anthropological 12
anti-Semitic 1–2, 27, 33, 62, 63, 72, 84, 125, 206, 218, 239, 249
    anti-Semite 2, 194
    anti-Semitism 2, 5, 13–14, 19–21, 26–27, 33, 38, 51, 63, 67–71, 74, 77, 115, 121, 132, 152, 187, 194, 198, 202, 219–21, 251, 252–53
apologetic(s) 64, 72, 82, 204
    apologist 26, 28, 62

apostasy 34
   apostate 10, 28, 49, 70, 115, 157, 212, 220, 235
apostle(s) 6, 9, 50, 60, 82–83, 100, 146, 189, 192, 204, 211, 240
Aryan 63, 68, 69, 238
aseity 44, 52, 54–56, 62
Asiatic 157, 162, 184
atheism 22, 27–28, 34, 38–39, 45, 93, 160, 222, 225–26, 229, 235, 238
   atheist(s) 10, 16, 27, 32, 35, 45, 80, 157, 203, 222–23, 226–27, 229–30, 232, 235, 245
   atheistic 10, 13, 28, 35, 37, 44, 49, 69–70, 82, 95, 160, 223, 226
atone(ment) 6, 47, 49, 67, 99, 114, 135, 157–59, 164, 197, 210–12, 245 (See Salvation)
   atoning 197, 212
autonomous 75, 115
awareness 12, 18, 147, 225, 226, 232

baptism 152, 181, 208
   baptized 27, 137, 180–82, 227, 235
Barmer Erklärung 68
b/Beauty 17–18, 21, 28–29, 40, 59, 114–15, 124, 138–39, 150, 158, 225–29
   beautiful 29, 41, 92, 116, 123, 139, 157, 203, 225, 232
belief(s) 2–3, 10–11, 12–15, 20, 25, 28–30, 33, 34–36, 39, 41–43, 49, 50, 56, 70–71, 74, 78, 80–82, 85, 90, 95–98, 126–28, 131, 163, 173, 180, 192, 203, 204–6, 211, 220, 223, 228, 233–35, 245, 250
   believe 1, 11–12, 50, 56, 73–74, 82, 89–91, 145, 152, 159, 164, 179, 182, 197, 206, 214, 227–29, 233, 251
   believer 32, 237
   unbelief 82, 84
Bible 1–2, 4, 9, 11, 13, 15–16, 18–20, 25–26, 32–33, 38, 45, 50, 54–56, 58–60, 63, 71–72, 75–76, 78, 83–84, 90–103, 106–8, 112, 121–22, 125–26, 128, 134–36, 138, 145–47, 149–51, 154, 162–63, 166, 168–69, 171–72, 177–79, 181–82, 188, 197, 204–5, 210, 212–13, 229, 232, 236–37, 241, 250–259, 261, 265
biblical(ly) 15–17, 20, 57–59, 62, 66, 91–95, 98, 101, 105, 108–10, 125, 134, 152, 188, 195, 236, 240–41, 255–56, 258–61, 264–67
bibliolatry 99
bless(ing) 77–80, 123–24, 133, 140, 171, 187
blood 21, 27, 47–49, 50, 67, 113–15, 126, 195, 208–12, 238
   bled 21, 210, 212
British 2–5, 20, 26–27, 38, 52, 71, 79, 85, 119, 131–32, 137, 189, 195, 219, 224, 241, 243, 253
   British empire 26
   British establishment 26–27, 38, 131–32
burning bush 59, 226

cancer 22, 28–30, 222–24, 236, 241–42, 244–46
character 2, 20–22, 71, 74–75, 115, 179, 181, 189, 192, 206, 221, 243–45, 251
chosen people 2–4, 6, 9–10, 15, 18, 20–21, 26–27, 33, 39, 55, 64, 67, 72–73, 76, 78–79, 80, 82–83, 89, 103, 126, 128, 132, 144, 152, 155, 178–79, 181, 196, 200, 205, 209, 213, 227, 245, 252, 255, 258–60, 267
   choice 3, 43, 202, 228, 232
   choose 1, 3, 77, 214
   chosen 2–4, 6–7, 9–10, 13, 15–16, 18–21, 26–27, 33–39, 55, 64–65, 67, 72–74, 76–84, 89, 103, 120, 126–28, 130, 132, 144, 152, 155, 158, 176, 178–79, 181, 194, 196, 200, 205, 209, 213, 217, 227, 237, 239, 245, 249, 252–53, 255, 258–60, 267
   chosenness 15, 78–79, 92, 252
   unchosen 15, 65, 77–81, 213, 249, 252–53
Christian(s) 1, 3– 5, 9–15, 17, 20–21, 27–28, 32, 35–36, 41–42, 45, 49, 60, 62, 65–66, 68–73, 76–77, 79–80, 82–86, 90–94, 101, 103, 106, 108, 111, 115–20, 122–25–27, 129–30, 137–38,

140, 146–48, 154, 157, 162–66, 173, 177–78, 180, 183, 191–98, 203–4, 208–9, 213–15, 217–18, 220–21, 224, 229–30, 232–33, 235–38, 240–42, 244–45, 247, 249, 250–52, 256–66
Christianity 2, 13–15, 21, 34–35, 41, 48–51, 62, 66, 68, 70–71, 74, 76, 84–85, 86, 92, 115, 157, 184, 192, 196, 199, 201, 209, 212–15, 219, 224, 232, 238, 240, 252, 258–59, 261, 263–64
   Christologically 181, 233
Christmas 137, 166, 171–75, 178–79
   Christmastide 174
chronology 106
church 2, 6–9, 12, 14–15, 32, 34, 36, 53, 62, 65–66, 68, 71, 82–84, 105, 107, 116, 121, 137–39, 155, 157, 168, 173–75, 178–79, 190, 195, 205–6, 216, 237
   ecclesial 6, 179
   ecclesiastical 111
Church of England 5, 13, 26–27, 33, 35, 70–72, 137, 171–73, 241
   Anglican(s) 1, 2, 3, 5–6, 12–13, 29, 62, 71–72, 83, 90, 109, 122–23, 131, 172, 174, 241, 251, 253
   Anglicized 7
   Anglo Catholic(ism) 32
   Book of Common Prayer 105, 171–72, 175
circumcise(d) 3, 195
city 70, 137–38, 200–201, 211, 225
civic religion 13, 20, 122, 32–33, 200
colonial(ists) 26, 156, 205, 206, 221
   colony 26
command(s) 25, 40, 115–16, 135, 142, 195, 237
   commandments 25, 75, 122
communism 230, 234 (See Marxism)
comprehension 16, 102
conscious(ness) 5, 12, 124, 128, 147, 162, 180–81, 192, 207, 213, 227, 231
consumerism 14, 62
conversion(s) 12–14, 21–22, 25, 28, 37, 39–40, 45–48, 51–53, 55–57, 59–60, 62, 64, 67, 69–71, 73–75, 101, 113, 115–16, 154, 157, 202, 212, 215, 219, 224, 228, 232–33, 235–36, 240, 242–45, 247, 249, 257
   convert(ed) 11, 14, 21, 45–47, 55, 108, 173, 195, 202, 215, 219, 237
correspondence 4, 25, 34, 98, 126, 209, 263
   letters 4–5, 25, 27, 38, 48–49, 57, 77, 80, 84–86, 89, 91, 92, 95, 98, 103, 157, 174, 188, 201–2, 209, 212, 219, 230, 237, 252–53, 260–64, 266
covenant 12, 15, 59, 61, 68, 73, 75, 78–79, 82–83, 112, 187–88, 195, 251
creation 4, 16–19, 58, 73, 80, 90–91, 94, 96, 133–36, 138, 140–44, 146–50, 153, 155–57, 167, 225–27, 257
   creative 134, 181, 228, 250
   creator 4, 21, 45, 94, 135, 149–51, 153, 184, 207
criticism(s) 17, 19, 130–31, 240
   critic 19, 181, 204, 230
   criticize 19, 26, 72, 122, 131
crucifixion 49–51, 148, 154, 158, 161, 166, 177, 210–12, 214
   cross 9, 18, 22, 31, 49, 82, 136, 147, 155, 163, 177, 180–82, 197, 208, 210–11, 214, 233–34, 237, 245, 250
   crucified 46, 99, 157, 176–78, 208, 214
cultural 1, 3, 7, 10, 12, 14, 22, 29, 33–34, 49, 67, 70, 84, 107, 212, 219, 222–24, 226, 229–30, 236, 238, 242
culture 4, 10, 12, 14, 21, 26, 37, 47, 51, 57, 68, 74, 81, 137, 155, 207–8, 218, 221–22, 228
cursings 3, 17, 117, 121, 131

damnation 2, 80, 126
   damned 80, 190–91, 192
Davidian 14, 19, 72, 168
dead 2, 6, 29, 41, 64, 114, 127–29, 142, 172, 189, 191, 201
   death 5–6, 14, 17–18, 21–22, 30–32, 49, 67, 77, 80, 98, 100, 108–9, 125–29, 131–32, 146–47, 151, 154, 157–59, 161, 164, 171, 175, 178, 182, 184, 201, 208, 210, 211–13, 219, 224, 228, 233, 237, 242–47, 250

Decalogue 125, 236–39
  Ten Commandments 33, 236–38, 258
democracy 79
  democratic 79, 202
demon(s) 4, 81, 158, 196, 199
  demonic 72, 196, 200, 209, 233
descend(s) 2, 9, 18, 69, 147, 172
  descending 18, 145, 147, 151–52, 183
desire 17, 20, 28–30, 35–38, 40–41, 43, 45, 85, 114–15, 121, 137, 150, 153, 197, 239–40, 251
destructionism 192
Deus abscondus 54
Deus dixit 64, 100, 146
dialectic(s) 5, 11, 22, 76, 82
  dialectical 17
disciple(s) 9, 18, 26, 81, 97, 101, 146–47, 176–78, 214
dispensation 237, 251
divinity 1, 18, 67, 138, 141, 149, 207–8, 235
  divine(ly) 3, 8–9, 16, 21, 28, 54, 58–59, 64, 80, 90, 100–102, 127, 130, 132, 134–35, 141, 149, 152, 158, 162–63, 171, 179, 182–83, 207–8, 213, 219, 231, 237, 251–52
divorce(d) 7, 192, 224, 236, 241–42
  divorcee 241
doctrine 16–18, 32, 49, 55, 62–63, 67–68, 78, 83, 86, 90–91, 97, 133–35, 141, 147, 149, 150–52, 154–56, 160, 167, 172, 178, 180, 182, 192, 204, 207, 212, 214, 241–42, 246
dream(s) 25, 146, 155–57, 181, 183, 239–40

Easter 137, 208, 229, 247, 262
Edwardian 13–14, 26–28, 31, 33–35, 38, 62, 218, 249
Egyptian 18–19, 145, 149–52, 159, 162, 184, 264, 266
election 3, 6, 64–66, 78, 135, 183, 206, 214, 260, 267
  electe(d) 6, 66, 78, 81, 237, 241
empire 14, 26–27, 38, 62, 64, 71, 131, 165, 218–19, 253

endure 213, 247–48
  endurance 128, 142, 200, 248
Enlightenment, the 3, 11, 13, 52, 62, 64, 66–67, 69, 79, 152, 171, 191, 204–5
  Enlightened 63, 70, 93, 138, 179, 253
enslavement 26, 123, 217–18, 220
ens realissimum 80
epiphany 22, 244–45
equality 79, 202
  equal 9, 34, 56, 79, 85, 146, 153, 192, 202, 220, 243
e/Eschaton 11, 76, 79, 81, 83, 126, 164, 173, 251
  e/Eschatological 38, 82, 119, 126, 155, 159, 173, 175, 197, 200, 202, 207, 236
  eschatologically 65, 214
  eschatology 155, 159, 173
eternity 2, 22, 34, 227, 244
  eternal 5, 17, 52–54, 57–59, 62, 65, 80, 90, 112, 126–27, 135, 149, 152, 168, 192, 197, 200, 215, 232
ethics 16, 57, 63, 75, 83–85, 94, 125, 215, 223, 252
  ethical 16, 76, 136, 235, 241
Eucharist 50, 152, 208, 209
European 3, 12, 18, 26–27, 38, 51, 63–64, 66–69, 73–74, 106, 116, 137–38, 145, 155, 157, 160, 162, 181, 184, 189, 191, 194, 206, 220, 222, 229, 238, 240
Evangelical(s) 3, 6, 33, 117, 255, 257–58, 265
existence 3–4, 18, 35, 45, 58, 61, 66–67, 73, 78–79, 83, 128–29, 134, 144, 149, 160, 196, 211, 245
  exist 14, 18, 40, 54, 84, 135, 141, 143, 183, 192
ex nihilo 18, 141
extinctionism 192

fact(ual) 2, 10–11, 16, 38, 61, 65–66, 71–73, 90–97, 103–4, 124, 129, 141, 147, 157, 172, 205, 220, 222, 235, 243–45

faith 12, 22, 27–28, 30, 34, 39–40, 45–46, 53, 55–56, 60, 63, 66–67, 69–70, 72, 79, 81–82, 84, 99, 107, 122, 126, 132, 145, 156–57, 188, 196–97, 200–202, 207, 217, 222–23, 229, 231, 234–36, 239–42, 244–45, 257–59, 261
faithfulness 129, 141, 142
fides quaerens intellectum (faith seeking understanding) 55–56 (See Anselm)
fall 3, 6, 20, 34, 50, 53, 58, 75–76, 81, 86, 128, 130, 174, 182, 190, 208, 211 (see original sin, sin)
  fallen 3, 6, 96, 125, 128, 146–47, 158–61, 178, 182, 190, 192, 202, 206, 230, 233
family 20, 22, 25, 29, 39, 66, 188–89, 192, 196, 229–30, 243
fantasy 41, 78, 118, 137, 181, 229, 230
  fantasies 73, 181
fear 17, 30, 75, 79–80, 109, 119, 218, 251
First World War 27, 28, 38, 74, 140, 175, 218, 238
flesh 26, 40, 47, 67–68, 73, 113–14, 183–84, 195–96, 207–9, 213, 237, 242
forgive 8, 55
  forgave 55, 232
  forgive(ness) 6, 47, 55, 76, 178, 207–8, 211, 238
freedom 62–64, 75–76, 91, 124, 157, 181, 220, 241
fundamentalism 95, 97, 99

genre(s) 16, 90, 92–93, 94–96, 98–99, 103, 166
gentile , 133,
gentile(s) 6, 12, 15, 20, 63, 65–68, 77, 81–82, 122–23, 130, 133, 143, 149, 169, 173, 178, 192, 195–96, 200–201, 215–19, 222, 237, 240, 245, 252–53, 261
glory 54, 59, 80, 86, 89, 97, 116, 135, 139, 141–42, 145, 168, 197, 233, 262–66

glorification 193, 198
glorious 6, 33, 54, 112
goddesses 48, 58, 149
God is God 53–56, 62, 257
  gods 21, 36, 40, 46, 48–49, 50, 54–55, 58, 69, 78, 134, 138, 141–43, 148–49, 151, 154–57, 162, 179, 183–84, 206–7, 213, 217–18, 230, 245
God was God 45, 52
God was indeed God 55, 232
good 1, 4, 31, 35, 59–61, 79–80, 85, 89, 94, 101, 115, 117, 119–20, 125–26, 128, 130–31, 139, 161–62, 165, 167, 171, 183, 189, 201, 215, 222–24, 226–27, 235–36, 238, 246–47
  goodness 1, 54, 80, 105, 124, 161–62, 226, 246
gospel 1, 6, 14, 35, 39, 46, 126, 191–92, 217, 220, 233
goy qadosh 15, 78
grace 28, 50, 57, 65, 76, 86, 135, 155, 182, 203, 208, 223, 225, 235
grammar 16, 31, 53, 107, 108

ha'am hanivhar 15
Halakha 11–12
harvest 17, 137, 147
hate 125, 127, 130, 132
  hatred 84, 122, 125, 131–32, 157, 192, 220
h/Heaven(s) 2, 4–6, 25, 38, 72, 76–77, 79, 87, 108, 122, 126–28, 134, 141–42, 149, 162, 165, 170–72, 175, 189–91, 193, 195, 207, 211, 217–18, 223, 227, 230–31, 234, 238, 256, 261, 267 (See hell)
Hebrew 1–11, 13–21, 25–27, 29, 33, 38, 45, 47, 48, 49, 50–52, 54–55, 56–57, 58–64, 67, 71–72, 74–75, 76–78, 80–83, 89–100, 101–7, 108, 109, 110–16, 120, 123–25, 128, 131–32, 134, 136–37, 138, 139, 142–45, 146, 147–48, 149, 150–51, 153–54, 155, 157–59, 162–63, 166, 168–77, 178, 179–181, 182–84, 187, 189, 191, 194–97, 200–1, 202, 204–6, 208–12, 213–15, 227, 229, 232, 234, 236–37,

239, 240–41, 249–50, 251–53, 257–58, 259, 261, 264–65
Hebraic 1, 5–7, 9, 11, 12–13, 17–18, 22, 59, 62, 65–66, 69, 81, 83, 93–94, 108–12, 115, 119, 122, 126, 131–33, 136, 140–41, 145, 148–49, 151–53, 166, 173–74, 176, 179–80, 183, 194–95, 198, 208, 213, 215, 236, 238, 245–46, 249–53
Hebraist 105 (See Synagogue)
Hegelian(ism) 10, 13, 27, 42–45, 52, 54–56
h/Hell 2, 4–5, 7, 38, 76, 126–28, 175, 189–93, 207, 261 (See heaven)
heteronomous 75
historic(al) 10, 16, 19–20, 89, 91, 92, 95–96, 98–99, 100, 102–3, 150, 205, 220
  historicity 15–16, 90–92, 89, 96, 100–102
history 16, 18, 33, 51, 54, 63–64, 68–69, 79, 81, 83, 94–96, 98–99, 103–5, 107, 111, 113, 127, 136, 146, 148, 154, 156–57, 162–63, 168, 179, 181–83, 192, 201–2, 205–6, 208–9, 213–15, 239, 251
holiness 15, 42, 60, 77
Holocaust 67, 72, 99, 126, 194, 210
holy nation 15, 78
  holy people 15, 78
human(s) 1–2, 8, 11, 13, 16, 27, 34, 37, 45, 47, 50–52, 54–55, 57–58, 64, 67–68, 78, 82, 86, 90–91, 96, 99–103, 107, 111, 119, 124, 127, 130, 135, 153–54, 157, 159, 160–63, 172, 182–83, 190–92, 195, 202–8, 210–12, 219–21, 223, 225–28, 232, 234, 237–38, 24–42, 246–48, 252
  humanist 146, 209
  humanity 2–4, 6, 8–10, 13, 15–16, 18–21, 37, 38, 39, 43–45, 51, 55, 66–68, 73–74, 80, 89–92, 100, 101–3, 107, 112, 125, 135–36, 144–46, 149, 152, 159, 161–62, 164, 176–80, 182–84, 188, 190–92, 195–96, 199–200, 202, 205–6, 210–12, 214, 218, 220, 237–38, 245, 252
  humanity of Scripture 16, 90, 102–3

humanoid 13
  merely human 13, 16, 96, 107, 127
humility 56
humor 4–5, 108, 116, 132, 251

I am that I am 45, 52, 54–56, 60–61
idealism 10, 181
identity 1, 2–3, 5, 12–13, 19, 63, 66, 80–82, 97, 125, 127, 163, 194, 200, 213
  identity politics 1, 2–3, 5, 12–13, 81–82, 127, 194
idolatry 38, 43, 130, 141, 153–54, 200
  idol 38, 54–55, 82, 230
illumination 21, 90, 155, 163, 213
imagination 28, 44, 154–56, 162, 180–82, 227
imago Christi 247
imago Dei 247
immeasurable 32, 54
immortality 141, 192, 211
immutable 54
i/Imprecatory 17, 117, 122, 124, 125, 127
i/Incarnation 1, 3, 9, 18, 45–46, 49, 51, 54, 57, 67, 76, 82, 111, 135–36, 147–48, 154–56, 160, 163, 166, 171, 178–80, 182–83, 199, 202–3, 204–7, 213–15, 227, 233
  incarnate 46, 48, 68, 99, 103, 146, 148, 155–56, 168, 183, 215
Indian 18, 145, 157, 162, 167, 184
inerrant 97–98
  inerrancy 98, 100
infinite 16, 34, 41, 54, 102, 136, 203, 231
injustice 19, 74, 154–55, 203, 230
i/Inkling(s) 1, 10, 13–14, 69, 70–71, 155, 183, 195, 253, 256, 258
intellectual 21, 28, 35–37, 40, 49, 60, 62, 64, 70, 95–96, 144, 172, 204, 213, 227–28
  intellectualization 56
  intellectualized 42
interpretation(s) 9, 18–19, 99, 101, 104, 146, 154, 156–57, 159, 163, 166–67, 169, 171–73, 176–77, 180, 204, 241

intertestamental 7–8, 11, 14, 119, 127–28, 143, 146, 155, 169, 175
intimations 18, 22, 38, 44, 146–50, 155–57, 59, 179–80, 181–84, 226, 233, 244
Ireland 25, 28
Israel 1–3, 5–8, 10, 15, 20, 37, 52, 57–58, 59–61, 63–64, 65–68, 72–73, 78, 79, 81–82, 83–84, 111, 119–20, 125–26, 128, 135, 138, 143, 146, 158, 165–70, 172, 175, 179, 184, 187–88, 195–96, 199–200, 203, 207–8, 213, 215–16, 234, 240, 244, 251–52, 256, 259–61, 266
Israelite(s) 14, 15, 33, 52, 59, 69, 72, 78, 73, 90–91, 111, 150–53, 176, 200
Israelitisch 14, 73, 64–69

Jew(s) 1–10, 12–15, 18,–22, 25, 26–27, 39, 47–49, 51, 55, 58, 61–66, 68–82, 83–84, 92, 110, 114, 116, 118, 122–23, 127, 129, 132, 138–39, 143–44, 146–47, 149, 152, 155, 158, 163, 169, 175, 176–78, 183–84, 189, 194–96, 202, 206–208, 213–14, 217–20, 222, 223, 226, 229, 235–41, 244–45, 249–53, 255–56, 258–61, 264, 266
Jewish(ness) 1–4, 6–10, 12–14, 20–22, 26, 28, 39, 52, 57, 62, 64, 66–68, 71–73, 76, 78–79, 82– 86, 90–91, 99, 111, 120–21, 125–27, 143, 146, 152, 158–59, 163, 172–74, 177–79, 183, 188–89, 191–97, 202, 207–8, 212, 214–15, 217, 222, 224, 228–29, 232, 234–39, 240, 244, 249, 251–53, 255–57, 259–61, 266–67
Jewish Question 62
Judaism 1–4, 7, 11, 13, 15, 21, 26, 28, 34, 57, 58, 66, 71, 75–76, 78–79, 84, 93–94, 112, 115, 128, 131, 151–52, 179, 195–96, 215–16, 222–24, 236, 238, 240, 242, 244, 251–52, 255–56, 259–61, 265–67
Jobian 22, 250
Judaea 20, 103, 138, 199
judge 8, 17, 110–11, 117–18, 120, 123–24, 126, 131, 170, 172, 174, 180

judgement(s) 17–19, 38, 65, 86, 110, 117–23, 126–27, 152, 155, 161, 164, 183, 192, 197–98, 233, 246
judiciary 17, 119, 124
just 12, 29, 39, 42, 47, 51, 65, 72–73, 79, 84, 94, 115, 120–21, 125–26, 137–38, 140, 155, 161–62, 168, 177, 181, 189, 192, 196, 203, 205–6, 215, 217, 220, 225, 232–33, 244
justice 17, 89, 108, 111, 118–19, 120–21, 125–26, 132, 141, 170, 174, 200, 223
justifiable 121
justification 122, 156, 178, 183, 196
justified 26, 121–22, 125, 131, 173, 220
justify 70, 125, 181, 196, 230

kill(ed) 8, 123, 147, 158, 201, 214, 230
kingdom 5, 25, 78, 126, 168, 174, 183, 201, 250
k/King(s) 7–8, 54, 58, 147, 165, 172, 187, 234
know(s) 11, 20, 25, 42–44, 52, 65, 81, 85–86, 97, 108–9, 112–13, 117, 129, 135–36, 152, 159, 164, 167–68, 177–78, 194, 197, 199, 203–5, 214, 218, 220, 229, 238–39, 243–44, 249, 252
knowing 11, 40, 54–56, 57, 75, 101, 112, 203, 251
knowledge 112

Lamb (The) 49–50, 79, 89, 158–59, 208, 210–12 (See Blood)
landscape 18, 34, 138–40
language 7, 26, 49, 53, 90, 108, 118, 127–28, 130, 143, 228, 238
l/Law(s) (The) 11–12, 15, 19, 25, 27, 47, 28, 57, 75–76, 82–84, 99, 112–13, 115, 122, 125, 131, 138, 141, 145, 152, 195, 201, 215, 223, 237–39, 241
legal 19, 173, 236, 241–42
legalism 86, 237–38
legislation 19, 125
legend(s) 90, 92, 214, 120

Indices

l/Liberal 1–2, 21, 78–79, 82, 137, 146, 206, 219–21, 241
 illiberal 21
life 6, 8–9, 12–14, 17–18, 21–23, 25, 28, 30–32, 34, 37, 39, 42, 47–49, 53, 58–59, 65, 74, 76–77, 79, 80, 83, 85, 89, 98, 101, 105–6, 108, 111, 121, 127–29, 136–39, 143, 146–47, 153–54, 157–58, 159, 161, 163, 179, 183, 191–92, 196, 201–3, 208–12, 222, 227–28, 231–36, 240, 243–45, 248–51, 253
 lifeblood 210–11 (See Lamb and Blood)
light 14, 21, 41, 56, 78–79, 82, 103, 108, 129, 135, 141–42, 155–58, 163, 172, 177, 182, 213, 225
literary 16, 93, 107, 164, 181, 220–21, 229, 234, 241
literature 16, 25, 31, 42, 58, 70, 92–93, 95–96, 98, 106–7, 111, 205, 220–21, 229
logic 31–32, 188, 235, 247
 logical positivism 13, 27, 38
 logician 31, 64
Lord 12–14, 17–19, 21, 29, 32, 45–46, 47, 50–52, 54–57, 59, 69–70, 74, 80–81, 94, 100, 109–12, 118–21, 125–26, 130, 132–33, 140, 148, 152, 163, 171, 174–75, 177, 192, 207, 226–27, 233, 237, 240–42, 245, 249, 252, 256–58
 LORD 33, 55–58, 60–61, 75, 77, 105, 108–9, 112, 114, 116–18, 121–22, 124, 126, 129, 13–38, 141, 142, 149, 151, 158, 165, 169–70, 172, 175–77, 187, 210, 249
 Lordship 54–56, 231
love 18, 20, 30, 34, 43, 45, 54–56, 77, 80, 86, 91, 105–6, 112, 114–16, 122, 125–26, 129, 131, 138–41, 153, 158, 183, 189–94, 197–98, 199, 203, 205, 208, 210, 227–28, 230, 231–32, 238–39, 240, 242, 247, 258–59, 265 (See *agápē*)

mankind 49
Marcionite 83

marriage 4, 21, 69, 179, 189, 191, 196–98, 219, 222, 224, 230, 235, 241–43, 246, 249, 259
 married 4, 66, 189, 222, 224, 230, 241–42, 246
 marry 4, 236, 241, 246
Marxism/Marxist 5, 22, 231, 245, 234, 245
matriarch 188–89
meaning(s) 6, 7, 9, 16, 18–19, 28, 33, 52, 57–59, 72–73, 96, 99, 106–8, 109–10, 146, 154, 156, 159–60, 163–64, 167, 169, 171, 176–77, 180–83, 189, 202, 212, 225–27, 245
measure(s) 110–112, 129, 156, 182, 233
mercy 12, 25, 32, 55, 58, 65–66, 81, 105, 118, 120, 169, 246
 mercies 25, 66, 115, 152
messenger 7, 158
m/Messiah 2–3, 6–11, 19, 26, 27, 48, 64–68, 76, 79, 82, 97, 125, 127, 129, 145, 159–60, 166, 167, 169, 171, 173–74, 178–79, 188–89, 191, 196–97, 206, 208, 213, 240, 253, 256, 260, 265
 messiahship 7, 8, 9
 m/Messianic 8, 11–12, 19–20, 65, 68, 82–83, 166–67, 168–69, 195–96, 236, 252, 255, 261
miracles 77, 79, 80, 91, 92, 94, 147, 148, 173, 175, 195, 204, 209, 213, 215, 263, 264
 miraculous 16, 94, 178, 204, 235, 242, 246
modern(ism) 7, 10, 13, 15, 20, 39, 62, 67, 70–72, 78–79, 81, 118–20, 124, 138, 152, 159, 182, 188, 191, 202–4, 238, 250, 252–53
monotheism 19, 149–51, 153
morality 13, 16, 222–23, 225
mortality 127, 141
mystery 34, 176, 223
 mystic 20, 34, 207
 mystical 28, 36, 40–41, 43, 58, 172
 mysticism 34, 64, 71
myth 19, 33, 35, 42, 48–49, 90, 104, 146, 154–57, 159, 163–64, 167, 182, 220
 mythology 34, 40, 89, 103, 100, 106,

279

157–58
myths 18, 30, 36, 49, 91–92, 96, 120, 133–34, 140, 146–47, 153–57, 160–62, 164, 179–82, 184, 205, 220–21

name(s) 7, 9–11, 19–20, 27, 34, 37, 39, 47, 54–57, 58–59, 61, 79, 83, 123, 129, 138, 142, 149, 165, 171, 178, 187, 188–89, 192, 195–96, 209, 226, 229, 233, 239, 263
naming 21, 47, 102, 213
narratives 91, 100, 163, 188, 204
nation(s) 15, 20–21, 26, 33, 37, 39, 48, 58, 65, 72–73, 76–79, 109, 81, 90, 118, 120, 124, 128, 131, 133, 136, 138, 142–43, 148, 159, 170, 172, 174, 187, 199–201, 205, 207, 213–215, 220, 252, 264
nationalism 20, 63, 201
nationalist(ic) 5, 63
nationality 21
National Socialist(s) 2, 5, 19, 68, 85, 194
National Socialism 2, 15, 51, 69, 72, 74, 194
Nazi(sm) 2, 5, 20, 68, 72, 194
n/Nativity 162, 171, 174–75, 178
nature 8–9, 11, 14, 18, 33–35, 37, 55, 67, 70, 90–91, 94, 98, 103, 106, 111, 115–16, 132–35, 140, 141–44, 147–48, 153, 157, 161, 171, 173, 183, 196, 202–4, 208, 221, 226, 238, 241, 251
nature myths 18, 147
Nazarene 2
neo-colonialism 221
New Testament 6, 8–9, 11, 13, 26, 56, 58, 68, 76, 84, 89, 92–93, 103, 121, 125, 147, 151, 166–67, 168, 184, 204–5, 212, 214, 235, 255–56, 259–61, 265, 266–67
nihilism 20, 27, 69, 132, 201, 250
northernness 33–36, 49

Oceanic 162, 184

ontology 59
ontic 59
ontological 58–59, 179, 242
oppression 19, 78–79, 132
Oriental 90, 156
original sin 1, 6, 128, 135, 159, 180, 190, 201, 211, 246 (See fall, Sin)
orthodox(s) 3, 10, 14, 21, 46, 62, 157, 203, 207, 222, 235, 241–42

pagan(s) 4, 10, 14, 18, 20, 33, 36–37, 48–49, 58, 67, 69, 73, 79, 81, 91–92, 94, 106–7, 112, 116, 120, 124, 131, 133, 140–41, 143, 145–46, 149–50, 152–56, 158–59, 160, 162, 179, 181–84, 189, 192, 196, 200, 218, 220–21, 237
paganism 151, 179, 216, 252
pantheism 226, 252
parable(s) 16, 95, 100–101, 117–19, 126, 236, 250
paradox 17, 21, 54, 64, 109, 128, 209, 226, 242
parallelism 108–11
passion 97, 106, 154, 158, 161–63, 210
Passover 21, 50, 153, 208–10, 256, 260, 265
p/Patriarch(s) 6, 54, 59, 149, 188, 215, 234, 236
peace 74–75, 130, 165, 171, 195, 210–11, 237
Pentateuch 33, 75, 83, 91, 95, 122, 155
Pentecost 137, 175
people 2–10, 12–13, 15–18, 20–21, 26–27, 29, 32–35, 38–39, 43, 47, 52, 55, 58, 61, 63–69, 72–80, 82, 83, 84, 85, 89–90, 95–96, 99, 101–3, 114, 117, 119–20, 122, 125–26, 128, 130, 132–33, 136, 138, 140–41, 143–44, 146, 148–50, 152–53, 155, 158–59, 165, 168, 170, 173, 176, 178–81, 183, 192, 194–96, 199–203, 205–7, 209–11, 213–14, 220, 223, 226–29, 230, 233, 236–38, 240, 242, 244–45, 249, 252, 255–61, 267
perceive 4, 20, 135, 183, 190, 226
persecution 47, 51, 74, 202, 229

personality 191, 200, 229, 235
Pharisaism 130
philosopher 5, 11, 27–28, 56, 62, 150, 154, 166, 204
philosophy 5, 10, 27, 34, 42, 52, 54, 106, 166, 181, 197, 203, 215
    philosophical 9, 10–11, 27, 32–33, 39, 44, 50, 69–70, 80, 94, 115, 152, 156, 181
pietistic 96, 123
piety 123, 131
pilgrim 21
pilgrimage 21, 27–28, 40, 224
Platonic 45, 106, 148, 163, 215
pneuma 91
pneumatology 91, 155
    pneumatological 91, 156
poetry 5, 16, 93, 96, 106–12, 115, 138, 153, 182, 213, 227–29, 257–58, 262–66
    poem 16, 19, 30, 109, 149, 157, 162–65, 171, 175, 178, 229, 234, 247, 264
    poet 16, 26, 29, 41, 96, 106–7, 115, 133, 138, 143, 154–55, 162, 180, 224, 228, 230–31, 234
    poetic 16, 93, 107, 109–12, 123–24
    poetic 110, 261
    rhetorical parallelism 108
politic(s) 1–3, 5, 12–13, 51, 56, 63, 81–82, 125–27, 194, 200, 221
    political 1–3, 5, 8–9, 13, 26, 74, 76, 85, 96, 101, 125, 202, 208, 234
    politicians 2
    politicized 4
    political 1–3, 5, 8–9, 13, 26, 74–76, 85, 96, 101, 125, 202, 208, 234
    politicians 2
    politicized 4
postmodern 81, 125
postmortem 233
praise 18, 73, 115–16, 129, 138–39, 141–43, 165, 226
pray 32, 35, 118, 129
prayer 31–33, 35, 45, 105, 113, 123, 170, 207, 210
prayers 30–33, 105, 202, 206, 217–18, 220

prefigurement(s) 18–19, 21, 94, 145, 148–52, 154–55, 156–58, 159–60, 162–64, 166–67, 170–71, 179–80, 182, 213, 256
prefigured 19, 146, 156, 159–60, 177, 184, 212
prevision 162, 164, 167–68, 170–71
prevenient 57, 155, 182
    prevenience 57
    preveniently 53, 57, 190, 247
pride 4, 12, 15, 77, 83–86, 115, 185, 239–40, 251
priest 1, 7, 58, 123, 150, 158, 168, 171–72, 241
    priests 7, 8, 78, 123
priestess(es) 58
primitive(s) 16, 25–27, 38, 95
prophet(s) 19–20, 25, 54, 78, 89, 97, 110–11, 117, 145, 149, 150, 155, 162, 167–168, 200, 204, 215–17, 226, 234, 236, 239
    prophecies 97, 167
    prophetic 19–21, 154, 158, 160–62, 166–67, 222
proposition 53, 83, 94, 101, 111, 146, 155–56, 182
proud 27, 86
Proverbs 5, 93, 108, 257, 265
Psalms 1, 3, 5, 16–19, 33, 39, 50, 65, 69, 80, 85–86, 90–97, 103–19, 120–25, 128, 130–46, 149, 150–53, 154, 159–79, 191, 195, 199, 208–9, 210, 213, 215–18, 220, 226, 250, 255–56, 258, 264–65, 267
    psalmist(s) 17, 114–16, 118–19, 122–23, 125, 127–33, 139, 141, 143, 168, 155
    psalmody 105
psychology 103, 160, 245
    psychological 12, 37, 42, 103, 192, 232
public school 13, 31, 33–35, 38, 50, 195

Rabbi 11, 72, 111, 126
    Rabbinic 11, 28, 57, 59, 265
race 1, 3, 13, 19, 80, 199, 214, 217–19, 237, 253

racial 27, 194, 218, 220, 238
racism 1, 21, 26–27, 218–219, 221, 229, 253
racist 1, 219, 221, 249, 253
rational 10–11, 203, 220, 223, 228, 250
rationalism 11, 205
reality 7, 16, 34–35, 40–41, 52, 57, 61–62, 68, 73, 80, 84, 96, 106, 109, 135–37, 147, 148–50, 156, 159, 180, 188, 202, 207, 210–11, 225, 234
real 10, 34, 37, 50, 68, 73, 80, 85, 90, 101, 148, 152, 161, 164, 175, 183, 190, 206, 211, 215, 223, 227, 231, 237
realization 8, 10, 44–45, 50, 52–53, 55–56, 62, 149, 153, 159, 226–27
realize 8–9, 26, 32, 40, 60, 79, 177, 187, 203, 227, 246
realism 5, 62
reascend(ing) 9, 18, 147
reason 2, 11, 35, 47, 70, 97, 98, 112, 145, 151, 152, 161, 162, 173, 175, 190, 197, 204, 205, 206, 218, 243
reason(ing) 11, 74, 90, 102, 107, 115, 135, 136, 180, 256, 257, 260, 264, 266
rebellion 132, 146, 189, 191–92, 211, 242, 250
rebel 18, 140, 250
reconciliation 14, 31, 120, 245
reconcile(ed) 6, 127, 211, 237
redeem(ed) 4, 8, 33, 127, 148, 190, 197
redeemer 8
redemption 8, 22, 48, 81, 127, 131, 135, 157, 164, 183, 212, 247, 251
Reformation(s) 32–33, 79, 137, 171–75, 219
Reformed 14, 52, 62, 76, 235
religion(s) 4, 8, 10, 13, 18, 20, 22, 26, 28–29, 32–38, 45, 49, 51, 54, 67, 69–73, 76, 78–79, 80, 86, 90, 112, 116, 122, 128, 130, 134, 140–41, 145–46, 148–51, 154, 156–57, 178, 181, 184, 189, 194, 200, 201, 203, 206–10, 214–15, 218, 221–23, 235, 240–41, 252–53, 259, 262, 264, 266–67
religious 1, 4–13, 17, 20–21, 28–33, 35–36, 40–41, 44, 58, 62, 64, 67–68, 72–73, 78, 81–82, 84–86, 93–94, 98, 107, 114, 127, 130–32, 136–38, 143, 146–47, 149, 150–54, 156, 172, 177–78, 179, 183, 190, 194, 200–8, 210–11, 213–15, 219, 221–22, 226–28, 232–33, 235, 237–38, 239–40, 244
irreligious 30, 42
Renaissance 79, 106
replacement theology 2, 15, 82–86
resurrection 6, 8–9, 18, 21, 30, 49, 51, 64, 82, 98, 102, 128, 135–36, 146–48, 154–56, 159–60, 163–64, 166, 177, 179–80, 182, 201, 204, 211, 214, 229, 233, 235
resurrected 26, 46, 66, 68, 99, 154, 157, 176, 183–84, 228, 232, 251
resuscitated 49
retraktation 14, 62
revelation 2, 9–11, 18, 20, 46, 51–52, 54–55, 57–62, 72–74, 76–77, 81, 90–91, 96, 102, 106, 108, 135–36, 140, 145–46, 148–49, 154–56, 159, 163–64, 166–68, 180–82, 197, 204–5, 207, 214, 221, 226, 233, 241, 245, 249, 252, 256–57, 260, 266
revealed 9–10, 22, 25, 45, 48, 55–57, 59, 74, 102, 152, 167, 187, 210–11, 217, 223, 225–26, 241, 244
rhetoric 82, 108, 193, 234
righteous(ness) 17, 21, 25, 65, 86, 108–9, 118, 120–21, 125–27, 131, 141, 159, 161, 170, 177–78, 192, 200, 207, 210, 217, 234, 249, 251–52
rightness 17, 226, 239
rightwis 121
rihtwis 121–22
self-righteousness 17, 86, 120–21, 131, 178, 210, 252
Roman Catholicism 33
Catholic(s) 3, 6, 32, 48, 65, 71, 83, 108, 117, 126, 209, 215, 220, 241, 260
rural 17, 84, 136–39, 215

sacrament(s) 21, 49, 166, 225–26
sacramental 21, 114, 225–27, 241–42
sacred 75, 89, 95, 98, 103, 111–12, 169, 190, 193
sacrifice 14, 20, 49–50, 58, 102, 112–14, 116, 158–59, 162, 173, 178, 183, 197,

200, 208, 210–12, 267
sacrificed 81, 178, 212
sacrificial 14, 113, 158–59, 190, 208
salvation 2, 3, 5–8, 16–18, 22, 33, 38, 49, 64, 66, 74, 79, 81, 83, 96, 99, 103, 105–7, 127–29, 135–36, 146, 157, 159, 166, 168, 181–83, 202, 208, 212–14, 217, 233, 236, 247, 252
save(ed) 6, 8–9, 17, 19, 49, 67, 120, 128–29, 155, 183, 212, 236, 239
Savior 7, 20, 72, 73, 83, 130, 146, 166, 197, 199
Sayings of Jesus 5, 17, 101, 108, 110–11, 163, 251
scandal of particularity 20, 203, 205
scapegoating 74, 160
science 16, 64, 112, 225
scientia 112
scientific 16, 70, 92, 95, 104, 112, 161, 202, 204, 246–47
Scripture(s) 3–5, 9, 14–16, 18–19, 26, 33, 49, 51, 62, 89–93, 96–99, 100, 101–3, 109, 113, 135, 145–46, 152, 159, 169, 172–73, 177, 181, 183–84, 191, 197, 204–5, 217, 220–21
scriptural 205
second meanings 18, 19, 146, 163, 164–165, 171, 257
Second World War 67, 123, 194, 231
secular 37, 58, 93, 96, 137–38, 146, 178, 203, 211, 241–42
secularism 14, 62
Sehnsucht 28, 36–38, 40, 42–44, 225–27, 257 (See Joy, name index)
longing 17, 28–29, 36–38, 40, 42, 114, 117, 119, 137, 200, 227
self-revealing 55
Semitism 2, 5, 13–14, 19–21, 26–27, 33, 38, 51, 63, 67, 69–71, 74, 77, 85, 115, 121, 132, 152, 187, 194–95, 198, 202, 217–221, 251–53, 264 (See Anti-Semitism)
Septuagint 57
shamans 58
Shekhinah 28, 58
Sheol 25, 128–29, 211
shrine prostitutes 58
simul iustus et peccator 66

sin 4, 6, 15, 17, 37, 83–86, 95, 118, 123, 124, 127–28, 130–32, 135, 159–59, 177–78, 180, 190, 196, 198, 201, 207, 210–12, 223, 246 (See fall, original sin)
Sitz im Leben 90
skeptic(s) 16, 204–5, 227
skeptical 26, 69, 166, 204, 206
skepticism 20, 69, 90, 115, 204
slave 26, 221
slavery 26, 184, 201, 217, 219, 239
sorrows 47
soul(s) 2, 28, 37, 41, 75, 108, 121, 128–29, 148, 183, 192, 211, 222, 231, 238, 250
souls 2, 47, 114, 127, 210
speech-act 17, 134, 135
s/Spirit 10, 15, 28, 37–38, 40, 42–46, 50, 52, 54–57, 62, 71, 101, 113–14, 144, 146, 157–58, 162, 167–68, 175–76, 180–82, 184, 190, 198, 217, 225–29, 232–33, 237, 239, 242, 247, 267
spiritual 15–16, 28–29, 30, 34–35, 39, 41, 50, 74, 95–96, 121, 138, 210, 224, 228, 235, 242, 253
spirituality 15, 32, 35, 77
status 2–3, 6, 9, 19, 21, 31, 39, 64, 69–70, 78, 86, 93, 114, 122, 125–26, 147, 176, 181, 191, 200, 233, 236
stereotype(s) 27, 39, 138, 219
story 2, 10, 16–18, 20–21, 35, 39, 49, 94, 95, 98, 102, 126, 128, 146–47, 149–50, 155, 159, 163, 182, 188, 203, 206, 214, 221, 224, 235, 241, 243
suffer 79, 89–90, 91, 145, 192, 214–42
sufferance 242, 247
sufferer 169–70, 176
sufferings 77, 79, 168, 177, 250
superiority 4, 15, 17, 26, 63, 78, 83–86, 172, 218–20
supernatural 1, 35, 56, 172–73, 175, 179, 209, 230
supersessionism 2, 13, 15, 82–86, 120, 266–67
supersessionist 83, 85
symbolic 188, 204
synagogue(s) 26, 48, 63,112, 169, 189, 226

283

syntax 16, 107
systematic 97–98, 104, 166, 168

Talmud 11, 28, 58, 126
   Talmudic 11, 59
Tanakh 26, 33
taught 30, 63, 93, 130, 177, 207, 223–24, 229, 251
   teacher 16, 20, 63, 94, 106, 150, 180, 215, 222
   teaching 28, 32–34, 63, 70, 83, 96, 112, 126, 130–31, 229, 251
telos 68, 164
   teleological 164, 168, 182
   teleologically 68, 164
temple 3, 8, 11, 14, 20, 26, 40, 48, 58, 83, 114, 133, 137–38, 146, 153, 158, 200, 208, 215, 239, 265–67
temptation 86, 130–31, 158
testament 2, 6–9, 11, 13–14, 26, 52, 56, 58, 68, 75–76, 83–84, 89, 92–93, 101–3, 112, 121, 125, 147, 151, 166–69, 184, 204–5, 210, 212, 214, 222, 235, 255–56, 259–61, 265–67
   testimony 20, 52, 99–100, 146, 177, 200, 214, 233
Tetragrammaton 57–58
t/Theology 2, 5, 12, 15, 22, 28, 62, 63, 64, 65, 66, 68, 70, 76, 77, 82, 83, 84, 85, 86, 91–93, 123, 140, 148, 151, 152, 154, 156, 166, 173, 181–82, 188, 211–13, 223, 226, 235, 237, 244, 245, 252, 256–62, 264–65
   theologian(s) 5, 9, 14, 26, 28, 46, 52, 56, 60, 62, 67, 76, 83, 93, 154, 168, 204, 209
   theological(ly) 1, 13, 16, 56, 63–65, 78, 99, 104–7, 140, 153, 166, 171, 182, 188, 226, 236, 241, 255–58, 260–61, 267
time 7, 8, 10–14, 29, 31–32, 34, 38, 40–42, 52–53, 58, 63–66, 71–72, 75, 92–93, 95, 97, 106, 115–16, 121, 129, 132, 135, 138, 140, 150, 152, 154, 161, 167–68, 172, 176, 177–79, 187, 193, 195, 200, 212, 214, 218, 220, 222, 224–26, 228, 230–32, 236, 242–44, 246–47
title 7–8, 37, 47, 56, 58–59, 237, 262
tradition 3, 4, 7, 9–10, 13–14, 26, 33–34, 58, 70, 90–91, 96, 101–3, 109–10, 135, 139–40, 147, 153–55, 166, 169, 175, 180, 208, 210
   traditional 3, 14, 17, 31, 62, 78, 83–85, 117, 126, 149, 173, 228, 235
transcendence 52
Transposition 90, 201, 257, 264
tribalism 3
   tribalistic 3, 5
   tribe(s) 3, 48, 54, 58–59, 90, 101, 122, 159, 183, 194, 201
Trinity 8, 40, 45, 58, 99, 146, 156, 167, 172, 195–96, 227, 266
   trinitarian 8, 9, 54, 62, 76, 227
   triune 40, 57, 62, 151
truth 4, 9, 16, 30, 34–35, 42, 51, 54, 56, 60, 73, 82, 89, 92, 98, 101–4, 106–7, 118, 125, 127, 132, 142, 145, 148, 151, 160, 162–64, 168, 174, 177, 180–84, 202–6, 208, 211, 221–33, 241
   true 11, 14, 21, 35–36, 40, 45, 49, 53, 58, 63, 71, 76, 79–80, 90–91, 94, 100–102, 106, 112, 119–20, 126, 135, 143, 145, 148–53, 155–56, 159–61, 184, 195, 197, 205–7, 210–11, 213–15, 223, 231–33, 235, 238, 241, 252
   truism 76, 171

unattainable 36, 40, 120
uncircumcised 195
undemocratic 79, 203, 215
understand 4, 9, 11–12, 20–21, 30, 40, 42–43, 50, 56, 59, 75, 89, 99, 101, 115, 145, 148, 161–62, 167, 173, 180, 191,

209–10, 212–14, 231, 237, 244, 249, 253
understanding 3–4, 6, 9–12, 14–15, 17, 19, 27, 35, 36, 50, 53, 55–59, 63, 75–76, 78, 82, 90, 93–94, 100, 102–6, 111–12, 117, 122, 131–33, 136, 143, 146–49, 151, 153–57, 160–62, 164, 166, 169, 174–75, 178, 180, 181–82, 196, 203, 205, 219, 226, 234–36, 242, 245, 250
universal(ism) 20, 64–68, 73, 94, 118, 135, 146, 149, 155, 162, 167, 179, 203–6, 228, 241 (See annihilationism)
unmoralized 252

vengeance 17, 121–22, 124–25, 132
veracity 48, 101
vision 68, 138, 226

war 27–28, 41–42, 63, 69, 71, 165, 171, 175, 201, 218, 221
Weltanschauung 14, 62, 72, 218
Western 20

w/Wisdom 16, 74–75, 102, 112, 122, 124, 145, 151–52, 154, 160–63, 168, 179, 235, 256, 260, 265
Wissenschaft 64
witness(es) 5, 9, 13, 20, 39, 48, 51, 69, 72, 78–79, 99, 101, 136, 171, 174, 178, 200, 202, 206, 213, 218, 234
witnesses 77, 100
worldview 27, 205, 253
worship 3, 12, 20, 36, 43, 50, 107, 112, 114–16, 133, 136, 138–39, 148–49, 151, 179, 200, 226, 252

YHWH 14, 17, 21, 29, 33, 45–46, 48, 52, 57–60, 74–75, 80, 114, 118, 137, 143, 148–49, 152, 176, 179, 196, 207, 213–14, 232–33, 239, 250 (See Name Index: God, *HaShem*, et al.)
Yiddish 15, 261

zeitgeist 62, 72
Zionism 2

BV - #0032 - 100323 - C0 - 229/152/17 - PB - 9780718896560 - Gloss Lamination